T0162819

You Don't Stop Living

A Family Cure For Cancer

Jack Dold

authorHOUSE®

AuthorHouse™
1663 Liberty Drive
Bloomington, IN 47403
www.authorhouse.com
Phone: 1-800-839-8640

© *2012 Jack Dold. All rights reserved.*

No part of this book may be reproduced, stored in a retrieval system, or transmitted by any means without the written permission of the author.

Published by AuthorHouse 4/10/2012

ISBN: 978-1-4685-7184-4 (e)
ISBN: 978-1-4685-7185-1 (hc)
ISBN: 978-1-4685-7186-8 (sc)

Library of Congress Control Number: 2012905410

Any people depicted in stock imagery provided by Thinkstock are models, and such images are being used for illustrative purposes only. Certain stock imagery © Thinkstock.

This book is printed on acid-free paper.

Because of the dynamic nature of the Internet, any web addresses or links contained in this book may have changed since publication and may no longer be valid. The views expressed in this work are solely those of the author and do not necessarily reflect the views of the publisher, and the publisher hereby disclaims any responsibility for them.

To Mary

An Inspiration For Everyone In Her Life

❧ ❧

Mary and Jack

Preface

I am writing this journal as a result of a chance meeting the other day in the radiation office at Epic Care Center in Pleasant Hill, California. My wife Mary was just finishing with her daily radiation treatment and we were talking to Janea, the super friendly receptionist in the front office. A woman was waiting for her appointment and somehow we struck up a conversation. She realized that Mary had had cancer, assuming the fact from the short crop of white hair that Mary now proudly reveals to her world.

"I am just beginning treatments", she said with more than a bit of trepidation in her voice.

"Oh, you'll be fine," Mary responded with a smile. "I'm nearing the end, and everything went very well."

"I just don't know what to expect," the woman said, and her daughter who was in the chair beside her nodded seriously.

"This is a great cancer center," I said. "They take extremely good care of you. We were as worried as you are, not very long ago."

The woman thanked us as we were leaving.

Just that. It occurred to me that maybe others who are experiencing the acute trauma of cancer as Mary did, would benefit from what we have just gone through, and more importantly, learned. Since I always have kept a journal of whatever happens in my life, important or not, I naturally began one when Mary was first diagnosed with a large sarcoma in her upper thigh. Her story, since the symptoms first appeared, has consumed more than a year of our lives, a year where we entered a brand new world for which we had very little preparation. As Mary's treatment nears its end, at least for the immediate future and we hope for good, it occurs to me that maybe it would have helped if we had a journal like mine to draw on for understanding and perhaps assurance. What we have discovered is the confirmation of an old adage that has almost become a cliché: "If cancer is not the worst thing that ever happens to you, it may be the best." The first half of that statement has been true for the first half of Mary's journey; the latter sentiment pretty well sums up the rest. Cancer for us began as a disaster, and it is ending as a triumph of sorts for Mary, an experience that she, and we, could gladly have done without, but one that has produced measurable benefits.

This journal is about Mary's illness, but it is also about the family and friends that surrounded her during that struggle. It is a declaration that in spite of the worst that may happen, life goes on, adjusts, adapts, transforms, and continues. This is a personal journal. It is filled with a hundred little stories, and some very big ones, such as the marriage of our daughter Anne, that happened in our family during the time of Mary's struggle, little glimpses that prove that in spite of illness, life does indeed go on, and often that life is what helps to cure the patient. You don't stop living just because cancer comes into your life.

Many things have changed in our lives, some decidedly for the better. We discovered just how incredible is the science that deals with cancer, how wonderful is the environment of skills and care that is confronting the disease. We also discovered the therapeutic effects of friendship and family love that can help to treat this dreadful malady. And lastly it is apparent that this experience has drawn everyone in our lives closer together, most especially Mary and me. It's hard to imagine that after forty-seven years of marriage you need to rediscover each other, but that is exactly what has happened. It has drawn everyone else in as well. If we didn't know how much our daughters and grandchildren loved us, we certainly do now.

Our family helped to cure Mary's cancer, was in fact, a major part of the cure. By family I don't just mean me and the girls, their husbands and their children. Family to us is everyone who enters our lives with love—friends and classmates, brothers and sisters, aunts, uncles, cousins—everyone. Everyone who became close to Mary and me became "Uncle Jim" or "Aunt Donna." Our daughters' close friends became adopted sons and daughters for Mary and me, and so, while we have two daughters, we have many more whom we think of as sons and daughters—Deb and Patrick and Brian, Nancy's high school friends in Massachusetts; Eric and Sully, Jim and Donna's son and daughter-in-law; even Walter and Chris in China, which is another story that will take longer to explain. Of course, Marty and Erik, our two sons-in-law, immediately dropped the "in-law" label and became simply sons. And then there is what the world used to call "the greater family," the uncles and aunts, the nephews and nieces, the "relatives," connected by blood or marriage, who often are scattered all over the country and even the globe. Since I am one of eleven children, and my Dad was one of fifteen, that is no inconsiderable number. We called on all of them in Mary's behalf.

How our family has answered that call for help, and how Mary reacted to their love is the story of this journal.

September

September 20, 2010

I was in China, with one of the University of California Alumni groups, when Mary was diagnosed with cancer. The word hit like a hammer to my temple, almost a crippling blow when I first heard it. It is what we were raised to fear—the dreaded "C-Word," not to be uttered out loud for fear it might hear you, like Valdimort in Harry Potter. We had other fear-inspiring words too, when Mary and I were growing up. We were in the era of polio vaccines, which brought hope in the war on that awful disease. My brother Bob and I had to move out of our small rented house in El Cerrito, because our roommate had tuberculosis. The house had to be fumigated and Hugh sent to a sanitarium. Jerry Lewis was beginning his telethons for muscular dystrophy. We had lots of fearful illnesses in those young days, but none quite as scary as cancer. That was the one you couldn't get out of. Cancer was the end of the line. All of us had friends and relatives, even schoolmates, who had succumbed to the dread disease; fear of cancer was endemic in those days.

The times have surely changed. Today we probably know more people who have survived cancer than those who have lost the fight. "He's in remission" has become a standard phrase, although most of us don't exactly know what that means, or what it doesn't mean. It is almost as common to hear that someone's cancer has "recurred," but our mind continues to stay back on the remission level.

Whatever our toned-down thoughts on cancer are now, they are only relevant if the person in question is not in your family. I found out in China that the word continues to be horribly frightening when it is used to describe someone you love. In that initial shock, my mind bounced back and forth between hope and despair on a plane that was completely outside of reason, as fear provoked tears and doubt battled with certainty.

Mary, as well as our two daughters, Nancy and Anne, urged me to finish the tour, assuring me that there was nothing I could do if I came home early that was not being done already. Of course they are right, but staying on the road certainly created in me a measureable amount of guilt. In my mind, I knew that Nancy and Anne would handle everything that needed to be done, would provide the love and attention that Mary needed at the moment. I was also certain that Mary would be accepting this diagnosis with the same unruffled demeanor that she has handled her entire life. For me to leave the group and rush home would almost be grandstanding; the girls can handle things as well as I. Sometimes it comes as a shock that folks can actually get along fine without you, but I finally convinced myself that my presence could wait.

Over the years my presence often waited because I have been "on the road" for almost forty years. In the 1970s, I was happily settled in as a teacher and vice principal at Bishop O'Dowd High School in Oakland, California. Then Mary's brother, George, and I decided to go into the travel business. George founded California Field Studies in California and I moved to New England to begin American Field Studies. Simply stated, we took school teachers on travel courses that earned them graduate credits. Field studies evolved into Golden Gate Tours, which we have run in California together since 1985. Since then we have taken groups, mainly senior citizens and university alumni organizations, to just about every part of the world. I have been away from Mary and the girls many times. The tour with Cal, the University of California at Berkeley, was to be my last, the beginning of retirement.

Even though I stayed to finish off that tour, I did make one vow in China that until Mary was cured, she would be the center of all of our attention, that everything else in our lives would take a back seat to her well being. That might seem a small thing to someone not familiar with the Jack and Mary Dold family, but it is not. Mary has never been the center of attention because she never wanted to be, and never has needed to be. She has always been that thoughtful mother and wife and sister and aunt and grandmother and friend who cared deeply for everyone in her life, did things for them, and never asked for anything in return, often didn't even know how to express her thoughts in an emotional way.

I vowed that Mary was about to get payback for the thousands of cards and gifts and Cenacle of Prayer enrollments, the hours of work, the unceasing attention to the needs of others. It is Mary who is now in need of help, and we will provide it without limit. It helps too that I have just retired, after almost forty years in the tour business. Without knowing a thing about Mary's cancer, I mentally checked off the next year as being consumed by that illness. I didn't know then how prescient I was.

Saturday, September 25

This morning I got back to our home in Green Valley, Fairfield, California, feeling very uncomfortable with the world I was about to enter, a world that now contained an unwelcome visitor—cancer. Nancy and Annie have given Mary all of the help and support she needs at the moment, have spoken with the doctors, have assisted her in the multitude of tests that are the beginning of her journey with this illness. They have gone through all of the GI tests, colonoscopy, x-rays, various upper body scans, blood tests of all sorts. Way back in the spring, Mary began complaining of having dry mouth and loss of appetite. She was losing weight in chunks, which we all assumed was the result of not eating enough. In fact, Mary had started again on the South Beach Diet, a regimen she and I had successfully followed a couple of years ago, only to begin putting on the weight again as soon as we finished. It includes two weeks of near starvation at the beginning, which I assumed was what Mary was going through. But the lack of eating became a worry, then a definite problem, so Mary went to her doctor, Dr. Vanita Jain, who instituted the search for the problem. Those tests were still going on when I left for China in September. Of course, they never discovered anything, until they decided on a full PET scan, for the first time bypassing the G.I. assumptions and expanding the search to below the waist. That's when they found the cancer. Nancy told me on the phone that they thought it might be Stage 3 or 4, that it was a tumor in Mary's inner thigh. She said there were smaller tumors elsewhere.

At that time, I didn't know what Stage 4 meant, that the disease had metastasized to invade other areas of the body, but I knew that any stage higher than one was bad news. The doctors told the girls that Mary's cancer was a sarcoma, a tumor in the soft tissue. Two of my college classmates, Tom Meschery and Donald Dirito had sarcomas, Donald's very recently. On the plane coming home I resolved to contact both of them as soon as possible, figuring it would be the first logical step to helping Mary.

Mary's regular doctor, Dr. Jain, contacted an oncologist named Shoba Kankopati, who was with the Epic Group at a cancer treatment center in Pleasant Hill. Mary met with Dr. Kankopati, Dr. Shoba as she is usually more easily called. She is a young, attractive woman, remarkably slim. Her family comes from Pakistan. Dr. Shoba called for a biopsy which another doctor, Dr. Kim, started a week ago, and then stopped, declaring that it was beyond his ability to proceed. Before he closed up the incision, he said that cancer was most definitely present. The girls were furious with his actions, saying he shouldn't even have attempted the biopsy if he wasn't capable of completing it, but I calmed them a bit, saying that at least he stopped and didn't blunder on, possibly making things even worse. Dr. Shoba also suggested a surgeon, Dr. Rakesh Donthenini, who would do another biopsy, hopefully this time a complete one. That was the state of things when I arrived at home.

Monday, September 27

I met with Tom Meschery this morning. Tom and I were classmates and basketball teammates at St. Mary's College half a century ago. He recently faced multiple myeloma, had a full body stem cell transplant and is apparently in remission. Years ago he also had a sarcoma in his lower leg. He told me that they removed the tumor before it spread and that after a year of scans he was declared cancer free. It has not returned, although the myeloma is a much more virulent form of cancer, and now absorbs far more of his time and attention. It was reassuring to know that he has beaten cancer twice, and he said he was confident that Mary would do the same. His sarcoma occurred some time ago, so he wasn't in a position to tell me much about the current state of treatment.

Tuesday, September 28

Another college classmate, Donald Dirito, is still in treatment for a sarcoma, again in his leg. Donald is a very meticulous man, and when he was first diagnosed, he scoured the country looking for the best physicians to treat his disease. He even flew to New York to visit with a doctor who was supposed to be the country's leading expert on sarcomas. I met with Donald today at his Volkswagen agency in Walnut Creek. He is a walking encyclopedia on the disease, and he filled me in on what he had gone through.

In New York he learned that the best surgeon anywhere was right here in the Bay Area. Donald pulled out his three-inch book of research notes on his effort to deal with his cancer. In front was a list of doctors rated by him from 1 to 10.

"This is the doctor who operated on me, Dr. Rakesh Donthenini."

"In Oakland, on Telegraph?"

"That's him. He's the best in the business."

"That's who Mary is going to see next week. He's supposed to do her surgery."

Donald tends to be very excitable and emotional. He nearly burst into tears when I told him that, so happy was he for Mary. "Then you have nothing else to do. Dr. Don is simply the best."

I can't express what this endorsement meant to me and Mary. We are neophytes as far as medicine is concerned. We are also products of the 1950s, which means we were raised to trust people in positions of authority—policemen, teachers, priests, parents. And that includes doctors, who back then were placed in a very high position by everyone. The fact is that neither Mary nor I are capable of distrusting people, so I was very worried about how to go about the process of picking the right doctors to treat her. Donald Dirito is capable of such an investigation, doesn't trust as well as we do, and he really has done our work for us. Of course, that also means that I trust Donald!

I am looking forward to meeting Dr. Donthenini.

Wednesday, September 28

Annie and I went with Mary to meet Dr. Donthenini this morning. He is a very impressive man, relaxed, confident, and handsome with a warm smile that immediately made us comfortable. He took us through the details of sarcoma, showing us the PET (Positron Emission Tomography) scan results where tumors were discovered. Mary has a large main tumor in her inner thigh and smaller ones in lymph nodes on both sides of her abdomen, plus a small one on her lung. He said that he was not concerned with the small tumors but the large one would have to be removed, since it was the source of the others. He examined Mary's leg, commenting obliquely that the first attempt at a biopsy had been done differently than he would have done it, based on the position of the cut, and explaining exactly how he would do it. He assured Mary that it would be as small an incision as possible. He wanted to do another biopsy immediately to determine the exact nature of the large tumor, saying that he would rather have an MRI (Magnetic Resonance Imaging) instead of the PET scan because it is much more detailed. His assistant, Jackie, would arrange for the MRI this afternoon and the biopsy tomorrow. We found that none of the imaging labs had any openings until next week, but that wasn't acceptable for Dr. Donthenini and he told her to check some others. She found a lab in Emeryville who could do the MRI this afternoon. The biopsy is scheduled at Alta Bates tomorrow.

I can't begin to say how reassuring it is to have a doctor who acts on things immediately. Of course, we could interpret the speed with which all of this is occurring as a bad sign that the doctor doesn't want to let any more time elapse before treatment begins because of the virulence of Mary's tumor. Still, it is refreshing to have such forcefulness called into service in your behalf. Mary's MRI was a detailed one, involving a long period in the tube with, as she reported it, considerable "noise."

We will get the word on the biopsy results next week. For this weekend, we decided to put everything into the background and drive to Nancy and Marty's farm in Eureka, Nevada, and let the family surround her for a few days before the biopsy hammer falls. Our daughter Nancy met her husband, Marty, when they were students at St. Mary's College in California. Marty was born in Eureka, Nevada, four hours east of Reno, on what they call "the loneliest road in America." About fifteen years ago, after the birth of Kasey, our first grandchild, they moved to Eureka, and bought a 640 acres, which was planted in high grade alfalfa.

They have fashioned a wonderful life for themselves and their two children, Kasey and Joshua. Nancy is a dietician, receiving her B.S. at St. Mary's and M.S. from Loma Linda University in Southern California. While Marty farmed, Nancy developed a career in long-distance nutrition, joining positions in Ely, Elko and Reno with fax and email. She is our in-house dietician and nutritionist.

Mary and I find that life on the farm, removed as it is from the bustle of the big city, is refreshing, a time where we can focus on the grandkids, and let everything else take second billing. Actually, truth be told, everything takes second billing to the grandkids, something that every grandparent readily understand.

October

Tuesday, October 2

I am sitting on the back porch at Marty and Nancy's, watching the sunset perform its magic on Diamond Peak across the valley. The kids' farm and school activities seem to be the exact elixir that Mary needs as she steels herself to face the medical problems ahead.

Kasey just drove by on Gold Street in her Ford Ranger on her way to Deanna's and the Eureka High Spirit Week Dance. Is that possible? Kasey, a junior in high school and driving? Where has the time flown, from when that beautiful little blond-haired, blue-eyed doll captured my heart more than sixteen years ago? If anyone were here with me right now, they would see a tear in my eye, hear the quiver in my voice. Kasey has grown into a complex young woman, a beautiful person of strength, and intelligence, of carefully moderated highs and soul-searching lows.

This week she has competed in volleyball, (I watched her play against a pair of teams, three wins, one loss, moments of joy, of depression, of triumph and loss), been quarterback in the flag football game, appeared as the junior class princess at halftime of the homecoming game, participated in the spirit week rally and snake run through town and tonight is at the dance. In school she has a killer junior year schedule—junior college classes on the computer in math and English; advance placement classes in civics and writing;

Spanish and chemistry. She will worry about each of those and she will conquer them all, because at heart, my gentle Kasey is a fierce and dedicated competitor. She takes everything seriously. Lord help you if you don't!

Yesterday I watched Josh play his first meaningful minutes in a varsity football game. You can't help but notice him—he is that little #13 who is a head and a half shorter than anyone else on the field, whose total body weight is a third of what the varsity linemen bench press. I watched him field a punt on the bounce, skid to his right through a big hole, then dart left into the open. The entire Eureka crowd rose to its feet with a roar because this little guy has captured their imagination, as he has all of his teammates, with his speed, his courage, and his spirit. "Shake 'n bake," they call him, a water-sprite of a boy skimming the surface of the field as he runs. He would have scored on that punt return except that a big lineman leveled him in one quick blow, planting him straight into the turf. He held on to the ball as his teammates plucked him from the ground, patting him on the helmet until he almost had a concussion. Nancy shrieked; Marty and I burst with pride. Josh has grown up too, a high school freshman now, and he doesn't yet know quite what to do with his newfound status. Nancy showed me a picture today of Josh and friends, including cute Beth Damele, who was wearing his #13 jersey. I asked him about that.

"Does that mean she is your girlfriend?"

"I don't know. I guess so."

That is as close to a firm declaration as Josh is likely ever to utter, and about as many words as he is able to string together at one time. Tomorrow he is sure to be a campus hero in tiny Eureka High School; today he is still my little buddy, a wonderful boy on the edge of becoming a wonderful young man.

How can I tell you about Mary?

She is the gentlest woman I ever met, unassuming, self-effacing, caring and loving. She lives her life for other people, always one step ahead in figuring out what they need and taking that extra step to make them happy, or comfortable. Mary has never really considered herself. I don't think the thought ever occurred to her. From the day we were married, my family took her in with universal love. In those days she wrapped every present especially for the recipient, carefully thinking out the things they liked and somehow putting that knowledge into the wrapping. For forty-seven years she has kept Hallmark cards in business with her constant flow of cards for every occasion. We even managed to find a "congratulations on your driver's license" card for Kasey this week. Without notes, Mary can give you the birth and anniversary date of just about everyone we know, and they will always get a card. She gets "thank you" cards for many of the cards she sends.

Nearly half a century ago, Mary handed me my life, certainly my career. For nearly half a century, she has stood behind me, alongside me, usually quietly and without demands. She let me define our lives, and she quietly chose to live hers with me, and I think we have done very well. Ours has been a phenomenal run. I remember vividly in 1974 when I had decided to leave Bishop O'Dowd High School in Oakland. I came home one night with a crazy thought.

"Hey Mare, how about we move to New England?"

It brought a now familiar response.

"Oh, I don't care." That translates as, "If that's what you want to do, go for it. I'm game."

And after a year of trying to start American Field Studies in Plymouth, Massachusetts, and after spending every dime we had, I almost quit and came back because I couldn't find an Eastern college to accredit the field studies I wanted to offer to school teachers. But Mary stopped me with the suggestion that I call St. Mary's College and see if they would take them on. Sure enough, American Field Studies was officially born and almost immediately prospered. Our success was founded on Mary's unbreakable faith in me.

And ten years later, after she had put down her roots in New England, I suggested that we move back to California, the field study business having run its course, and my company beginning to leak red ink. She didn't want to move, but she did anyway.

Perhaps twice in all those years we raised our voices at each other, and I can't even remember those times. Instead we created a life that has no internal turmoil, where we tried very hard to understand each other and steered clear of tangles and misunderstandings. Without question I am the vocal part of our team, the one who was always talking, always out in front showing off, but it was Mary who gave me all of her support and encouragement. We were never alike, but we love each other deeply.

Monday, October 4

We met for the first time together with Dr. Shoba Kankopati. She is one of seven oncologists at the Epic Care Center, a full-service cancer treatment facility on Taylor Blvd. in Pleasant Hill. She had the biopsy report from Alta Bates and went over it carefully prior to making recommendations on the treatment Mary would receive. Dr. Shoba confirmed that the tumor was indeed malignant. It was very large, essentially stretching from just above Mary's knee on her left thigh nearly to her buttock. It is embedded in the muscle and soft tissue. She said that they had agreed it was a sarcoma, but couldn't determine what type. It seems there are a hundred different types of sarcomas, but Mary's, given her symptoms and the largely mucous content of the tumor, is something different. She said that she sent the biopsy report to the local cancer committee for analysis and also to the cancer center at Boston's Brigham and Women's Hospital. Unless the biopsy is analyzed differently, she intends to begin a "normal" chemo treatment, although sarcoma cancer is always dealt with surgically and the tumor eventually will have to be removed. She wants to try and shrink it first because its size would be difficult to operate on. She also recommends that Mary should have a port installed, which will greatly facilitate transfusions, chemo drips and blood work. The port, installed in outpatient surgery, is inserted in the upper chest below the skin, tying directly into a main vein.

Mary is piling up a good number of scars and she hasn't yet gotten to the actual surgery. She has two relatively small biopsy gashes, and now she will have another in her upper chest, just under the shoulder. Seems like they could just install a general zipper somewhere to give them access to the interior. Thus far in our lives, neither she nor I have had much to do with hospitals. She has a significant scar from a gall bladder operation when we were in Plymouth, and I have a similar one for appendicitis back in the 1970s. That's it. As far as our medical system is concerned, the two of us are pure novices, naïve and generally uninformed. Neither of us had heard of these cancer centers, which apparently have popped up all over the country. They offer literally one-stop shopping, where you meet your doctors, get your chemo and radiation, get scanned and tubed and MRI-d and X-rayed, have your blood analyzed and get counseled all along the way. The nurses are all geared for cancer treatment, maintain a wonderfully upbeat attitude, and make you feel very good. Quite simply, the Epic Care Center in Pleasant Hill takes most of the pressure off the disorientation you feel when you first encounter cancer.

Wednesday, October 10

10/10/10, at precisely 4:00 p.m., Annie and Erik Gibson got engaged, ensconced on Montana de Oro State Park Beach, somewhere south of San Simeon. And the entire Dold family celebrates with them! Their impending engagement is probably the worst-kept secret in our family history. It actually is a long and torturous path that got them to that beach, and I am thrilled for Annie, and for Erik as well. It is also wonderful news for Mary, given the uncertainties of her treatment, and will provide her with many new avenues of interest over the next six months. The date has not yet been set, but Annie, who is a meeting planner with McKesson Corporation in San Francisco, has compiled a list of four possible dates from late March to early May of next year. Of course she is now beginning the formal planning process, something she undoubtedly inaugurated months ago, if you judge from the size of the binder she has already assembled.

This should be a classic wedding because Annie is a professional romantic and has been dreaming and mentally planning her ceremony since she was about ten. As the father of the bride-to-be I have no illusions about the nature of the event and have prepared for it along with John Rohan, my financial counselor. I will probably appear to be fiscally dragging my heels at times, and perhaps even be heard to utter a loud "NO!" here and there, but this is our daughter, and as was the case with Nancy, Mary and I are going to make this an Occasion, which of course will have a price tag. Mary's present condition makes it even more exciting because it will give her a definite goal to shoot for.

Tuesday, October 14

We still haven't heard the final results of Mary's biopsy, which was done almost two weeks ago. All we know is that Mary has a sarcoma tumor in her leg and that it is Stage 4 cancer. I have spoken with Dr. Shoba a couple of times, but she says that the Tumor Board can't agree on the type of sarcoma Mary has, and they haven't heard a word from Boston. It's apparently quite an odd tumor, almost all mucous, and so soft that even though you know it's there, you can't feel it at all. There is no bulge in Mary's leg, no hard knot under the skin.

I asked Shoba if this thing could be growing that fast that it just happened and is more or less exploding. She said it is a very fast growing cancer, but that the dry mouth symptoms and loss of appetite go back to last spring so that is probably when it started. She isn't sure if chemo is the answer to this form of cancer, repeating her earlier statement that sarcoma is always treated with surgery. But chemo might shrink the tumor and then surgery would be a bit easier. I must say it is not comfortable to hear that the experts can't agree on what is wrong, but Shoba told us that none of the local oncologists disagree with her tentative treatment plan. There are seven oncologists based at the Epic Care Center, so it is hard to see how we could have better treatment.

Sunday, October 17

I think we are calling this an "engagement party," because Nancy and her family have arrived and she has organized the event. She started with a "few family and friends" which would include our best friends, Jim and Donna Schafer and their son Eric, his wife, Sully, and daughter, Kinsey. Sully and Eric are expecting their second child tomorrow but we will still only have to feed three of them today. Our friendship with Jim and Donna goes back to the 1960s and our first houses, which were directly across the street from each other. Jim and I had each bought a new car for our wives, and we were backing them out of our driveways, being careful not to hit the kids who were playing in the street. Of course we collided! The two of us got out to survey the damage.

"Looks like they are dented about the same," I said. "I'm Jack."

"Yeah, I'm Jim. Want a beer?"

So we re-parked the cars and went and had a beer. We have been closer than family ever since.

The party numbers expanded when I invited our friends Cole and Marcia Buxton, and then Nancy Bagnato and Brian decided to come. Cyndi at Golden Gate Tours for some reason put out an APB, which snared Bob and Anne Hagler, my old college coach, and Mary's brother George and wife, Gayle. Yes, it's an engagement party, as well as a good-wishes party for Mary who starts chemo shortly.

I can't recall any time in the past few years, in fact, any time since she graduated from the University of San Diego, that Annie has looked any happier. She is positively glowing, which makes me smile with everything in my being. She is so special to all of us, and it has been a long and arduous route to arrive at this happy moment. And Erik, who has a tile and stone business, and whom we have known for many years, also looks very relaxed. It wasn't long ago that he had requested a meeting with me to ask for Anne's hand, and I will never forget the nervous man who walked into our house and sat with me for a while. It had not been an easy course for the two of them, who had been quite serious more than five years ago, only to have their relationship fall apart. They are back together and far stronger for having negotiated the winding road to this place. I couldn't be happier for them. Erik now has a son, Clayton, a wonderful little five-year old. The only sensible thing for Erik is to move his business from Phoenix to the Bay Area, something I told him I would insist on. Annie already has a home in Pleasant Hill. And they have many opportunities in this area, given Annie's position at McKesson Corporation, which is a good-paying job with an outstanding medical program. Annie doesn't try to hide the fact that she wants to become a mother, yesterday if possible, and the medical plan is crucial these days. It will be difficult for Erik and Clay to move, but in the long run, a better chance for them to succeed financially. That is all a long way down the road. Right now we need to raise a glass of champagne and shower these two, these three, with our love.

Wednesday, October 20

Dr. Kim is implanting Mary's port today. After his aborted biopsy, we found it a bit disconcerting that he was selected to do the port, but Shoba assured us that he was the resident expert in such things, the man who installs all of the ports for the Epic Care Center. Nancy and Annie were none too happy about it, but I calmed them down a bit, telling them that if we trusted Dr. Shoba to do Mary's major treatment, we had to trust her judgment in this matter too. This is new stuff for all of us, and I can't see any way ahead if we don't trust the people who are doing the work.

Mary's port was installed at John Muir Hospital in Concord. Dr. Kim went straight at it and finished with style. Mary now has a "sub-cute" depot for needles and prods that should take care of most of the fluids she is going to need over the next year or so. I suppose in a way that is a sort of zipper, obviating the need for poking around looking for a vein.

The thing itself is called a Bard Power Port, a small triangular device with three little bumps on top, which show the nurse by feel where to insert a special needle (called a Huber needle) for any injections. When you consider that Mary is going to be getting chemo infusions, blood work, possible saline solutions, and other fluids, it makes great sense to have this port. Otherwise her arm would have tracks like a heroin addict before a month had passed.

The port can be left in as long as there is a need. Mary was told that she would have to have it flushed every month or so when it wasn't being used regularly, and that it would be removed some time in the future when there was no more chemo or frequent blood draws. With the port in, the schedule is ready for the beginning of chemo, something we are both dreading mightily.

Thursday, October 21

It is an important day today. I was going to call it "tough" or "scary" or any number of other not so great adjectives, but I think "important" is a good description. Today we go to the Epic Cancer Center in Pleasant Hill where a nurse practitioner, Donna, will give Mary the complete lowdown on chemotherapy: what it accomplishes and what effects it has on the human body. It is interesting how commonplace the word has become, even shortened in popular parlance to "chemo" and spoken of as routinely as hip or knee transplants, and for that matter, heart bypasses. Our medical skill and knowledge have so increased, just during the last quarter of our lifetime. Cancer is being dealt with today, and it is being defeated.

Mary knows that, and for that reason it does not feel today that we are going to an execution. I can remember that awful phrase, "terminal cancer," being used not so long ago. Today medical science refuses to consider any illness as "terminal" and they have the skill to back up their position. We are a bit frightened today by the effects of the treatment, rather than the cause of it. Mary knows she is going to feel awful for many months to come, that she will lose her hair, of which she has always been very proud, that she will have her routine altered as completely. But both of us are certain that there will be a happy outcome to this whole ordeal.

Annie is joining us for the briefing. When Mary was first diagnosed, the girls decided that one of them needed to be present at all meetings so that we would be sure to hear everything. I have to admit that it does work. It is amazing how many things get past you in a conversation that a second or third set of ears picks up. That is particularly true of something as complex as cancer, the various treatments involved, and most importantly, the massive array of complications associated with those treatments. I think the hardest thing of all, except for the actual disease of course, is coming to grips with all of the aftereffects, especially of chemo—the nausea, blood cell complications, emotional pitfalls, skin problems, and so on. Mary asked about a book that had been recommended by my sister Janet, *Taking the CAN out of Cancer,* and Donna was nice enough to give her a copy. When we got home, I decided to read it and was immediately struck by the fact that it was written by four women, all cancer victims, who between them have had a century of treatments and almost a score of different cancers. I am not sure at all that is what I would like Mary to read. It is difficult enough to deal with your first episode, without the awful thought that you might have several different recurrences in your future.

Everyone talks about not believing all of the horror stories that people tell you about their own experience with cancer and chemo, and then everyone proceeds to tell you about even more grisly things. I got through that book and decided to just take parts out of it that I think Mary really needs to know and forget the rest. Mary is not going to be one of those cancer patients who makes it a quest to learn everything she can about the illness. That isn't the way she is. "Just tell me what I have to do and I'll do it. Don't bother with all of the other jazz." That is Mary. She will face up to anything put before her, but she is most certainly not going to scrounge around and find more things to worry about than she already has.

My feeling right now, before she starts chemo Monday morning, is that she needs to be concerned with about three or four things— exercise, diet, and drinking enough water. And she needs to tell us, and her doctors, whatever she is feeling or whatever she notices is happening with her body. All else can be dealt with as it occurs. She is so mentally strong that she really doesn't need to be scouring the Internet for more and more information. Hers is a very basic outlook on life. I'll try to do the reading and worrying.

Friday, October 22

I decided back when Mary was first diagnosed that I would set up an email system to alert our friends and family about Mary's condition and update them whenever something important happened. I have often thought that one of the most difficult things for friends is dealing with the lack of information. When someone dear to you gets sick, you never know whether you should call and ask how they are, or just wait and see what happens. I have always felt that it is the duty of the family to let their friends know what is happening. I have several cousins who have beaten cancer or are presently fighting it, but I almost never hear how they are doing. I suppose we feel it is an imposition to phone, that someone who is sick gets tired of answering the same questions, but down deep I have a suspicion that maybe that isn't true. I think that emails are a perfect solution. With a single report I can alert everyone in our family, and with a separate batch, tell all of our closest friends. I can also let them know how Mary is responding, whether she welcomes phone calls, or would rather be left alone. To be honest we just don't know how she is going to respond to all of this, so I plan on becoming a reporter to keep people informed. I think it will work fine. My first report announcing Mary's diagnosis, went out today. The response was almost instant:

> Aunt Mary, (and family!)
> Oh no! I'm so sorry to hear about this. You will be in our thoughts and prayers every day. Hang in there.
> I just know that you are going to be fine. It might not be a peaceful few months ahead but I have a feeling that you will be back to normal in no time.
> Please keep us on your email updates (or Mom can keep us in the loop).
> With love and hugs,
> Sue, Dan & boys xoxoxoxo

Susie O'Connell is our niece, my brother Bob's daughter. Her email, which was predictably the first to arrive (Susie is super organized!), was the beginning of a deluge of responses. Every one of my siblings responded and just about everyone on my friends email list. For Mary it was heartwarming, something that could only inspire positive feelings in the struggle ahead.

Monday, October 25

Mary starts her chemo this morning. Nancy, Anne and I accompanied her to the Epic Cancer Center at 9:30. There she was warmly welcomed by Alice, one of the nurses in the chemo center, who promptly hooked the IV-unit up to her new port. It is really amazing, like an electrical outlet that they plug into to draw blood and drip the medicine. She was given some medications first to prevent nausea, more or less to prepare her for the poisons that are about to start flowing through her body. She also got an infusion of steroids before the actual chemo began. Today she is being introduced in a gentle way, with a half-hour of Gemzar, the first medicine that will begin to attack her cancer. Dr. Shoba stopped by to see how she was doing. She reported that they still haven't gotten the final study of Mary's biopsy which was sent to Boston right after the biopsy was done. They have yet to pinpoint the exact form of cancer that Mary has. Shoba had convened a meeting of the seven oncologists in the area who agreed that Mary should start chemo anyway to try to shrink the tumor, and she will adjust the treatment if the report from Boston indicates that the cancer requires it.

Mary took the entire morning in typical style without a hint of complaint and, I might add, without a hint of any side effects. What were we expecting? That her body would just start shaking and fall apart, like she was just bitten by a cobra? I think I thought something like that, that the "poison" would have an instant effect. Such is the fear that the very word "chemo" inspires. We were finished at 11:30 and promptly went out to lunch. From there Mary accompanied Nancy and Annie on a wedding dress hunt, off to try out various styles. It remains to be seen whether Mary will have any of the dreaded side effects today. Those may be forthcoming, but at the moment, all is well.

Tuesday, October 26

Hi all:

Just a quick note to let you know that Mary's first chemo session went very well. As far as we can tell, there are no noticeable effects yet. She had an infusion of a chemo called Gemzar which is one of the less invasive ones. Next week they add a more powerful one, Taxotere, to the cocktail. To date, they have still not identified the exact form of sarcoma (I think there are almost a hundred different). They sent all of her biopsy data to Boston and have a team of seven oncologists conferring out here. She will have two weeks of chemo and then they will do an MRI to see whether the main tumor has been reduced.

As always, Mary is very upbeat, and not quite willing to accept that there is any problem at all. She told me to read up on everything because she has no intention of doing so. "Just tell me what to do and I'll do it," were her exact words. Yesterday and today, she, Annie, and Nancy spent all their free time looking at bride, maid-of-honor, and mother dresses. A date has been set in April but I will let Annie announce it formally.

Mary truly loves all of the cards and emails. And she has no trouble at all with phone calls. Feel free to call any time. I think it is a happy thing for her to hear from all of you.

I'll keep you updated if there is anything new.

Love,
Jack

We are holding our breath, waiting for the dreaded side effects to hit—bone ache, nausea, dizziness, weariness. But none of those came up today and we decided that it takes a bit longer for the chemo to have its effect. Besides she only had a short infusion yesterday, not the full four hours. That will come next week. Nancy is staying with us until Wednesday which is great for Mary who is about as close to her daughters as a mother can be. And Nancy has helped get our refrigerator and kitchen properly stocked for the weeks ahead.

Wednesday, October 27

Still no reaction to the chemo. Alice, the nurse at the Cancer Institute, said that Gemzar is a strong chemo, but the really strong one comes next week with Taxotere. We are thrilled that Mary is handling the first infusion so well. Dr. Shoba only smiled when we bragged to her that Mary was doing so well. She said that the true test was yet to come. Nancy went home this morning, so I am in charge the rest of the week. We decided that we would move over to Annie's house on Sunday and Mary will stay there next week, because she is scheduled for daily treatments after the double dose of chemo on Monday. Part of the treatment with chemo is an infusion of steroids, and it really pepped Mary up, so much so that she had a hard time sleeping last night. She was zippy all day today and ready to take on the world.

I went to the Mark Twain Luncheon Club today for the grand unveiling of *Mark Twain's Autobiography*. It has been edited and published by the Mark Twain Papers Project at the Bancroft Library at UC Berkeley, headed by my good friend Bob Hirst and has been very much anticipated. Twain dictated his autobiography mostly from 1906-08, stipulating that it not be published until 100 years after his death, namely 2010. He allowed random chapters to leak out now and then during his last years, but the entire work is being seen for the first time. This is only Volume 1 of three and it is an intimidating 725 pages of very small print. I have a feeling that many people will use it as elaborate furniture. I intend to read it from cover to cover because I want to see if he could maintain his humor even in his 70s. Besides, after organizing and running four different tours on Mark Twain's life, and listening to Bob many, many times, I figure I have already heard a great deal of what this incredible author had to say.

Thursday, October 28

For the first time, Mary is showing some slight effects from the chemo. Today she is has less energy and no desire to do much of anything. I can't say we are relieved, but yesterday I kiddingly asked her, "What the hell is wrong with you? Get sick, will you?"

Sunday, October 31

Mary decided to move to Annie's house this morning. She lives in Pleasant Hill, only a few blocks from the cancer center. Mary will have daily treatments after the second chemo treatment, and this will save a lot of driving time. We filled a box with Nutritionist

Nancy provisions, took a few pillows and blankets, and a half dozen books. One of the issues with chemo patients is that their immune system gets weak and you have to be very careful about infections. So Annie had a cleaning company come in and work over her whole house, to get whatever extraneous germs that could be zapped. I will stay home with Maddie, our cat, and keep our home warm and cozy. Mary has her first double dose of chemo tomorrow, a combination of Gemzar and Taxotere, both very strong mixtures. Tonight she preps for the cocktail with a dose of Dexamethasone, a steroid that helps prevent fluid buildup. Mary had her first real reaction to anything with those pills, finding it difficult to sleep, so amped up was she and "ready to roll," to use her term for feeling full of energy. She takes those steroids today, tomorrow and the day after the Taxotere. Actually, they gave her liquid Dexamethasone with her infusion of chemo last Monday, and she will get it with all of the treatments.

November

Monday, November 1

Today is Mary's first major dose of chemo. Dr. Shoba said that the Gemzar attacks the cancer cells that have split, and Taxotere takes out the whole cells by invading them and freezing them. Of course they both kill good cells too, which is why they will start daily shots and blood tests this week. They are most concerned with the white cell counts because they operate the immune system, and when their count gets low, Mary will need injections of Nuprin to boost the levels. The same with the red cells, but they are commonly replaced by transfusions if the level gets too low. Technicians also monitor the platelets which must be maintained between a state of excessive bleeding and clotting. Mary got four separate "pharm" infusions before the actual chemo to help with the nausea and bone ache that usually follows. We are totally impressed by the science of this whole thing. I can't say enough about how much I appreciate this Cancer Center, which is officially called the California Cancer and Research Institute. It is totally self-contained with the lab facilities, MRI and PET scan capabilities and all of the infusion systems, not to mention a very caring nursing staff that is upbeat, professional and disposed to hug you. Actually Alice and Liliana hug everyone, including us spouses who are just tagging along for support. It took about four and a half hours for Mary's entire treatment today. She was very energetic

Tuesday, November 2

There is still little sign of side effects and we are thrilled, but also waiting for the hammer to fall, which everyone says will happen. Mary has injections of nuprin every day this week, with blood tests every other day. So far the cell counts are doing fine.

Thursday, November 4

Hi all:
Just a quick note to keep you up to date on Mary's progress. She is finishing her second week of chemo and seems to be doing great. Today she was a bit tired, which was the first indication that she was even getting the medication. Thus far she has experienced no real side effects. She has next week off and then starts a second cycle a week from Monday. After that two-week cycle they will measure the tumors and if they have shrunk, they will do a third cycle and then operate to remove the sarcoma and the two lymph nodes in the groin area. We are just keeping our hopes up that there will be considerable shrinkage.

Thank you so much for the great outpouring of love and care. Naturally Mary has started a new collection of cards, emails and letters. We have moved to Anne's house because it is only a couple of blocks from the cancer center. You can reach her there. We will probably come back home next Tuesday during her week off.
Thanks for everything.
Love,
Jack

Mary is pretty much socked out this morning, with no energy and no desire to do anything except lie on the couch and watch TV. But she is so tough, and even today, she accepts her weariness with a smile and lots of grace. She just assumes that it is the price you have to pay to get better. It is the way she has approached this whole illness, asking only that she be told what she needs to do. Mary is one of the strongest people I know in that respect. She makes no assumptions, no demands, and is perfectly willing to accept whatever comes along. I haven't the slightest doubt that whatever she is faced with she will deal with it in her usual way and get over it.

Tuesday, November 9

Mary gained a pound! Every time she goes in for a consultation with Dr. Shoba, they check her weight, because they are very concerned that she not lose any more weight. Of course, what they are afraid to tell her is that she is even graver danger from my cooking than from the cancer. I want it recognized that I have been beefing her up during my tenure as Chief Culinary Advisor and Provider. Just last week I served my bride pork chops stuffed with apples and walnuts. I will admit that I bought them already stuffed, but *I put them in the oven and turned on the correct oven, that is, the upper oven!* And I overcooked them to the point where Mary didn't have to worry about trichinoses, tape worms or anything.

My best thing as a chef is opening cans of cut green beans, but I also make a wicked Caesar salad so long as everything is in those packages you buy at Safeway. Once I even used leftover chicken to make a *Chicken Caesar Salad*. I think that was probably the apogee of my culinary career to this date. I can also pour chocolate sauce on top of ice cream, cook steak and hamburger rare, garnish cottage cheese with raspberries, and once even with sliced peaches. I have also gotten very good at won ton soup, which Fred makes for me three times a week down at Happy Garden. He even gives me a small Tsingtao while I am waiting.

Generally Mary deals with her own breakfast because Nancy gave her a bushel of fiber to be ingested along with the three gallons of water daily. Lunch I prepare in restaurants, and I might add that

I do a very good job at selecting them once Mary tells me where she wants to go.

No, thus far she is in very good hands. I considered actually opening her Betty Crocker cookbook and surprising her with something truly spectacular, like mac and cheese or sauerkraut and bratwurst, but I really have to consider that overexciting Mary at mealtime could cause bad cholesterol or maybe rising triglycerides. This is a time for calm.

Wednesday, November 10

The emails continue to pour in, from three generations of family members as well as friends from as far back as grammar school. One of Mary's closest school friends, Jovita (Jo) Kerner, sent my original email to all of their grammar school mates at the School of the Madeleine in Berkeley. Another broadcast Mary's medical condition to her classmates at Holy Names High School in Oakland. She is hearing from some old friends she hasn't seen in decades! Each morning I run off copies of the emails she has received the day before and give them to her with breakfast. She is starting to look forward to "mail call."

The Cancer Institute phoned today to ask Mary to come in for a blood test. She doesn't have any chemo this week and so no shot to keep her white blood cells up, but they are concerned lest those anti-infection cells fall to a dangerous level. Everyone was thrilled that not only were the white and red cells way above normal, the platelets had also risen almost back to normal. Yesterday they told us that for platelets Mary was at the nadir of the cycle, the lowest point in the curve. I could hear her grousing, "Why don't they just say 'lowest point'? Why do they have to find a word like 'nadir'?" (That's why I put in "apogee" back earlier in this journal because of course that is the antonym for nadir.) "Why don't you just say 'opposite'?"

She was very bright-eyed and energetic this morning, so after the blood test we went to lunch out in Danville and a bit of browsing around Elegant Clutter, which is already completely filled with Christmas. We didn't buy a thing because Mary said, "You have to have time to shop in places like this." She is going to bring her sister Barb there next week, maybe for the entire week.

Back at home, she dismantled Halloween yesterday and that is safely transferred to the garage, in orange and black tubs, and today she installed Thanksgiving. I could only find a weird green-colored tub at Target today, but that seemed satisfy her for the Thanksgiving theme.

Thursday, November 11

Nancy flew into Reno today, where she was picked up by Marty and the kids on their way here. I think that Mary really is enjoying the family and friend closeness that her illness is causing, not only in emails and cards, and phone calls, but also in the presence of her daughters. I find it very moving to see their concern and love so visibly expressed. And of course, Kasey and Josh give their love naturally and fully, with big hugs, cuddling and care. These few weeks since Mary was diagnosed have given us a close view of just how well we have done in creating a close and loving family. I am so proud!

Chuck and Margaret Pedri came by early this evening, having just returned from their adventure in Italy, France, and Spain. Chuck, whom I have known since grammar school, through high school and college, moaned about the amount of driving involved, something I had warned him about, but they seem to have survived their three-country jaunt. We had finished dinner by the time Nancy and Marty and the kids arrived, so it has been a full day for both of us.

Friday, November 12

Marty dies if he has nothing to do to keep him busy. We puttered around the yard this morning, with me blowing leaves all over the place and Marty installing a watering timer near the garage. Annie has a cake-tasting appointment in Vacaville this afternoon, so all of the girls and Josh, who has Erik's power of attorney to select the cake, headed for shopping. Marty and I continued with leaf stuffing and general cleanup for a Cal tour reunion scheduled for tomorrow. By the time we were finished I realized that we had used up all of the jobs I had mentally assigned to next week. What on earth am I supposed to do with all of those days?

I decided that at 4:00 p.m. it is really 5:00 in Daylight Savings Time, so we quit, got ourselves a drink and sat on the back porch watching Mt. Diablo change in the twilight. It is my favorite time of day, both here and in Eureka. I love to sit on the porch with a fine libation and contentedly watch the day end. Both Diamond Peak in Eureka and Mt. Diablo here manage to grab the very last rays of the declining sun.

Saturday, November 13

This afternoon we host the reunion of the participants of U.C. Berkeley's Nevada Geology trip that I did last August. This group is special because we spent two nights in Eureka on the trip and had dinner at Marty and Nancy's house. The folks were all excited to see them and the kids again. For almost twenty years I have scheduled a dinner following each tour, where folks can bring their pictures and memories and reminisce about the experiences. I will miss these parties, most of which we have hosted at our house over the years. The folks from Cal are so gracious, and they always are startled and quite pleased with our house and gardens, both of which come as a surprise. Green Valley, where we live, surprises people because almost nobody knows that it is here, one of the great well-kept secrets of the Bay Area. The houses around us are all hidden on large lots, two to ten acres, fully forested in old oaks, with stunning views of Mount Diablo, framed in the valley about thirty miles in the distance.

Just about everyone who was on the Nevada trip attended the party today, which will be the last of these reunions we have planned, unless we decide to have one for the China trip sometime after Christmas.

Sunday, November 14

Marty, Nancy and the kids go home today, leaving early at 5:30 because Josh has CCD and Confirmation studies at church and Nancy has to read for the Mass. Last night, before they went off to dinner at Shaw's, Kasey asked me to read her latest essay for her college writing class.

"Are you crazy, Kasey? You're asking Papa to read your paper? You'll be crying!" That was both Nancy and Annie in unison.

"I want to learn to write! I don't care. Papa, will you read it?"

I read it after they left, and I have to admit, I pretty much trashed it from start to finish. I couldn't help it; it was just as it had happened with both Nancy and Annie when they were in high school. Kasey's writing was all over the place, with repetitions, redundancies, grammar problems, and so forth. Thank God I didn't have a red pen, but the black ink pretty well obscured the essay, which was about diet and health. I knew what Kasey wanted to say in the piece, but it was pretty well hidden.

They got home fairly late, and because I knew they were leaving early in the morning, I went over the essay quickly with her. She was indeed near tears, and I couldn't get to sleep for an hour, so bad did I feel for not having been gentler with my corrections. But she bravely took the paper, and put it in her bag.

"I'll just rewrite the whole thing, Papa."

Nancy told me that on the way home, Kasey was pretty upset, telling her that that there was nothing in the essay that I liked, an observation that was probably true. But surprise, surprise! The next day I got a completely new essay, incorporating many of the suggestions I had made to her. It was fundamentally better writing, but still had many of the problems that young writers are likely to have in setting down the logic of their thoughts. But this was a major improvement, and my corrections were considerably fewer, and more to the point as far as writing techniques are concerned. Now I can point to a sentence and tell her to expand it, and I can show her that "international foreign countries" is redundant. I emailed it back immediately.

A third essay arrived the next day. It was so far improved from the first effort that it would have been impossible to say that it came from the same source. Kasey took my criticisms and in three days, completely rewrote that five-page essay, arriving at a work that elicited a single correction out of her grandfather. I can't even say how proud I am. Her introductory comment: "It is so frustrating. I know what I want to say, but I just can't say it right." I don't remember ever seeing a student progress faster than she has in these few days. Her essay may not yet win a prize, but the thought process has undergone a fundamental change, and her writing can only improve as a result.

For all of her young life, I have watched the way Kasey learns by blocking out everything outside, concentrating completely on the project, and listening intently to the instructions. She does that with volleyball, basketball, piano, dance and I am sure in every subject in school. When she is in that mode, she is total concentration and dedication. And she will do the work required! How I love her!

Monday, November 15

Dear Aunt Mary,

I hope you can hear our daily "God Bless Aunt Mary and get that cancer out of her body" prayer that we say each night at dinner and at bed time. We also have an 8 year old friend who is fighting cancer and her name is Mary Kate. Mary is a powerful name. Her cancer cells are gone right now and yours will be soon.

Hang in there and think of this "lack of hair period" as a time to focus on your beautiful blue eyes, perfect skin and beautiful smile. Your hair was just distracting from all that sparkle!!

I love you and just know that you are going to be ok.

Uncle Jack – you hang in there too. I trust that you are a pretty good caretaker—you can show off your skills right now. Just don't get too cocky. Aunt Mary will be back in charge in no time.

xoxo
Sue (Dan & boys!)

Round Two! Mary starts her second cycle this morning, with the short infusion of Gemzar. All of her blood counts are doing well, either on the high side or smack in the middle of normal. We had a meeting with Dr. Shoba to discuss what their plans are. I have to say, it is not the most optimistic report I have heard. Actually, she admitted that they really don't know what Mary has. They are certain it is a sarcoma, and they have ruled out a condro sarcoma, which is ligament and bone-based, much more difficult than the soft tissue tumors. But they have never seen what Mary has, nor has the cancer center in Boston where the biopsy was sent. Shoba called it an "undifferentiated muchoid sarcoma," which means it is producing mucous and they don't know anything else. She said that sarcomas are rather rare, and this one is extremely rare, in fact, it seems to me, so rare it is unique. Her plan is to have this second cycle of chemo and on December 1, do another PET scan to measure the tumor and make sure it has not spread. If the size has been reduced or the growth stopped, they will do one more cycle and then operate. If it has grown, they will operate immediately and take it out. The ominous side comment was that if the tumor has spread significantly, they may decide that the operation would be useless. She didn't really say that very loud, and I don't think that Mary heard or understood what she had said, but I did. I am just praying that at least, the cancer has not spread. Lord, give us that much!

After Mary had gone back to the infusion area, I asked Dr. Shoba if this was a fast-growing cancer and she said it was.

"Could this have grown this big in a month?

"Yes. Mary's symptoms are so strange, with the weight loss, dry mouth and no pain.... "

Tomorrow I will make an appointment with Dr. Donthinini, the surgeon who will operate after the PET scan.

Tuesday, November 16

> Dear Mary and Jack,
>
> Thanks for the update. So glad you aren't having too much in the way of side effects Mary. I think we're lucky that they've come a long way in making chemo less debilitating. Now about being bald, I'll bet you

look a lot better than I did with my big ears sticking out! I couldn't believe how much I resembled my dear brothers! I gave up on the wig after getting a headache and switched to hats. Just last week I went out for the first time without a hat. It's still very short and my ears still stick out but I've gotten great feedback. Who cares if it's true that I look chic! You are so often in my thoughts and prayers Mary and I picture us both in my mind as healed. Happy Thanksgiving.
Love to you and all the family,
Jan

My sister Janet has been emailing Mary constantly since I first informed the family. Janet is just finishing up with uterine cancer and has been a model for all of us in remaining upbeat and dealing with everything with strength and grace. I love Susie's emails because she is such a cheerleader, and Janet's express the voice of experience. We have heard from several friends and relatives who have endured and overcome cancer, whose voices are fundamental in building Mary's attitudes toward her treatments.

Mary's hair has started to fall out. I think there are few things that could be more traumatic for her, so proud has she always been about her beautiful silver hair. People have always enthused about her natural "frosted" look, and indeed it is the perfect frame for her features. She reminds me always of dear "Auntie Ag," Aggie Brophy, who had similar silver locks and was very fastidious about her looks. Ag suffered through chemo and had to resort to a wig, although it must have hurt a great deal. Mary, who was always very close to Ag, at least has her example in this thing. Yesterday she appeared with a cute little black hat that Jackie Olson from Cal had given her, declaring that she didn't want the hair falling out when she was out in public. Today she is going down for a "pixie cut" and will shortly be wearing the wig she and Annie bought a couple of weeks ago. As horrible as the disease is, I think this loss of hair is almost as bad. But like everything else she does, Mary's attitude is, "there is nothing you can do about it, so stop moaning and get on with it."

Wednesday, November 17

I had a fun talk with my investment manager, John Rohan this morning, and it had almost nothing to do with our IRA and investing, the fragile stock market, the inane national government, Obama, or anything really interesting. Well, it did open in a natural way:

"Jack, Wells Fargo is not part of the GM IPO that is coming out today. I can't get you any of the stock."

"I wasn't even going to ask that," I lied. John and I have been sparring ever since I told him to order me a thousand shares of Ford when it was $1.50, another thousand at $4.50 and a third at $10. Every time he told me I was crazy. It reached $17 the other day and now he is kicking himself. So it is natural that both of us will buy GM as soon as it is available. Even the government can't screw up the first month of a new stock. That will happen as soon as people realize what they have done, putting their faith in anything that is "run" by the government.

We really got the enjoyment out of our conversation when we started discussing the cost of modern weddings. Thus far, I have been astounded by some of the fees that wedding schemers are asking, and apparently getting. Nancy and Marty were married twenty years ago, so that is the blueprint for Annie in her planning. At that time, Jim Fidelibus was the photographer of choice for Nancy, and I remember being shocked at his $1500 fee. But at least I got to enjoy the autographed pictures of Cheryl Tiegs and Christie Brinkley when I went to pay the bill, because Jim was the Sports Illustrated swimsuit photographer in those glory years before 3-D and body painting. Naturally Annie made an appointment to see about getting him for her wedding.

"We are in luck, Dad. He only had a couple of dates available and April 9 is one of them." She said this with a slight break in her voice that I have come to learn has something to do with price.

"How much?" I figured I may as well cut right to the chase.

"Well there are several different plans."

"How much?"

"Well…"

That was one too many "wells" and I immediately threw Mr. Fidelibus out of my check book.

"There is one plan for about $3000 (translation: $3795 + pictures), but the one I would want runs from $7000 to $12,000."

I simply laughed, which always makes Annie defensive, but this is really funny. I wasn't laughing for effect; I was astounded that anyone could have that kind of nerve.

"Does he know that everything is digital these days? He doesn't have to buy film, you know."

"That is kind of expensive, isn't it?"

"No, it's kind of ridiculous."

That's my favorite word, always has been, because so much in life can be brought in under it. The girls are used to it, and they always react badly when I use it, but holding things up to ridicule is part of my nature. If I don't, I feel I might explode some day, and they wouldn't like that at all.

"I have a couple of other photographers to meet with."

"Good."

On to the wedding cake. I saw one on TV the other day. $2000! The bride-to-become asked how many that would feed, which as we all know is not the real question. Nobody "feeds" on a wedding cake. Very few of us are in enough of a state of sobriety to even taste it by the time it is stuffed unceremoniously into the gaping maw of the dutiful groom or smeared over the luscious lips of the doting bride. This particular two-grand concoction, which could also serve as a bunker along the Maginot Line, could scratch out 200 slices.

"Oh, that is perfect!" oozed Bridezilla through her collagen lips.

What in hell can be perfect about a cake that costs $10 a slice? And it's not even a real slice, but rather a little square piglet that doesn't have enough moisture in it to wet your eye teeth. $10 a slice!

Annie had an appointment last Friday to interview a cake in Vacaville. Josh was commissioned with Erik's power of attorney to select the cake, an expertise Josh comes by genetically, being Marty's son. He and I had a nice discussion of cube cost before they left. My idea is to buy a tiny bride and groom at Michael's and a half dozen sheet cakes at Costco, stack them up and go at it. I don't think Annie is going to go along with that suggestion. All I can do is hope that Josh likes something cheap; otherwise I am taking the cost of the cake out of his inheritance.

Did I mention the bridal gown?

Not having anything functional to do today, I decided to get a haircut. Mary's hair loss pains me, probably more than her, because it is such a shock for her, a visible sign of the illness that we are focusing on. Pam, at Big C has been cutting my hair for years. She always greets me with "Short? Medium short? Trim?"

"I want it really short," I said, and I explained Mary's hair loss.

"Okay, I'll cut it really short," she said and started clipping away. She got it to where there was still a style, but at that length the cowlick that I have always hated was sticking straight out, admirably marking me as a late bloomer for the Little Rascals.

"Buzz it!" I whispered.

"Are you sure? Well, okay!"

I have to admit, I always wanted to try that line, but at 250 pounds and seventy years old, it just doesn't seem like it fits with my state in life. Brian, our quasi-adopted son in New York, told Mary that he was going to shave his head in support of her cancer, but Brian is young enough, and goofy enough to do that. A couple of days ago I considered shaving my head, but then I remembered that as a young boy I used to bang my head on the iron bars of my bed, and I have a sizeable lump there to this day. I would look like a tennis ball with a big zit on top if I were bald. So buzz is as far as I can go without seriously disturbing anyone who happens to see me.

It took Pam about five minutes to finish the fleecing, and there it is, a short crop of hair surmounting my ears. I realized that I must look a lot like my sister Janet whose hair is just growing out from her own cancer experience. I like my new "do"! That bothers me a bit, because my intention was to do something brave for my Mary, but how can it be brave if I like it? Anyway, when her hair is gone, mine will almost be, and I intend to keep it that way until hers starts to grow back. Besides, I know that she is going to giggle every time she sees me right now. That's the way she is. And giggling can't be bad for her health.

Friday, November 19

I don't know what happened to yesterday. There was just nothing I could think of worth writing about. So that is what I am writing about today, yesterday's nothing. It is an interesting thing, this retirement, interesting because I begin to realize how my life was completely structured around my job for the last fifty or so years. I got up at a given time, usually around 6:30 or 7:00, even when I was on the road; I stopped for lunch around 12:00, because that is when you have lunch; I was home usually for dinner by 6:00 or so. All of those time markers are now gone, replaced by getting up whenever I wake up; lunch maybe, probably not; dinner could have been lunch. I do have a new time mark however—a drink on the porch at 4:30. It used to be 5:00 but that was daylight savings time and it is now almost dark by 5:00. Since these changes have been made, I don't think it is necessary any more to tell a friend, "Let's have lunch this week." It could just as easily be breakfast or dinner since the day is now simply a succession of hours not necessarily tabbed for any one duty or confined by time restraints.

I think I will eventually start assigning things to given times. I would like to write at a certain time each day because, like jogging or working out, it almost takes a specific commitment in time to get it done. I am not sure I can be a haphazard writer, even though my writing is the essence of haphazard. And I want to have a certain time for reading. I decided yesterday I was going to read the complete works of Ernest Hemingway and I started right in with *Across the River and Into the Trees*. My selection may have killed the resolution in its infancy, because that is one of the most inane books I have ever struggled through, a meandering of words and dysfunctional ideas to no discernable purpose. I am 200 pages into it and still don't know what the title is supposed to mean. It took me 150 pages to figure out that he was talking about World War II instead of World War I. But I am determined to finish it so that I can have an opinion about the book. I wanted to start with *A Farewell To Arms*, to help me in writing a book about an old friend, Boris Kastel, but I can't find it, a serious hole in my "complete" Hemingway.

Thus far I have had plenty to write about. In the first month of my retirement I started writing a novel about domestic terrorism, which I have named "Crosshairs America." The book took only a month, simply poured out of my brain almost without coaxing. Then I took on a really stiff challenge. Years ago I taught with a couple, Boris and Eva Kastel. Eva is a German Jew who escaped with her family from Berlin in 1937 and settled in Uruguay before coming to America in 1949. Boris was a Croatian who had an incredible history, as did his father—Olympic skiing competitor, world traveler, swimmer, kibbutznik, Tito Partisan, Italian Underground fighter, Nazi hunter. On his death, I promised Eva that someday I would write his story. I began to fulfill that promise just as Mary got sick. I am writing it as a novel because I don't really have enough information to make it non-fiction. And if those two projects aren't enough, I also have this journal to keep me busy.

I am not sure what role travel is going to have in our retirement at the moment, and won't be able to figure that out until we get Mary's cancer dealt with. I have a feeling that the next year or so is going to be spent pretty much at home, all the more reason to get myself organized.

If I didn't have this stuff to talk about today, I would probably be skipping today in my journal, just as I did yesterday. But then I would have had to write this tomorrow.

Saturday, November 20

Mary, Annie, and Donna are off to a Christmas boutique this morning, early. Normally Mary sleeps in until 9:00 or 10:00 every morning, but she hasn't had the incentive of Christmas decorations. She was up at 8:00 this morning and ready to roll by 8:30, already worried that "all the good stuff" would already be gone at the boutique.

There was nothing else for Jim and me to do except watch the Raiders and 49ers get butchered by Pittsburg and Tampa Bay respectively. It has been a pretty bad weekend for Bay Area sports with those two awful performances by the local heroes. Cal got stomped by Stanford yesterday and, even though Stanford is a local team, Cal is more local. The Warriors were down by thirty in the first half to LA, and even the Sharks lost. That is the price for being genetically unable to go Christmas shopping the week before Thanksgiving, Christmas shopping I might add that takes far more than the fifteen-minute endurance test that Jim and I would tolerate.

In spite of the fact that "everything good was gone," the girls still came back with bags of stuff, having gone off to other stores that had sufficient stock for their needs. Probably because we are in a near economic depression and the government is urging us to buy more stuff, Christmas shopping actually commenced about three weeks ago, before Halloween, when Home Depot put up all of their phony Christmas trees and started selling outdoor lights. In past years, Mary, Nancy, and Anne would get up about 5:00 a.m. to stand in line in the rain at Target to be the first in the door on Thanksgiving Friday, but nobody is waiting that long this year.

Sunday, November 21

Hi all:

Tomorrow Mary completes her second cycle of chemo. She will then have a week of blood tests and shots to keep her white cell count up. On Dec. 1, they will do an evaluation PET Scan to see what has happened to the tumors. We are all hoping that the chemo has shrunk them. If that is the case, she will have a third cycle of chemo and then they will operate. If the tumor has remained about the same size, they will operate immediately. The third alternative, that the cancer has spread, is something we don't want to consider. Mary has been amazing throughout. As expected, she has lost most of her hair, and that was traumatic for her, but she remains in great spirits and without much else by way of side effects. Of course she started decorating for Christmas yesterday, and is planning her annual Christmas party.

Again we thank all of you for your prayers and good wishes, emails and cards. I credit them for keeping her spirits so high. As all cancer patients have discovered, the disease has brought our family much closer together. Josh even wrote a long letter, and for a freshman boy that is saying something!

Love,

Mary and Jack

Monday, November 22

Mary has her second big chemo day today, the end of the second cycle. It is a 4.5-hour sit, with both Gemzar and Taxotere going into her blood stream. Before that, she gets a mess of other liquids—Benedryl to counteract the Dexamethazone, which counteracts the Benedryl. She also gets a slurry of Zantac to fight heartburn and one other bag whose name and function I don't know. Last night Mary had to take Dexamethazone pills in preparation for the Taxotere, pills she takes for three days. It is a steroid and wires her up considerably. She probably took them too late last night and couldn't get to sleep. I woke up about 3:00 and she was gone. I checked all of the logical places, figuring she couldn't stand my snoring and went to sleep in another bedroom. I found her downstairs, sound asleep on the couch. It wasn't my snoring at all, so I took back my resolution to move to another bedroom so she could get a good night's sleep.

This afternoon she was talking about sleeping downstairs and complained that she had stepped on something when she got off the couch last night. It was squishy. It turned out to be a piece of the chocolate coating from a Klondike bar that had fallen onto the rug.

"How did you know it was a Klondike scab?" I asked innocently, knowing full well it had been deposited by me since I find it hard to eat one of those things without losing some of the shell.

"I tasted it," she replied innocently.

"You tasted something you just walked on, that had fallen on the floor," Anne exclaimed, astounded. "Like the Baby Ruth bar in 'Caddy Shack?'"

"Yes."

"Mary," I lectured, "You are getting daily shots to keep your white blood cells growing so your immune system stays viable, and you are eating things that fell on the floor."

"Well, it was four in the morning, and nothing happened."

"What, germs aren't active at 4 a.m.?" Anne editorialized with her best daughter-preacher voice.

"What's the big deal? It was a stinking Klondike bar! And I was sleepy. Besides, nobody saw me do it."

With that Mary rested her case, fully satisfied that everything is normal. I felt good about it because she never asked who dropped the chocolate in the first place. I am mad at the cat, because lapping up stray food bits is what we keep Maddie around for.

Annie took Mary to the wig shop after the infusion. Her hair is splotchy at best and she has decided to shave her head and end the struggle for the time being. The woman at the shop offered to cut her hair and get it wig-ready. I asked Mary if she had a thing to hang the wig on, and she assured me there was one in the attic. But Anne was insisting that they get a rack at the wig shop.

"See if they have one that looks like Catherine Zeta-Jones," I suggested, but I only got double scorn back in reply. The wire frame they brought back didn't look like anyone glamorous, not even Madonna.

Mary continues to get all sorts of cards, letters, books and flowers from all over the country, even a couple of fruit baskets. It is so wonderful to watch her happiness at the consideration and love of people. She may be getting a small inkling of just how important she has been to her family and friends. Even casual friends and clients who have only met her a time or two are responding to the natural goodness that she has always projected. And all the while there is still a steady stream of cards flowing out of our house, for birthdays, anniversaries, Thanksgiving, and Cenacle of Prayer petitions. I would say the flow is about perfectly balanced in both directions, probably for the first time in Mary's life.

And the emails! I love reading the emails as they are also pouring in, each perfectly suited to the personalities of those sending them. Some people complain about the computer age and how everything is so mechanical these days, but I think that emails are one of the really positive results of the technology. They are easy to do and actually are the closest thing we have left to writing a letter. Emails are so much more immediate than using the postal service. I am also finding out what I suspected before Mary got sick—that it is great to hear from friends and family when you are ill. People shouldn't worry about "disturbing" the invalid; the disturbance is a healing thing. By communicating with emails, you are able to tell everyone how you feel and what they can do to help.

Tuesday, November 23

Mary has six straight days now of Nuprin shots, a chemical that gets to the bone marrow and starts rebuilding white cells. Yesterday the blood counts were way up, the white cells far above the normal and the reds only slightly down. It's amazing, for the first time in our lives we are even considering the makeup of our blood. Normally we just put a bandage on a wound to stop blood's flow, or we give blood, as Mary used to do. But we never stopped to think exactly what blood does or that it has all sorts of component parts. I guess I have always heard of various types of cells in blood, but now we not only have white and red cells and platelets, but we have neutrophils and lymphocytes, monocytes, hemoglobin and hematocrits. And there are numbers attached to each of those, some of which are completely unfathomable. What, for instance, is a white blood cell count of 21.1 $10*3/mm*3$ supposed to mean? I suppose it's important for someone to know because the normal count is supposed to be between 3.5 and 10. Suddenly our world is filled with things like MCH and MCV, RDW and MCHC. Mary's MPV was 7.0 $fm*3$, right smack in the middle of normal. Who could have guessed!

I used to be confident if the thermometer read 98.6; I could call a doctor if it was seriously high or low. I figured my blood pressure should be my age + 30 over about 70. Then I started worrying about cholesterol, until I discovered that there is both good and bad of that stuff. I never did figure out triglycerides. But now there are dozens of numbers you have to brag about, sort of like your credit score. I do like the printout they give us at Epic Care Cancer Center. We get all the abbreviations and readings and normals and such, but then there is column 4 which simply reads "H" and "L." High and Low I can handle.

Thursday, November 25

Happy Thanksgiving! Even with all of Mary's medical problems, we really do have much to give thanks for this year. The family started gathering yesterday when Marty, Nancy, Kasey and Josh arrived from Eureka. Erik and Clayton motored in from Phoenix-

San Luis Obispo this morning. We are now nine! That alone is plenty to thank the Lord for—a new prospective son and grandson.

We are having our feast at Anne's this year, where she and Erik are cooking and the rest of us will sit around, watch football games and observe Clayton chasing Josh all day. For Josh the shoe is on the other foot for the first time. In past family gatherings, Josh has been the chaser, usually of Geoffrey if he is around, and even though Geoff is a very good athlete, he would be exhausted by the end of half a day. So now it is with Clay and Josh. It only took about an hour and Josh was beginning to drag, letting out a moan every so often about how Clay just wouldn't stop. Get used to it, Josh!

Last night Mary stayed up until midnight baking pies. She promised Annie an apple and a pumpkin, but we warned her about overdoing it when the Nuprin is trying to drag new blood cells out of her bone marrow, but Mary's answer is always, "I'm sitting around anyway. What's the big deal?" As a result, much of today she is asleep on the couch as we get ready for Thanksgiving dinner. The problem is that Mary has her infusions on Monday and it takes until Thursday for that poison to start causing strain on her body. Thursday has been the bad day each week since she started chemo, and today she is beginning to show the fatigue. My guess is that tomorrow she will be wiped out.

I got an email from Walter (Shui Heng Yong) in Beijing yesterday which I find remarkable. It is a Thanksgiving thought, something he has done the last few years as he has gotten closer and closer to America in his way of thinking. I read it before dinner tonight:

> At this moment of time, there is someone far far way, also close by, who sends you Thanksgiving Greetings. On this day (and on any other days) we should be thankful that we are alive and living a comfortable life as it is, how it is. Let's be thankful to anything we have, anything we don't have, anything we will have, anything we will not have.
>
> We are thankful, we have wives, husbands, child (children), housing, food, clothes, friends, friendship, love, care, nurture, anything we have in life now

because we are better than billions of people, luckier
than billions.

That is very well said. It was accompanied by a startling slide
show from around the world, showing just how bad it is for those
billions of people more unfortunate that we are. Looking around out
table, I can only say, "Thank you" from the bottom of my heart.

Walter Horatio is one of the gems of our lives. In China he is
Shui Heng Yong. He was the first man I met in China when I first
went there ten years ago, and he has been my travel companion
there ever since. It is very difficult to describe him. I would say he
is the smoothest man I have ever met. Very handsome, fifty years
old, with a smile that instantly attracts you, he is a facilitator, a man
who gets things done. Over the years I must have written a hundred
descriptions of Walter and I keep adding to them. He is one of those
"one name people." Everyone who has ever met him remembers
him immediately and smiles at the mere mention of "Walter." His
brother's name is Chris, Shui Jing (Jing means crystal, hence Chris.)
Several years ago, Mary and I attended an elegant dinner at Tommy
Toy's in San Francisco with Walter, Chris, and a crew from China
TV. After about six toasts led by Mary with *baijou*, the Chinese fire
water, Walter, Chris and their cousin, whom we knighted with the
Western name of Rolf, requested that Mary and I adopt them as
sons. All three now call Mary *ma ma*, and me *da*. And we consider
them to be our sons.

Friday, November 26

They call this "Black Friday," a ridiculous name for the biggest
shopping day of the year. I looked it up on Wikipedia and discovered
that the name comes from Philadelphia, coined by the Philly police
because Wannamaker's Department Store always had a huge sale
Friday after Thanksgiving, and there were so many people downtown,
the traffic accidents and injuries were always the biggest of the year.
But merchants across the nation started marketing that Friday as
the kickoff of the Christmas season, and they didn't think that a
day called "Black Friday" was a very good advertisement to attract
shoppers. "Join the sale and end up in the hospital, or morgue!" So

they spun the thing to mean that this was the first day of black ink for merchants around the nation, and that version has more or less stuck, although nobody really seems to know for sure. Mary and the girls used to get up at 5 a.m. to go to Target and Mervin's, but this year Kohl's and others upped the chaos to advertise 3 a.m. openings for "bargains." We have so matured that everyone slept in at least until 8:00.

As I suspected today is a lost day for Mary. We went in for her shot at 9:00 and then breakfast at Annie's. She slept until breakfast was served, got up to eat, and then while the kids all went to the Exploratorium in San Francisco, she and I went home, when she crashed. We thought we might meet everyone at Jim and Donna's but Mary was just not up to it. This is her Thursday this week.

"I feel like I'm carrying a heavy weight on my shoulders," she said. "It just weighs you down."

Saturday, November 27

Marty started looking for handyman jobs early this morning, so I asked him to free up the lock and doorknob on the back door. Done! Then he suggested that we start bringing in the Christmas decorations from the garage, and he recruited Josh to join us. Done!

"I need to get all the Christmas trees (Mary had eleven last year) out from under the house." Done!

Erik, Clay and Annie arrived and Erik was recruited.

"Can you get the extension ladder behind the garage?" Done!

"Can you help me clean out the gutters?" They have been clogged for several rain sessions in the last year, but the guilty ones are at least thirty feet up and I really can't trust myself on that ladder any more. But I can trust Josh to scramble up to the roof line especially with Marty and Erik supervising. Even the most difficult of the drains, the one on the front corner, was cleared in less than half an hour. I just "managed" to clear a whole month of retirement work in less than a morning. It is wonderful to have staff!

And Mary does as well. Once we got all the decorations (ninety tubs to be precise) in from the garage, Anne, Nancy, and Mary started dragging out carolers and "deckies," as Mary calls them.

Marty, Erik and I hung all of the garlands in the dining room, and all of the wreaths around the outside of the house. And the girls polished off most of the bar, the living room and dining room. That is no easy thing. There are more than seventy Byers Choice carolers in the dining room alone, with lights, boughs, nativity sets and all sorts of other Christmas items to worry about. And it is also not easy putting your soul into it as Mary does.

"You want me to put that where?" an incredulous Anne exclaimed when she was handed a rather ugly Santa and told to sit him on a shelf among the coke bottle collection. "He won't fit there." Mary had to climb on a ladder and show her how he could fit, leaving Anne shaking her head in disbelief. I always used to say that when Mary was in a decorating mode, you didn't want to sit or stand in one place for more than about twenty seconds or you would have a bow taped to your butt and a garland encircling your brain. Nothing has changed.

It was about three or four hours of the most joyful family life I can recall, all of us working to lighten Mary's load and to fill her house with its usual incredible Christmas cheer. I can't think of any gift that will be more appreciated by her this year, and it was pure fun to give.

Sunday, November 28

For the fourth day in a row, we are in at the Epic Center at 9:00 for Mary's shot. We drive for half an hour and it takes about thirty seconds for the doctor to give the shot. We stopped at Anne's to take her out to breakfast, did a brief bit of shopping and headed home, where Mary laid back one more time to recuperate from the last chemo installment. Tomorrow she gets her blood taken and a final shot and then has the week free from treatment. But Wednesday is her big day, when she gets a PET scan to measure the tumor, which will determine future treatments. We can only pray!

Monday, November 29

I am sending all my good vibes and prayers your way this week. I've emailed both Nancy and Anne to lend my support from afar.

Here is a quote that I found that I shared with a friend in town whose 8 year old daughter is fighting (and beating) Stage 4 cancer. My friend really found some comfort in it and I hope you do to:

"When you get to the end of all the light you know, and it's time to step into the darkness of the unknown, faith is knowing that one of two things shall happen: either you will be given something solid to stand on, or you will be taught how to fly."

– Edward Teller

I love you all,
Sue

Who else but Susie will console a cancer patient with a quote from the father of the H-bomb? Teller, by the way, was a next-door neighbor of Mary's on Hawthorne Terrace in Berkeley when she was a kid, not a very friendly one according to her memories. But I do like the quote Sue sent.

Mary woke up this morning late, the first day in five where we didn't have to be in Pleasant Hill at 9:00. She went to take a shower and found that her tumor had ballooned out terribly. Her inner leg had grown several inches, about half a football in size. It is bad enough that cancer is that insidious thing inside of you that you can only measure with angst, something you can't see, and in Mary's case, can't even feel. You know it is working its foul mission unceasingly in your body, and you know its destructive abilities, but there is nothing externally that you can do about it. The doctors assure you that their medicines will work, and you trust them with all your soul because there is no alternative to trust. Actually there is an alternative, but despair is not a thing that a sane person wants to choose.

Now, suddenly, there is a gigantic growth that can be seen, and your heart just stops beating. At least mine did. Mary showed me that bulge in her thigh with not an ounce of worry or emotion, figuring that it was some easily explained natural thing. Why would you worry about it?

"Jack, this sucker has grown." I don't think she even used the exclamation point.

"My God, Mary!" I did the correct punctuation. "What happened?"

"I don't know. It was just like this when I went to take a shower. It could just be water, or something to do with the medication. No big deal."

I immediately called Dr. Shoba, but she was with a patient. We have to be in for Mary's shot at 12:15, so I figured we would see the doctor then. But she was off at the hospital by the time we got in there. And she was with another patient when I called later in the afternoon. I finally talked to her about 5:30 this evening, and she apparently had not been alerted that this was an urgent call. We will see her, unfortunately, at 8:30 tomorrow morning, but I doubt there is anything that she can do. Mary has her PET/CT/MRI scans Wednesday at 1:00 p.m. so that will tell us what is going on. I hope Mary is right.

The days are creeping by. It feels so unusual to have no focus on my time, to just be standing still or walking in sand, with nothing to aim for, except for the hope that whatever news you are going to get isn't bad. Mary is bearing up under that strain exceedingly well, at least I think she is. Even after all these years, I still find that I can't always read her, or know what she is thinking or how she is reacting to something. Oh, I can tell if she thinks something is stupid, or not worth worrying about, but where she herself is concerned it is almost impossible to tell if she is worried, upset, fearful or resigned. She doesn't have any telltale signs about herself, because she has always lived her life about other people. At times I just want to yell at her and tell her to cry, or worry out loud, or complain. But I know I will never see that happen. I love her for that. I wish I could do it.

I awoke about 2:00 a.m. and Mary was gone. I found her reading in Nancy's room, wide awake, unable to sleep. I was in the same boat, but have learned that if I can't sleep, I need to get up, walk around a bit, type something, or watch fifteen minutes of ESPN, and then I get right back to sleep. Mary was determined to finish her book tonight. She was already on page twenty-three. There is no point in urging her to get back to bed, because she is going to do what she wants anyway. I have also learned that long ago. My system worked well for me because I was soon sound asleep. Mary waited a few chapters.

Tuesday, November 30

Mary and I decided to spend today sitting in one place or another. It started with that tumor yesterday, when Mary calmly showed me that the thing had "exploded" in her thigh, doubling in size, from unable to be seen to obviously a problem. We left for Pleasant Hill at 8:00 for a meeting with Dr. Shoba, who was at a loss to explain the sudden growth, assuring us that cancer never acts that way, with such an explosion. She posited three or four possibilities:

It could be a blood clot, which happens frequently with cancer patients. I asked if there would be bruising with a clot, and she nodded, and even though there was no bruising, she still held that out as a possibility. The bulge in Mary's thigh was just as soft as the tumor had been.

"It could be dead tissue from the tumor," Shoba said hopefully, but it didn't seem like she was very convinced of that possibility.

"Or it could be that the tumor has actually grown. Is there any pain?"

Mary shook her head, not showing the least concern about the whole thing.

"Well, we can determine the first one," Dr. Shoba told her. I didn't ask about the fourth possibility. "We can get you an ultrasound at Diablo Hospital. That will tell us if there is a blood clot and may show the tumor as well."

She asked Mary about other concerns—appetite, bowel movements, headaches. Mary reported that the second round of chemo had a bunch of bad side effects, mainly fatigue, but also the recurring dry mouth, as well as occasional diarrhea, constipation, a couple of bouts of dizziness, and a continuing lack of appetite.

"Are you drinking water?"

"Not really."

"Did you take Immodium?"

"No."

Shoba didn't even raise an eyebrow. I protested that Mary had to be forced to eat, to drink water.

"It's okay. We'll hydrate you here, Mary. Come back after the ultrasound. I'll have Alice reserve a chair."

We sat for two hours at Annie's until the ultrasound appointment, then sat a couple of hours at the hospital. Our sit continued for two more hours back at the Cancer Center watching the saline solution drip, one slow drop after another for a liter of time. I started counting the drops as they fell from the plastic bag suspended over Mary's chair and soon gave up. I asked Alice if she knew how many drops there were in a liter of saline solution, but she only walked away laughing, shaking her head. Dr. Shoba came in to tell us that the ultrasound showed not a single aberration in the leg, didn't even show the tumor.

At 5:00 we were finished, heading home, having logged a day of no progress, a day of sitting. Tomorrow, with the MRI and PET/CT (Computed Tomography) scans, we will find out what is happening.

December

Wednesday, December 1

Neither of us was particularly worried about the importance of today. I think we have figured out that there is nothing we can do to influence the findings of the PET scan that Mary has this afternoon. Because we, and Dr. Shoba, think that she will be having surgery soon, she is scheduled for all three imaging systems today, the MRI being a more detailed and precise picture of her body that is required for surgery. At 1:30 I left Mary ready to be inserted into that loud tube for the MRI and went to have lunch with Tim Brophy, a former high school student of mine who has become a close friend. I picked Mary up at 4:30, stopping at Wendy's for a couple of large chocolate Frosties, one of the few things Mary is willing to eat these days. I dropped her off at home and drove down to Happy Garden for another bucket of Fred's wonton soup, which she will also accept.

Dr. Shoba called right after I got home.

"I have good news, Jack. The tumors are all reduced. The two lymph node tumors are reduced by more than 50 percent and the tumor on the lung no longer appears on the scan. The sarcoma in the leg is necrotic. It is dying."

"What a wonderful word, Doctor—necrotic!"

"I like it a great deal too. It might be my favorite."

"Does the scan tell you what the large mass is on her leg?"

"That's all dead tissue and fluid from the tumor."

It is a strange thing that both Mary and I expected positive news. I couldn't explain it, but both of us knew what the call would be. Oh, it is a wonderful feeling, better than wonderful, but it evoked more relief than elation. Of course, from Mary's standpoint, she now has another cycle of chemo to endure, which is the result of the discovery that chemo is working. The feeling is that the smaller the tumor gets, the less invasive will be the surgery to remove it.

It was a joy to send out my emails tonight, and to hear Mary calling the girls and Donna, Barb, and George. Tomorrow we have not a single thing to do except decorate for Christmas.

I sent this off right away:

> Dear Family:
> Since it is good news and I told everyone that December 1 was a big day for Mary, I figure I better get this email off quickly. We have great news! Mary had a PET scan and MRI today. It showed that the tumor on her lung is gone, those on the lymph nodes were reduced by 50%, and the main tumor in her leg is dying. That comes after a huge scare on Thursday when the leg tumor more than doubled in size. The doctors didn't have a clue what caused that and suspected a blood clot. But a sonogram showed nothing. They now think that the excess is dead tissue and fluid from the tumor. Great news! She has been scheduled for one more round of chemo, since it is working, and then surgery after New Year. Thanks for your many prayers and good thoughts. So far they have worked! We will now get busy decorating for Christmas.
> Love,
> Mary and Jack

Thursday, December 2

> Hey Papa!
>
> I just heard the good news about Grammy! I am so happy!!!!! Grammy sure is tough. :)
>
> Here is another one of my essays. I really strug-gled on what would be appropriate to start it, so I don't know if my opening is very good. I don't mind a paper that has way more wrong things than right things! I want to fix them. Anyways, I will see you very soon for Christmas!
>
> Love Always, Kasey
>
> P.S. Are you smiling?

Kasey's was one of thirty-three emails that poured in after my latest report on Mary. It made both of us smile. I can't think of any time that I have felt closer to everyone in our life. Isn't it strange how something like this draws everyone together? But in Mary's case, there has been such a lifetime of thinking about other people that it is completely normal. I am so proud of her!

Friday, December 3

This morning we meet with Dr. Donthineni. Having gotten the great news from Shoba, we now have to find out when they can do the surgery. Dr. Shoba says that sarcoma is always a surgery cancer; it can't be cured by chemo or radiation. I was a little disappointed that Dr. Donthineni had apparently not been informed about the MRI results when we met, but he assured us that was not important at the moment. I will get a CD tomorrow and bring it to him. The main thing is to get Mary ready for surgery, which will be no easy matter. She needs at least a couple of weeks after the last chemo infusion for her body to gain some strength. She will have a couple of appointments with the surgeon before she is ready. It is a very difficult surgery to say the least. Anything that the tumor in her thigh has touched has to be removed, including ligaments, muscles, etc. If the affected lymph nodes are close enough to the main tumor they can be removed in the same operation. If not, a second operation will be necessary, perhaps done by a general surgeon instead of Dr. Donthineni. Mary will then have at least four days in the hospital and several weeks to recuperate, at which time she will begin another batch of chemo rounds. I wasn't sure whether the total would be six cycles including the three she has already had, or if there is an additional six. Radiation is also in her future. If she has another six cycles that means four months after they start. She will also have to have rigorous physical therapy to get her leg working properly again. I am thinking that the 4th of July celebration at Nancy's may well be her coming out party. A long six months is in front of us.

We agreed to a tentative date of January 6 for the surgery. Mary wasn't completely pleased with the date, thinking it is a desecration of Little Christmas, but since Dr. Donthineni only operates on Thursdays, there is not much else we can do except delay, and that is not an option.

Saturday, December 4

To say that today is part of a weekend has no significance for us retirees. I think I have finally lost the meaning of weekend, although Saturday is still marked by college football, and Sunday is pro football time. But they play games on Monday and Thursday as well now, so maybe pro football is retired too.

We are into our storm season finally, where every third day a new batch of rain hits the coast, wets down the gardens and departs to dump snow on the Sierras and then continues east to Nancy and Marty's farm. It is nice, but I have tried to make working in the yard part of my daily schedule these days, and if it's raining, that is out. I am also really trying hard to have at least two hours of writing every day, but I am not completely succeeding with that resolution. "Boris" is coming along, now into Chapter 12, and almost moving him out of high school into the "real" world. I shudder to think how long that book is going to be by the time I get him to New York in 1950, marrying Eva. He is still in high school at 350 pages, and I haven't yet gotten him into a kibbutz in Israel, driving a truck in the Sinai, in the '36 Olympics, or into the Italian Underground and Yugoslav Partisans in World War II. Oh, yes, and Nazi hunting in Argentina after the war. I feel like I'm writing an old version of *Forest Gump*.

Meanwhile the main concern is Mary. I have to admit that trying to make life easier for her these days has given me a completely different view of the job of the "housewife" in our society. That is a lot of work! It's not so much that it is wearying or overly stressful; it's just that it never lets up. I will be happily doing something and suddenly realize, "Oh damn! I have to get us something to eat." Now if everything were normal, that realization would result in us heading for Happy Garden or Mary's Pizza or some other restaurant and getting dinner. But Mary doesn't eat anything like that these days, so it means a trip to Safeway, and putting something together.

And now, after dinner I have to actually load the dishes in the dishwasher, where before I just rinsed them off and left that chore for Mary. Then I have to wash the suckers! I admit that Mary had to show me what soap to use and where to put it and what setting buttons to push, but I was able to absorb that fairly quickly, having to only ask three times. The worst thing though—*you have to empty the dishwasher and put the damned dishes away!* If this keeps up I'm even going to have to learn how to turn on the washing machine and drier too.

I knew I had to learn all this stuff when one day I found that the bed wasn't made and we were heading to Pleasant Hill for Mary's treatment. In all of our years of marriage I can't ever remember Mary leaving the house with the bed unmade. She would rather be caught in a wreck with dirty underwear than have someone walk into our house and find dishes in the sink or the bed unmade. That's when I knew that something was very, very wrong. So I started making the bed when Mary was taking a shower, and washing the dishes before going to bed. I also decided to wash the pots and pans and other stuff that doesn't get put in the dishwasher. I even use soap on those things!

For all of our marriage Mary and I have laughed that she is Mrs. Inside and I am Mr. Outside. She takes care of the house; I do the garden. She takes the garbage to the back door and I deposit it in the garbage can. She decorates for Christmas inside; I handle everything outside and make sure that every bush has a light on it. It has always worked. But now, I am finding more and more that I am working inside, and I think that is the main reason that I am feeling disoriented. I fear that when Mary actually beats her cancer and is fully in remission, without any more chemo or radiation or Immodium or Zantac or steroids or marijuana brownies (someone sent her some, but she was terrified to try them), I may have been drawn irrevocably into the interior of our house and may never be able to escape. I remember when we were first married and I was the only one who knew how to diaper a baby or iron a pair of pants, how hard it was to teach those skills to Mary and then forget them myself.

I have never been able to cook, am not even capable of boiling water without burning it. But now I am in charge of keeping Mary not only alive, but in some semblance of well-being. That would normally be a monumental task, but in this case, it is a task that only results in a tremendous feeling of guilt on my part. Simply put, Mary doesn't want to eat anything. When she first got sick I was so proud of myself, serving her fresh shrimp for appetizers, soup, and Caesar salad, maybe with a chicken breast or steak. All of that I could cook, especially the fresh shrimp. I can barbecue stuff but I don't consider that cooking. And I can make a Caesar salad because you can buy those bags at Safeway. I can boil Campbell's soup, and I can even place a can of string beans in a pot to heat. Voila! A four-course meal. I was so proud.

But gradually, as the effects of the chemo plug in, Mary's appetite is disappearing and her repertoire of things to eat is shrinking drastically. Right now she is down to milkshakes, Wendy's Frosties, chicken noodle soup, won ton soup, and ice cream, washed down by water and little red bottles of Boost.

"Why don't you make her some smoothies?" friends have asked. That would mean I have to learn another domestic machine.

Sunday, December 5

There is nothing to do today except sit around and watch the 49ers lose.

Monday, December 6

Mary starts her third round of chemo today, getting the single dose of Gemzar at the center. I left her all hooked up, with Alice and

Liliana happily ministering to their patients. Downstairs I picked up the DVD of Mary's PET/CT scan/MRI and drove it to Dr. Donthineni's office in Oakland. I then ran down memory lane with a salami and Swiss sandwich at Genova's, the original site (though today not the original restaurant) of that great deli chain. Then I stopped for a beer at the Kingfish, across from an apartment that brother Bob and I rented during my senior year in college. By the time I got back to Mary, she had been patiently waiting in the lobby for forty-five minutes. I guess I got carried away with my nostalgia.

She should be in pretty good shape for the next couple of days because part of the treatment is that dose of steroids. That jacks her up for at least two days, probably will inhibit her sleep, but they gave her Benedryl to counteract that. It's another of those Catch-22s that crop up throughout the chemo program—one drug has an effect that is countered by another drug which takes a person back to the condition they were in the first place, or to another condition that requires counteracting drugs to counter.

Thank God the cancer cells don't get so confused.

Tuesday, December 7

It's Pearl Harbor day. Hard to believe that is almost seventy years ago. I was alive when the Japanese hit Hawaii, but I couldn't tell you about it, being less than two years old. I do remember fragmental pictures of World War II. I remember walking, probably with Janet and Bob around Woolsey St. collecting bacon grease in #10 tins to be taken to the Lewis Store for a few cents, our war effort, however small. I can remember the rations, particularly of gas, which made driving a luxury. I remember hiding behind the couch during blackouts, with a siren going, scared out of our wits and picturing the chaos after the bombs such as we saw on the newsreels at the movies on Saturday. I remember visiting Aunt Ruth, who had a map of Europe with pins, showing where Uncle Larry was fighting. He was the only member of our family who had to serve in active duty. Tiny bits of memory, but at least enough to keep me aware of the incredible struggle that the invasion of Poland and France and the attacks on Pearl Harbor, China, and the Philippines caused for the world. That so many people could have died is unfathomable; that our generation and our children should ever forget is unforgiveable. I suppose that if we are to make the mistakes of our fathers, it is necessary to forget World War II.

Today is also the birthday of our next door neighbor, Dennis Adair. I always kid him that it is so cool that the Japanese put on such a fireworks display just to celebrate his birthday, but they anticipated Dennis by two years. We walked a bottle of wine over to him anyway, and then stayed to finish it off. It was good to get Mary out of the house somewhere other than to the cancer center.

Wednesday, December 8

In the old days we would have gone to church today, since December 8 is the Feast of the Immaculate Conception, one of the sacred Holy Days of Obligation in the Catholic Church that we all faced when we were young. They were an odd bunch, those holy days; I think there were ten of them, including Easter and Christmas—All Saints Day, where you recovered from Halloween (really All Souls Day); August 15, which I think was the day that Mary was assumed into heaven, called the Feast of the Assumption when we were young, but something else now; Mary got assumed, but Jesus ascended, which was also a holy day, forty days after Easter. Then we had today's holy day, the Immaculate Conception, which commemorates the fact that Mary was conceived without the stain of Original Sin I remember some comedian, George Carlin I think, talking about the irony of "The Holy Family"—a family where the husband got no sex, but the wife had a kid, the kid, a spoiled only child, didn't listen to his parents and ran away from them all the time. There was more, but I can only remember so much irony. My favorite was the Feast of the Circumcision, which occurs on New Year's Day. One night we were having dinner at home with ten or twelve friends and family. Annie was about eight, I think, and we were recalling the Feast of the Circumcision.

"Daddy, what's circumcision?" Annie inquired loudly.

"Well, sweetheart, when a boy is born he has a flap of skin around his penis. For medical or religious reasons, that flap is cut off. That's circumcision."

Annie rose and threw up both arms. "One sentence! He answered that in one sentence! That would have taken Mom two weeks to explain."

She was such an actress!

Today they call the Circumcision the "Solemnity of Mary," whatever that means. And how could I forget, my Dad's birthday was also a Holy Day, January 6. I will always believe that Dad was the only person in all of history who was born on Epiphany in Epiphany (South Dakota). No wonder they declared that to be a holy day!

I forgot the rest of the Holy Days of Obligation, so I looked them up on the Internet. Here they are:

- 1 January: Solemnity of Mary, Mother of God
- 6 January: the Epiphany
- 19 March: Solemnity of St. Joseph, Husband of the Blessed Virgin Mary
- Thursday of the sixth week of Easter: the Ascension
- Thursday after Trinity Sunday: the Body and Blood of Christ
- 29 June: Solemnity of Saints Peter and Paul, Apostles
- 15 August: the Assumption of the Blessed Virgin Mary
- 1 November: All Saints
- 8 December: the Feast of the Immaculate Conception of the Blessed Virgin Mary
- 25 December: the Nativity of our Lord Jesus Christ (Christmas)

I got a kick out of it because the article says that the last synod, or whatever, declared that the bishops have the authority to flop any of these they want over to a Sunday and thus take away the obligation of another Mass day for the Mackerel Snappers. Speaking of which, if I were now roasting in hell for having eaten meat on Friday back in the 1950s, I would be hotter than the hell I was in. I think that the bishops actually did zap at least three of those days into Sundays because I don't remember March 19, except at the feast of St. Joseph (It came two days after the more important St. Patrick's Day which is a holy day only in Ireland and Boston). I also don't remember any

Solemnity of Sts. Peter and Paul, or Thursday after Trinity Sunday, unless that was Pentecost. I suppose it could have been.

Thursday, December 9

It's a day to just slug around. The toll from chemo usually hits Mary on Thursday and builds through Friday and into the weekend. Yesterday she spent the whole day out on her own, with a doctor's appointment with her GP, Dr. Jain, then lunch with her sister Barbara and shopping and dinner with Annie. I declared shopping to be a form of exercise for her, which was well received. All of the doctors have advised her to exercise more, something Mary bravely fights, but when put into a context of shopping or going to lunch, it is a little easier to take. Eventually we are going to have to get into a real routine because she is going to need her strength when we get to the surgery stage. After surgery, it will be formal physical therapy.

Eating for Mary these days is a real problem. The fact is that nothing tastes good for her, and most of what I can prepare makes her gag, not because of the chef, but because she has simply lost her taste buds so to speak. Dr. Donthineni had a name for that, which I should have written down, because it was a cool word, but he said that it was quite common for cancer patients to lose both their appetite and their desire to eat. For Mary it comes down to one thing—soft foods. I can get her to drink smoothies and shakes and I'll start learning how to whip out things on the blender. Anything else she can't take.

It seems to me that there are a whole string of Catch-22 things about cancer. One thing always leads to a consequence, often its opposite. For instance, if Mary tries to force foods, her body will reject it, usually through diarrhea. That necessitates Immodium. The Immodium results in constipation, which requires a pill or two of Dulcolax to soften up what got hard because it had been too soft. Catch-22! The other day, Dr. Shoba said that the swelling around the tumor in her thigh was caused by water blockage because of the tumor. She said she could give Mary a diuretic to take out the water, but then she would probably become dehydrated. Last week she had to have a saline solution infusion because of dehydration. Let me get this straight—she is generally dehydrated except for her left thigh which is retaining water. Couldn't we just drain the thigh into the rest of her body?

And so it goes! The chemo results in all sorts of new problems, each of which has a solution that may well result in a new problem, which requires a remedy that gets you back to Go, where you either collect $200 or go straight to jail.

But all of this provides those of us in the cancer environment with something to do during the day to keep up our interest.

Friday, December 10

I am back in the swing of writing! For the last several weeks it has been like pulling teeth to get me to sit down for more than five minutes and write anything. My book about Boris has languished; this journal about Mary has been sporadic. But today I actually have the desire to write again and the words have simply poured out of me. I feel like I just took a big dose of mental Exlax, and I feel normal again. I always believed that we operate on biorhythms, that all of us have high and low energy days. I also have always believed that you should be acutely aware of how much energy you have, and should consciously recognize the highs and lows, especially the highs. Once you identify one of those highs, you need to act on it and keep working until it runs its course. A high biorhythm time is gold—you don't want to let it pass without being productive.

Saturday, December 11

My old Plymouth returned today! It has been gone or lost for seven or eight years, since Johnny at High Tech towed the carcass away without a working motor, without brakes, without healthy upholstery, unpainted, unchromed, unusable. Johnny dragged it out from behind the garage and carted it off, assuring me that he could fix everything in no time, it being such a simple machine, compared to modern cars. For years I would exercise my visitor rights to that old Plymouth, a '49, that I bought in the early 1980s from an old man in the woods up in Boxboro, northern Massachusetts. Then it only had 40,000 miles on it and was a perfect car to drive in Plymouth the one mile from home to work. I felt so wonderfully eccentric! We dragged her out to California in 1985, towed behind the moving van and it has essentially sat for twenty-five years doing nothing but rust and rot.

Over the years of Johnny's ministry, he has rebuilt the engine, ($3500); painted it an awful color of red/purple, resanded and repainted it an awful color of green/blue, resanded it and repainted it the green I picked out in the first place. He sent the carcass over to a Vietnamese guy in Fairfield name Chang who redid the entire interior ($2500). Finally he replaced the starter, generator, brakes, water pump, steering gear, fixed all the lights. And here it is! The horn doesn't work yet; the speedometer needs a new cable; the gas gauge is broken, but by God, my car is back! I even cleaned out enough room in the garage to fit it in, if I Vaseline the front end to allow the door to slip past the hood.

"Johnny, I'm afraid to ask what the bill is!"

"I don't have a bill. Just give me what you think it is worth. Take your time. You have as long to pay me as I had the car."

Nancy arrives tonight, making yet another trip to cheer up Mary and help her with Christmas. She is also coming to spend a day with Deb, who is flying from her home in Massachusetts to San Francisco tomorrow for business meetings. Deb Woods-Joyce and Nancy were best friends at Plymouth-Carver High School when we were living back East. Since then she has become another of our "adopted" children. Actually, Nancy is coming from Reno, because the kids are playing basketball in Virginia City, so she is already more than halfway here.

I was very pleased at dinner because Nancy was highly impressed with my menu: cracked crab, fresh salmon, asparagus, and spinach salad. Those things I can cook, because they take no expertise at all, no recipes, no thinking, but it is very difficult to learn to cook with Mary in her present state. I have to admit she had a few crab legs and a tiny bit of salmon, a miniscule amount of cottage cheese, and mandarin oranges. That is more than she has eaten in two weeks, except for soups and chocolate milk shakes of one form or another.

I think it's because Nancy is here. We both have great respect for Nancy's expertise in nutrition, and frankly, Mary is scared to death that Nancy will think she is being unhealthy. I may have her phone every night to badger her mother about proper diet, but I don't think it is fair to impose too many rules on Mary because it is difficult to put yourself in her position with a body full of poison to which each person reacts differently. Mary is doing as well as can be expected at the moment.

Sunday, December 12

Deb Joyce got to the house just before noon, having taken a red-eye from Boston. She wandered in bright-eyed and happy, joining Nancy and Annie in bonding with Mary—our three daughters.

I so love watching Mary with them. The love is measureable, the result of a lifetime of doing things for and with the girls, time that basically has been free of turmoil where they are concerned. Early on, I told Mary that I would do the disciplining with Nancy and Anne, and I let them know very clearly that in a fight with their mother, they would probably lose in my eyes, so they never bothered. They have grown closer together as time has passed, and now they are essentially of the same mind in most things.

Of course, as the children of an ailing parent, Nancy and Annie are totally concerned with her well-being, and as such they are likely to be a little more demanding than I am.

"Mom, did you drink your water today?"

"Mom, you have to have more proteins. You need at least three Boosts a day if you aren't going to eat anything solid."

"Mom, you have to exercise. We are going for a walk this morning."

Mary returned from a half-hour walk along Green Valley Road, clad palely, all in gray, her face matching her sweatshirt,.

"How was it, Mare?"

"Oh, it was wonderful." Accent on the no exclamation point!

"We're going shopping now, Dad," one of the girls said.

"Not with me," their mother said, forcefully, plopping down on the couch without removing coat, hat, or gloves. She tuned in to the Hallmark Channel and prepared to settle in for the rest of the day to recuperate from the "exercise." I have been reading about Gandhi, and I think that Mary has discovered a form of non-violent opposition to her daughters' "suggestions."

So at 1:00, Nancy, Annie, and Deb went shopping, a mini-marathon that would last until 7:30, when they finally returned loaded with bags and presents. Nancy would say that she has no choice. In fact, she did say that, because there are no stores in Eureka and she only gets one or two days to do her shopping for Christmas. Anne would never even try to make an excuse for shopping; she has been a pro at it all her life, perfectly capable of walking into a store, carefully examining every single item in their inventory and walking out without buying a thing, carrying just as much energy and enthusiasm into the next store. Deb, like our friend Donna Schafer, simply gets dragged along by our daughters. Deb and Donna are amateurs who remain more or less in a state of reverent shock when they see the girls in action. I think that Annie is a natural born shopper; Nancy has learned the skill and taken it possibly to a higher level than her younger sister, but she may have the benefit of a more expansive credit card, and I feel sure that Annie will eventually get into her volume class.

This evening, the girls and Mary carried the energy right into present-wrapping, filling three rooms with conversation, wrapping paper and debris, leaving a mountain of boxes, colorfully wrapped, around the tree. We are almost ready for Christmas.

Mary has just about finished decorating the ground floor, with only one or two venues yet to be filled. The girls' bedrooms upstairs remain, but I have no doubt she will finish by Christmas. In normal health, she would start at 9:00 and "putter around" all day and well into the night. But these days she can only muster energy in half-hour spurts, maybe three or four times in a day, so the effort is, of necessity, much more spread out. But it is still a labor of love, and one that only she can do, at least in her own mind. I could probably place every caroler and every nativity set into its proper place, but Mary would have to move them around to get them looking perfect, and she would be absolutely right. I have tried to put stuff up and it looks stupid until she comes around, "sproofs" them up a bit, and makes them look wonderful. Mary's Christmas "deckies" have become the stuff of legend. There are more than 500 of the Byers Choice carolers, 150 nativity sets from around the world, dozens of Santa Clauses, at least a dozen trees for African animals, patriotic USA, children, Beanie Babies, and so on. All of these are carefully placed in suitable vignettes with boughs and garlands, occupying every square inch of flat space in the house. There is literally too much for the eye to take in, and the array increases every year.

Monday, December 13

Mary has her last chemo infusion today at noon. This will be the end of the third cycle. She will go in every day for the next seven to get a shot of Nuprin and/or a blood test to make sure her cell counts are okay. So far they have been fine the entire time, the red cells and platelets just barely low and the important white cells way over normal. Of course, today she felt very good, the best day in a couple of weeks, but that will change as the double dose of chemo takes effect later in the week. But thus far, her side effects have been pretty much limited to fatigue, not the other kinds of things that the cancer books talk about—neuropathy, nausea, swelling, etc. Now she has off until after the surgery, which is still scheduled for January 6. Mary has decided that the Feast of Epiphany may be a good omen, and if not that, then my dad will certainly be looking after her on his birthday.

Nancy and Deb both left this morning, after whirling through the house, making beds, doing dishes, cleaning wherever it occurred to them or wherever they happened to be standing. Tomorrow I will engage Rosemary, a professional who cleans for Mary every so often in normal times, to do a thorough job of cleaning preparatory to Christmas. She has been coming in on a regular three-week basis since Mary got sick. I may be capable of doing the dishes and occasional other chores in the house, but vacuuming, dusting, and other cleaning is, in my mind, a job for the pros. And Mary hasn't raised a single objection, although she likes to get out of the house when Rosemary and her daughter are in cleaning. I always smile because whenever Rosemary is scheduled to clean the house, Mary runs around the day before and cleans everything in advance. Heaven forbid that a cleaning service comes to your house and actually finds it dirty. If it were me, I would deliberately work in the mud outside and track it all through the house just to get my money's worth the next day. But then again, I am only in the opening stages of being a Hausfrau. But I swear, the day I catch myself cleaning up in advance of the cleaning lady, I will resign and move to Samoa.

Tuesday, December 14

Hi all:

Just a final Mary update before Christmas. Today she finished her third and last cycle of chemo, a double shot, before she takes a break prior to surgery. She has about three weeks to get her strength back, with surgery scheduled for January 6 at Alta Bates. We will get the details of the operation from her doctor on Friday this week. It will be a serious operation, because they have to remove anything in her leg that the tumor is touching, so she has been advised that there will be a significant program of physical therapy afterward. She will then be scheduled for up to six more cycles of chemo and probably radiation. Right now it would be wonderful if we could look to the 4th of July at Nancy and Marty's as her "Coming out Party." Meanwhile, Mary has stayed in very good spirits, with the main side effects of the chemo being fatigue, but none of the more sinister ones that she could have gotten. The girls and Deb were all here last weekend decorating, wrapping and talking, so they left us in great spirits. We feel very blessed for the way things have gone thus far, and that certainly includes all of your good wishes and prayers. On January 6 we are certain that Herman will be looking down and smiling at Mary. Have a wonderful Christmas if we don't see you. We are looking forward to the "California Party" at Ed and Jeanette's on Sunday.

With love,

Mary and Jack

Amazing, how the chemo schedule dominates the day these days. Mary doesn't have any more infusions, but she gets the Nuprin every day this week. For some reason they scheduled them all in mid-afternoon, so we spend the morning "filling in" the time until we drive to the Epic Center for the shot. It is about a thirty-five-minute drive. The shot takes about three minutes and then thirty-five back home. With a stop at the store, it is now 4:00, almost time for a drink, scotch for me, Boost for Mary. I sometimes put water in my scotch so as to be a good example for her in water consumption. We have never really figured out just how much water she is supposed to drink. Basically she drinks a glass of water whenever I get the urge to nag her. With the girls around I seldom have to nag because they are so good at it, but I am developing the skill because of necessity. If there are three things that Mary is not too keen on right now, they are eating, drinking water, and exercise. For some reason the cancer people make a big deal out of all three.

Wednesday, December 15

There's nothing to talk about today, so I guess I'll fall back on my good old big toes. I woke up last night with both of my big toes absolutely freezing, at least mentally frostbitten. It is really hard to find a blanket of something that is capable of just warming up the big toes when the rest of your body is sweating. I put on a pair of jogging socks and that seemed to handle the problem.

For several years I have had problems with my feet. It usually feels like a line of pebbles is lodged right behind the toes and in front of the balls of my feet. I lived with it for quite a while, and then decided that I should tell the doctor. He sent me to a foot specialist who examined my feet and sent me to a neurologist. She examined my feet and sent me to a physical therapist who told me to sink my feet into a tub of white rice and crinkle them around for half an hour or so every day. Can you imagine how embarrassing it is to have someone show up at your house and you are bathing your feet in rice? For several weeks I had recurring nightmares that someone had mistaken my foot rice for Uncle Ben's and had served it to me for dinner, toe jam and all.

It seems I have a sort of secondary neuropathy in my feet. That means that the nerve endings are losing their strength and causing the blood flow to stop. But it isn't the main nerves; that's why they called it "secondary." It is the smaller nerves that sort of run out of steam before they actually get to the toes. The neurologist said that I should do a stimulus program by rubbing my toes with a variety of different textured surfaces to get the nerves working. I tried that right after the rice, tickling them with a feather, and pounding them with a hammer. Did you know that you can't tickle yourself? Not even your highly ticklish big toes. And all the hammer did was blacken the nails, which were so angry they left my body entirely. I finally decided that I had lived with my toes for my whole life, and why should I worry about them now. I'm 80 percent or so done with them anyway. So now I find that if I simply ignore them, they don't bother me.

Except at night in bed when they get cold! It is really curious how that all works. You can't just have one cold big toe. If you're going to have one, you have to include them both. I think there is some main line up by your buttocks that sends out the codes and it never learned to send a signal to just one toe. So both big toes get cold if one of them feels like it. Some nights it will be the two little toes on the other side of the foot, but both toes on both feet have to suffer the same, whether it be cold or pain or whatever little toes need when they feel like acting up. There are days when the pebble line runs all the way across my foot/feet, and others when both of them got sick of throbbing and don't send out any signals at all. I ignore those days too.

One of these days I'll have a real nerve problem and I intend to ask the doctor about how both feet have to feel the same thing all the time. I'm sure they have a multi-syllable name for it. If they do, I'll commit it to memory because it is so cool to be able to tell your friends you have some exotic ailment that you can barely pronounce. It took me two years to remember neuropathy, but now I'm ready for bigger game. I wonder what you would put the rice in if you had a nerve problem in your buttocks.

Thursday, December 16

Nothing. Mary is starting to wear down, as is usually the case at the end of each cycle. She'll be rocked tomorrow and it may carry into the weekend as well. It seems to build each cycle, I suppose because more and more of the Taxotere is in her body.

Friday, December 17

Mary could barely stand this morning when I came home from my morning coffee and muffin. She was panting heavily, and very wobbly.

"Have you eaten anything?"

"No, I'll drink a Boost in the car."

"No, you'll sit down and drink it right now."

"We'll be late for my shot."

"You can't be late. They give it to you whenever you get there."

Mary has a respect for doctor's appointments that approaches reverence. Even though she has probably spent a year of her life waiting in doctor's offices for a physician who is chronically late, she still thinks she has to be on time herself. At the Epic Care Center, if we get there half an hour early, like we did yesterday, they give her the shot immediately. If you are late, they give it to you immediately. An appointment time is like lines on a road in China—they are merely suggestions. But Mary's Holy Names training is so strong that she hyperventilates if she is two minutes late. She did stop this morning, sat down and drank her Boost in a civilized manner, from a cup, instead of ripping the seal off with her teeth and drinking from the bottle. But that is all she would take. I have to admit, it is frustrating to want something very badly for a person and have them completely unresponsive. You think it is your duty to insist that they eat, for instance, and plainly put, they can't. I was thinking it must have been that way for the family of Karen Carpenter, the singer, who died of anorexia. They must have tried to get her to eat, and she must have been unable to do so. How discouraging. I almost feel that way with Mary. It is obvious that she has lost a lot of weight, and it is just as obvious that for health and well being she has to eat, to get the nutrients she needs to live. But she can't. Most things, no matter how simple, gag her when she tries to swallow. I can't imagine that, thinking that I would eat paper if I knew I needed it. But watching her these days, maybe I wouldn't.

We meet with Dr. Donthineni this afternoon. He is a very personable man, very comfortable and comforting, not at all the uptight, highly strung professional you encounter so often with doctors. Today he reviewed the two MRIs Mary has had. It seems that all of the tumors are necrotic in their core, dead with live cells on the outer edges. All have shrunk considerably, by almost half. She has two small nodules on one lymph node, but only on one side, where before they told us that the lymph nodes on both sides were affected. As Dr. Shoba said, the nodule on the lung is gone.

"I can easily cut out the tumor in your leg," he said confidently. "I have done a hundred like it."

He told Mary what to expect, that he would have to remove the muscles where the tumor is, but explained that the muscles on the inside of the thigh are not vital, as those are on the outside. She will have a bit of adjustment but not too much. He said that the tumor on the lymph node is in the stomach area and that will probably be more sore than her leg. After the surgery, she will have to start daily injections of Coumadin to prevent blood clots. Mary cringed a bit when he told her she could administer them herself or have me do it. That will be interesting to see which of us ends up as the administrator.

We had originally been told by Jackie, his receptionist, that the operation would be on January 6, but the doctor said that he was asked to be the main speaker in a conference that week, so he would like to move the surgery up before New Year's Day. I think that both Mary and I are fine with that, because the sooner the tumor is gone, the happier we will be.

"Let's just get rid of the sucker," was the way Mary put it, causing Dr. Donthineni to smile.

All of that business taken care of, I asked him where in India his family lives.

"Hyderabad," he answered, saying he left for England as a little boy.

"We were just in Hyderabad, two years ago," I told him, to

his astonishment. Apparently not too many tourists ever get to Hyderabad.

"We spent a day in Cyberabad," I said, referring to the massive IT section of the city that has been taken over by just about every high tech company in the world.

"That is very near my home."

"It is surrounded by slums of the worst sort," I said.

"That's it!"

That began a discussion of India and the terrible conditions most of the people have to endure. We all agreed that It is a very depressing place to visit, not one that has any quick solutions.

Mary's surgery will certainly end our New Year's Eve plans. In fact, with the operation on December 29, she will still be in the hospital at New Year, opening 2011 in a very inauspicious manner. Or maybe not, depending on the efficacy of the operation. I would expect that the girls will opt out of any plans that take them very far from their mother, so I will have to tell Cole that we won't be going to his place at Tahoe, as we had planed. It has been a long while since we spent New Year's Eve at home. Come to think of it, we have never spent it in a hospital either.

Saturday, December 18

A simple shot of Nuprin this morning at 9:00. Mary is still pretty shaky. We stopped by Annie's to discuss shopping plans, but it was evident that Mary was in no mood to hit the stores. It took us quite a while to get her to tell us what she needed to buy, almost as though she was afraid that we would object. But finally Annie pried a few items out of her and agreed to pick them up this afternoon. We headed for the Hickory Pit for breakfast, but Mary only ate about five slices of banana and shut down. We dropped Annie off back at her house and headed home ourselves to put Mary to bed. She will be better tomorrow.

Sunday, December 19

My brother Ed and his wife Jeanette are hosting the Dold Christmas brunch today for those few of us who are still living in

California. Isn't it interesting that our family of eleven kids, just about all of whom were born in California, are now mostly living outside of the Bay Area, indeed east of the Midwest? There are only Mary and I, Clayton and Hilda, Linda and Mike, and Ed and Jeanette in the Bay Area. Gini is still here too, but her family is all in Seattle. I suppose we have to consider Ken and Elaine to be Californians, but Susanville is more Nevada than California. And Linda Jo and Gorden are in Reno. Now that I think of it, I'm wrong, because that is seven of our eleven who are still in the West, with Bob and Gail in New Hampshire, Tim and Patty in West Virginia, Janet in Maryland, and Carolyn in Minnesota.

A few of us gathered today in Montclair: Linda and Mike, Clayton and Hilda, Mary, Annie, and me, and Ed and Jeanette with their kids Geoff and Michelle. A big winter storm is raging this week, which pretty much closed down the Donner Summit, preventing sisters Elaine and Linda Jo from getting here.

Mary was wigged out for the first time in public, wearing her silver wig that so closely approximates her normal hair. She promised Annie and me that she would beg out of the party if she started feeling bad, but she hung right in there to the end and seemed to have a good time. Of course, she was asleep within seconds of getting back home. She had her normal shot this morning at 9:00, and had to get up a bit earlier to dress and get ready for the party. It was a big day comparatively speaking, for her, and she did well with it.

It was nice to see Geoff, who hasn't changed much with his first year in college at U.C. Davis, and Michelle, who is in her last year at Bishop O'Dowd, student body president no less, getting mentally geared up for the rugby season and college entrance applications. It is amazing how fast time passes, but we already knew that.

Monday, December 20

This morning I discovered that Wayne Newton and Brenda Lee are the same person. For weeks now we have been listening to Christmas carols on XM Radio—"Traditional Holiday" for us old guys who like to listen to Glenn Miller, Bing, Frank, Nat, Doris Day, Ella, and the Lennon Sisters with Lawrence Welk; and "Holly" for the youngsters who want to hear Smashing Pumpkins mouth

"Jingle Bells," or Barenaked Ladies (who are all male) singing "An Elf's Lament." Generally, I like the old songs because to me, they are Christmas, but Mary prefers songs "that have a good beat," so she opts for the "Holly" stuff. Simply by accident, I listened to Brenda Lee and Wayne Newton back-to-back. You couldn't tell them apart! All this time we thought Wayne Newton was in the closet, when he was actually walking around in plain sight in drag. I discovered shortly afterward, listening to Chuck Berry singing "Merry Christmas Baby," that he's really Pearl Bailey. And I have always believed that Michael Jackson and Donny Osmond are clones, one race removed, and remained that until puberty hit one of them.

It is getting harder and harder to deal with the songs of Christmas. They seem to be able to take any subject and worm it around to make it sound like it belongs. Elvis sings "Blue Christmas" and Jo Stafford belts out "Christmas Blues." First of all, Christmas is red and green, period! What's this blue stuff? Every so often you see a house decorated with blue lights, Totally wrong. Now Mary tells me that is for Hanukkah, but who ever heard of Jewish Christmas lights? Blue is out; so is blues. That aforementioned "Elf's Lament" deals with the elves wanting to unionize because they are underpaid and underappreciated and forced to make junk toys that are beneath their craft level. What kind of Christmas spirit is that?

We got kind of excited when we heard Vic Damone singing "Christmas in San Francisco," a song I hadn't heard before. It's the only Christmas song I've ever heard that brings in Chinatown and actually has a line that rhymes with "pork." I was taken back a bit however when old Vic crooned "Christmas in San Francisco, looking like some wonderful fairyland… ." Tony Bennett, whose signature song is about San Francisco, voiced the same theme, singing about the "gay feelings" of the season. But in those old days, PC wasn't so strong, in fact, didn't exist like today. I heard Johnny Mercer say that the "fat guy" was coming to town, and later referred to St. Nick as "that old guy." And what can we say when the Spinners tell us that they are "dreaming of a white Christmas"?

Most of the singers and groups are definitely tied to one or the other genres; they're either traditional or they're copycats. I recognized only three singers who are able to jump from one channel to the other—Elvis, Johnny Mathis, and Tony Bennett. Their voices seemed to be accepted over all the decades. I think that I put Mathis and Nat King Cole as the two best at singing carols—their voices so mellow, the phrasing wonderful—and if I had to pick a female singer, I would say Ella who can sing like Streisand, but doesn't have as big an ego. The group that does Christmas best, hands down, is the Mills Brothers, who can pull off all the old carols with the warmest of feelings. They just sound like Christmas. Of course Mary and I grew up with Andy, Perry, Bing and Frank. Nobody in modern music can match them, nor can they match the songs. Today I heard The Waitresses singing a thing called "Christmas Wrapping" and I got mildly ill. Later Right Stuff chimed in with "Christmas List," intoning the perfectly seasonal thought that "I want the whole list," and "If you give me everything, I won't be happy. Ah yes, the Chritma $pirit!

I was trying to decide who was the worst singer to attempt an album of Christmas carols. I more or less cringe when the world's tenors make an attempt. Pavarotti can manage the big classical stuff like the "March of the Wooden Soldiers" and "Handel's Messiah," but the other guys sound like wimps with things like "Jingle Bells." Andrea Bocelli tried that song and the only note he got right was the final "night," where he could let loose and sound tenorish. Placido Domingo stumbles along trying to tell us "Santa Claus is Coming to Town," sounding very much like Tennessee Ernie Ford tiptoeing through the tulips. Worse than Placido though is Willie Nelson hoping Santa would bring him some joints if he was really good. For a while that one got my Worst Carol Award, until "America's Poet," Bob Dylan, took the mike. The Singing Dogs have more on-key notes than that fraud. He nearly fell asleep telling the kids they "better watch out." I think his big brass bed was too close to the recording studio. Dylan should be summarily taken out and whipped if he ever leaves his cave again and appears in public trying to "sing" anything. Not to sound too old fashioned, I have also selected a worst among the traditional singers. Nothing can match the ineptitude of Rosemary Clooney and Gene Autry flattening "Jolly Old St. Nicholas." Just because he wrote "Rudolf the Red-nosed Reindeer," cowboy Gene thought he could sing. He brought Rosemary down to his level. An interesting song I have never heard before was Cary Grant singing "A Christmas Lullaby," a perfectly beautiful poem about a grandfather tucking in his lovely granddaughter. There was music, but he only managed to mouth a phrase here and there. I kept waiting for him to intone "Judy, Judy, Judy. ..." It would be cool if that were his granddaughter's name.

My favorite song on the "Holly" side is without question Bruce Bedsprings doing that much overplayed "Santa Claus is Coming To Town." He rocks that out and just makes you feel good. And hands down, my favorite Christmas carol of all times in Nat King Cole's "Christmas Song." And I hate the taste of roasting chestnuts.

Is there any singer who puts a smile on your face any better than Dean Martin? He literally sings a smile through the radio. He's certainly not the best singer of all time, but he just seems always to be having so much fun.

After listening to these two stations for about two weeks, I am thoroughly fed up with certain songs. We know that Santa is coming to town. Everyone with a bad voice tackles that song because you really don't have to sing. You hear less and less of the old hymns: Joy to the World, Little Town of Bethlehem, First Noel, even Silent Night. Jingle Bells hangs in there, but nowadays Jolly Old St. Nick, Santa Coming to Town, Little Drummer Boy, are more in vogue and mostly secular. Then Grandma gets run over by a reindeer, Snoopy toasts the Red Baron, and a guy yells "Alvin!" at the top of his lungs. That's the Christmas spirit these days.

The most inane "song" has to be the "Twelve Days of Christmas," which has been sung in every language, by every sort of singer, with every variety of 12th Night gifts. A Brown University group called Grex Chattertockarum sings the whole thing in Latin, "Duodecem Dies Natalis." John Denver even tried to sing it with the Muppets, Miss Piggy telling everyone in the world that she got five gold rings. I made a compilation of gifts from a couple dozen different 12-Day versions:

12 Howling kitties (Parody)
11 Diaper wipings (Christmas with a baby)
10 Madoff ponzies (Business)

9   Finding parking spaces (12 pains of Christmas)

8   8 million dollars (Baby Tigga)

7   Packs of smokes (Second City)

6   Harvey Wallbangers (Christmas Spirit)

5   Flanle shurts (Redneck)

4   Jelly donuts (Twin Peaks)

3   French friends (Elmo)

2   Pogo Sticks (Disney—Winnie the Pooh)

1   Cadillac to put it all in (Ghetto)

Just to set the record straight, the twelve days begin with Boxing Day, December 26, and end with Twelfth Night (January 5), filling the space between Christmas and Epiphany. Of course, that only comes to 11 days if you count on your fingers. I figure Epiphany, January 6, must be the 12th Day of Christmas. That's when the wise guys brought their gifts.

Christmas music is a fertile field for editorial opinion and it gives me something to think about when we're on our way to the cancer center. Mary has her last shot this morning. She will now be free from chemo, shots, and other medications for more than a month, and may not have to have any more of the Nuprin either. But her pre-op meetings will start sometime this week I am sure, because her operation is only four days after Christmas. She is still pretty rocky from the three rounds of chemo. This morning she had lost another five pounds, not a good thing, since she is going to need her strength for the surgery. But there is just no way to get her to eat anything substantial. We just have to keep our fingers crossed that she will be all right.

Tuesday, December 21

There is nothing that is cancer-related today! Mary can sleep in without the threat of shots, infusions, or anything. We are still worrying about her eating habits. Marcia Buxton tells me I should buy a Vita Mix machine, which apparently can make a juice out of anything—asphalt, soil additives, old socks, anything. "You can disguise what you are giving her," Marcia said with conviction. I'll have to talk about that with Cole. We are meeting this morning for breakfast, for no other reason than to BS about life, worry about the present and the future, and treasure the past. It is a skill that we have had all our lives. We met at the Hickory Pit in Walnut Creek, an old standby way back to the days when it was Emil Villa's on 44th Street in Oakland. Mary and Annie and I had breakfast there last week, so I suppose we are once again good customers.

I finished up my Walnut Creek time with some random shopping at David M. Bryan, my favorite store, mostly because they have marvelous stuff that has no practical use, unless you go to the kitchen department. I always go for crystal and knickknacks that clutter up the top of furniture or the shelves of china cabinets. Plus they wrap everything for you, which is the main reason I like it.

My last chore of the day is to fill my green garbage cans with dead leaves. It's not easy these days because of all the rain we've had, but I have piles stored up for times like this. I have found in my retirement that filling those cans is one of the sure things in my existence, something I have to do simply because it goes against my grain not to use something I am paying to dispose of. I suppose if I could get a dozen of such chores, I could fill several days of my week. I'll wait until the summer to find out.

Tonight I have to look forward to the Beef O'Brady's Bowl in Jacksonville, which pits the University of Southern Mississippi against Louisville. I haven't catalogued the bowl games for several years. The names continue to change, getting more bizarre every year. I am starting to look back with feeling on the good old Poulan Weedeater Bowl, which now is one of the old favorites. There are now thirty-five officially sanctioned bowls in college football, and they don't end on January 1. It used to be that the colleges felt the football season was too long and the athletes had to be back in class as soon as possible. That's the reason they give to explain why they don't have a National Championship tournament—"Our *student athletes* need to be in the classroom." Bull! First of all, half of those *student athletes* never graduate. Either they get drafted or they flunk out; most are semi-literate at best. Cal, that incredible institution of higher learning in Berkeley. has graduated only 20 percent of its basketball players in the last ten years. My guess is that the number is lower for footballers. This year there are, count them, seven bowl games after January 1, with the Tostitos National Championship Bowl (Isn't that a ridiculous name?) in Glendale, Arizona, on January 10. There are six bowls on New Year's Day: TicketCity Bowl, Outback Bowl, Capital One Bowl, Tostitos Fiesta Bowl (Tostito's can afford two BCS bowls?), and the semi-traditional Gator Bowl, and yes, thank God, the unattached, un-sponsored, unadulterated Rose Bowl, the "Granddaddy of them all!" However, it no longer pits the winners of the Big 10 and the Pac 10, because Oregon is in the National Championship game and Stanford, who came in 2nd in the Pac 10, can't be in the Rose Bowl because Oregon isn't.

The names continue to make one smile. How can you be serious in the face of the GoDaddy.com Bowl in Mobile, Alabama, which pits Middle Tennessee against Miami (of Ohio)? Or the BBVA Compass Bowl (Pittsburg vs. Kentucky) in Birmingham, the Kraft Fight Hunger Bowl (Nevada vs. BC) in San Francisco, or the Meineke Car Care Bowl (South Florida vs. Clemson)? I can't even say Chick-fil-A Bowl without cracking up. I suppose it would be serious if I was from South Carolina or Florida State, but come on, eat beef! There is a Little Caesar's Bowl, a Franklin American Mortgage Music City Bowl, the New Era Pinstripe Bowl, the Bell Helicopter Armed Forces Bowl. The longest name goes to the San Diego County Credit Union Poinsettia Bowl. In case you missed it Northern Illinois defeated Fresno State in the uDrove Humanitarian Bowl and Troy whipped Ohio in the R+L Carrier New Orleans Bowl. BYU wiped out UTEP in the New Mexico Alphabet Bowl. (I made up the alphabet part.)

Friday, December 24

To all of our family:

Mary and I send out heartfelt best wishes for a wonderful Christmas. We thank each of you for you warm thoughts and prayers over the past months. We think an end is in sight. Mary goes in for her surgery on Wednesday, Dec. 29, where they will take out the large tumor in her leg and two small ones in her lymph nodes in the stomach area. After that they will take her case to what they call "the tumor board," a consortium of hospitals at Stanford, Cal, Sutter (Alta Bates) and others to determine the continuing treatment. Apparently nothing is very normal about her cancer.

The chemo has been tougher on her as each cycle progressed, but she will now be free of it for at least a month, and we hope her appetite will return. We are celebrating Christmas Eve at Anne's, complete with Stroganoff ala' Mom, and will have Christmas at our house with the entire family.

One of the best things about this experience is how close it has brought everyone, both friends and family. Our hope is to continue that feeling through-out the coming year--a perfectly do-able New Year's resolution.

Our love to all of you and your families.

Mary and Jack, Marty, Nancy, Kasey, Josh, Annie, Erik and Clay

It's Christmas Eve and that means Stroganoff for dinner tonight. As long as I can remember as a kid, Mom always served Stroganoff on Christmas Eve, cooking two or three huge pots of the beef-laden sauce which she poured over mounds of rice. Bob, Tom, and I would easily put away three plates each, so I suppose it was a perfect meal for a family of eleven kids and a modest budget. But I will never forget the taste! I suppose over the years I have eaten a dish called "Stroganoff" many times, but none of them ever came close to Mom's. Wonderful memories are evoked the second I taste Mom's Stroganoff as cooked these days by Nancy and Annie; it makes me a kid again. Mom's Stroganoff was distinctive, one of those dishes that you never forget the flavor, like linguini and clams at the Cellar in Monterey when I started the field studies back in the early 1970s. I have scoured the world looking for that wonderful taste, finding it only at Del Monico's in New Haven and a little restaurant in Rome. It is that way with Mom's Stroganoff. She gave the recipe to Nancy and Annie and they are the only ones I have found who can make it to taste like Christmas Eve in 1957.

Because of Mary's illness, the girls decided that Annie would host Christmas Eve and Nancy would supervise the turkey dinner at our house on Christmas. Most of the morning today was used up cooking the dinner we will eat tomorrow. Josh has duties helping Grammy with her apple pie, including picking the Granny Smiths off of our tree. Kasey always works on the turkey dressing. Usually Mary makes cranberry sauce, but we are falling back on her reserve supply this year.

We got to Anne's around 5:30, greeted there by Erik who made the long trip up from Phoenix yesterday, arriving about midnight. Passing the Church of Christ the King on our way, we noticed that the parking lot was fairly empty, so we quickly decided that the 6:30 Mass tonight was perfect for us. Mary had said that the kids really liked Midnight Mass and we were going to that marathon tonight, but Kasey and Josh quickly squashed that idea and we gladly joined the "Kids' Mass." It is awful to have to report, but we were all thrilled that it only took half an hour, Father Joyce, being eminently practical, not wanting to drag the service and sermon out too long for the young ones, to the delight of the old ones.

Saturday, December 25

It's the first track on Ray Coniff's Christmas Album, "Jolly Old St. Nicholas." We aren't sure when we started using that as the signal for the kids to come running to the living room to see what treasures Santa has left them, but we simply can't have Christmas without it. The minute those notes hit the air waves, Kasey and Josh roar down the stairs and into the living room. In the old days we made movies of the event, and once Mary sent Anne and Nancy back upstairs because they didn't show enough enthusiasm for her taste. Kasey offered to let me do the run with them this year, but it kind of reminds me of Pamplona at the start of bullfight season, and I was afraid I would get trampled, or worse yet, fall down the stairs and break a hip or ear or something. After all, Kasey takes only about four steps to make it down the whole winding staircase.

The Santa world is much altered these days, probably because of the Internet. Santa has competition now that he never dreamed of before Rudolph started guiding him around. He can't just bring a portable radio or model car. Kids need laser-guidance, and Ipod-Yahoo-Kodak-flashlight cell phones. You have to know what equipment the kid already has from outside sources, and even with FaceBook, Santa is hard pressed to keep ahead of the information glut. So it is down to the very latest version of the cell phone (with a flashlight and an airhorn, please) and a sock full of little things that don't absorb too much of the memory in the kid's computer brain. Life Savers still work and, in some cases, even Peeps.

The adult world on the other hand is not nearly as frivolous as the kids. Marty got very excited over Josh's new remote-controlled helicopter yesterday, but he completely exploded his joy-meter when he opened his new electronic-controlled model airplane, with a three-foot wingspan. Mary and I are astonished by the challenge of our new Wii games, which will now allow us to play darts, tennis, croquet, pool, box a few rounds and work out with Jane Fonda without ever leaving our house. Of course, we will have to phone Annie or Josh to get instructions for turning the system on, but we have been doing that ever since they went away from telegrams, Victrolas, and crank wall phones.

This year was supposed to be a reduced Christmas, but the living room was even more filled with wrapped things than ever. Kasey and Josh made a spectacular haul of warm clothes, jewelry (for Kasey) and tools (for Josh). It always amazes me what gift the kids will get excited about. But when you think about it, a toddler will get more excited by the crinkly paper that a stuffed animal is wrapped in than the panda itself. There is always some seemingly unheralded thing that completely draws their enthusiasm. We are the same. My best thing is a coffee cup signed with love by Marty, Nancy, Kasey, and Josh, one of those gifts that Nancy has a habit of creating in the solitude of her farm and the Internet.

Erik has taken over the turkey duties in the family. He was busy in the kitchen by the time the second of five NBA games was half over. We more or less slugged the day away. Mary is really rocked out now by the accumulation of chemo, feeling extreme fatigue, bone ache, and flu symptoms. She vowed to get up by the time dinner is served, and indeed, appeared in the early evening nicely wigged out with her traditional Christmas blouse and holiday decorations.

It bothers her that she doesn't have the strength to celebrate as she wants, but the family is so solicitous and thankful for every effort she makes that it doesn't matter. It is amazing that the house is at least 90 perce% decorated, a monumental accomplishment, given the fact that it was mostly done in twenty-minute increments when energy came and was quickly dissipated.

We can only be thankful this Christmas for everything we have. Certainly Mary's cancer has thrown a hurdle before us, but we have Erik coming into the family and his beautiful son, Clayton. We have a sparkly-eyed Annie planning their wedding, a granddaughter who grows more beautiful and interesting by the day, a grandson who is growing up right before our eyes. Marty is really our son, and we have two daughters who could not be more beautiful and loving if they tried. We have a hundred times more good things in life than we need, now even a perfect, green '49 Plymouth, and a complete collection of every Beatles' CD in existence. Life is indeed good, to be treasured daily.

Sunday, December 26

There is nothing to do today but eat turkey sandwiches and sit around and watch the 49ers and Raiders get eliminated from the playoffs. Mary never did get out of bed today and by the time I looked up from the TV it was dark outside. I love our new Vita Juice mixer, which I think is capable of chewing just about anything into a liquid. Right now it churns out two glasses of protein-calorie shakes for Mary's consumption. Later I can get to bar drinks, fruities, and other useful things. I think I may also be able to save money on the garbage bill by juicing everything and washing it down the sink rather than filling the cans. Compost should be no problem at all anymore.

The fact is that Nancy's concoction seems to be working. Mary emerged from the bathroom this evening moaning that she had gained two and a half pounds. She has lost more than forty pounds already and that is quite enough. My fear is that tomorrow's Pre-Op at the hospital will show her too weak for surgery, and that would not be a good thing.

Monday, December 27

Mary went this afternoon for her pre-op session at Alta Bates for a thorough check-out prior to her surgery on Wednesday. We arrived a little after 2:00, late by Mary's figuring, but it is really hard to be late in a hospital because you always have to sit around for a half hour at least before anyone decides to see you. In this case, Mary had half an hour of form filling to do, so the actual arrival time was moot.

Her pre-op consisted of blood pressure, chest X-ray, urinalysis, blood work, and EKG. We didn't get any of the results, but Mary got a kit that discussed pre-op, post-op, pain treatment, diet, exercise, etc., so we assume that the operation is still on schedule. She will report on Wednesday at 1:00 p.m.

Tonight we switched floors at home. Until now, I have watched my football and NBA games upstairs, and Mary absorbed 400 Christmas shows on Hallmark in the family room. But since she has been pretty much wiped out the last few days, she is staying upstairs most of the time, so I have moved downstairs. I think that Hallmark and NFL are just about polar opposites, or one of us would be able to adjust and we could live on the same plane. Last night we also moved into separate bedrooms, which is really temporary. A couple of nights ago I woke up to find her asleep on the couch downstairs, driven there by my snoring. But she badly needs her sleep these days, so I am moving into Anne's room until after the operation.

Tuesday, December 28

Aunt Mary,
We are sending all our prayers, good vibes, and positive energy across the country to you tomorrow. Just keep visualizing a cancer free body (and go ahead and visualize yourself as 20 years younger, too! What the heck.

I'm glad you had a nice Christmas. It's times like this when your daughters can rally and show you all they have learned from you over the years of Christmases together. I bet they are pros just like you.

We love you and look forward to the "all clear" email
in the weeks ahead!!
Xoxoxoxo
Sue and the boys.

Today is a day of nothing to do. There are no doctors' appointments,
no Christmas duties, no jobs to do outside because it's raining. It's a
day to catch up on this journal, write a little bit about Boris in Israel
(He's joining a kibbutz today and falling in love with a beautiful
Jewish girl.) Maybe I'll start reading one of the books I got for
Christmas. Otherwise, I can feel my gut growing from eating too
much.

I counted fifty-four turkeys walking across our hill this morning
as I was finishing my shower. It is amazing what our bathroom
offers up by way of wildlife. Mary and Annie will never forget the
morning that I yanked them out of bed to watch a trio of pileated
woodpeckers doing a *ménage a trois* dance around one of the oak trees.
From our bathroom window I can observe the squirrels stealing
seed from the bird feeders and have been known once or twice to use
my air rifle on them. One morning, standing there in my Jockeys, I
counted sixteen different species of birds, and on another day I found
a pair of red foxes almost invisible, sleeping among the rocks. Our
bathroom is like a forest blind, a perfect place to discover things. It
has occurred to me that if I could find a toilet seat that was about 4'
high, I wouldn't have to stand any longer.

Nancy and Annie both come home again today, in preparation for
Mary going to the hospital. Annie has adjusted her work schedule
to fit Mary's, and Nancy has endured that seven-hour drive from
Eureka countless times. For a while, they were positively human
dynamos in directing Mary's activities, sometimes leaving little or
no room for Mary and me to have an opinion. I understand perfectly
their reasoning, knowing that they wanted the very best for Mary
and making sure we knew how to proceed. One day early on I took
them aside, and as gently as I could, explained that Mary and I had
actually been making decisions for forty-seven years together and

we haven't completely lost that ability, even in our dotage. Both girls laughed and admitted that maybe they had been a bit "forceful" but that they just wanted what was best for their mother. I told them that we wanted the same thing and loved them dearly for feeling as they do. Believe me, I knew lots of parents who aren't blessed as we are with children who express nothing but love—all the time and without limits.

Nancy was going to take her VW from Nevada yesterday, but it is snowing on Donner Summit, so Kasey ordered her to take the big car with the 4-wheel drive. "You will be all by yourself, Mom. But we'll be fine, because we're going to be with Dad." See, it's a trait that has been passed down to each of our generations! Marty and the kids will be driving down for New Year's Day on the weekend and to be with Mary in the hospital. To be sure they may come over the summit in snow shoes, but Marty will get them here.

Sue and Dennis next door called to see if they could visit tonight, which of course sent Mary into a flurry of decorating, cleaning, and bed-making. It doesn't matter that they are not going to see any of that; it is enough that Mary thinks they *might*. It bothered the girls to see her scurrying around, and they yelled and scolded to stop her, urging me to agree. But I don't. Any exercise Mary does is good, even if it has no purpose. She has been totally unmoving for days. Even a little moving around can't hurt her because she is going to need all the strength she can muster in the coming weeks. Besides, when you are sick, what do you have left but your dignity? For Mary, the Christmas decorations are her signature, and every time someone sees them and is stunned by the scope of them, she puffs out just a little bit with pride.

Right now she can use all of the acclaim, all of the confidence she can muster. I know how tough it has been for her because on several occasions she has left the house with untidy spots here and there. That simply doesn't happen. I took over the sink duties quite a while ago, but I have to admit, to my shame, that I hadn't always noticed whether the bed was made. But today, because Sue and Dennis are coming over, the bed is made, the dishes are done and the rooms have been "froofed."

Wednesday, December 29

Today is a very big day in our lives. Except for Mary's gall bladder and my appendix, we have never had surgery. It is really nice to have Nancy and Annie here. Right now they are sitting on our bed, advising their mother about what to pack for the hospital. If I tried that, I would receive a deaf ear from Mare, who would regard any suggestion as silly, but when the girls tell her something, she listens. There is a life lesson there somewhere.

We are due at Alta Bates at 1:00, and her surgery is scheduled for 2:30. I have no idea how long it will take, but I assume it is fairly complicated with all of the things that have to be taken out along with the tumor. Lots of friends and family are waiting for a report, which I think will be my duty tonight.

This morning Mary was very nervous, understandably so, because this is a big operation she is facing. Before Mary went into surgery, Dr. Jason Sloan, the anesthesiologist came to discuss the operation with her. He is a young man, and according to both Nancy and Anne, very much a "hunk," with a wonderful manner and genuine concern for his patient. He carefully explained the whole procedure, what position she would be in with each of the two operations, how he would monitor her and what she could expect during and after the procedure. And the whole time he was holding her hand!

"Don't worry," he added. "I am wide awake and I have already had lunch."

Dr. Donthineni expected the operation to take about six hours, but it took less than five. Afterward, Dr. Sloan found us in the lower waiting room to tell us that Mary was perfect under the anesthesia. "She is amazing," he said. "She is small, and very nimble. It was easy to move her around."

I have heard Mary referred to as many things—caring, loving, gentle, etc., but I have never heard someone say she was "small and nimble."

Dr. Donthineni also came to see us in the waiting room afterwards. He explained that he removed the large tumor, which required the removal one of the two hamstring muscles in that leg, but he assured us that she can do fine without it. He also zapped the two tumors in the lymph nodes. He said that we probably wouldn't have to worry about daily shots of Coumadin, a blood thinner, which Mary or I would have to administer ourselves, something that was a major concern for Mary. And he said that she would not be doing much exercise for at least a month while they monitored the healing of the two incisions.

"It will be a couple of hours before she is in her room. You could go out for dinner."

"No, we'll just stay here until she's ready to see us," I told him.

He got a big smile. "I'm going to want you guys to look after me if I get sick."

It was everything we could have hoped for. Mary was very bright and cheery when we found her in her room, 1615A, even cracking her usual jokes. Annie and Nancy simply light her up, and I am so happy they were both able to be here. I don't think I have ever seen the reciprocal love between the three of them so beautifully expressed.

Jason Sloan later dropped by her room when he was off duty. He just stood there smiling when he saw how perky Mary was.

"Are you happy with the results?" he asked me.

"We sure are. Are you?"

"I'm really happy. She is an amazing lady."

Thursday, December 30

Hi all:

We have very good news. Mary's operation went extremely well. It was scheduled for six hours, but they were finished in four and a half. She came out of recovery in half the expected time too, and at least for now is very much alive and perky. They took out the big tumor in her thigh and two smaller ones in the lymph node near her stomach. She now has at least a month of recovery time before she has to start chemo and/or radiation. They are taking the biopsies to the Tumor Board to determine the next step in the process. She will be at Alta Bates (Room 1615) for at least four days so that they can monitor the healing process and get her started on light therapy. Thanks

you all so much for all of your love and prayers. They
are working.
With much love,
Mary and Jack

There was an incredible outpouring of love in response to my
latest email, probably the greatest New Year's gift we have ever
received, more than thirty emails from family and friends all over the
country. I shouldn't be amazed at the outpouring of love for Mary.
She has never asked anything from anyone, and that fact is quite
evident in the love she generates, seemingly without even trying. She
was very feisty when I arrived at the hospital this morning, sounding
very much like her mother whenever someone tried to cut in front of
her in the line at the grocery store.

"I have to get out of this place!" she groused the minute she saw
me. I regard that as a very good start, because anger shows more life
than fatigue. She was talking in one of her quiet voices, as though
afraid that Sandra in the bed next to her would hear her, the kind
of voice she used to adopt when the girls brought up anything to do
with "S-E-X." It seems that the hospital staff wasn't quite as quick
as she thought they should be, and the food wasn't something she
wanted to try, and they put her in a chair and forgot to come back
and get her for a long time, and . . . and. . . . It was great to see her
full of angst about stuff that doesn't matter, because if she was in
pain, or there was a genuine problem with the hospital, it would
be awful. My guess is that she was also under the influence of pain
killers, which often cause anxiety if not anger in patients. I'll ask the
nurses about it.

Friday, December 31

New Year's Eve! Until Nancy mentioned it, I never even thought
about what we were doing tonight. Originally we were going to

Cole's at Lake Tahoe, but Mary's illness cancelled that idea. Jim and Donna asked me if we wanted to join them at the Wine House at Oakmont, but I declined that when we realized that Mary would be in the hospital. Yesterday, Nancy asked me about it, and I drew a blank. We agreed that we would try to book an early dinner and then visit Mary at Alta Bates and go to Annie's or our house after that for the actual dropping of the ball at Times Square and the ushering in of the new decade. I figured I could get us an early reservation at Spenger's or someplace like that, and decided to call Jim and Donna and see if they wanted to join us.

"I don't like Spenger's," Jim announced emphatically. "I'll call you back."

He called back to say that he had scrounged us a table at Trader Vic's for 5:30, something only one of their board members could have accomplished. Even though we were there last week for Christmas, it is always a treat to go to Trader Vic's, because in my mind it is one of the best restaurants in the Bay Area. .It is one of the culinary institutions of the area, maybe even of the nation and the world. It was founded in Oakland, California, as Hinky Dinks by a local man, Vic Bergeron. It expanded phenomenally, especially when a contract was signed to put a restaurant in all of the Statler Hilton Hotels. When that chain folded, however, Trader Vic's went into a steep decline. Our friend Jim Schafer, was asked to come in to restructure the company, even though he is a developer, not a restaurateur. The chain has come back to life, opening restaurants throughout the Arab world and Far East. Jim has stepped down as CEO and is now a board member.

So it was decided, another family meal at the Trader's, and a continuation of our string of New Year's celebrations with the Schafers. I can't even think of when the last New Year was that we didn't share with Jim and Donna. It goes back to when we first returned from New England, which is twenty-five years ago. There was a time when all we did was meet for the bowl games. At that time, I was in the middle of my college jersey collecting and had hundreds of sweatshirts and T-shirts. I would bring the shirts for just about every team in the bowl games. With each game, Jim would wear one of the team's shirts and I would wear the other. Whoever lost, dumped his jersey on the floor and we walked all over it for the rest of the day. The winners were hung in glory on the walls. I think my proudest moment in those days was having a sweat shirt from Eastern Carolina U.

"You certainly don't have one of those," Jim declared, happy to find a school I hadn't visited. But I pulled it out of my sack and amazed even myself.

From those "simple" days we began our long string of touring, beginning with the Canadian Rockies and a marvelous week at the Jasper Park Lodge and Chateau Lake Louise. We had wonderful times in Phoenix with Annie, in Santa Fe, Monterey, even Eureka at the Opera House. Then on to China, three times, Thailand, Taiwan, Korea. Who can forget the frigid day shopping for warm clothes in Seoul? We went to Guatemala, Nicaragua, Costa Rica, Panama, Vietnam and Cambodia.

No, New Year's is a Dold-Schafer time, and I am very happy that, as unstructured and last-minute as our celebration was this year, it was spent properly, with our best friends.

January

HAPPY NEW YEAR!!!!

Saturday, January 1, 2011

It's 1-1-11! That's the kind of date that Mary lives for. The only ones better, in ascending order are 1-11-11, 11-1-11, and the ultimate, 11-11-11. At 11:11.11 on November 11th of this year, Mary is going to drink a glass of champagne.

But regardless of the numerical date, they have ruined New Year's Day. Gone are the final bowl games of the year. All that remains that is important is the Rose Bowl, and this year that doesn't even contain a Pac-10 team. Since Oregon is in the Tostito's National Championship game on January 10, they wouldn't let the next Pac 10 team come this year, so Wisconsin is playing Texas Christian U. of all teams, making the "Granddaddy of All Bowls" a sham, a mere shadow of what it used to be. I decided that it would be a good time to visit Mary, when the Rose Bowl was on. Secretly I knew that I would probably turn the TV on in her hospital room, but I vowed not to turn on the sound.

Can you believe it, they don't have ESPN at Alta Bates Hospital! Not only did I not have the sound for the Rose Bowl, I didn't even have the picture. TCU won the game anyway, which I suppose is good, because we were raised to hate the Big 10. But times have changed. Sully went to Wisconsin; our niece Cheryl and her husband, Adeeb, did as well, and our next door neighbor Sue is also an alumnae, but who really cares? The Big 10 now has sixteen teams and the Pac 10 has twelve. Nothing is sacred any more. We let a batch of Texas Christians come in here and steal our trophy all because Oregon is playing in Glendale.

Mary was super today. When I got to the hospital, Nancy, Annie and Kasey were just finishing up. Cole, Marcia and Marsha's sister Jacqueline were there too, and we made a nice compact crowd. But the centerpiece, the star, Mary, is sitting up, bright and happy, very alert and as we are getting used to saying, perky. They took her epidural out this morning, and also removed the drain from her major incision, so she is now on oral painkillers, but not using them. Probably tomorrow, when the heavy medication has worn off, there will be a drop in her energy and enthusiasm, but it sure is nice to see her like this now. She is walking very well, without the walker, just using her medication stand for support, and doing several laps of the floor. She has been practicing getting into the bath tub, putting on her pants and socks, and generally performing the feats that will get her sent home. Someone told me it was a bad idea to let them discharge you on a weekend, although I have no idea why. It was agreed that Mary would come home on Monday. I will arrange for a nurse to come to the house once a day to help with changing her bandages and exercising her. It will be nice to be back together in our own house. As easy as it is to deal with Alta Bates, it is still at least a 45-minute drive each way, with a hospital atmosphere at the end of the drive.

It has been impossible for the two weeks around Christmas and New Year to figure out exactly what day of the week it is. I suppose that is because the holidays fall on Saturday this year, and it seems like they should be Sundays. But that doesn't explain why Wednesday feels like Friday and Friday comes three times each week. There is no way in the world that today does not feel like Sunday, and I keep trying to find the 49ers game on TV to no avail. Tomorrow, when it really is Sunday, it will feel like Monday and I'll probably miss the game entirely. Annie and Erik left after dinner tonight. Nancy, Marty, and the kids leave tomorrow. It will be very quiet for a while around the house, at least until Mary comes home on Monday.

Monday, January 3

Mare comes home today and I am in charge. Someone told her yesterday that the checkout time at Alta Bates is 11:00 a.m., so I arrived around 10:00 to find her lying askew on her bed with that look she gets when she is disgusted, sort of pursing her lips up on the left side with a roll of the eyes. It is a body-language way of calling everyone involved "turkeys."

The hospital staff didn't really deserve the editorial. It seems that Debbie, the floor nurse on Mondays, was waiting for me to arrive to show me how to administer the Lovenox injections that Mary is going to need for the next ten days. The thought of giving them to herself was totally repulsive to Mare, and the thought of me administering the needle only slightly less so, but still the better of the two options. I have to admit, the thought of me sticking those needles in her stomach was one that made my own stomach more than upset, but I am learning lots of new things these days, so why wimp out on this one?

Actually, it's not difficult. You just select a good region of love handle, clean the area with alcohol, pinch a chunk and press in the needle, which is rather short and very thin. As you reach the bottom of the syringe push, a safety cylinder reacts and pushes the needle right out, protecting you at the same time. You just pick a different side each morning, moving up and down the abdomen. Mary has been getting a lot of injections in that area at the cancer center, so her stomach looks somewhat like a war zone right now. But there is still space for a few more shots.

Having learned injecting, we waited for the discharge officer to come by and tell us what they had arranged for home care and to take care of ordering prescriptions and other necessities. They presented us with a fine two-wheeled walker. I was pushing for a golf cart, which Obamacare says you can get, but nobody here is politically informed. Finally, just after noon, Mary was wheeled out to the car and we headed for home.

"It's a lot easier ride today than four days ago, huh Mare?" I asked and got a ready agreement. All in all, even though sometimes the folks at the hospital didn't move as fast as Mary wanted them to, Alta Bates was wonderful. The admission process was quick and efficient;

the surgery staff very friendly and accommodating. Dr. Donthineni is one of the most assuring doctors I have met, very professional, wonderfully casual in his conversation and approach. His confidence spreads immediately to his patients and their families, no small thing when your wife is going to come out in six hours with two major holes in her body. Actually, today is the first day I looked closely at Mary's incisions. The thigh operation virtually opened the entire upper leg, easily a 12"-long incision, while the stomach cut is about half that size. Both appear to be healing nicely.

I am frankly amazed at Mary's ability to walk, even by herself, with no cane, walker, or anything. I had an image of her being bed-ridden for a month, since they took out the hamstring along with the sarcoma. But she is walking fine, only slightly slower than normal. Once we got into the house, she promptly (gingerly I'll admit) ascended the stairs to the bedroom. No big problem. If anything, getting into and out of bed is difficult because of where the incision is in her leg, but all in all, she is in remarkable post-operative condition. Now she again has to put up with my cooking.

Tuesday, January 4

I thought it would be cool to have some bleached jeans. Last week Nancy showed me how to load the washer, where to put the soap, softener, and bleach (which I thought were all packaged as one in Tide or Dove or something), what temperature and style to wash stuff in, and so forth. She didn't actually show me where to turn the damned thing on but eventually, by pushing every button, I found the secret. She even showed me how many sheets I could wash at once, a good thing, because in my mind, if you are washing sheets, you naturally wash them all. Why would there be a limit? She did tell me that you only use the little tub that says "bleach" with the white stuff.

My figuring was this: If I stick my one pair of Wranglers into the machine to get them whiter, there is not enough volume to carry off the deal. So, since bleach is also used with white stuff, why not just throw in all the socks and undies and do the whole thing at one blast? That way you don't waste water, electricity, soap, and all that. Al Gore would be pleased—no carbon footprint here.

The jeans never got white at all! As a matter of fact, I don't think the bleach is everything they brag about, because my jockeys never got white either. And my white socks, which I wear every day, now match my jeans beautifully. I am giving up on the bleach cycle completely. The girls can figure that out.

Gabby, the nurse from Sutter VNA, came by around 10:30 this morning. She represents another of those incredible health services that America has, seemingly without very few of the citizens knowing about it. The service provides for post-hospital care in the home by RNs, therapists, and specialists, completely covered by Medicare. Thus far the expenses for Mary's cancer have come to $117,000, totally covered by our health care system. That is incredible! The next time that someone complains to me about our health care in America I am going to deck him or her. It is absurd to think that our country is not taking care of its people, at least the people who have worked their butts off, paid their taxes and earned their retirements. If Mary's experience is any indication, our system works, works beautifully. Because we have had very few illnesses, we haven't been aware of medical costs or services. It has come as a complete surprise to us that the system really does work.

Gabby told me that she or another nurse would come only a time or two, and that one of her jobs today, besides giving Mary a complete checking over, was to see how I would clean the incisions, change the dressings, and give the Lovenox shots. We had been told that the nurses would come every day and do that stuff, but apparently, as the head of the domestic household, those duties fall to me. Because the nurses aren't going to be doing any of those things, dutifully, I shot Mary up in the gut under Gabby's watchful eye. Then we put the bandages back on the wounds and she was gone; Mary is exhausted; and I am heading for Safeway.

Mary is no longer under the hospital clock and I had forgotten the urgency of meal times when watching over a loved one. I re-learned it quickly this morning when I found out that there was not even a small box of cereal in the cupboard, and Mary only will accept Cheerios. I did have milk, but I no sooner got home from Safeway with my cereal, then I realized I haven't considered lunch or dinner. How on earth do mothers do this stuff, every day, every week, every year? In all today, I made four trips to stores and virtually bought nothing. I picked up Mary's glasses at Costco, got her CPAP (Continuous Positive Airway Pressure) machine fixed, picked up wonton soup at Fred's (he gave me a free Tsingtao as a New Year's present), and got some irrelevant groceries again at Safeway. At the end of the day, I poured a scotch and figured that in fourteen waking hours, I have not accomplished a single thing that was productive. Except give Mary a shot and write this journal.

Wednesday, January 5

Mary started to feel a little pain from her incisions yesterday, and popped the first of the Vicodins that they have lavished on her for the past two months. She has a bottle of fifty from each of her biopsies and another forty from the installation of her port, and yesterday they prescribed another eighty. I could be temporarily wealthy selling pills on the street corner with all the painkillers they are handing out. No wonder there are all sorts of people hooked on them. Mary finally broke down and took one, the first since they removed the epidural last week. Yesterday, the visiting nurse, Gabby, told her it was best for her recovery to take some of the pills because the goal of therapy and recovery is no pain. She had me get a flashlight so she could examine the incision areas closely, and I got a really good look at Mary's rear end. The scar will pretty much cover the whole thigh, twelve or thirteen inches long. For the next two weeks I will check the area for any signs of infection. The problem for Mary is that it runs right up to where she would normally sit, and that area is a little redder than the rest. So she basically has to sit on one cheek for a while, and that is causing the pain.

I am driving in this morning to pick up Mary's older sister, Barbara, who no longer likes to drive as far as our house. She and Mary can have lunch together and I will escape for a few hours. Planning lunch is no easy thing, what with Mary's limited repertoire of edible dishes, but I picked up a pot of won ton soup from Fred last night, and I can always get Mary to eat a slice or two of sourdough bread if there is *real* butter to apply. Actually, that doesn't sound like a bad lunch.

What a change has occurred in our kitchen! For years I was

really proud of myself as a modern husband because I have always taken the dishes from the table to the sink and cleaned them off in preparation for the dishwasher, something by the way, I have always considered ludicrous. Why on earth do you buy a dishwasher if you have to wash the dishes first before you put them in? Anyway, Mary would never let me actually insert the dishes because she said I do it wrong, so I would just stack them up, leaving the dirty pots and pans in the sink and consider myself sensitive. I could always tell when she was coming up to bed because I would hear the sounds of pots and pans clanging, her last chore every night before turning off all the lights.

Well now I get to do the whole thing! Not only do I get to cook, I also get to do all the sensitive male things leading up to loading the dishwasher. Then I get to again switch roles and put the dishes in! Mary taught me where the soap goes and what cycle I am supposed to use. So now I am fully functional in the kitchen. The full realization of the magnitude of this change only hit me later—I now have to *unload* the dishwasher too! And put all the clean dishes away. That's a bitch! For a while I just left them there and used the dishwasher as a cupboard, but then the dirty dishes started stacking up. Sometimes it's painful to be reasonable.

Thursday, January 6

Happy Little Christmas! Today has always been a big day in our family, because of my Dad's birthday. He would have been 105 today, but he is still alive to me. Every so often I get a warm feeling that is very powerful, and I know it is him. Happy Birthday, Dad.

Of course, this is also Little Christmas for Mary, the last day that the Christmas decorations have to be up. In past years, she has dragged out the dismantling of the house for a week or more because it is such an enormous chore. This year she may have help from Marcia and Donna, and I will insist that she allow the help. It is not always easy to get Mary to accept assistance on either end of the decorating process. Lord help us if we put a Santa in upside down!

The therapist, a young woman named Sharee, came in for the first time this morning, taking Mary through a few stretching and bending exercises. Actually she is doing great. The major incision is healing well, and she has remarkable mobility, given the length of that scar. She is able to walk up and down stairs fairly easily, and gets out of bed better each day. They will take the staples out next week, something she is not looking forward to. Sue next door told her that Dennis almost died when his staples came out, and Mary heard other horror stories as well. I have to admit, the job doesn't look easy, especially since there is some swelling around the incision in her leg and the staples are pretty tight. Doctor Donthineni offered to take them out if Mary was more comfortable with him doing it, but Nancy says that nurses may be better at it than a doctor. I have the feeling that we will just take our chances with the nurse.

Friday, January 7

I am not making a list! Nancy tells me that I should start keeping a list of what supplies we need, groceries and household items. That is taking this one step too far. For over fifty years I have been going to Home Depot and Orchard Supply Nursery, Yardbirds, brickyards, and bird supply stores and I always come back with less than I needed so I would have an excuse to start swearing when I ran out of stuff. I refuse to be so organized that we have everything we need all the time. What kind of life is that? Boring, that's what! Nancy even started a list for me, taping it to the cupboard in the kitchen, writing down things like toilet paper, and milk. She doesn't look at life like a man does. If you run out of toilet paper you use Kleenex, and if you run out of that you get some newspaper. If that fails you just tiptoe over and take a shower. *Then* you go get some toilet paper at the store, along with the Chronicle as backup. There are a dozen surrogates for milk—Diet Coke, 7-Up, scotch, orange juice. If all else fails, try water. You don't need a list for that. All you need is a McGiver mentality and a tiny bit of flexibility. Okay, so I ran out of applesauce for Mary this morning. Did I panic? No. I substituted some Boost chocolate pudding which is perfectly understandable, and I have a dozen little pots of Jello right behind that if she doesn't like the pudding. In fact, she didn't and I tried it myself. It tastes like crap. But I threw in a few extra Cheerios and brought her a knife to slice a banana. I'll get some applesauce this afternoon when I go to the store, if I don't forget it.

On a more important note, I saw fourteen cedar waxwings in the maple tree this morning! The last time I saw some in the yard was March 10, 1998. Now that is a long migration!

Mary's appetite has come back nicely. Last night she actually agreed to eat fish and chips from the store near Costco. That is a major change. She is now eating breakfast every day, soup and even a tuna sandwich for lunch, and a variety of things for dinner. I know she is worried about gaining weight, and she is in fact retaining water because she has largely lost the love handles I am supposed to shoot up every morning, but that will change as her general health improves. I can't believe that I am actually starting to think about and understand things like nutrition and good health. By the time Mary is completely well there are going to be hundreds of things I am going to have to unlearn. She admitted this morning that she intends to milk her windfall as long as she can.

Saturday, January 8

"How was your day today, sweetheart?"

I now know that that is one of the stupidest questions in the history of mankind. Ozzie always asked Harriett; Desi asked it as he was taking off his hat and coat and handing them to Lucy. Mrs. Cleaver, Mrs. Partridge, Mrs. Everyman has been asked that question on every segment of their TV shows. Archie never asked it because it never occurred to him that Edith ever had a bad day. The answer was always the same—"Fine, how was yours, dear?"

The next question should have gotten hubby decapitated. "What did you do today?"

"Oh, nothing."

What that really means:

I did six loads of wash. Doesn't he even know how to wipe himself?

And I cleaned up the dishes from last night's party. Why is it always his friends who show up unannounced and stay late?

I vacuumed the house. The jerk commented last week that there were dust devils under the bed. That's where he should be living.

I washed the windows. Another comment from last month, and a job he should be doing.

I went grocery shopping. His next question is going to be "What's for dinner, honey?"

I took the dry cleaning down. He's sure to bitch about the cost. I had to put it on our credit card. But I'll be damned if I'm going to iron his shirts and denims.

I picked up Sally and took her to her dance lessons and Jimmy to band practice.

I got his registered letter at the Post Office.

I took the dog to the vet for his rabies shots. I should let him just bite someone. The dog that is.

I weeded a patch in the garden, where those flowers died he forgot to water. Oh, maybe I was supposed to water them.

I had the car washed, because he is always moaning that he keeps forgetting to do it.

I watched The View, Opra and Ellen to find out if there is anything worth thinking about out there.

He says, "Well, my day was a bitch. The morning was one phone call after another. And three of them were from my fraternity brothers. Don't they realize I have real work to do? I met Joe Blitzflizt for lunch at Trader Vic's. He's backing out of our club presidency, and I might get stuck with it. I got together with the sales staff at the Sheraton Palace. That is a great bar they have next to the Garden Court. Great margaritas!"

Oh, I forgot. I cleaned out the cat's litter box too. And by the way, I didn't ask you how your day was. I already knew.

And then Desi would pour himself a drink, plop down in the big chair and moan—"Damn, what a day! What's for dinner, honey?"

I cleaned out the litter box yesterday. It is one of the chores I am discovering that Mary has always done. It has no intrinsic value except possibly preserving good health and maintaining a pleasant quality of air in the house, but otherwise, you can't really write about it or brag about it, like you might about good margaritas or hung-over friends. The same goes with washing clothes. I did a load yesterday because Mary's ace bandages needed cleaning, and I threw in some sheets, socks, towels, and stuff. No real value there either, unless you aren't willing to live like a frat boy and just throw everything in the corner and select your outfit by the smell test. I gave Mary her Lovenox shot, lit a fire downstairs and served her dinner there, until the ball game came on and she retreated upstairs. I went to the grocery store (but I didn't make a list!), and I remembered that Mary needed milk and applesauce. I admit that I forget to get something to cook for dinner tonight, but I am getting used to three trips to the grocery store every day.

Back in the old days, I never was able to buy everything I needed, no matter what it was, except yellow bricks. If I needed sand, I always ran out three-fourths of the way through. I never had the right screws, the correct tool, enough posthole concrete, rubber hose washers, soap, paint. It is awful to run out of paint, like I just did staining the garden boards, with seven feet left to go. So it is nothing to go grocery shopping and come home one can short of a six-pack.

Actually, I like the grocery store. For one thing, the shoppers are better looking than in Home Depot. And I have noticed that so long as you have more than beer and ice cream in your basket, all the ladies talk to you, thinking, I am sure, how nice it is to meet a sensitive male. Just today, the lady in front of me at the check-out stand, a very attractive blond, 45-ish, was checking out and the Filipino bag girl asked her what one of the boxes was.

"Kotex!"

"What do you use that for?"

She pointed to a corner of the store. "Honey, I'll meet your over there and explain it to you!"

She turned to me with a big grin. "Isn't that cute?"

The check-out guy's cheeks turned rose red. But as one of the "girls," it didn't even faze me. After all, I had fresh corn and applesauce in my basket. And no beer.

I cooked Mary some Genova raviolis tonight. Now that may not seem like much, but it involved two completely separate cooking skills. I boiled water and I drained. I'm not going to claim any credit for thawing the sauce out in the microwave because I am convinced that microwaves are a form of magic and can't actually be considered cooking. But I did boil water without burning it, timed the little squares for five minutes (or when they pop up to the surface) and drained them in a colander. For me I consider that a geometric jump up in the culinary skills. I even washed the colander afterwards (with soap) even though it was very evident that it never got dirty. Fortunately Mary couldn't tell that those ravs were filled with artichokes, something I had overlooked at Safeway. Why would anyone fill anything with artichokes?

Sunday, January 9

Women can fold things in threes. I have never figured out why they do that, or for that matter, how they do it. A towel rack in the bathroom won't hold two towels folded in half. You have to fold them longwise in threes. Why would they do that? Obviously it is on purpose because otherwise they would make wider towel racks. And I tried this morning folding pillow cases into the nice little squares that Mary achieves. It can't be done unless you can three-fold. That's ridiculous! So as a form of minor protest, I put all of the pillow cases onto the shelves as rectangles. Nothing can be divided by three unless it already has a three in it, and I haven't found a single three in any towel or pillow case in the house. I'll bet nobody alive can give me a logical answer on this one.

And why does Mary insist on putting in the toilet paper backwards? It makes no sense to have the roll unwind from the back. For one thing, you usually can't even tell where to grab it, because the end is hidden behind the roll. All toilet paper should be installed properly, so it unwinds from the top, exposing the end square directly in front of your eyes, where you can even find it in the dark, a thing that happens more often as you get older. Backward installation is one of the primary reasons our country is not operating properly these days. Too many people are frustrated the minute they get up in the morning and sit down. There should be an arrow required on the outside of all rolls of toilet paper so even the illiterate can't become disoriented.

Jim and Donna came over early this afternoon, and the process of de-Christmasing the house commenced. With their help, as well as with Erik's and Annie's later on, the family room and the pub

(Mary always wanted an Irish pub in her house, so we built one in) were finished today. We also got all of the empty tubs staged for filling in coming days and weeks. Even Mary was heard by Jim to muse—"Sometimes I wonder if this is all worth it." Frankly, with all of our kidding, I hope she never loses her enthusiasm for the Christmas season. It is something I am very proud of in her, and in our life together. If you can't go overboard on something, what good is anything?

I think that she has fully retrieved her appetite. Today she ate completely normal meals with good portions at breakfast, and pasta and pizza for a late lunch/dinner, finished off with ice cream. It can't be long before she is worrying about gaining weight, thank the Lord.

Monday, January 10

I was insulted by a misogynist this morning! What a jerk! I was minding my own business in the flour row at Safeway, and this guy stops me.

"What do you think is the best cake mix?"

"What?"

"My wife told me to buy cake mix. Women are always doing things like that. How in the hell am I supposed to know what's a good cake mix? Ask me about beer."

"So you expect me to know about cake mixes? Do I look like Betty Crocker?"

"Hey, man, I'm sorry. It's just that you looked like you know what you are doing in this store. I'd rather ask a guy than one of these gals. They'd think I'm a big jerk."

"Trust me buddy, they'd think you were cute. I'm the one who thinks you're a big jerk." Imagine!

Breakfast: Cheerios with banana, sourdough toast slathered in butter, orange juice, and a large glass of milk. How far away can she be from a Valley chorizo scramble, eggs Benedict, or a farmer's breakfast? It has been so long since Mary has had a normal meal that I had forgotten what it was like.

This week Mary is supposed to get her staples out, and we will see Dr. Donthineni to determine the next step in her recovery. The VNA nurse is due tomorrow for the metal removal and a final checkup of the incisions. Mary keeps calling them "wounds," and I have tried to tell her that an incision is not a wound, since there probably was no malice intended. I'll ask Dr. Donthineni about that.

Big bird day this morning! First of all there were seven Western bluebirds perched in the maple tree, darting down every few moments to gorge themselves on the toyon berries that are fully ripe now. There they compete with the robins, which also arrived this morning. But the highlight was a beautiful, tiny ruby-crowned kinglet, which posed in the sun on the garage door so I could actually see the crown, a first for me. The last such sighting in the yard was in February, ten years ago. I have kept my bird log for about fifteen years, and it is amazing how the migration patterns appear. I always thought that you would see more species in the summer, but it is the opposite for us "warm weather" areas. Winter is the big time. This morning, in a matter of five minutes, I counted thirteen different species of song birds in the yard, plus crows, vultures, some yellow-billed magpies and various blackbirds down in Rockville. If I saw twenty species on a bird walk in China, I would be thrilled beyond recall, but here there is such variety that with a walk in Suisun Marsh or on Highway 37, I could easily find sixty.

Tuesday, January 11

It's 1-11-11, one of Mary's lucky days. She should have been a numerologist or born Chinese, because she loves symmetry in numbers. Actually, it is a good day, because Sue arrived from VNA Hospice to take her staples out. It's something Mary has been dreading, mainly because Dennis Adair and a couple of others related horror stories about their staples being pulled. Sue assured her that she would be as gentle as possible. Mary popped a Vicodin earlier this morning just to be on the safe side.

It was actually a piece of cake. Dennis is such a wimp! Mary said it was like a little pin prick here and there but most of the twenty-five staples came out without anything at all. Sue thinks there was a hard knot under the skin on the stomach incision, so I called Dr. Donthineni's office and made an appointment for this afternoon. He wants to see Mary anyway.

The doctor feels that bump is just a collection of dead blood, backed up by the incision. He said he could drain it, along with water buildup in Mary's thigh, but that it is better if the body does it naturally. However, if they are still there when the chemo is finished, he said he may have to drain them because Mary will then have radiation and that tends to make the body retain fluids.

I was shocked that he kept referring to the incisions as "wounds," so I reprimanded him.

"A wound is something that results from an attack with malice. I have been lecturing Mary that it should be called an incision."

"Well, when it is as long as that one on Mary's leg, I would call it a wound."

I like Dr. Donthineni!

Wednesday, January 12

I think I hit a muscle or something when I gave Mary her injection, because she let out a yell. I must be getting blasé about needling her and will have to be more careful. It is amazing what you can learn when you have to. I would never have considered sticking a needle into anyone or, for that matter, anything, but when the need is there, you just have to do it. It does help that the Lovenox needles are pretty short and very thin, and it also helps that Mary has decent love handles. I don't know what you would do with someone who had a washboard for abs, stick it in his or her butt I suppose. As Dennis said, these shots are "sub-cute," which I infer means in the fleshy part of the body under the skin and over the muscles and bones. We are almost done with these barbaric things. But they seem to be watering Mary's blood down nicely because there are no signs of clots up to this time.

Mary was rather full of energy today and completely boxed up the entire upstairs deckies. I pulled all of the wreaths off of the windows and started stacking the tubs out in the garage. It doesn't really take that long to dismantle Christmas, just a lot of work hauling very heavy plastic tubs out to the garage. Who would ever guess that nativity sets would be so heavy?

To my despair, I tried getting fancy for dinner. Safeway's butcher shop had elegant looking chicken breasts, (maybe "luscious" would be a better descriptive for breasts.) stuffed with asparagus and cheese.

Why not?

Following directions I pre-heated the oven, proud of myself that I knew I was supposed to do that, although I think the oven does it all by itself. I even figured out that you have to push "start" when you set the timer. I did exactly as I was supposed to do, cooked those things the correct amount of time at the correct heat. They weren't very good. Actually, I thought they were awful, but Mary wasn't so critical. In fact she almost ate the whole thing. So she was hungry! I forgot completely to bring her lunch today. I made up for the bad breasts with ice cream.

Thursday, January 13

It is the last day of Lovenox, the last injection. I guess yesterday I didn't hit a muscle, because there was no dark mark on Mary's handle. I have to admit, I am thrilled to be finished with that blood thinning, and I know Mary is. Of course, she would take that instead of the chemo if they gave her the option.

"Dad, you know it is okay to buy food for more than one meal," Nancy scolded me the other day, when she found out I was going off to Safeway every afternoon to get something for dinner. Actually, that thought had occurred to me, but I discarded it as impractical when Mary wouldn't eat anything. I didn't want to get stuck with stuff spoiling, so I never bought more than I needed for one day. I think I would have a hard time buying a whole bunch of stuff at the grocery store. I have always marveled at the ladies who hit the check-out stand with a basket chock-a-block with stuff, and I have almost fainted when I saw some of the grand totals. The other day, a lady almost hit $500 with her cart, and I vowed never again to buy more than fifteen things so I could use the express line and avoid these overachievers. How can you deal with a grocery bill that big? I had considered trying to fill the whole cart to overflowing just so I could experience the ultimate in household providing. I would positively die if I had to come up with $300 or $400 at Safeway. On the other hand, it didn't bother me in the least to shell out $325 for Marty's impact screw driver at Home Depot before Christmas, and many times I have filled a cart with flowers and plants for the yard totaling similar amounts, several days in a row. What's wrong with spending money for tools and garden needs? But groceries? Come on! That should be done with moderation and good sense and a half-empty cart.

Annie and Erik came over this evening to take Mary to dinner, at the grill in Suisun. I met Tim Brophy and Nick and Dan Buscovich, all former students of mine at Bishop O'Dowd, at the Round Up in Lafayette. It is wonderful to be on a friendship basis with the "kids" I taught forty years ago. I think that Nick was in the very first classroom I ever walked into, a sophomore world history class. I remember being scared stiff to be in front of a bunch of kids, but I got over it quickly. Monsignor Donovan, our principal, had told us rookie teachers, "It's either you or them. Either you control your classroom or the kids will control you." I remember taking that to heart, and grabbing the first kid I saw who was smiling, yanking him out of his desk and whispering, "If you ever do that again, I'll kill you." It was Ed DeCoit, who remembers the moment vividly today, telling me recently it was the most exciting thing that happened to him in high school. For me too. Of course, today I would be in jail.

After graduation Nick became a Moonie, actually the Rev. Moon's personal bodyguard, married one of his daughters, and had two lovely daughters go through Bishop O'Dowd. Dan and Tim were classmates in the Class of '69, one of my favorites. How they have changed!

What hasn't changed is the Round Up, a bar that was going strong when I was in college, a dump of a place, back then a "bucket of blood" that attracted a rough crowd and underage St. Mary's students. It hasn't changed one bit, still has an unpaved parking lot of rocks and mud, scruffy pool-playing clientele, Boston-like barmaids, and no recognizable décor of any sort. There it sits, on a central corner of downtown Lafayette, a sturdy, unmovable rock in a tsunami of architectural change.

We went to the St. Mary's-USF basketball game afterwards. When I was playing, that would have been one of the crucial, rivalry games of the year, and even now, the gym was sold out. But the rivalry is gone. There wasn't a single untoward incident on the court, no fights in the parking lot, no vulgarities hurled by the rooting sections. If fact, there wasn't even a discernable USF rooting section to be found. Whatever happened to the good old days? St. Mary's won fairly easily. Once again, they have a pretty good team.

Friday, January 14

Gabby was here this morning, checking on Mary. I think that will be the last of the home care nurse visits because we go back to Shoba Kankopati next week to resume the chemo treatments. Mary is resigned to them, although now that she is feeling better, it is difficult to gear up again. But there is an end in sight, and the cure is worth all of the weariness and ache. I say that, but I am not the one having to endure the process. This morning Barb related the horrible effects of chemo on her son Raymond twenty years ago when there was little knowledge of the treatment and what to do about the side effects. Things have progressed remarkably since then.

Saturday, January 15

The only reason I know this is the weekend is because there are NFL football games on TV. Otherwise, this could be a cold, foggy Tuesday, just like last Thursday was, and next Sunday will be. We are in the tule fog season, and each day is as remarkably gray as the last and the next. There is nothing else to do but ignore the weather and concentrate on more important things. For instance, a bumblebee came dive-bombing onto the railing as I was standing on the deck this afternoon. After his crash landing, he sat there shivering, wondering what happened to all of the California sunshine that was supposed to be here when he woke up from his winter hibernation and decided to buzz around and stir things up. His neighbor probably told him that the daffodils at Dold's place had pushed up, so it must be spring. So he takes off, finds his fat little body being weighed down by fog vapor, and does a forced landing on our deck. I have always loved bumble bees. I once lost a race with a bumblebee, running into a 25-mph wind. It is one of the most humiliating moments of my adult life, losing to a creature that is aerodynamically impossible. This rotund little dude came struggling up behind me, got in my wind stream if you can create such a thing running 2-hour miles, and then drafted right into the lead. I definitely saw him look sideways at me before he bumbled ahead. I think there was a leer on his face. I just know that the minute he got out of my sight he collapsed of a heart attack, but what good does that do me now? I suppose that he would say that it proves that white men not only can't jump, they can't even run very well.

Like I say, foggy weather doesn't leave you much else than to think heavy thoughts and impose them on whoever will listen.

Sunday, January 16

Mary was up early, at 10:00, wearing red going-out clothes, and ready to roar. We went off to breakfast and then to the store to buy stuff for dinner tonight, as well as a dozen or so Hallmark cards for her weekly mailing. Jim and Donna are coming over this afternoon, as well as Cole and Marcia Buxton. Cole and I were in the first grade together, at St. Augustine's in Oakland, and went through grammar school, high school and college together. At least until our sophomore year at St. Mary's College, when he went into the Marines to fly jets. We remain the closest of friends.

This was really our first solo hosting of anything since Mary got sick. She feels well enough these days to shop, and socialize, something nice to see. We both know that chemo is going to start again pretty soon, so she better enjoy the relatively good health while she can. I have read that your body doesn't actually get rid of the chemo poisons for about a year, so her "good" health is surely relative, but still something to be thankful for. Yesterday we completely finished dismantling Christmas. The boxes and tubs of decorations are all stuffed into the right side of the garage; the number of large containers now reach the century mark. Mary is about ready to pull out the bins of decorations for Valentine's Day and Chinese New Year, both of which thankfully rely heavily on the color red, and thus are entirely compatible. Thank God St. Valentine wasn't born around the same time as St. Patrick because red and green would look like we were bringing back Christmas for an encore.

I had a nice discussion with Donna and Marcia while we were cleaning the dinner dishes, about issues pertaining to the household. I learned all sorts of interesting things that I never could have guessed. For instance, you can thaw out frozen shrimp by washing them in cold water. Now who would have come up with something like that? I would have opted first to just stick the whole bag in the microwave or at least in the oven. If I even thought to use water, it would never be cold, but as hot as I could get it. But cold water? Why not just stick them back in the freezer?

"So, do you soften butter with cold water?" I inquired with just a small bit of irony seeping through my teeth.

"No, you could stick it in the microwave," Donna suggested. Marcia chose to just scrape it onto the French bread and stick the whole thing in the oven.

This is a whole new experience for me, discussing domestic husbandry over the dishwasher, comparing soaps and softeners, thawing techniques, and so forth. Jim sat out in the dining room with Cole the whole time, worrying about what was happening to my thought processes. I didn't bother to ask him what brand of soap he uses.

Speaking of which, as I recall, we only had a couple of choices in soap when I was a kid. I know Mom had Tide, and I think I remember Duz, because "Duz does everything!" Well, not any more. Nothing does everything these days in the soap game. It's like baseball—you have starters, and middle relief, and set-up guys and closers—in soaps. I went to Safeway the other day because I noticed the supplies in the laundry room were running low. I know Mary uses Tide liquid, and Downy softener. They have an entire row of Tides these days! I measured—the aisles at Safeway have 7 shelves on each side. There are 25 feet of seven shelves filled with a bewildering array of Tide clones. I suppose you could just buy good old Tide, Tide Nothing, (They call it "Acti-Lift) but how would that look in the check-out stand? You have to have Tide Something—Tide with Fabreze (whatever that is), and Tide with Downy, and Tide with Clorox. I'm not sure if that is different from Tide with Bleach. I took a few notes. There are the four I just mentioned, and all four also come in Tide HE (It stands for "High Efficiency"). It occurred to me—why would you not want to be highly efficient, even if you're not a soap? What is the rest of the Tide stuff—LE, for Low Efficiency? But back to that low stuff, there is also Tide Coldwater Liquid, Freshness, and Freshness Sport. There is Tide Free and Gentle, which also comes as LE and HE, with and without Fabreze, bleach and Downy. Then there is Tide Pure Essential and Pure Essential with a Touch of Downy. Down the road there is Tide Coldwater HE and Tide Total

Care HE, and Tide Free for Coldwater HE. There is a whole line of Free and Gentle Tide, and a bunch of Stain Release Tides and when all else fails, you just want soap, they have Dye and Perfume Free Tide.

Have we become blithering idiots? Most surely, YES!

Tuesday, January 18

I don't know what happened to yesterday. All I know is that I woke up this morning and it is already Tuesday. We have a meeting this afternoon with Dr. Shoba, who will resume her care of Mary now that the surgery is finished. She and Dr. Donthineni are passing her back and forth. Dr. Shoba will inform us today what further treatments are in store for Mary, undoubtedly more chemo and probably radiation. I think that Mary is resigned to whatever comes, although now that she knows the real effect of the chemo, she is not as glib about the whole thing. We now know it is poison, and something that simply has to be endured.

Our meeting went very well. Shoba is thrilled with the pathology reports of Mary's surgery. Essentially the large tumor is gone, with just a few small active spots found. Dr. Donthineni took out two lymph nodes, only one of which had a very small tumor, only three millimeters in size. She is bringing the report to the oncology team at Epic Care tomorrow for a group consultation, and next Monday the Concord College of the Tumor Board is meeting to discuss Mary's care and treatment. She doesn't want to begin any treatment until the incisions are fully healed, since chemo can be very destructive and can impede the healing. We will meet with Dr. Shoba on February 1, as well as Dr. Kenneth Chao, the radiation oncologist. I told her that whatever the treatment, we wanted Mary to be chemo free at least a month before Annie's wedding, and she assured me that they would be sure to make that possible.

For us that means two glorious weeks of Mary feeling good, at least as good as can be achieved with the remnants of chemo still in her body. She has been eating normally for a week now, and this didn't even seem to add any weight, as she tipped the scales today at a sprightly 154.

Wednesday, January 19

Mary's first day of relative ease, physical and mental. There is nothing to think about as far as treatments go—no chemo, no shots, in the stomach or otherwise, no pills, no steroids, nothing! For me it's Wednesday, and I have two large green waste containers to fill, the one constant that has been with me every week since I retired. I would feel awful if I didn't get those tubs filled and had to pay for them anyway. It's a Protestant Ethic sort of thing, a needless waste. These days, filling them is not that easy. We have had weeks of drippy fog without letup, and the leaves that are lying around or even piled up are soggy, cold and heavy. By the time I get the containers filled, and they hold a great deal, I can barely move them. I dread the day when they are so heavy and I bounce them down the brick stairs and a wheel falls off. I have picked up all of the easy leaves this year, so what remains is up on top of our hill or down a steep slope at the bottom. But I have made up my mind that I am going to have a leaf-free yard at least once before I keel over, and there is no year like the present.

Other than that, there is not much happening, except to continue writing about my Boris. In four chapters I have had him in a kibbutz in Palestine, driving a truck in Egypt, skiing in St. Moritz, at the University of Vienna, and now he is in Garmisch-Parteikircken trying to win the Olympics cross country ski event. The man never sat still!

Tonight I am taking Erik, Tim Brophy, and Cole to the St. Mary's-San Diego game. Originally it was Annie's idea, since USD is her Alma Mater and SMC is mine. She and Erik and Mary and I were going to go. But then after I had bought the tickets, she discovered that she *had* to be in Hawaii, inspecting hotels, such as the Ritz, the Hyatts, and other swank resorts. Since she wasn't going to be here, Mary didn't want to go. It's just as well, because her backside isn't really up to hard bleacher seats. So it is boys' night out. We all met at the Hickory Pit in Walnut Creek where we completely went overboard on ribs, and then went to the game. It was supposed to be a big blowout for St. Mary's, but San Diego hung in there and made somewhat of a game of it. It is interesting to see how quickly the St. Mary's community has gotten spoiled by their recent teams. They went to the Sweet 16 last year in March Madness and now that is expected. They are pretty good again this year, but I don't think as good as last year. But they are 15-2 and that ain't bad.

Thursday, January 20

Just a quick update on Mary's progress. She is doing very well, feeling almost good, and eating almost normally. The Boost shakes are temporarily on hold! Her oncologist is taking the pathology reports from her surgery to the Tumor Board on Monday. Apparently hers is a rather new form of sarcoma and they all want to consult on the ongoing treatment. She is slated for at least two more cycles of chemo and then radiation. Because of Annie's wedding, they may reverse that so that she feels good in April. Anyway, her outlook is extremely positive and we are looking ahead with optimism. Thanks again for all of your love and concern. Mary and Jack

Friday, January 21

A note from my sister:

Dear Mary and Jack,

Many thanks for the update. So good to hear you're feeling pretty good, Mary, and have more of an appetite. Know you'll be glad to have the chemo and radiation behind you. Glad too the doctors can work with you so you'll be feeling good for the wedding. I just saw my gynecologist for my quarterly check-up and all looks well. So looking forward to the wedding and time with the family. I'm going to Minnesota today. I really know how to pick my winter travel spots!

Take good care.

Much love,

Jan

Big day today! I knew that the moment I saw Mary completely wigged out. She and her friend Jovita are going to their class reunion at Chevies in Emeryville. Mary really is almost back to normal in appearance, attitude and appetite, although her energy is still a bit low. But she was all excited to be able to get into her car and do something for herself after all these weeks.

I am going into Castro Valley for another interview and lunch with Eva Kastel. She is the most amazing woman I have met in a great long while—eighty-eight years old next month, but with the brain and body of a woman in her sixties. She teaches yoga classes three days a week and takes two advanced classes herself. She is in a couple of book groups, is president of Baywood Retirement Home, and maintains a daily schedule that would wear anyone out. She refuses to use any elevator, and walks, like any good German woman walks, at double speed. Our meetings and interviews have been a highlight for me this past year, as we try to dredge up memories of her and Boris for the novel I am writing. Every new batch of memories contains new surprises. For instance, today I learned that Boris' name really was Otto, and that he had at least three passports under fictitious names, including an Italian passport that he was still using in his old age.

I asked her how he was able to stay in the country after they got married in 1950. After all, he had arrived on some sort of travel visa, ostensibly to go from Montevideo through New York and ultimately back to Yugoslavia. But they had a whirlwind romance and marriage and he never did go home. Eva said she had never thought about it, but one day Boris simply came home and announced he was now a U.S. citizen and that was that. She says he never took a test to her knowledge and surmised that the "organization" he was tied into must have gotten his citizenship worked out. That organization is another real mystery. Eva says it was definitely Communist, that he had been trained in Moscow and was working for the Communists when he came looking for Nazis in South America and further, he was definitely in their employ when he was here in California. He never spoke of the organization and she never knew exactly what it was. He always swore he was not a Communist. His life gets more amazing with every new discovery. (Later I found a number of articles about a secret service group that was trained in Moscow for Tito, men who were sent around the world in search of Ustaše and Nazis who were wanted in Yugoslavia. This makes more sense, because Boris always considered Tito to be more of a Socialist than a Communist, and it fits with other stories Boris told.)

Saturday, January 22

Father Leo appeared at our front gate this morning. I forgot to turn on my cell phone, and when I did, at 11:00, there was a message from him that it was 10:30 and he was at the front gate. Now that is patience! Leo Dummer and Ron Carignan were the first Oblate priests, from the Oblates of Mary Immaculate (OMI) to come to Bishop O'Dowd High School. He remained a pillar of the school until he left in the late 1970s and moved to a mission in Zambia. He is a wonderful man, garrulous, caring, very well informed and highly talented mechanically. He almost single-handedly created Zambia's first real radio station during his years down there. Mary and I shared a fine dinner with him and Ron Carignan in Livingston, Zambia, when we were there. Our friendship with those two priests and Father Paul Waldie are those of a lifetime. Paul will marry Annie and Erik in April, and our hope is that all three of them can be here for the wedding.

Leo has aged quite a bit since I last saw him, has two new knees and is almost completely white-haired, but his energy and enthusiasm are the same as ever. We had a nice lunch in Suisun.

Sunday, January 23

I saved $39.28 at Safeway today! That is what my Club Card receipt told me when I checked out, and I am thrilled. So grateful was I at the savings that I went right over to BevMo and with my club card and there I saved another $42.37 buying completely unnecessary booze and wine. That's $81.55 in one day! Of course I spent almost $200, so I couldn't really say that it was an economical day. Of course, I probably could have bought the same groceries at Lucky Store or maybe even Raley's for $39.28 less and the same liquor at Costco for $42.37 less. But then I never would have "saved" anything.

Michael and Julie Petrini came over today, the first time they have been here, since the house was brand new. Michael took my job as vice principal at Bishop O'Dowd when I left for New England and the travel business. I managed to burn the steaks, and we managed to overcook the baked potatoes, but the tossed salad came out perfect, probably because Michael tossed it. But we had a very enjoyable day. Michael has been deathly sick the past year with a rare blood disease that resembles bone cancer. He was treated at Stanford, and had to rent an apartment near the campus for more than a year to be close to immediate aid. He received a stem cell transplant from his sister, which seemed to be working but then apparently collapsed. However, his blood has continued to be healthy, a complete mystery for the Stanford doctors and researchers. Now he is back to work as the chief fund raiser at Bishop O'Dowd and is fattening up nicely. I think that he is the only connection still at the school that goes back to my days there.

Monday, January 24

Jackie Olson, the director of alumni travel at U.C. Berkeley, and I had a fundamental difference of opinion today. A few nights ago, when I was unloading the dishwasher, it occurred to me that if you put the silverware in handle first, you had to take them out with the useable side, the blade of the knives, the tines of the forks, etc. That is very unhealthful, since your fingerprints are all over the very places where someone's tongue is going to be. It seems to me that you ought to put it all in the other way, so that you remove the pieces by their handles, subjecting nobody to your germs during the next meal. Jackie stubbornly objected, asserting that the racks are not made for handle-first loading, that the slots are too small and you couldn't clean as many pieces at one washing. She also said that you ought to clean your hands before unloading the dishwasher anyway and then there would be no germs to worry about. That is perfectly ridiculous. I have been studying this whole hand-cleaning phenomenon. If you actually washed up every time they tell you to, you would have no time left in your day for anything else. You may as well buy a big dishwasher and deposit yourself in it and never come out. And if you ever do get out, be sure it is head first, because your feet might just infect somebody.

Mary is definitely feeling much better. She was off this morning to have lunch with Barb. And tomorrow she has advised me that she is taking BART over to SF to have lunch with Annie and then to spend the afternoon looking for a wedding dress, for herself, mother of the bride. I think it is wonderful. She is looking better every day, and obviously feeling chipper. Too bad she will have to go back into chemo, but at least she is having a week of feeling energetic. We are even going to drive to Nancy's on Wednesday to spend a few days with them, and watch a few of the kids' basketball games.

Wednesday, January 26

This may be the last time in quite a while that Mary feels like riding for seven hours to Nancy's house. Or should I say to Kasey's and Josh's house? Of course we always want to be with Nancy and Marty, but let's be honest, we grandparents measure our joy at this stage of our life with the young ones. As much as I love my daughters, and I love them with everything I have, I love Kasey and Josh without limit. As Kasey used to say when she was little, "I love you to the moon and back. Twice!"

Both of the kids are playing basketball this time of year. I always watch the games with mixed emotions. On the one hand, I was raised playing basketball. There was hardly a day during my high school when I didn't play, and I coached at Bishop O'Dowd, which had Northern California's premier high school basketball program in those days, winning the state title a couple of times. The basketball skills of the Eureka kids can't compare with those in the city, if for no other reason than they don't play enough games and never get a chance to face the best competition. Besides, both Kasey and Josh have so much more to do in their lives—work, studies, music, dance, dirt bikes, guitar…and sports. In no way can you call their lives "one dimensional," as you might the soccer or basketball star in Oakland or San Francisco.

But as limited as the general level of the games are in Eureka, the competition is just as fierce. I think in many ways it is healthier competition, because the kids play largely for the fun of the game. In a school as small as Eureka High, every kid has to play, almost every sport, or there won't be enough to field a team. Josh has only three boys in his whole class! So even the fat kids play, and are welcomed, and win or lose, they have a good time. And after all, isn't that the very definition of the word—game? When I see the pressure, the stress that is so evident in the city game, you can hardly suppose it is fun for all concerned. On the other hand, here in Eureka, all of the parents and grandparents show up. They root for all of the kids, not just their own, and they go home, perhaps disappointed, but certainly not shattered. And the kids go on with their lives, putting the game, win or lose, behind them almost immediately. Robert Frost said he could sum up life in three words: "It goes on."

Mary did just fine on the ride up, propping her left side up with the little whoopee pillow she drags around these days, absorbed for most of the trip in her latest book. I love watching her read, grabbing her little dictionary every so often to look up whatever word she has stumbled over, carefully writing down the definition in her journal. She eventually transfers her new words into a computer list Annie started for her. I have mentioned that what she is creating is called a "dictionary" and she really doesn't have to make her own, but it is the accomplishment that is important for her. The effect is striking— Mary is now using words she used to laugh at not too long ago, even though she sticks by her most common concept—"Why do you need a fancy word when you already have a perfectly good common one?" I have to admit, I am also flattered because quite often, her pocket dictionary doesn't contain the word she is seeking, and I become the court of last resort.

We stopped for lunch at the Slanted Porch in Fallon, a very fine restaurant with surprisingly good food, prepared with imagination and served with a friendly smile. It was one of our discoveries on our recent geology trip for Cal.

We made it out to Nancy's by 5:00, even beating her in from Elko where she is working today. I went into town to watch Josh's practice, while Mary settled in. Tomorrow the games start.

Thursday, January 27

It was very moving to see all of the Eureka women come over to greet Mary tonight at the games. More than ever I feel that we have become in a small way part of the Eureka society, bona fide members of the town. All through the evening, ladies came over to tell Mary how good she looks, or to inquire about her illness and to wish her well. It is how the country people are—thoughtful and caring. Of course, Mary was all wigged out tonight, and looked great. Several remarked on what "good color" she had, and probably all of the men failed to realize that it wasn't really her hair. On the other hand, Mary did look good. Amy Damele brought her a padded chair to take the edge off of the hard bleacher seats, and we were all propped up against the wall in the top row of the stands. And there we made our stand, for two games.

The opponent tonight was Round Mountain, from Smoky Valley on the way toward Tonopah. Kasey's Varsity Girls game is first. Eureka came out pressing, and within a few minutes it was obvious the game would be a rout. I love Kasey's team. Right now they have ten girls, all of whom can play very well. The coach, Mr. Fujii, who is also the school principal, generally rotates five at a time, so they are always fresh. There isn't a lot of drop-off between the first and second string, although the first string guards are much more aggressive than the next two. The game came close to being too big a blowout. Schools are fined by the league if they win a game by more than fifty points, something that would have happened tonight by the end of the third quarter if Eureka hadn't decided to drop their press and shoot nothing but 3s, most of which they missed, and retreat into a box zone defense where they didn't contest any shots.

Josh and Andrew are on the JV team, but since there are only five actual players on the varsity, they also suit up for that too. The rule is that they can only play five quarters in any given day, so if there is a JV game, they might play two or three quarters there and then be eligible for two or three in the varsity game. Both of them would be better off sticking with JV because they are growing and learning to play, and the more court time they get the better. Andrew is more aggressive than Josh and fits a bit better into the varsity game. Both need another year of learning. Josh made several beautiful drives over the weekend which is a portent of what he can become. When he gets a lane, usually from the left side, he flies into the basket so quick that it is actually startling. But he doesn't have the confidence yet to expand his scoring with floaters and pull up jumpers. He will learn and develop the confidence, if he is willing to practice what he doesn't yet know.

Actually, next year, Eureka could be pretty good if Josh and Andrew become the guards they have the potential to be. They also will have Tanner back, the best player on the varsity this year, and Dakota, who is only a sophomore. The fifth player should be Kevin, who is still awkwardly gangly, but has improved greatly in many ways. He will probably keep growing, and can actually jump well, so Eureka should be very good for the next several years.

As for Kasey's team, they are fun to watch. As with everything she does, Kasey is extremely competitive, going after loose balls and rebounds with real energy. I have always been amazed how she competes on the inside. She did that years ago in soccer, perfectly happy to be in the middle of the scrums, and she does that in basketball. She doesn't start this year, although she easily could, and I don't think she gets enough minutes, but she just keeps plugging along, even when she is disappointed. I love that in her. Volleyball is her first love, but she will continue to improve in basketball too.

Friday, January 28

Josh and I went out to Black Mountain to get a load of rocks for my garden. Long ago I decided to design part of our front yard with a black theme, and Marty directed me to a lava mountain about seventeen miles out on Sadler-Brown Road north of the farm. It is the most curious mountain, one whole side covered with black rock, heavily fractured, perfect for my walks and walls. Doris Sloan, my geologist friend, said it was once a lava flow that cooled quickly and shattered. The rocks are dense, very heavy, dark gray on the inside, and black where exposed to the sun and elements.

Today's opponent is a league game for the kids—Carlin. This time there is a JV team, so Josh plays in the first game, and then again in the third game with the varsity. Kasey plays in between. Josh is more in his element on the JV level. He started the game with

Andrew on the bench, and the team really struggled to score at all. Josh played three quarters and Andrew two. When they got in the game together, the whole pace picked up, and Eureka made a fine comeback, with these two pesky guards flying around the court.

Kasey's game was much tighter than last night's, but the varsity girls won handily in the end. The varsity boys struggled again. They are really almost a dysfunctional team, with an offense that is too advanced for their skill level, and really no guard play at all. There are three boys who are about 6'3" and fairly active, the best of the bunch being Tanner, who is a junior. I think their time will be next year, but they are going to need some coaching, more than they have now.

Saturday, January 29

These are the big games today—literally big. Owyhee is in town, and they are some very BIG kids. Owyhee is an Indian Reservation up north of Carlin, and they must play a lot of basketball, because these kids, many of whom approach obesity, do know how to play. Last year, Mr. Fujii ran a new team into the game every four or five minutes and literally ran the Owyhee girls into the floor. It is almost painful to watch some of these girls try to run up and down the court, but they do compete and are very effective. Tonight there are four games, JV and varsity for both boys and girls. We got to the gym just in time to see the JV girls go into overtime tied at 47 in what proved a very exciting game, won eventually by Eureka. Unfortunately Josh's JV game was not competitive, the Indian boys towering over the Vandals, and one boy in particularly racking up more than twenty points with the same left-handed layup, over and over again.

Eureka's varsity girls almost ran their opponents out of the gym in the first quarter, racing to a 15-point lead, but then they ran out of gas. Mr. FujiI was not there, apparently having been sent to the hospital with chest pains yesterday, and the stand-in coach forgot that these girls are used to going all out for most of a quarter and then getting spelled by the second team coming in en masse.

She opted not to substitute tonight, and she almost ran her own team into the ground. The game tightened up until Eureka finally lost the lead in the second half. But the girls came back, finally making 5 clutch free throws in the last couple of minutes and winning by half a dozen. It was a very good game, but from our standpoint, not as satisfying as it could have been because Kasey saw almost no action.

February

Tuesday, February 1

This is another of Mary's big days, which seem to be coming fast and furious. We begin this morning with a consultation with Dr. Kenneth Chao, one of the radiation oncologists at the Cancer Center. In our last meeting with Dr. Shoba, she told us that there would undoubtedly be more chemo as well as radiation in Mary's future. I think that the last couple of weeks, where Mary was eating normally again and feeling pretty good, have dropped her guard a bit, and she is beginning to think that the crisis is over. Today I fear she will be yanked back to reality, that the cancer is still with her, insidiously, and that the fight is anything but finished.

Dr. Chao is a young, friendly Chinese man, well spoken and confident in his expertise. He embarked on a careful and thorough explanation of exactly what radiation is and how they use it. After examining Mary's incisions (as well as removing a staple that had been missed by the nurse at home), he explained that radiation is aimed at the old tumor sites, more or less as preventive maintenance (adjuvant therapy) to obviate a return of the cancer to those areas, especially along the incision lines. He then went into the possible side effects, the most difficult of which is called lymphodema, where the arm or leg swells up, possibly a permanent condition. This is no simple matter, but as he called it "a permanent quality of life adjustment." I saw Mary shudder slightly at his description. There are other possible side effects of radiation as well, but not quite as drastic as that.

He then talked about the particular cancer that Mary has, which doesn't have a name, simply an "undifferentiated sarcoma." He told us that it is new, something they are trying to figure out, and as a result they aren't completely sure how to treat it.

"The least we want," I told him, "is that this cancer be named for Mary."

This evoked a fine laugh, and from that point on, Dr. Chao called it "Mary's Cancer." We all want our fifteen minutes of fame!

But he said that at this point, because chemo had worked wonders on her tumors, he would not do radiation at all, but rather go back to some more cycles of chemo. If the first treatments had not been so successful, radiation would have been useless. If, after several more cycles, the PET scan shows no more signs of cancer, then he would recommend radiation as a follow-up treatment.

That treatment is daunting—five or six weeks of daily sessions. They only last five minutes or so, but are given every day, thirty-four in all until they reach a total of sixty *gray* (Gy), 1.8 Gy per session. The radiation actually destroys the DNA of the cancer cells. Dr. Chao said that they triangulate the laser to meet at the cancer site rather than just barging through good tissue. He said he would tattoo Mary with small dots in three areas to achieve the triangulation. This is way above our comprehension. Chemo, which we can regard as a medicine without worrying about the exact contents or makeup, is easier to accept, but this photon radiation or radiation therapy is high science. We can comprehend chemo as putting poison in your body to kill cells, grudgingly accepting the fatigue and nausea. But this radiation stuff is scary. If the cancer is gone, what cells are they killing? And is it worth the 25 percent chance of a serious lymphodema resulting? But thus far, the doctors have led us along a straight line of cure, so it is going to take more faith in their knowledge to finally get to a conclusion.

Even then, the "conclusion" of cancer is a dubious thing. Almost every type of cancer eventually recurs, so insidious are the tiny cells that have filtered through the blood system. But the doctors talk of eight to ten years of healthy living, and that is worth fighting for at our stage of life.

I asked Dr. Chao where in China his family lived. They came from Beijing and Guangchao, so they cover both the Mandarin and Cantonese cultures. We had a brief laugh over learning the language. I like him a great deal. He is very casual and very human with a nice sense of his craft. We will take his advice.

Upstairs we moved to a second meeting with Dr. Shoba, who is making the final decisions on Mary's treatments. She is more relaxed with us now because the chemo was so spectacularly successful. It seems that Shoba was holding her breath mightily hoping that the treatments would be efficacious. They were, apparently more than anyone could have wished.

She said that just yesterday the "Board" met and spent more than an hour discussing Mary's Cancer. It is new and treatment is a matter of opinion. Six or seven local oncologists from the major hospitals attended along with several physicians. "A lively discussion" was the way that Shoba described the meeting, with many conflicting opinions on treatment. One oncologist proposed no more treatments; another asked why they didn't take out the lesion on the lung. Another wanted to change the chemo cocktail. Shoba's reply was that the current mix of Gemzar and Taxotere worked extremely well, and why change something that works?

This was an interesting explanation of a group of doctors that, confronted with something new, battle it out to come up with a treatment. It reminded me of listening to Marty and about five other farmers discussing how to plow a particularly difficult field. They all had their opinions but in the end, Marty made his own decision which wasn't in accord with any of them. I hope that Shoba's decision works out better than Marty's that time! He plowed the field so well, the next big wind blew all the soil away.

But Shoba's reasoning makes sense. At the beginning they weren't sure of what the chemo would do, but they were thrilled with the results. If there are any cancer cells left in Mary's body, and it is probable there are, then it is logical to assume that the chemo would take them out, since it already pretty much killed a huge tumor in her leg. Alice, in the infusion center, has to get the Medicare folks to approve the new cycles, but we expect to begin the chemo again next Monday.

Free of doctors, we headed to find a place for lunch. After several months of Mary feeling bad, it seems a bad idea to waste a perfectly beautiful sunny day doing nothing.

"Let's go to Clayton for lunch."

"Clayton, why there?"

"Because it's different and you've never been to Clayton for lunch."

Mary gave me one of her best eye rolls and we were off to Clayton. Actually, while in college, I did a paper for Brother Matthew, a perfectly awful history teacher, on Clayton. As I recall, they had just finished a very famous poltergeist experience in the small town, and everyone was buzzing about big rocks flying over buildings and chandeliers crashing to the floor. But that wasn't exciting enough for Brother Matthew, so I looked into the obituaries for half a dozen months before my assignment, and found an old 90-year man who had recently died, and "interviewed" him for an in-depth discussion of the brothels of Clayton during the old coal mining era. I came up with an extremely lurid account, which fully appealed to the chastity vow of the good brother.

Anyway, we had a very nice lunch of fettuccini and linguini vongole at La Veranda in Clayton, a fine use of a nice day feeling good.

Wednesday, February 2

I am the one who is nervous today, because I go to Tony DeMeo's office for my annual physical. Now that Mary had to discover a completely unexpected cancer, I am not at all sure I want to undergo a long series of blood tests and other poking and pressures. No choice! Everyone says you have to get an annual physical, and missing one is worse than missing confession after a particularly spectacular impure thought back in grammar school. What would people think if I don't pee in a cup and stick a stick into my stool—on time?

Tony didn't even yell at me for hitting 260 again. That's probably because he matches me in girth and the last time he yelled, I yelled back at him and prescribed the South Beach Diet for his rotundency.

He knew he needed a diet even more than me, so this time he left me alone and concentrated on finding something else wrong with me. Cholesterol is fine; blood pressure was great; EKG was normal; triglycerides were a bit elevated but I blamed Mary for that, forcing me to join her every night with ice cream. He was starting to panic as he ticked off things that were okay, even poking into my privates and finding no enlarged prostates or dysfunctional liver. No need for FloMax or Cialis. Then he failed to find a pulse in my left ankle. Finally!

"You are going to need a Dopler LLE," he announced, writing me out an order for one doctor Gregory Rhodes. "You are supposed to have a pulse in both of your legs."

So that's it. My legs are fine except that there's no blood running in one of them, and the knees hurt and I have neuropathy in both feet. What's the big deal? He's just mad that my Vitamin D count was above normal.

Thursday, February 3

It's a lovely, cold, sunny day and we are just sitting around contentedly, taking our blood pressure readings. Both of us are under orders to log in our blood pressures for the next two weeks. I went down to CVS to get a new machine. It took me quite a while to find one that would register both of us at a happy 123/73, which we will log in every day until the paper is full.

Seriously, Mary's BP was sky-high yesterday, something like 153/103, when they took it at the radiation office and again upstairs in oncology. But today it is back to normal, probably because she isn't sitting in the chemo room being nervous. She seems so relaxed all the time, but I have the feeling that the proximity of all of those chemicals does get her heart beating faster than she thinks. It would certainly bother me.

The center called this morning to inform Mary that she has been cleared for next Monday, so that is the commencement of stage three as far as I'm concerned. Stage one was the initial chemo infusions; stage two, the surgery; and now we are hopefully in the final stage—preventive maintenance. Of course there is also the mysterious radiation stage ahead somewhere too.

Saturday, February 5

I just couldn't help myself. For the past year or so I have been loading black rocks into our Saab in Eureka. When I decided to take out our lawns, this black rock was perfect for the area just below our deck. It has taken more patience than I usually have with such projects but I have persisted in operating in increments of about 800 pounds a shot. I figure I have about three more loads and I'll be finished with that area.

But then I decided to take out the big lawn in front of the house, and I have scribbled paths around and through the plot, paths that are going to require a large number of rocks. Life is too short to try to fashion that area out of black rocks from Eureka! So today I went over to the Rock Source out near Travis and bought myself 5000 pounds of moss rocks. I am a little concerned because they are dirt brown instead of black, but I figure the brick stairway is a legitimate transition zone and should allow the color change to be made. I am considering using red lava pebbles for the walkways instead of the black lava I used on the first project. Red goes much better with dirt brown. Anyway, they dropped my 2.5 tons of rocks in the driveway last night, and I am going to have a chiropractor appointment on Monday for sure. There is no way I am going to allow a nice rock pile to sit around dormant for very long. It is nice to be back to work! Compared to other projects I have done on the hill, this one is pretty tame. For the "Yellow Brick Road" that winds around the north side of the hill, I used up 6,000 bricks, which at five pounds each comes to a tidy 30,000 pounds. To that was added about 60,000 pounds of big moss rocks for the planters and sculpture circles. So this lawn project is child's play, which is good because there's not much left of what used to be my back and hips.

Sunday, February 6

Annie was dressed for the occasion. So was Erik, but you expect it of him, outfitted as he was with a fine John Elway sweatshirt from Superbowl XXXIII in 1999, shorts and flip-flops. But Annie! She was sporting a brand new referee striped shirt, matching black sweat pants, hair in pig tails, and black glare patches under her eyes. Now that should be *de rigueur* for a Superbowl party hostess!

Green Bay plays Pittsburg today, two teams that most people can identify with, without the anti-city hatred that attaches to places like New York, Chicago, LA or Detroit. I mean, who can root against Green Bay, a city of 100,000 fanatics who sit in Lambeau Field frozen for seven months of the year? Pittsburg is a little harder for the non-Steeler fan, mostly because of the jerk they have playing quarterback, Ben Rothlenberger, who by all rights should be in prison for statutory rape a couple of times over. But hey, this is sports in America, and there are no punishable crimes if you are a big-time jock. I think that because of Rothlenberger, most of the country is rooting for Green Bay and their squeaky clean quarterback, Aaron Rogers, who has finally stepped out of the shadow of Bret Baby-faced Favre. Everyone at Anne and Erik's house is pulling for Green Bay, although there are a couple of garages on the block who are Steeler loud.

The game saved the event. Christina Aguilera completely butchered the National Anthem, leaving out "o'er the ramparts we watched" and later cramming in "what so proudly we watched," instead of "what so proudly we hailed." That would probably have been okay, because we have arguably the most difficult anthem in the world to sing, but she butchered the correct words with what I suppose was her singing. First of all, she had long stringy, snow-white hair that made her look like a wicked witch in drag, and then she made the colossal mistake of actually opening her mouth. Every note had four or five versions as she stumbled around hoping to find the correct pitch, and in some cases the right note itself. One paper described it as turning every sentence into a paragraph. It was awful.

Half-time featured the Black Eyed Peas, a curious mixture of Fergie, dressed as a space traveling halfback with glittery shoulder pads and fortified boobs, and three leather-clad, somewhat plastic-helmeted creatures who rapped and sputtered through songs. Only Annie knew all the words and for most of those songs there weren't any discernable words.

The game was great, Green Bay streaking to an 18-point lead and then holding off Pittsburg 31-25.

Monday, February 7

Mary resumes her chemo today. She has had a month and a half, since December 13, of no chemo infusions, and in spite of her very complex operation, her health quickly improved. Right now she is close to normal in the way she feels as well as in appetite and outlook. Both of us know that will not last when the chemo reenters her blood stream. But she should be okay this week and maybe next, until the strong dose of Taxotere hits.

I have an appointment myself today, with a doctor named Gregory Rhodes in Walnut Creek to see if he can find some blood down near my feet.

I dropped Mary off at the Cancer Center and hurried off to my own appointment. Annie is picking her up when her infusion is finished. I left Mary nervous as a cat, because she may have to use her cell phone to call Anne. Mary is positively frightened of that phone, afraid to push any button, I think because she thinks it is a tool from Mission Impossible and will self destruct if she opens it. She never turns it on, because she says nobody knows her phone number, which means she never checks for messages which she would get if the phone is turned on, that is, if she got any messages from people who don't know her number. I think that is approximately the reasoning involved. But today, I made her turn it on, got it recharged, and showed her, once again, how to get hold of Annie. We'll see.

As for me, I never knew that they could measure your blood pressure in your feet. But they did, and found out that I actually have blood flowing down there on both sides. I already knew that because neither of my feet was pale white, or in danger of falling off. But Dr. Rhodes did say that there is an artery blocked in my left leg, so I will get a sonogram and find out where and why. He isn't too concerned because the blood pressure is fine.

We took Anne to dinner tonight. Erik went back to Phoenix to finish some jobs he started, as well as to earn a little money to pay for the honeymoon. As we dropped Annie back at her house, we noticed a big box on the front porch from Macy's and her wedding registry. It was a Bissell vacuum, and Annie was completely overjoyed.

"Erik totally laughed at me when I put this on our list. He said that nobody would ever buy this for us. I love this wedding stuff!" It was from Erik's best man, a perfect gift that could only be purchased by a guy, when you stop to think about it.

Today I started my wedding diet, my push to be able to get into my tux and look splendid for the photographer. I am back on the South Beach Diet, with which I lost almost forty pounds a couple of years ago. Or was it last year? Whichever year, all the weight I lost got found again and I am exactly where I was when I started that diet the last time, 262. I figure it would be a good goal for April to get down to about 230. It's a great diet, almost as good as the one Mary has been on, but hopefully without all the medical problems.

Thursday, February 10

We may have started a tradition today. I met Cole for breakfast at the Hickory Pit, something we did last month. I have always said, "Twice makes custom," so now it is a custom, which I think is the last step before a tradition. Yesterday I invited my ex-partner, brother-in-law George to join us, and that made it doubly enjoyable. I think we will try to do this once a month, maybe down the road dragging Chuck into it as well. It is nice to just sit and reminisce with old friends without the complications of job, families, and other stuff. Nothing really gets accomplished, but you certainly feel good doing nothing.

Mary is so much like normal these days. I almost forget what it was like when she was in the full throes of chemo and cancer worry. She had her first Gemzar infusion on Monday, but as was the case the first time around, she is showing no outward effects, except she was all wired up on Monday night from the steroids. Jackie suggested she get a prescription for Atavan to get her some sleep after the Dexamethasone drip. Isn't that interesting—you get your chemo and they give you Dexamethasone to keep you from getting nauseous, and then you take Atavan to relieve you of the side effects of Dexamethasone. There must be some additional antidote for Atavan. But it is really neat to see Mary able to be her old self. Actually I think she is better than that. I think the whole cancer experience has given her a new outlook on life. She is more outgoing, more confident, and certainly more playful than before, something you notice when she is interacting with Annie or Nancy. She is loving life more. I find myself forgetting the awful feelings we had not very long ago.

We were halfway through dinner at Trader Vic's this evening when I realized that Mary had her wig on. It looks so natural, so close to her real hair and style that it is impossible to tell. As a matter of fact, Krishen and Jennifer Laetsch didn't have any idea that it wasn't Mary's real hair. We are celebrating their recent marriage tonight. Krishen is the son of Mac Laetsch, former botany professor and vice chancellor of U.C. Berkeley, with whom I have traveled on more than twenty-five alumni tours. Krishen and Jenny have been living together for nineteen years when all of a sudden they decided to get married, in a totally private ceremony with a dinner at Cal's Faculty Club afterward, attended only by their parents and Jenny's son Charlie. Mary and I wanted to celebrate officially with them and we had a wonderful night.

Saturday, February 12

Mary and Anne met Donna, Sully, and Kinsey this morning to buy a wedding dress. For two-year old Kinsey, of course! She is tabbed to be the flower girl at the wedding, and has to be pinked out properly. They are doing their shopping at David's Bridal in Pinole, which Anne describes as some sort of ghetto boutique. "Did you see all the women looking at bridal gowns? Every one of them had tattoos." These days, a place like David's talks to you only if you have an appointment, something that apparently is as hard to acquire as tickets to the Oprah show. So Kinsey, properly escorted, sampled a variety of red dresses, which she will wear in pink. It is a complicated process, this marriage thing these days, one that no guy will ever understand and one for which all he needs to know is what his checkbook balance is.

For my part, I am fully engaged in ripping out the big lawn in front of the house. Last week I bought my moss rocks and started lining paths. Today I finished all the paths, and the last rock fit *exactly* in the last hole! Such a thing has never occurred before in my entire history of rocking. I always run out before I'm finished. I was so proud of myself today I looked around to see whom I could brag to, but sadly everyone was out bridaling. Of course, I still need another load of bigger rocks to build a large oval planter in the middle which is going to hold a sculpture yet to be determined. I visited Phil Glashoff this afternoon for ideas and think I have found exactly what I had in mind. It occurs to me that I have no cause to complain about wedding costs when I compare them with what I have spent on landscaping over the past twenty-five years. So I will dutifully write Annie's checks and shut up.

Sunday, February 13

Today I was out digging in front and heard noises in the garage. Mary has become a human cleaning machine and has moved out to the garage! And there she was, under the sink, digging out old fertilizer bags, garbage, a variety of birdseed and mouse droppings. Ugh! I told her to get out of there because even though she is feeling good, with her upcoming chemo she doesn't want to get sick. But once she starts, there is really no stopping her. In her mind, the garage is now simply an extension of her hall closet, which gets "cleaned" every few weeks. In that case cleaning means taking everything out, putting it in the hall and putting it right back in, throwing nothing away. It is simply reorganizing. But in the garage there is decades of detritus and Mary is actually filling barrels of things to be discarded. I simply sat and watched in awe.

I should have helped her, but I am in the process of developing a theory for Mary, which I am calling, for want of a better name, "Controlled Reentry." Since Mary has gotten sick, everyone thinks that they, or I, have to do everything for her. That's fine when she needs such help, and when she is looking for assistance, when physically she either can't do something or in doing it she might have a relapse. But I have watched Mary all these years. She detests being considered helpless or unable to do something. As she gets better now, she has to be allowed to do things for and by herself. I don't think it does her any good at all to keep her permanently helpless.

Monday, February 14

It's Valentine's Day. And everywhere, men are rushing to florists to buy flowers. Well, actually, most of them are going to Safeway or Home Depot because flowers are cheaper there. Even at Safeway, where I have been buying Mary a dozen roses for $9.95 ever since she had her cancer, the price is now $19.95 for these few days. Tomorrow it will be back down under ten bucks.

I was at David M. Brian's last week, where I always go to get my gifts because they wrap them nicely. My friend Pat, who has been selling Waterford bowls to me for years, talked me into Pandora bracelets for my girls. These are the new, far more upscale versions of the Italian charm bracelets which all the girls had and which Mary still wears. They are simple silver-braided chain bracelets that accept sterling (or if you are totally foolish, gold) charms. You keep adding to them until you are in need of a second. I'm not certain that my discretionary money will outlast the fad, but at least Mary, Nancy, and Anne got their first charm.

Kasey emailed me asking if I would be her Valentine, and I replied that I became her Valentine almost seventeen years ago and will be for the rest of my life. Isn't that cute! But true! I have to ask about Josh who, as a two-sport hero, is bound to be inundated with precious thoughts from the girls at school. I don't think he is completely affected by the attention yet, but his time will come. I have noticed that several of his girl classmates make it a point to give him a big hug after every basketball game. I haven't seen him actually hug back yet, but he will.

Last year we tried to go out to dinner on Valentine's Day, and it was a Faz Restaurant disaster, so this year I told Mary we were staying home, and I would cook whatever she wanted. It is so easy to cook cracked crab! It was one of my finest gastronomical triumphs—cracked Dungeness crabs and green salad with balsamic vinegar, won ton soup from Fred's, and ice cream with chocolate sauce, strawberries and whipped cream. And nary a stove burner was ignited!

Today was also the tough chemo day for Mary. We got to the Cancer Center around 10:30, with Mary literally ablaze with Valentine decorations, including flashing lights for a necklace, candy kisses for earrings and red everything, including hearts attached to her bright red cancer cap. She was a pure delight for Alice and Lily in the infusion room. Mary is becoming a recognizable personality there, a very positive, optimistic image for all of the suffering patients. I am proud of her. Today she is there for 4.5 hours with the Gemzar and Taxotere and all of the other stuff they pump into her.

Tuesday, February 15

"Wow, plug an engine into Mary. Look at the dexi-blush!"

I had just told Mary that she was about as red as a sliced beet, and she thought it might be her first hot flash moving in. But Alice's exclamation told us that it is a result of the Deximethasone she takes twice a day for red blood cells that are wiped out by the Taxotere. Whatever it is, it made her face light up like it was still Valentine's Day.

This is our week of drive-by injections, shots of Nuprin, mostly meant to stop nausea and build more white blood cells to replace those that Taxotere kills. We take thirty minutes to drive into Pleasant Hill, two minutes to get shot, and thirty minutes home. Breakfast at the Waffle House has become part of the routine if the shot is in the morning; we don't have a restaurant for afternoon injections. Too early for a bar stop.

Life has become pretty basic, these last six months—up when we wake up, the day centered around Mary's cancer treatment, a stop at one store or another for groceries or general supplies, maybe a ride in the country. For me there is usually a bit of writing, an hour or two, more if the spirit moves me.

For Mary there is an unending task of cleaning out drawers and closets, rooms, garage, attics, or if she has lost energy, just sitting and watching Hallmark shows where good always triumphs. And for both of us there is always a bunch of books awaiting our attention. It's really not a bad existence, certainly one that is keeping our blood pressure low most of the time. I think that when Mary is finished with chemo and radiation, we will start putting a future into our daily thoughts. Until then, we'll slog along contentedly, doing things that fill our day. Haven't we always yearned for a time when there was no pressure, no deadlines, a time to just sit and read a book?

Thursday, February 17

The kids are playing in their sectional tournament tonight in Reno. Josh's varsity team barely squeaked their way into the weekend and isn't expected to go very far, not past tonight actually. But Kasey's team is another matter. They have only lost a couple of games this year, and are really fun to watch. They are expected to win tonight, and play for the sectional championship tomorrow. I think that they are assured of going to the state tournament if they win tonight. Mary and I were going to go to Reno to watch, but the weather has been getting progressively worse all week. Snow has dropped almost to the 2000' level, which isn't far above Sacramento. I really don't want to take Mary into that kind of weather, so we decided to back out and root the kids on from long distance. Today really is the start of the three-day Presidents' holiday weekend and it is going to be a mess going to the Sierras no matter what the weather.

I took Mary in this morning for her Nuprin shot. She is starting to drag a bit, which reinforces my decision not to go to Reno. In the past, Thursday was always the beginning of her heavy fatigue after the Taxotere infusion. We really don't know what to expect this time around, because she has a smaller dose, but on the other hand, there are much fewer cancer cells for the poison to attack, so I wonder if the chemo will be harder since it is mainly going to kill good cells.

Chuck and Margaret came over tonight, down for their monthly provisioning at Travis Air Base grocery store. Chuck was supposed to go to the dentist, but the traffic was so bad he never got there. It is really raining, and streets are flooded all over the place. I-80 is also closed from Applegate on, which makes our decision not to go even smarter. We had a quiet meal at home, thanks to Mary's Pizza Shack. I like having Chuck and Margaret visit, because Margaret was a head nurse in the ICU of several different VA hospitals, and she can answer lots of questions that Mary might not be comfortable asking doctors.

Friday, February 18

Around noon, the bottom fell out. Mary is completely shot, sick to her stomach, aching all over. I called the cancer center and cancelled her shot this afternoon, since she wasn't in a condition even to get out of bed, much less go anywhere. I was working in the yard and came up to check on her. I found her lying on the floor of the bathroom, not moving. My heart stopped beating.

"Mary, are you all right? Did you fall?"

"No."

"What happened?"

"I just slid down to here. I didn't feel like getting up."

"Well, you have to get up. You'll catch cold down there."

It took some doing to get her back on her feet, and she collapsed completely into bed, unable to move. I don't think I have seen her so sick. She hasn't had a bowel movement in a couple of days, and she has sharp pains in her stomach. It is impossible to move her, even a little bit, without causing considerable anguish. For the first time since she has had cancer, I gave her one of the anti-nausea pills, Ondansatron, which was prescribed right at the beginning. It did help for a while, but then the stomach cramps resumed with even great intensity.

Annie and Erik are heading up to Reno, so I called her and asked her to get some laxatives on their way here. I administered a good dose of Milk of Magnesia, and Mary settled in for a long night. It is heart-wrenching to watch someone you love in such distress. I called Jackie Olson to get her description of what she went through with her post chemo side effects. She described exactly what Mary is experiencing. I suppose it is a comfort to know that there is nothing out of the ordinary in the pain she is feeling, but it is awful to watch. I would much prefer to be suffering it myself than to watch her go through that. I slept in Anne's room tonight, not wanting to wake her with my snoring, if she was able to get some sleep.

Saturday, February 19

Mary seemed a bit better this morning, so we went in to Pleasant Hill for her shot. Since it is a holiday weekend, our regular doctor, Dr. Shoba, is off, and the other doctors take turns with these nuprin shots when the office is closed. This weekend, Dr. Birnal Patel is standing in. I told him that Mary was experiencing a great deal of nausea and pain, something she didn't have during the first chemo cycles. He barely listened, gave her the shot and said, "Well, I'll see you tomorrow."

"Wait a minute," I said. "Aren't you even going to examine her?"

He took a very cursory look, felt her stomach and told her to take some Zantac.

That was the high point of the day. By noon, Mary was even sicker than yesterday, vomiting and moaning, unable to move, even to roll over. I had to lift her just to get her into a position where she could take a sip of water or take a pill. I have heard the nightmare stories of people in this stage of chemo treatment, those who swore if their cancer ever came back they would never go through it again, and now I understand what they were talking about. We say that chemo is a poison worth enduring, given what it can do to save your life, but in the middle of an episode like Mary is having, I think that must be questionable.

"This has been the worst day of my life," she moaned when I got her ready for bed tonight. I believe it.

Thank God for all the house chores! All day I was like a fish out of water, trying to get my mind off of Mary's travails. So I did four or five loads of wash, probably shrinking most everything, but that is irrelevant. I moved a ton or so of rocks out in my landscaping project, wrote a really shitty chapter in "Boris" which I promptly tore up, and generally got nothing much accomplished. I do have clean socks though.

Sunday, February 20

One problem is solved! Mary's constipation came to a thundering halt around 4 a.m. But she looked awful when I woke her to go in for her shot this morning. She is even weaker than yesterday, probably because she hasn't been able to eat anything, or more exactly to keep anything down that she tried to eat. But she tottered in to the cancer center, got the shot, and then pretty much collapsed. She was able to keep one of my shakes down, which is good. I filled it with enough proteins and calories to satisfy a whole day's needs, so at least she isn't going to get sick from that standpoint.

I know how sick she must feel because she lay all day propped up in bed without once turning on the TV. Fortunately she had company. Maddie, the cat, lay with her all day without making any attempt to move either. I think she is feeling Mary's pain and just wanted to share it with her. The pain bothers me. She didn't have any such side effects from the first three rounds of chemo. I am starting to think that there is something else at play. Cole and I talked about that today. Sometimes when you are concentrating on an enemy, to put it into military terms, you fail to see another enemy sneaking up on you. I switched to Nancy's room tonight. My back and hips can't take another night in those twin beds!

Kasey called. Her team won their Thursday game in Reno by thirty, and on Friday they won the sectional tournament in a close game. And last night they beat Virginia City to win the whole North Section. They go to the state tournament next weekend in Las Vegas as the #1 seed. Go Vandals!

Monday, February 21

"Jack!" Mary screamed around 5 a.m. I came running in. She was in terrible pain, with a sharp stab in her right side, unable to move, even to prop herself up to get a drink. She has been overdosing on ginger ale the last day or so, and it is starting to bother me. Something is nagging in the back of my brain that this isn't normal, but I don't know what it is.

I called the oncologist who is on call at the cancer center, Dr. Patel, a perfectly useless physician in my opinion, to tell him Mary wouldn't be in this morning.

"Something is wrong," I told him. "Is this normal for a chemo patient to have no side effects for three cycles and then suddenly have this kind of discomfort on the next round?"

"No, that isn't normal." That was all he could say.

"Then I'm taking her to the emergency room."

"That might not be a bad idea."

That was the extent of his professional expertise. With great effort and pain, Mary got out of bed, heavily leaning on me. I got her into the bathroom and onto the toilet. From there we managed to get her socks and pants on.

"Don't bother with a shirt," I said. "You can stay in your pajama top."

"And screw the bra," she whispered in one of the most un–Mary statements I have ever heard her utter.

It took fifteen minutes to get her down the stairs and into the car. I decided right away that I wouldn't take her to North Bay Hospital in Fairfield because I have seen their emergency room filled with farm workers, and jammed like a busy bus station. Besides, I don't speak Spanish.

I told Mary we would go to Alta Bates in Berkeley because that is where she had her cancer surgery and they would have her records there. But she was so weak, by the time we reached the Benicia Bridge, I had changed my mind and opted for John Muir in Walnut Creek, which has a 24-hour trauma center.

We were just pulling up when a man came running with a wheelchair and Mary was taken in to an empty waiting room.

"My wife is in considerable pain. She is a cancer patient on chemo, and something is wrong."

Within fifteen minutes Mary was triaged and taken up to an examining room, where a nurse, Brenda, came in and took over. In less than half an hour, a dozen different nurses and specialists arrived. Mary had shockingly low blood pressure, heart fibrillations, and a pulse that was racing at nearly 170. Brenda was instantly alert, and called for an x-ray and CAT scan. She said that they had called in a surgeon and he would be here shortly. She was quickly hooked up to a saline solution, given pain killers (morphine), and antibiotics, a level of activity that made me very, very nervous.

Dr. Brian McGuinness walked in, a very young surgeon, forty at the most. "Mary, we have looked at the data and you have a hole somewhere in your intestines that has to be dealt with immediately."

"What do you mean by 'immediately'?" I asked.

"I mean now."

"And are you talking surgery?"

"Yes."

There is a shock that comes with something like this, a decision to be made based only on the word of someone you only met two minutes before. All of a sudden, we were confronted with such a decision.

"Can I call another doctor I know?"

"Mr. Dold, we have no time. Your wife is in life-threatening danger."

"Will you be the surgeon?"

"Yes."

"Are you good?" It was the only question I could think of.

"I am very good."

I looked at Mary, who was as mentally agitated as I was. "Go for it," she whispered, the pain making the decision, even if her brain was confused.

"When do you want to operate?"

"Now. I have an operating room reserved. We have called in an anesthesiologist. He will be here any minute."

"How long is the operation?"

"Two to three hours. It is very complicated." Dr. McGuinness explained that he couldn't tell where the hole is, that it could be an ulcer, a hole in the colon, or an appendix, but there was air in Mary's stomach and that meant peritonitis was already there.

I was terrified.

"Is there a chance that she might not make it through the operation?"

"There is, but if we don't operate she won't live until tomorrow."

"Doctor, we are placing all of our trust in you. Please take good care of her."

They didn't even bring in an operating gurney, but took her right from the examining room on the bed she was in. I followed along, totally numb, up a floor and into the operating area, where we were met by one of the male nurses who would be in the operating room and who would keep me informed if there were any problems. I didn't know what to do about the girls. I just sat there for a minute and cried, until Mary brought me up short with her typical, "What's wrong with you?" That jolted me back to reason, and I dialed first Nancy and told her what was happening. Amid the silence on the phone, I said, "Here is your mother," and handed the phone to Mary, who comforted her older daughter. Next I called Annie. Same thing. Both joined me in tears while Mary remained a rock of strength in her own solid way.

The anesthesiologist arrived, Dr. Neil Chaddha, and Mary was taken off into pre-op, departing with a quiet, "I love you." It was one of the hardest moments in my life. I went out to my car and for fifteen minutes fell completely apart, before I called each of the girls to tell them in detail what had just transpired. I asked Annie not to come by at the moment, that I would call her when I knew something. I realize now that was a very selfish thing to do, but I just didn't want to talk to anyone, not even the daughters I love so much. With not a shred of logic, I went off to get a double cheeseburger and large chocolate frosty at Wendy's, one of Mary's typical orders, and returned to the waiting room at the hospital. It wasn't long before Annie called and said she didn't care if I didn't want company; she was coming anyway. I had called Mary's siblings, George and Barb, plus Jim and Donna to let them know. Within half an hour George and his wife, Gayle, arrived, followed by Annie and Erik, and then by Jim and Donna. Barb would have come too, but she no longer drives after dark. What friends! Cole called to say that he and Marcia were coming down from Tahoe and would be there by 11:00 or so, but I told him we would be gone by then and I would see him in the morning.

I figured the operation, which began around 3:00 would be over by about 6:00. 6:00 came and went and at 6:30, I went up to surgery and asked what the progress was.

"Dr. McGuinness is just finishing up. I'll ask him to come down as soon as he is finished."

Around 7:00 he arrived at the waiting room, with a reassuring smile that was positively a gift from heaven.

"Mary is out of danger at the moment and in post-op. It was a very difficult operation. She had a rupture in the colon. I had to cut out a section."

"Was there a lot of infection?" I asked.

"She was filled with it. Everything in her stomach was swelled up."

He described the operation briefly to everyone there, but all I could really hear was that Mary was all right, that they had found the rupture and were able to fix it. I purposely put off all other details for later. That was enough. We were told that she would be out of post-op in about an hour and a half and we could see her then briefly.

Off we went to the Hickory Pit for dinner.

Around 9:00 Annie, Erik, and I were back at the hospital, ushered in to Mary's room in ICU. And there she was, calm, with good color and looking far better than she had looked any time in the last three days. We made small talk, held hands and silently said "Thank You!"

Nancy was sitting in her car in our driveway at home, having arrived just before me. The minute she had heard about Mary, she jumped into her car and started down on the familiar seven-hour ride. Earlier in the day she had driven home to Eureka from Reno, another four-hour ride. But this is Mom who is sick, and our daughters have no sense of time, space or effort where she is concerned. How I love them!

And so the emails started flying again.

Dear Family:

I'm afraid I have another difficult report on Mary. For the past three days, she has been suffering from severe stomach pains, which at first we attributed to the double dose of chemo. But this morning the pain persisted, so we went into the emergency hospital at John Muir in Walnut Creek. She was immediately operated on for a perforated colon, and her condition was considered life-threatening. Happily the operation was a success, although they took out part of her colon and were able to stop the peritonitis that had reached a severe state. Mary is in the ICU ward at John Muir and should be out of there in a couple of days. We expect she will stay at the hospital for at least a week. Needless to say, the cancer treatment is on hold for at least two months. It has been a very difficult week for her, but her last comment when I left her tonight was, "At least I'm going to get a good night's sleep." God love her!

One of these days I'm going to have a completely good report.

Thanks again for all of your prayers and good thoughts.

Love,

Jack

Tuesday, February 22

Dear Friends:

I have so not so good news about Mary, totally un-
related to cancer. Last week she was feeling very bad
and we assumed it was the side effects of the chemo.
But yesterday the pain was intense I took her in to
John Muir Emergency in Walnut Creek. They quickly
found a perforated colon that had spread peritonitis
everywhere. It was about a three-hour operation but
they were able to stop the infection and cut out part
of the colon. She is doing well, I suppose I have to
say, but is in intensive care at John Muir. I expect she
will be in the hospital for at least a week. Needless to
say, the cancer treatment is now on the sidelines for
at least two months. Give me a call if you have any
questions (510) 816-4486.

Jack

Nancy and I got to the hospital shortly after 9:00, when visiting
hours begin in the Intensive Care Unit. Mary was all wired and
tubed up with half a dozen drips going at once, a catheter draining
one side and her new stoma bag on the other. She was awake and
remarkably lucid, given the extreme trauma she has been under, not
just yesterday with the surgery, but for the last four days. They aren't
letting her drink or eat anything, not even a sip of water.

Dr. McGuinness told Mary that they will be very careful in
putting anything into her stomach until it is somewhat recovered
from the cleaning that was administered. They are also extremely
concerned with Mary's heart rate, which has been fluctuating
violently at times. She is now hooked up to a heart rate monitor that
sets off an alarm when the beat rate gets too high. It was going off
rather frequently. The doctors believe that it is due to the extreme
trauma that Mary has endured and that her heart will come back to
normal with rest. But they aren't taking any chances. They already

did an EKG and have ordered an echo cardiogram later today, which will show any scars or tears from the past few days.

In mid-morning, I called Annie to tell her to tell Erik that he should not feel obligated in any way to punch a time clock down at Mary's room, that he should take care of his own things and not feel he has to come to the hospital every time that Annie does. He was probably happy to hear that, because guys his age usually aren't very comfortable hanging around hospitals. Anne came to join Nancy in Mary's room and I took off to do some errands. We have decided that we should stagger our visits so that Mary only has to deal with one of us at a time and so we can get breaks ourselves. Barb showed up in mid-afternoon, a bit of a surprise. They only allow two visitors at a time in ICU, and they have to be immediate family. I am sure that Mary is going to develop several new sisters over the next week or so, and maybe even a brother or two.

Kathy, the "Swat Team" nurse, arrived to explain the colostomy surgery and the operation of the stoma bag. Essentially, Dr. McGuinness cut out the section of the colon or large intestine which had the hole. He then moved the intestine so that it exits on Mary's left side. The mouth of the intestine is called the stoma, to which is attached the bag for stool disposal. I am sure that Mary is dreading this whole thing, and to be honest so am I, but there is nothing that can be done about it. It is most certainly better than the alternative. I think it is amazing what you can accommodate yourself to when you have no choice. Kathy had a booklet entitled "Living with confidence after colostomy surgery," which she briefly discussed, taking us through several body plans and maps, and explaining the disposal system. She handed the book to Mary, who briefly glanced at the cover and handed it to me.

"I don't have to read this. Jack will tell me what I need to know."

That in a couple of sentences is Mary's approach to living—don't clutter her up with too many details. It has nothing to do with my telling her what to do; actually it is more like my doing what she expects me to do.

Wednesday, February 23

Annie is adjusting her time between conference calls at work, taking care of wedding details, and visiting Mary. Where the latter two tasks are concerned, she and Nancy are like a tag team, working together beautifully and seamlessly. Annie's big project right now is getting her wedding invitations out. Nancy worked on part of it; Annie on the other. Because she wanted special stamps for the RSVP envelopes and the outer envelopes, she has ordered 61¢ stamps with her and Erik's childhood pictures. And of course she has special address and return labels.

Meanwhile Mary continues to improve, although she is extremely limited in movement, and still is on a fast regimen. Since she has been in the hospital, she has become quite verbal with visitors. I remember vividly when we were first dating. Mary could go an entire night without talking if there were other people around. Over the years she has developed more confidence and has become more verbal, but now she will talk to anyone non-stop until they leave the room. Of course she is a bit drugged up, being fed a steady dose of pain killers which have to have an effect on your thought processes. But it is fun to watch and listen to her go on. She is very precise with a voice that is somewhat clipped. A doctor came in today to check her out. In short order Mary gave him her general medical history, every vitamin and prescription she presently uses and the dosage, and most of the past medicines. I was impressed. I couldn't list two of the prescription pills I have taken in my life, and I haven't just undergone major surgery.

The lack of water in particular is bothering her. I'm not sure I understand the prohibition, but I am not about to question Dr. McGuinness at this point, and none of the ICU nurses seem to question it at all. They gave Mary a little sponge ball on a stick that she can put in a glass of water, soak up a bit and suck on the ball. Mary took that one step further and asked for a glass of shaved ice to get the ball even colder. She has already worn out several of the little sponge balls, but it is getting her a bit of water and keeping her mouth and lips at least damp.

"If you're not coming in here with a tall glass filled with ice shavings and ginger ale, don't even bother coming in," she told one doctor who reacted in a startled fashion. It's certainly not the normal greeting a medic gets walking into an ICU room, but Mare is far from "normal." We are all laughing at the mental gymnastics she comes up with to get a drop or two of the precious liquid.

We also got a good laugh, except maybe for Mary, when the cardiologist who came to check out her heart got a little confused. I noticed that he was directing all of his conversation toward Nancy, who has an aura about her that seems to command attention. Finally he handed her his card telling her to call if she had any questions. She handed it to me, saying, "You should probably have this, Dad."

"Dad?" he said, considerably startled. "Aren't you her husband?"

"No, actually I'm this one's husband," I said seriously, pointing to Mary.

"Oh my God! I'm so sorry."

He retreated from the room about as embarrassed as a man can be. I'm not sure Mary was happy to have me as her son-in-law, nor Nancy to have me as her husband.

"Oh, that happens all the time," the day nurse laughed. "We see a lot of that around here."

"A lot of what, dirty old men and young chicks?"

"Exactly."

They have monitored Mary's heart carefully since the minute she arrived. She has been getting a Digoxin drip to calm down her heart, and it seems to have stabilized everything. What don't they have a drip for?

Nancy left for home around 3:00 today, which means she won't get back to Eureka much before midnight, especially if she stops to shop in Reno or Fallon on the way. Tomorrow morning, Marty is driving the school bus to Las Vegas with Kasey's basketball team, which won the northern section and is heading for the state championship tournament. They all think that they have a great chance to win the state. Wouldn't that be something! Nancy is waiting until Josh is out of school tomorrow and then they are driving to Las Vegas. Mary and I had considered going but that was before the operation. Now we aren't likely to go anywhere much before Annie's wedding in April. We'll root Kasey and the Vandals in from long distance.

Thursday, February 24

It's my 71st birthday, but sometimes I feel like I'm 100. Once again the year has flown by. Imagine being 71 years old! When we were kids, 71 was dead, but now they try to spin it that we are just getting started. Getting started is being able to move any part of your body after getting out of bed and stumbling around for fifteen minutes trying to get something to work without hurting. We always say that after a while, birthdays don't count any more. I truly believe that, but maybe I would be a little more excited and energetic if it weren't for Mary's condition.

When I got to Mary's room this morning, she was sitting up in bed with a wet wash cloth draped over her head. Propped carefully on top of the washcloth was a little pile of ice shavings.

"Cooling off, are you?" I asked. A dumb question.

"I don't care if it drips. It feels good."

Mary has gotten lots of mileage out of her glass of shaved ice. She uses it to wet her mouth, cool her face, and now it is a general body cooling agent. They haven't yet given her anything to drink so she can't dump her ice into ginger ale, for which she has great yearning. Interesting, that started last weekend when she downed several cans of ginger ale in short order, a craving that concerned me but I can't say why.

I went in to the hospital this morning carrying my own birthday present so she can give it to me. It was a box of Presidential wooden blocks which you arrange in the proper order, perfect for a barely pre-dementia male! I noticed that Mary is getting a little bit loopy at times, announcing that Jim and Donna were just here, or that Deb is waiting out in the hall afraid to come in. I think it must be the pain medication they are giving her. If it gets any more pronounced, I intend to ask them to change, at least the dosage if not the outright medicine. Mary is making up all sorts of activities for the rooms next door or across the hall. She hasn't been out of her bed once since she arrived, but she has the complete story on all of the rooms. She accuses one man of dragging off her nurse every time she wants to come to see her.

Late in the morning, she picked up her call baton and called for the nurse.

"Please send my Lift Team in," she requested with great assurance.

"Your Lift Team? What's that?"

"Two young guys who lift me back into bed. They got me into the chair earlier."

That night I found she also has a Line Team, a nurse whose specialty it is to find veins for sticking in needles. Mary's left arm swelled greatly today and they are concerned that the transfusion needle may be leaking. So they are moving it to her other arm, but the regular nurse couldn't find a vein. In comes the Line Team! As Jim always says, it's nice to have staff.

Friday, February 25

Hi all:

Mary has been progressing as well as can be expected. She is still in intensive care at John Muir Hospital in Walnut Creek. They will keep her in ICU until she is able to eat a reasonable meal and get rid of it. They are being very cautious about infections, since her stomach was almost completely infected. They have also been carefully monitoring her heart which was beating in all sorts of odd ways. Today she got her first small food and drink. She is very upbeat, very alert, talking almost constantly with anyone who will listen. I must say the nurses all love her. But she is still very weak, unable to walk and barely able to sit up by herself. It will be a long process of physical therapy before she is able to get around.

Once again, we thank you for all of your prayers and good wishes. To quote Mary: "When it's your time, it's your time. I guess this wasn't mine!"

Thanks and love,

Jack

Mary was definitely not in her best form this morning. She was pretty much subdued when I arrived.

"There's been a lot of pain and prodding this morning," she told me in her hospital voice, which she has developed to relate everything that is going on. "Dana (her RN today) is pretty gruff. I'm used to a gentler hand."

Before long, the therapist came in to begin Mary's exercises. She tried to beg off, but therapists are used to this, almost never having the luxury of willing patients. She started with simple toe flexes, which Mary was barely able to do at first, but then she got into other simple leg and knee exercises all done while lying back. Things got very difficult when Mary tried to sit up and eventually get off the bed into a chair. She really can't move. It is almost as though she is having to relearn everything. Because she hasn't been getting any food or liquids except the saline drips, they said she would be retaining large amounts of liquid, and she is quite bloated. But even given that, I was surprised at how difficult it is for her to make even the simplest maneuvers. I am thinking that we are going to have to make special arrangements at home, because certainly at this point, we could never get Mary up to the bedroom. We'll see how the next week goes, but she is going to have to do lots of therapy.

The pain medication plugged in with a vengeance this afternoon. Mary has been having mild hallucinations since she has been in here, mostly concerning imagined visits from various friends and family. But today, with Annie and Barb there, she went off on how everyone she thought loved her was outside plotting her end. She thought almost everyone she knows was out in the hall whispering. When Anne said it was just a bad dream, she blew up, apparently using some very un-Holy Names vocabulary, insisting that everyone was plotting against her.

When I got there, Anne had been gone a while, considerably agitated and Mary had settled down a little bit, but still insisting that Jim and Donna had been in to see her and George was always lurking around outside. Deb was manning a computer out in the hall. I quietly explained that the pain medication was responsible for that, that only immediate family could visit her and nobody but me, Annie, and Barb had been there.

"Well, I know what I saw, and nobody is going to tell me differently. You're the only one so far that isn't plotting."

I just grabbed her hand and held it. No point in arguing with a dream. They agreed to change her medication to a different class of pain killers, but the current dosage will take a while to wear off. I spoke to Dana, the nurse on duty, whom Mary had called "gruff," explaining that Mary had been having quite a time of it, apparently because of the pain medication.

"Oh, believe me, I know!" Dana laughed, holding up her hand to dismiss the whole thing. "She was using quite a vocabulary. But we knew it isn't normal for her to swear because she wasn't using the words very well. She's such a dear."

They agreed to change her pain killer, a drug called Dilaudin, an opiate that obviously does strange things in Mary's head. Dana warned me that it would be a day before the new stuff took over. This explains her rather unusual behavior since she got into ICU, the periods of relative anger, the things she was seeing in the hall, as well as all of the visitors she thought she was having. Not to mention her longshoreman's vocabulary.

Saturday, February 26

Hi all:

Another quick update: Mary was released from Intensive Care this afternoon and is now in the post-op center at John Muir Hospital. She is doing very well. She can take calls and receive visitors up to 9:00 p.m., John Muir Hospital, 1601 Ignatio Valley Rd., Walnut Creek, C 94598 (925) 939-3000. We think she might be home by Tuesday or Wednesday. Having watched her, I think she would welcome calls during the day. She seems to like to talk more and more!
Jack

Mary was pretty tired this morning, with a listless look in her eye. She had a full breakfast in front of her which she hardly touched, but she assured me she was eating lots of food. Not! Her RN was busy changing her bag, which seems to have overflowed, so I suppose she is consuming enough of something to keep her stoma working.

Maria, her RN today, said that they were still concerned about the level of antibiotics that were needed to fix her stomach, but she said that the heart concerns were now over. In fact they have removed the medication that was dripping for that purpose. Maria said that they have talked about moving her today to a post-op care center, but then she thought she would ask the doctor to delay that until tomorrow.

About 11:00 the physical therapy team arrived. Mary had already told me to send them away, but yesterday I noticed that even though she protested that she couldn't do any of the exercises, once she started she perked up almost instantly. So today I told her she had to do the therapy because I wanted her home as soon as I could get her there. She reluctantly agreed and I left her in the hands of the therapist and headed home to toss some rocks around and break a sweat.

I got back just around 3:00 to find that in fact, she had been moved. She is now in room 583 of the same West Wing, in a lovely private room that is spacious, very bright with a great view of the new hospital wing that is opening in April. She has a new light in her eyes and she is now very alert, and seems much happier than before. Her new RN, Julie, came by with ice, water and other things, and stopped briefly to talk, remarking on how unbelievable Mary's recovery is.

A bit later, Dr. McGuinness came by to see how Mary was doing. He is almost shy, very self effacing, but I would say also very charismatic. He also looks at Mary as something of a miracle.

"I can't begin to tell you how grateful we are to you, doctor," I told him. "The other day required an act of complete faith and trust on our part, and you repaid that in a way we can never express. Thank you."

He was positively embarrassed. "Mary's recovery is all the thanks I need," he said. He also told us that he had been extremely worried that she would not survive the operation, that the infection had proceeded too far.

Tonight Annie and Erik came by, as did George and Gayle. She can now take phone calls, get visitors all day up to 9 p.m. and can get flowers as well.

To me she is a miracle, and if not that, then at least one helluva tough woman. Same thing.

Sunday, February 27

Mary was up, sitting in her chair when I arrived this morning. She had already achieved one of her goals from yesterday, walking into the bathroom to obviate the use of the bedpan. She was having breakfast, and this time most of the Cheerios were gone. Slowly she is starting to eat again, but I can really understand her hesitancy, given the vagaries of her stomach condition. Plus there is always *"the bag."* Neither of us has the slightest idea how to deal with that. She just doesn't want to hit it with too much all at once, and I think that is very wise.

We continued an ongoing discussion with nurses and doctors about the numbers of the white cell count. It seems that about 8,000 is a good, normal number. Yesterday the nurse told us that Mary's count was the highest she had ever seen and they had been worried about it. What I don't understand is that with cancer, they worry about the number dropping as a result of the chemo, and this weakens the immune system. Mary missed two Nuprin shots last week, and her cell count was very low when she came into John Muir last Monday. Shoba, her oncologist, came in immediately and gave her the two Nuprin shots she had missed. Now it seems the cell count shot up way beyond what it was supposed to be. If it is heading up, why have Nuprin?

I asked another doctor today. He said that the body manufactures white blood cells as it needs them to fight disease. Mary had a massive attack of peritonitis, forcing her body into its defensive mode. So great was the danger, the bone marrow, which creates these white blood cells, went wild, fighting the infection, churning out an impressive 70,000!

"You have very robust bone marrow, Mary," he said with great admiration. And that explains the numbers, I suppose. I don't think I have ever heard someone praised for the quality of their bone marrow and I intend to brag about this at our next cocktail party.

Around 11:00, Tiffany, the physical therapist arrived, full of vim and vigor. She was shocked to see Mary sitting up already.

"How did you get here?" she asked in amazement, since yesterday it had taken took two strong men to get Mary out of bed.

"I had to go potty, so I asked them to get me up."

"You walked into the bathroom?"

"Yes."

"Would you like to go for a walk outside?"

"Sure, why not?"

And so off they went, Mary pushing her walker, Tiffany dragging along the medicine tower. They just got outside when Jim and Donna arrived with two enormous balloons, a rose, and an Oscar figure. They too were stunned to see Mary walking. I had told them last night she couldn't even get out of bed.

And so it goes. Mary is amazing everyone who comes by, with her inner strength, with her sense of humor, with her down to earth common sense. I am bursting with pride just watching them be amazed.

Monday, February 28

I am beginning to come down with a cold, so I told Mary I would only be in to see her briefly today. But I have a surprising stand-in. My sister Janet flew in to San Jose this morning from Baltimore. She called me from the airport and said that she was driving straight to the hospital. That is wonderful, the ultimate in "visiting the sick." She and their school friend Jovita, were great company for Mary all day long, three high school classmates jabbering away, while I hit the sack at home and tried to sweat out the beginnings of the cold. Janet agreed to come out to our place tonight, so we will have some time to talk. She looks good; her hair has come back curly after her own sessions with chemo, and she has lost some weight. I think she is as active as ever, constantly with one or the other of her five grandkids on a trip somewhere in the world. She has forged a nice life for herself after her husband Dave passed away.

Somewhat later it dawned on me what an extraordinary gesture, what a fantastic gift she had just presented to Mary, dropping her normal routine and flying out to visit her in the hospital. It isn't just the expense involved; it is the immeasurable gift of love and friendship. I am embarrassed, because Janet has just gone through her own major bout with cancer, and I am sorry to say, the thought of flying out to comfort her didn't enter my mind. I can guarantee her and everyone that I won't overlook such a thing in the future. God bless you, Janet!

I reconnected with another old friend today—Barny Quinn. Barny's husband, Art, was a professor of rhetoric at Cal, a delightful man who became a good friend. Barny always said that Art and I were like twin brothers, with the same interests, the same graduation date, and we both had Woodrow Wilson Fellowships. We had piled up almost identical books at home. We figured out that we even played basketball against each other in high school. Art died of a brain tumor just as he had become a highly praised author, one who almost won the Pulitzer Prize for his work on Colonial America. It was a horrible shock for Barny who went into an eight-year mourning. We lost track of each other because she told me it was too painful to see me because I reminded her so much of Art. But on my recent China trip, a couple from Berkeley, Frank and Pat Meghetto, gave me a note from Barny and her phone number. She had finally remarried and felt she could now resume her former life friends. So I called her tonight.

It is a strange world! Barny remarried a man, Bill Rosso, whose former wife was Sue Woodward, the sister of one of my closest high school friends, Dick Woodward. He answered the phone, and we had a great time reliving the details of the Woodward family before Barny came on the phone. She is as bubbly as ever and we talked a mile a minute until Janet arrived and I had to hang up. I look forward to getting together with them once Mary is home and feels better.

March

Tuesday, March 1

I am happy to report that I have blood in both feet. At my annual physical last month, my doctor, Tony DeMeo, said he couldn't find a pulse in my left ankle. I didn't think it was much of a big deal because I have feeling in that leg and no pain. The vein must just be hiding. But that's not good enough these days, so he sent me to Dr. Rhodes for a Doppler Test, a sort of MRI that tracks blood lines. That test showed there were indeed blood vessels right down to the toes, and a concluding blood pressure test on both feet confirmed a pulse. I think that they were more concerned, as I am, with the possibility of diabetes than anything else, but that seems not to be a problem either. I told the technician when I arrived that I was not willing to hear any more bad medical news, since we have had quite enough of that already with Mary, and she promised that she would only tell me nice things. She kept her word.

Mary may come home tomorrow, although her white cell count is still high and they are monitoring that closely. As long as it remains high, they know her body is continuing to fight infection, and they fear any recurrence of the peritonitis. But they are taking her off of the antibiotics drip this afternoon, so she will start fighting whatever is left on her own. She remains so upbeat, so strong, that she really is an inspiration to everyone who sees her. I love her more each day.

Thursday, March 3

Mary had a bad day today, a combination of things that probably started yesterday. The SWAT nurse, Leslie, arrived in the morning to show us how to change the bag. She found that the stoma had pulled away from the stitches a bit and showed us how to apply powder and medication. She also changed all of Mary's steri-strips that were used in place of staples in the incision.

That was fine until the afternoon, when the bag pulled away under a heavy load and leaked down Mary's incision and onto her clothes. The new nurse, a young one who may never have changed a bag before, called in help and two of them labored for half an hour getting Mary cleaned up, with a new bag, new steri-strips and new clothes. I think that took a lot out of her, because such a thing could easily happen at home, and when you are new to the stoma game, it can be very disconcerting.

She was decidedly weary when I got in around 11:00. We have another meeting with the other SWAT nurse, Kathy, who is going to show Mary how to change the bag herself, as well as how to empty it in the toilet. I think for the first time, the reality of Mary's condition actually hit her. She is going to have to do this for at least six months and then look at another operation to reconnect her colon. It was a very difficult blow for her, one of her worst, I think. It seemed to just drain the energy out of her, and she has remained close to listless all day. The therapy nurse, a pretty, upbeat young woman, came in at 3:30 and took her off to learn how to walk up stairs. Cyndi, the office manager of Golden Gate Tours, found them on the stairs, just in time to realize that all of them were locked out of the hospital. Fortunately they had cell phones and could call for help. But for Mary it was another tiring event.

The internal medicine physician arrived in late afternoon. He is not sure we should plan on taking Mary home yet because her white cell count is still elevated, more than 20,000. He is afraid of a hidden pocket of infection that her body might be fighting. Dr. McGuinness came in even later and ordered a CT scan for Friday. So it appears that Mary is here for another day or two. She told me this afternoon that she would rather stay here if she is not feeling well, and I fully agree. She had some pain in her stomach, enough to call for medication, and some cramps near her stoma. Nerves are probably involved but I want her feeling good when they finally release her.

Friday, March 4

It was almost lunch time and Mary was still waiting for her CT scan. Finally the RN brought in a vial of some vile liquid that she dumped into a glass of water for Mary to drink, a dye they use for the scan, which is scheduled for 2:30. I left to get some lunch while Mary stayed in bed wishing she could have lunch. I figure that wish is worth a lot because it means that she is starting to want to eat again. She is getting thinner by the day, her arms and legs reducing noticeably although her stomach is still pretty much distended.

The CT scan is intended to show if there are in fact pockets of infection, "abscesses" is what Dr. McGuinness calls them, in areas of the stomach that the blood vessels, and hence, the antibiotics, can't reach. If there are, he said that they can drain them and get medicine into the specific areas to kill the infections. All of the doctors agree that Mary's white cell count is going down daily. That fact and the lack of any fever points to the conclusion that she has successfully fought off all of the infections, but they aren't taking any chances.

Late tonight we were told that there are three small areas of fluid that have collected. Dr. McGuinness said he was going to consult with the radiologist to see what he suggested. He thought that they would probably drain the fluid, test it for disease and go from there. That won't happen until Monday, so Mary is definitely here for the weekend. That is starting to get old for her, but she is keeping up a smiling face.

Monday, March 7

I would have gotten to the hospital early today, but I locked myself out of the house. My keys were in the jacket I wore yesterday, and the garden key was nowhere to be found. I was forced to get one of the tall ladders, walk it around to the back porch, climb onto the roof and let myself in one of our bedroom windows. It could have been worse.

Anyway, Mary was still in her room when I arrived. I thought that they might do the draining of the fluids early today. It was late morning when they sent a gurney to fetch her down to CT Scan where she was put into one of those colonoscopy half dazes while they inserted a tube into one of the pockets and attached a drain sack to her side. She is acquiring quite a collection of bag attachments!

It wasn't until late afternoon when Dr. McGuinness arrived. He took one look at the liquid in the drain, labeled it "sero-sanguinous," and bestowed a happy smile on Mary. "That's not an infection," he declared. "It's clear, and no pus. That's great." He was so happy for Mary, you could feel it. She has literally captivated everyone at John Muir who has met her.

"Do you think she can go home tomorrow," I asked hopefully.

"I think so. I'll come by and check the drain in the morning and if it is the same, we can take it out. Then we'll give Mary a final examination and maybe let her go home."

Today is starting our third week at John Muir. It is a wonderful hospital in every way, but a hospital is a hospital, and home is better. This is an exciting day, even if St. Mary's did lose to Gonzaga tonight.

Tuesday, March 8

It took Mary sixteen days at John Muir to bag her first turd.

As awful as carrying that pouch around can be, there are lots of aspects of it that can be comical in a sick sort of way. So many different things can happen when your waste disposal system is on your side. I was wondering, for instance, if they have bigger bags for full-figured people. I mean, that little thing that Mary has hanging off of her wouldn't last long if my processing plant was feeding it. It's okay for petite little Mary, but I'm afraid its capacity would be sorely taxed to accommodate a sausage egg McMuffin-Big Mac appetite. Admittedly we have a two page list of things you probably shouldn't even consider eating, such as beans, broccoli, asparagus, cauliflower, cucumbers and other gas-producing edibles. But they have no restrictions on meat of any kind, and you can have anything with white flour base, and potatoes. I suppose three-finger poi would be questionable and fry-bread. Thus far Mary hasn't felt like really digging into her trencher, limiting herself to five grains of white rice, a chocolate milk shake, a bit of soup, hot chocolate, half a ravioli, and a few saltine crackers. It would have been interesting to examine the contents of her morning deposit, come to think of it. Lots of things are interesting.

The worst part of the morning is that the fluid collected in her drip is not sero-sanguinous any more. I noticed it was pretty cloudy when I examined it, and sure enough, Dr. McGuinness immediately went deep into thinking when he arrived.

"I'm going to have to get this analyzed," he said reluctantly, fully realizing that Mary was in her seventh straight day of being released tomorrow. She was so upbeat when I arrived today that it hurt to watch her hear the doctor say he was keeping her for another day. She took it gracefully because that is the way she is, and besides, what could she say? But I could see the slight deflation in her whole carriage and I could taste the disappointment, because I was feeling the same. I honestly think that most if not all of Mary's doctors and nurses have come to adopt her. She has answered everything they have thrown at her with calm and dignity and always that little shy smile. She never complains, ever. Except perhaps when that Dilaudin got her amped up a few days ago. And she always has a good word for everyone.

I guess I help with that too, because I always get the nurses and doctors to talk about their own lives. Today for instance, Mary's RN is an exotically beautiful young woman named Aasiqa, with the most marvelous hairdo that positively goes in every conceivable direction, on purpose I think. Yesterday she told us it was a Persian name so I thought she was Iranian. But today we found out that she is from a small village in Tanzania, out on the western edge of Serengeti. *Nataka pomba biridi*, I told her, and she let out a good laugh. "I'd like a cold beer too!" She was so thrilled to find someone who knew even a few words of Swahili and had actually been to her home land that she stayed and talked a while. I wondered out loud with Mary yesterday, how many different nationalities a hospital like John Muir has on its staff. Lord knows the Caucasians are certainly in a minority.

Leslie from the SWAT Team came in this morning and walked Mary completely through the dumping and changing of her colostomy bag. It is quite a process, but Mary carefully worked her way through each of a dozen steps. I think it is interesting how something as basic as our waste system becomes so intricate when the natural way is removed. But it is still incredible that science has found a way for people to keep leading a productive life when not too long ago, they would have been dead. As with everything, Mary accepted Leslie's patient instructions with good grace and calm demeanor. She got high praise for her ability to handle the whole thing. This is about the third or fourth time that either Leslie or Kathy has walked us through changing the colostomy bag. I don't have any doubts that either of us can do it rather easily.

So tomorrow, for the eighth straight day, Mary is going to come home.

Wednesday, March 9

> Hi All:
> Mary came home this afternoon. Finally, after seventeen days in the hospital! Her white cell count is back to normal, no fever, no apparent infections. Amazing! Naturally she is tired, but we are delighted to be able to get "back to normal." The cancer stuff is off for at least 6 weeks, so she has time for a breath of air, and a wedding.
> Thanks for all of your love and prayers. You can probably phone her any time. Neither illness seems to have curtailed her talk on the phone!
> Jack

Mary did come home today! Dr. McGuinness arrived at 6:30 this morning to see her and declared her infection free. Finally, her white cell count has come down just about to normal, meaning she is not fighting anything of significance. And the fluid from the stomach drain tested out okay so he took out the wire drain they had installed a couple of days ago. Mary is free to head home!

There is a whole routine they do when you get released from any hospital. Here at John Muir the least attention seems to be paid to the insurance subject, probably because they know everything there is to know about Medicare and Blue Cross. But it is refreshing, given the other places that spend an hour on such details before they even examine you. There is a medication profile they have to fill out. Each of Mary's doctors has to sign off on her. Dr. McGuinness did this morning. The oncologists who have been coming in daily don't have to sign off because they're from Epic Cancer Center and were seeing Mary purely out of professional care. Dr. Wasserman, the internal medicine physician, is in surgery this morning and as soon as he is out, promised to come and see Mary and sign off.

"At least you'll get one more "free" lunch," I consoled her. Which doesn't amount to much because Mary has reduced eating to three spoons of white rice, a bit of apple sauce, two bites of sherbet and a cracker or two. Oh, and one chocolate ice cream-Boost milk shake.

Finally the docs signed off, the head nurse, Roxanne, came in with the papers, and Mary was free to go home. I went to get the car and pull it around to the Emergency Entrance. I was surprised when Roxanne dispensed with the Lift Team and wheeled her out the door herself with a nurse's assistant behind pushing a cart with all of Mary's flowers. I really believe that Mary became an inspiration on the fifth floor, a woman who always had a smile and good word for all of the couple dozen nurses, students and assistants who gave her service. She has endured two incredibly difficult surgeries, had her life style fundamentally changed, conquered a near fatal infection and excruciating pain, and never voiced a single complaint. Those in the healing business couldn't help but be impressed. That Mary was universally respected was evident throughout in the caring looks from the doctors expressing true affection and in the tenderness of the nursing staff. For her calm and accepting demeanor, she was gifted with extraordinary care at this wonderful hospital. If it is possible to take positive feelings away from such an experience, John Muir Hospital and its staff inspired such feelings in us.

A major question for both Mary and me was how she would deal with the stairs at home, all sixteen of them. I never doubted that she would just set her mind and walk right up because I saw her grit her teeth when we left for the hospital and walk down them. And that is just what she did. Actually, I had to slow her down going up. The therapy nurse, Laura, had suggested that I put a chair at each landing to give her time to rest. Mary didn't want time; she just motored up.

She had worried about getting into our high bed, but I had brought up a wooden box we use to raise the Christmas tree every year and that made an easy step up to the bed. Mary plopped right in, let out a deep sigh and settled back. A week ago, she couldn't even lift her knees in bed. Now she is moving with her walker and doesn't really even need that. Remarkable!

So it is back to supplying the house and firing up the blender. It is nice to be home.

Deb is flying in tonight from Massachusetts for Annie's shower on Saturday, and Nancy and Kasey are driving down. All three of them are due to arrive around 11:00 tonight. And they did, all exhausted. They showered Mary with weary love and hit the rack. Tomorrow is time enough for complete attention.

Thursday, March 10

Sometimes I just don't understand a woman's thinking. Yesterday I was checking out the beds for Nancy, Deb, and Kasey and found that one of the twins wasn't made. So I got the sheets and made it up. Did you know that you have to put the top sheet on upside down? And it's all because when you fold it back over the blanket, the pattern shows up. Heaven forbid that the back side of 4" of sheet should ever be viewed by the sleeper! I have to admit, I did that on only one of the beds, so you could say that in our guest room, Annie's old bedroom, we have bi-sexual sheets, one done reasonably and one done the other way. My favorite sheets are the wine-colored ones that Mary uses for our bed. They are the same color on both sides! I'm sure she has a fancy name for that color, like sparkling burgundy or native zinfandel, but both of those are wines. However . . . I have watched Mary carefully examine the top sheet to figure out which side is the good one, and then she turns it upside down! I have tried to picture what would happen if the sleeper woke up and found he was looking at the stitched side of his sheet. That's nightmare fodder.

I also noticed that there is no way to fold sheets up to the size of those in Mary's linen closet unless you can do thirds again. I have finally mastered the three-fold towel, but I can't quite get the rectangle Mary gets in her folded sheets. I think there must be a double triple somewhere in there. I know they do that just to keep us guys confused. There ought to be an easier way. Over the past few weeks I have actually found a way to fold the top sheet of our California king into a square. I was so proud of myself that I got overconfident, and started in with the same system on the bottom sheet. Wrong! There is actually no way to fold a fitted sheet. First of all, you can't find the corners unless you are willing to be satisfied with the stitched corner of the fitting. But then you can't get the damned sides into the middle. I finally found a system that works for me. I fold the top sheet to determine the size I want for the bottom sheet. Then I just crumple that one up to that size. I figure it doesn't matter if there are folds or creases because it takes a weightlifter to fit the thing on the mattress anyway, and once it is stretched out there are no creases. There is no need ever to fold a fitted bed sheet. Period!

Speaking of changing things, we now have to get into a routine about changing Mary's colostomy bag, which will occur twice a week. Thus far she has only used a one-piece bag, a curious thing where you have to cut the opening to the size of the stoma. There is also a two-piece contraption where you just unsnap the bag to change it, something Mary will probably prefer. But for now, with everything new and hands clumsy, changing that bag is a two-person chore. I think it is amazing that it doesn't seem to bother Mary at all, and it certainly doesn't bother me to help her. For our entire lives we have been scatologically prejudiced. One of the few words that can't be uttered on radio or TV is "shit." And yet it is the most basic of all natural things. Mary's condition has made me view shit somewhat differently. I can't say I am coming to like it, but it no longer bothers me to view it clinically or even have to handle it. Let's face it, "shit happens" and sometimes you just have to deal with it.

Showering is another new thing for Mary. Of course she has incisions making a map out of her body, several of them still in the healing process. And she has a wound from the stomach drain they installed a few days ago. Then there is the stoma, and the bag, or both. Today she timed her shower so that she could take it without the bag, something that is easier. More remarkable was that she could actually get her legs over the tub and into the shower with a bit of help; two or three days ago that would have been impossible. She surprises me more every day.

Friday, March 11

The girls left this morning for San Francisco. Today is their Dold-Plaskett-Joyce girls' day in the big city. Mary was supposed to be joining them but that is not thinkable. Her goal is Annie's bridal shower at Trader Vic's tomorrow. The girls are staying at the Sheraton Palace, getting their spa experience and hanging out at elegant places tonight.

For Mary and me, we are looking forward to meeting her new home care nurses from Sutter Health. They arrived around 1:00 this afternoon, two of them because one was learning the system. They worked Mary through a variety of questions concerning her past medical problems, her current mental attitude, and of course her current physical condition. It started a little stilted but gradually Mary's grace and ease calmed them down a bit and the meeting was more than useful—it was enjoyable. They actually timed Mary walking from a sitting position to the door and back—thirteen seconds without any aids. I was very impressed. I think it is a world's record for that distance.

Other than that I spent the day moving rocks in the front yard, trying to get the whole project finished before Annie's and Erik's wedding April 9. My sculptor friend, Phillip Glashoff, came by late to figure out how we are going to install a surprise for the centerpiece. The thing weighs more than 700 pounds, and it will probably take a backhoe to lift it into place. I have to put down a concrete pad to hold it. But the really hard work is already done, so I feel certain that I will be finished in time.

Saturday, March 12

We figured that I should wake Mary up at 9:00 to make Annie's bridal shower at Trader Vic's by 12:00. Jim, who is as nervous as a cat when he is running one of his dinners or parties, called me last night to let me know that they would be serving the lunch at 12:45, so we didn't have to get there right on time if Mary needs the leeway. I assured him that we would be fine. I got Mary up around 9:30, and into the shower. Nothing moves fast these days, because Mary is always dealing with various body parts that hurt or don't work well, or are just sore from being her age. She has been pointing toward this event for a couple of weeks, probably when she first woke up in the ICU at John Muir. This has been the goal in all those long days and nights. There was absolutely no way that she was not going to Annie's bridal shower.

I discovered that she even has a new dress for the occasion, blazing red, and she has already figured out how the bag would work with it. To say that she was nervous would be the understatement of the decade. She fidgeted around in the bathroom with creams and soaps and other stuff, then went to work on her contacts. They didn't work! One of them actually bent in half and wouldn't unbend, causing a level of frustration that almost brought Mary down. My job was simply to keep her going, so we threw away those uncooperative contact lenses and inserted new ones. So far so good. Now to the red dress. At first she thought it wouldn't fit at all, but once we got everything in the right place, it was beautiful, needing only a safety pin in the décolleté, which she said she would apply in the car. Panty hose.

"Are you kidding, Mary?"

The panty hose got nixed. Since I help to apply everything, that far exceeds my grade level. I can urge socks into place, and start panties, and gym pants. I even do shoes and slippers. Mary opted out of the shoes with low heels for a pair with no heels, but I convinced her that slippers were safer until we got to the restaurant. She actually had brand new pink slippers that went well with her dress. I assured her that she could just as easily wear those slippers right into Trader Vic's, but I knew that idea wouldn't fly at all. Out came the wig, which really does look exactly like her real hair, and she was just about ready to roll. By now it was nearing 12:00, but I figured we still had forty-five minutes to get down I-80. No problem!

We actually arrived around 1:15. Unbeknownst to us, there was a St. Paddie's Day parade in San Francisco this morning. The freeway was stopped cold near San Pablo. I took off at Albany, and wandered across Albany, Berkeley, and Oakland to Emeryville. God bless her, Mary never uttered a word of complaint, even though I am sure she was dying to tell me I was taking the long way around. But we got there. Jim, Cole and Eric were there to greet us.

The shower for Annie is sponsored by Donna and Sully, and since

Trader Vic's is part of our family tradition for big events, Jim in his role as board member got them to open the restaurant for this special occasion. Normally they are closed on Saturday until dinner, but Jim and Donna and Sully went completely overboard for Annie. It was absolutely special. Since Cole dropped off Marcia and Eric brought Sully and the babies, and I came with Mary, Jim also had a men's dining room set up separate from the ladies.

On arrival, Mary discarded her slippers, slipped on the shoes, and prepared for a grand entry. She used her walker about halfway into the restaurant. I asked if she wanted to dispense with it and enter the party room on my arm, a suggestion she quickly accepted. She entered in style, to a loving ovation from all of the women present. And when she took off her coat, revealing that sassy red dress, she got another rousing round of applause. It made me feel so good to see her positively glowing. If you saw her face this afternoon, you would never know that anything bad had ever happened, so happy and alive she looked. Nancy went around and told all the ladies that if they wanted to talk to her mother, they would have to go to her because she wasn't going to move. It was a wonderful moment, a wonderful afternoon, not only for Mary, but for her daughters, all of her friends and family. And for her husband as well.

Sunday, March 13

Mary was wiped out today. No wonder. It is a day to just slug around and lie as low and quiet as possible.

Tuesday, March 15

Mary has a male physical therapist! Won't the girls be impressed! His name is Khelmer, a Filipino Elmer, and he is perfect for Mary— young, soft-spoken, and encouraging. He worked her gently through some beginning exercises and outlined a program he wants her to follow, even leaving her with ankle weights to strap on to build up her leg stamina. Sutter VNA is a wonderful program, taking people out of the hospital but still giving them professional care. Khelmer, and his associate, Joanne, will be visiting Mary twice a week. The RN care also comes twice a week, on Monday and Thursday, to supervise the changing of the colostomy bag and to monitor her vital signs and incision healing. On Friday we begin what will probably be a long line of doctor visits, as Mary gets inspected by the many physicians and surgeons who have worked on her. We really ought to swap houses with Annie just to save on gas. It is now a $75 fill-up every three days, given the larceny that is taking place among the gas companies, government, and speculators. That's another subject!

Wednesday, March 16

Joanne, the occupational therapist came by just after noon. She showed Mary various ways to get on her socks, pants, etc., how best to handle the shower and cleaning, and what exercises she needs to get back to normal living. It was agreed that one visit would be sufficient, because Mary is getting better each day and is pretty well able to get around on her own. The familiarity with the colostomy systems is growing, and it won't be long until it is second nature. Hopefully, at exactly the time she is completely comfortable with everything, it will be time to reverse the colon and get her working normally.

I am having dinner with Mac Laetsch tonight at the Faculty House at Cal. We have talked about getting together for months, but I haven't been able to get away for one reason or another. I never realized how confining it is to care for someone on a 24-hour basis. Mary has nurse care now almost every day, so someone has to be here to let them in. She needs rides to the doctors. And of course there is the meal schedule. I now have a completely altered admiration for what we blithely called the "stay-at-home mom," when we were growing up. I don't think that men could ever fully appreciate what that involved, especially when pre-school children were at home. You simply have to limit your day to their needs. Of course with children, you can pack them up, strap them into a car seat and go somewhere, but wherever you go, they go with you. Even so, you are restricted completely by concern for them. Lord help the dumb husband who comes home and complains about how tough work was, or if he is allowed to do that, Lord help the poor stay-at-home housewife!

Anyway, I phoned Annie and asked if she could come over and be with her mom, which of course she agreed to do. Mac went overboard with his dinner, ordering two huge T-bones, a special bottle of wine and all the trimmings. The manager at the Faculty Club is Indian, and there is an ongoing competition between him and Mac as to who can be the most obsequious in their manner. It is fun to listen to, with Mac talking the typical Indian-English of the British Raj. "I am knowing….!"

It has been one of the special joys for us, traveling on more than twenty-five Cal trips together. As Mac says, "We have spent a year of our lives together." It is really more like two years, given the many organizational trips, meetings, and dinners we have had together—a strange partnership of the tour manager and professor. But we have become close friends, probably on a different plane than the rest of our friends, on both sides. I am Mac's non-academic friend, and he is my professorial mentor. I prize the relationship highly, even though he is a card-carrying liberal and I'm most definitely not. Anyway, it was nice to have a few hours off, not thinking about how difficult the times have been for Mary. You have to have such diversions every so often, both for your sake and for the sake of those for whom you are caring. I think the last few days I have been somewhat of a pain in the butt for Mary, because I am trying too hard to take care of everything, not letting her get back on her feet on her own. She is doing that anyway.

Thursday, March 17

Of course Mary is wearing a green shirt with shamrocks all over it. Isn't our house all decked out in green? Last weekend, the girls dismantled Valentine's Day and installed St. Paddy's Day, transferring from red to green. Mary's only comment was that there must be another tub of green still in the garage, "because I have a lot more stuff than this." Annie would have jumped all over her for that comment. "Mom, we took the time to do this and all you think of is we should have put up more. Be happy with this." But that is the way Mary is where decorations are concerned. There always must be more. Things are going fast and furious this year, from Christmas to Chinese New Year to Valentine's Day to St. Pat's to Easter and then a general celebration of spring before Memorial Day and the 4th burst out in red, white and blue.

Yesterday I poured a concrete circle in the front yard, the pad for the sculpture that is coming in next week. I had it all poured and floated when the RN arrived and I left to take care of that, completely forgetting that I had to smooth everything out again when the water drained off of the top. This morning to my horror I remembered. I came out to find my circle was still round, as I had intended, confined by the rocks I had installed around it, but the top looked like Lake Superior in a gale, all wavy, and far from level. Phil Glashoff will get a good chuckle out of it. His sculpture sits on a sheet of steel, so it would have been nice if the pedestal is flat and relatively level. I may have to introduce a layer of sand. I'll call it "artistic."

Friday, March 18

It is pouring today, really pouring. I looked at the long-range weather forecast and it shows rain for the rest of the month. I have to have a few good days because I want to finish my project and it is tough in the rain and mud. I had three mature dogwoods delivered this morning and Elisio, the Mexican man who helps me in the yard, and I will plant them tomorrow, rain or shine.

Nancy arrived around 11:00. She and Annie are taking Mary back to the wig maker to get her wig adjusted. The girls said that the wig was too big when they saw Mary at the shower, so it has to be re-sized, since Mary has lost considerable weight. I think down deep that she is thrilled with the weight loss, concerned only with the bulge that her colostomy bag might display. It is probably the most expensive diet in the history of the world. By the time they were finished today, the girls bought Mary a brand new "more sassy" wig.

Around noon, we all met at Scott's Seafood in Walnut Creek, a perfect place because they have indoor valet parking and it is a short walk to the booths for eating. More and more I prize the four of us, Mary and me, and our two daughters who want nothing more than to make us happy. What a gift! I don't want ever to underestimate what Mary and I have achieved in raising these two beautiful women. They are their own persons, each unique, but they are our daughters and they always tell us that. We see that in the care they take with us, in their own life styles which mirror in many ways that of their mother, and in their approach to life, which I have aided. How we love them! We just don't want ever to take them for granted. And we will never let them take us for granted!

This afternoon we have a follow-up meeting with Dr. McGuinness. We are a little concerned about the shape of Mary's stoma, but don't think it is anything serious. He met us as usual, smiling and casual, treating Mary as though she were his mother. It is difficult to describe the feeling we have for him, since he is literally our savior after that terrible arrival at John Muir Hospital. He examined Mary and pronounced her perfectly fine. We presented him with a bottle of Dom Perignon as a small token of thanks. He received it with the most embarrassed look on his face, saying that it wasn't at all necessary, but adding that his wife loved champagne and would certainly enjoy it. Meeting Dr. McGuinness will always be one of the high points of this entire narrative. He is a physician whose sole purpose is to heal, who remains humble and caring in the very face of his success. Thus far, we have met many such healers, but none I think so self-effacing as Dr. Brian McGuinness.

Saturday, March 19

Mary was out much of yesterday, so she is knocked out today. I have found that one of my main tasks is to monitor exactly how much activity she can handle. She wants so badly to get out, and to get her life back to some semblance of normal. Neither of us even dare to remember that when she is finished for the moment with this colostomy stuff, she has to go back to thinking about cancer. She has an appointment with Dr. Kankopati on April 4, and then we will put everything else off until after the wedding.

Tuesday, March 22

I took a break from house duties this morning to go get our taxes done. Is that a break at all? Actually it felt like one, because I was out for a whole morning, even if it means that I'll probably get depressed by how much we owe Uncle Sam. I got home to find Mary dressed and sitting downstairs, looking every bit healthy. This afternoon Martin and Sheryl Raumann came by from Lodi, and they were stunned to see how good Mary looked. They were expecting some sort of almost-cadaver, with sunken cheeks, dead eyes, and sallow complexion. What they discovered was Mary sitting on the couch looking alive and, my favorite word these days, perky. She is also comfortable enough with herself that she didn't even bother with a hat or head covering of any sort. Her hair is beginning to grow back, maybe half an inch worth, but it is covering well. She actually looks great without the hair, because her face is so alive these days. I find it interesting that when she is lying in bed, she looks completely exhausted and sickly. The minute she gets up, she transforms, perks up, and smiles a whole lot. She is also discovering that she has a very cute little smile that lights up whoever is talking to her, almost a flirt smile, and she is using it more and more. I would say right now that folks who haven't seen her since she got sick leave her feeling better than when they arrived. They come to cheer her up and end up getting exactly that from Mary.

Michael Petrini called the other day. His wife Julie just went through two back operations, including a fusion. The whole time she was in John Muir, Mary worried about Julie, asking me to find out if she was getting any help at home. I asked her if she was volunteering to leave the hospital and go help, and she almost said she would.

"Jack, Julie got a get well card from Mary," Michael said with astonishment in his voice. "She had to have sent that from Intensive Care. It was dated the 25th."

"Yeah, she was in Intensive Care then," I said, looking at my date book. "She sent a steady stream of cards out of there."

"That's incredible!" Michael said. It is.

Sunday, March 27

Mary continues to improve remarkably. In the past week she has become just about self-sufficient, getting out of bed without the box-stair I had installed there, able to walk to the bathroom, dress herself, and traipse up and down the stairs. More and more often I find her installed in the rocking chair watching TV or reading. For the longest time she didn't have the energy to read at all, but the books are again stacked around her and she is reading well into the night.

Because of that, I have moved into the guest bedroom. My snoring is as macho as ever, which was okay as long as Mary was getting to sleep before me. But now she is staying up much later than I can endure, so it is easier to move to another room. That will change soon because our house is about to get very full with the wedding approaching.

About the only thing still bothering Mary is her colostomy bag. It continues to be a two-man job replacing it. Mary prefers to do it lying down, but she can't really see the stoma that way, so I get actively involved. It is amazing to me how quickly you lose your repugnance for feces when you are literally handling it all the time. Like so many things in our lives, that whole thing is less important than we make it. Our visiting nurse, Sue, watched us change Mary's bag the other day. Actually Mary wanted to change it by herself, but the process got bogged down and she was getting frustrated, so I jumped in and finished it for her.

"You two are really a team!" Sue observed. "How long have you been married?"

I told her forty-seven years and she was astonished.

"Do you fight all the time?"

"No, actually, never. Oh, about sex a couple of decades ago, but we don't remember."

"That is amazing."

Mary got out several times last week. She and Annie went to pick up her new wig on Thursday. It is rather stylish, making Mary look about ten years younger, maybe more. She will be a knockout at the wedding. She was out on the town just about every day, having lunch a couple of times. But she has to be a little careful. I have monitored her time, because it will do no good at all if she exhausts herself today and gets sick tomorrow. Generally if she has been up and out for half a day, she will be pretty much wiped out the next day. It is astonishing how much energy she has, but I think she has to be prudent because she is still susceptible to getting run down and sick. The main goal remains the wedding. After that she doesn't care much.

Weeks ago, Mary found a dress for the wedding. She has worried first that it wouldn't fit any more because of her weight loss and second that the stoma bag would bulge and show. In fact, neither of those worries is warranted. Mary has lost almost fifty pounds and thus far, in spite of a returning appetite, hasn't gained much back if any. And most of the preconceptions about the stoma bag are unfounded. It hangs discreetly down her side and really isn't much of a problem, especially over a relatively short period of time. The wedding is only a bit more than a week away, and things are starting to heat up with the plans. Of course, Annie is in charge of everything, and she is doing an extraordinary job. If she is nervous, it is impossible to tell. About the only frustration she ever shows is trying to corral all of Erik's friends, who tend to be off fishing and hunting or watching a ball game or something. But even there, Annie is winning the battle. Of course, she has her sister who is about as talented a backup as ever volunteered. And Mary is no slouch either when it comes to putting on big events. We have always had major soirees in our family, back to when I was teaching and would "drop in" on Mary with a busload of hungry students looking for lunch. Annie and Nancy were raised with tour busses stopping at our house in Plymouth for cocktails and dinner, and we have never had a simple birthday party. Every year Nancy hosts a crowd, sometimes a huge crowd, at her home in Eureka for the 4th of July. And of course, Annie is now coordinating meetings and seminars for McKesson Corporation. Neither knows the meaning of simple. Erik has no idea how lucky he is that his only major role in this upcoming nuptial is to show up, say the correct words, and smile a lot.

My "surprise" sculpture arrived today. Philip Glashoff is a local man who has been fashioning figures out of junk metal for years. He is remarkable, not only with his welding skills, but with his imagination. I think that Philip looks at a piece of junk and sees something immediately. I have been buying his sculptures since we moved into Green Valley in 1986. They started with a 10' White Rabbit, whose ears were fashioned out of airplane propellers. Philip added the Queen of Hearts, the Mad Hatter, and a hookah-smoking caterpillar over the next few years. Hook, with Tinker Bell and a crocodile fill the middle of our yard. Finally I added a yellow brick road to the north end, a major highway to a tree house I built for Josh and Kasey. Philip's son, Chad, has created all of the Wizard of

Oz figures to line that road. In all, I have about twenty-five Glashoff sculptures and several from other artists filling our hillside, hiding behind trees, peeking out of shrubs. None of them comes close to creating the reaction of the one we placed today. It is a twelve-foot-high artist's palette, supported by the brush pushing through the thumb hole, alive with all of the most vivid colors. It is the first thing you see when you drive up the lane to the house. I love it, because it makes absolutely no sense to be standing in front of a modern "Victorian" house. The girls' reaction? I would call it subdued. My palette will grow on them. It is way too heavy to move.

April

Tuesday, April 5

Folks are starting to arrive for the wedding today. Walter and Chris (Shui Heng Yong and Shui Jing) come in from Beijing just after noon, so I am heading for the airport. Chris also has work to do at Ananda Travel in San Francisco with Vicky Lee, the tour operator who has administered all of our Far East trips. We dropped him off at the Ananda office on Powell St., where Vicky met us on the curb for a fast hello. Walter is staying at our house, at least for a couple of days, when he will shift over to Donna and Jim's house.

Mary has an appointment with Dr. Shoba in early afternoon, escorted by her daughters. Nancy arrived yesterday to give Annie support, though she seems hardly to need it. I love to watch the girls working together on something. They are so different, and yet in many ways they are so the same. That they have become such close friends and so attached to their mother is one of the most treasured things in my life. I am glad that they get the chance to go with Mary to talk with Dr. Shoba today.

Mary got a fine evaluation from Shoba. Everyone at the Epic Care Center is impressed by how well Mary is doing. She is off from any treatments until after the wedding, when we will discuss a program of radiation.

Wednesday, April 7

Father Paul Waldie arrives from San Antonio today. He is such a special man, another integral part of our family, who has been the priest for our family since I met him at Bishop O'Dowd. I think he is the finest priest I have ever met, a man who is solid in his position, who treats everyone before himself, whose liturgies are legend. He baptized Annie when he was principal at O'Dowd the year I left for Massachusetts. He married Nancy and Marty when he was pastor at St. Rose's in the San Fernando Valley. He baptized Joshua in our living room here at Green Valley, and he officiated at the funerals of both Mom and Dad. It has been several years since I last saw Paul, probably when he was the pastor at St. Benedict's in Seattle. Since then he has spent several years in South Africa and is now at the Oblate Seminary in San Antonio. He said he was thrilled to be asked by Annie to officiate at her marriage sacrament, saying that he didn't think that at his age anyone would be interested any more in having him at their wedding. That is the perfect indication of the humility of Paul Waldie. He lives for other people, his life devoted to service and giving. I can't think of anyone I would rather have marry my daughters. Since he is arriving a couple of days early I am looking forward to many good discussions about life and living. Paul is a curious sort of liberal-conservative, honoring the old ways in many things, but constantly pushing for new applications and ideas. He gives the most incredible liturgies I have ever experienced. I can't wait for Annie and Erik's wedding.

Friday, April 8

At Erik's request, I made reservations for ten or twelve to play golf this morning at Green Valley. Actually ten guys arrived at 8:00 a.m. Jim and I opted out, citing medical reasons, most of which are in our heads, so Walter, Jim and I rode around with Walter photographing and Jim and I advising. To keep play moving we decided to play "best ball," where the best shot of the foursome is the one everyone uses for the next. It was fun watching Josh, in his first-ever round of golf, as he utilized a perfect baseball swing to hack and chop his way around, every so often getting off a decent shot. On the last hole, his drive was the best of the foursome, and you should have seen him preen and strut! Afterwards I promised I would get him lessons the next time he came down.

"Oh, I don't need them, Papa. I already know how to play!"

At 3:00, everyone met at Christ the King Church in Pleasant Hill for the dress rehearsal. The church has a Wedding Coordinator, Rosemary, who takes her job very seriously, walking us laboriously through every single bit of minutia she could conjure up. Father Paul was barely tolerant of her officiousness. He tends to want ceremony to flow from the participants, not be installed by decree. But Rosemary lined us all up in the vestibule, where she admonished each of us to stay completely out of sight until the very moment we were to enter the central aisle.

"You're great, but you can't have your arms folded," she commanded Gwen as she was about to take her stroll.

She wasn't quite sure what to say to Katie, who came next, nursing Paige under a clever nursing apron. "You're not going to be nursing tomorrow are you?" she asked uncertainly. I would have paid Katie to say she was.

Annie, of course, comes in last, holding her ribbon bouquet from the shower at Trader Vic's, but we were held back for a whole minute after Nancy had occupied the aisle all by herself.

"You have to build the suspense, Anne. Just wait until people start getting nervous."

I couldn't see Rosemary's face when my cell phone went off as Annie and I were walking toward the altar.

Finally we were all properly seated, we went through the readings. Jim was first with his John gospel about love. He hammed it up perfectly, arms waving, pointing, spread wide to take in the heavens, and finishing with a flourish.

"You could be a professional reader, Jim," Rosemary gushed, causing Jim to preen with self-esteem. Annie groaned. Paul grimaced.

Paul gave a little speech, telling all of the participants that they should be very serious about their role in the success of Anne and Erik's marriage. He asked the men why they had accepted Erik's invitation to join the service.

"I thought there was money in it, Father," Mark Schlichter said.

Paul will probably incorporate that idea into one of his future sermons.

Afterwards we all retired to our house where we hosted the rehearsal dinner for the wedding party and anyone who is from out of town and staying at the hotels in Green Valley, about eighty folks in all. The highlight was the margarita machine that Nancy managed to rent somewhere, a devilish contraption that turned out drinks that were way too tasty and way too easy to drink. I do believe that Annie's head found out what it is like the morning after a bachelor party. But she is young and will most likely be able to adjust tomorrow morning in time for the wedding.

We decided on a barbecue with pre-made salads. Our biggest concerns were the weather and keeping Mary from doing anything. It hailed mightily last night, but tonight was clear, although cold. Folks are attending from 12 states and 3 countries, Walter and Chris from China being the winners of the longest trip contest. Mary, who loves flags, insisted that I get all of the state and country flags, which we installed on the gazebo. It was a great reunion of family and friends and it was nice to meet some of Erik's family, his mother, Gail, and Aunt Midge, and several of his cousins and friends. They have come a long way, from Southern California, Colorado, Tennessee, and Texas. His friend, Mick, who is a chef, did a fabulous job on the tri-tips. Now it is time for the wedding!

Saturday, April 9

Annie and Erik got married today! How long have we waited for this moment, when we would see the radiant smile on our daughter's face light up Christ the King Church? She stood there holding Erik's hand, the two of them alone on the altar in front of a church full of friends and family, and they commanded the scene. I am not sure I have ever seen Annie so confident, so relaxed, so happy. It was her moment.

Of course it was also Erik's moment, but for some reason weddings are the domain of the bride. On reflection, it is for good reason. Who else waits, hidden from sight in the vestibule, for the music to change, the trumpets to salute, the audience to anticipate? The bride!

"She is such a beautiful bride!" they will whisper. Have you ever heard a similar remark about the groom? Did Wagner ever create a grand entrance for the groom? Have you ever heard the song, "Here comes the groom?" The groom is the guy in the rented tux, standing in the front with his buddies, waiting like all the rest of the people for his bride to arrive. No, it is the bride who fills the wedding with her presence. Here she comes, in a stunning dress, her hair carefully quaffed in a style never before seen. She is veiled, trained, bouqueted— radiant, led to the altar by lovely maids, on the arm of her proud tuxedoed father (whose tuxedo I might mention was not rented!).

I watched the preparation for this day, not always with dispassionate eye, but always with interest. Twenty-one years ago we went through this process with Nancy, but I have forgotten many of those details. Anne has been a wonder to behold in this preparation, putting every meeting-planner skill she has acquired at Golden Gate Tours and McKesson into action as she methodically mowed down the manifold details of her big day. I have marveled at the five-inch binder filled with brochures, websites, phone numbers, price lists, addresses and contacts. I think she sprang into action about four months prior to Erik realizing that he was going to ask her to marry him. He really never knew what hit him! I recall Annie announcing that she and Erik had agreed on a wedding "in the spring," and that she had picked out five potential dates from March to May. Two things were immediately necessary to tie down the date—a church and a reception hall. I remember quietly recommending our own Green Valley Country Club, which wasn't at first a top choice. But gradually, as costs became apparent and dates were limited, Green Valley became the site, and her own parish in Pleasant Hill, Christ the King, a great church with cooperative priests, the wedding scene.

That's when the real fun starts, when the bride has picked her date and venues. That's when the discussion turns to budget into which must fit photographer, videographer, florist, music (disk jockey or band), food, wedding dress, bridesmaid dresses, mothers' dresses, hair styles, makeup, toes, fingers, massages, general wardrobe, candles, table decorations, wall decorations, limos, escape cars, rehearsal dinner, post wedding brunch, hotel arrangements, maps, guest lists, invitations, showers, priest, gift registrations, guest books, wine, champagne, dinner menu, bachelor party, bachelorette party in Las Vegas, wedding rings, tuxedo rentals, table arrangements, flower girl, ring bearer, church music. Annie's book expanded as she put all of this into her system, working up "do-lists" and memos with all sorts of check points and, I might add, checks.

It was not an easy time for Erik. He has been slowly moving his things—furniture, tools, clothes, and other things from Phoenix to Pleasant Hill, and that includes moving his business as well. He has had to deal with his son, Clayton, who is going to be torn between a mother in Phoenix and a father in California, a father who has raised him carefully and lovingly, and who has not been apart from him for more than a few days since he was born. And Erik has to establish himself in the tile and stone business in a new state, building his business from scratch. It doesn't help that the commute between Phoenix and Pleasant Hill takes at least ten hours and several hundred dollars in gas. He has made that round-trip many times since the wedding date was set. I know he was more than happy to turn over the wedding planning to his fiancée.

Annie got enormous encouragement and support from her sister. There may have been times when Nancy was a teenager and Annie was a pest, where their friendship was not fully formed, but today they are close to inseparable. Both are inveterate organizers, but they approach their task from different angles. It has been fun to watch them arrive at decisions from differing paths and then fully agree on the decisions. Both of them are shoppers. Both of them are imaginative and unafraid of trivial obstacles. Both of them can manipulate the Internet with ambidextrous skill, using both sides of their brains as well. In a perfect world, both could easily operate without a budget, but happily have agreed to accept one.

And what of the mother of the bride, that iconic person who features prominently in every wedding? Everyone who knows us is aware of Mary's medical problems, but few would be aware of just how active she has been through this whole process. She has been involved in just about every discussion on all facets of the event, not always physically involved because of constraints imposed by her two operations, but through meetings, emails, and phone calls, Mary has been with Annie and Nancy every step of the way.

For the past month, she has been enduring the highs and lows that naturally follow such difficult surgeries. Not only is there the physical drain from more than one major surgery, five days in Intensive Care, and seventeen days in all in the hospital, but there is the added, mostly emotional drain from the reality of wearing that colostomy bag and the complications that arise from that. Naturally Mary was concerned that the bag would show beneath her dress or would be the source of any number of imagined complications. But as the wedding day approached, she became more and more confident, not to mention more energetic. For the past ten days she has been often out of the house shopping with the girls or having lunch or dinner, and her spirits have risen tremendously. She was ready for the big day.

I can't even begin to describe my emotions when she appeared on the stairs at home in her stunning dress. She says the color is "mushroom" but it is a sort of steel blue-dark gray-purple-brown gown with Victorian style and Mary flare. She wore the new "sassy" wig the girls bought her, with veil and flower-bow on the side, black pearl necklace and earrings. She looked twenty years younger.

Annie decided that since the church is so far from our house and the reception, it would be best to charter a mini-bus to take the bridesmaids, bride, and parents to the church and back to Green Valley after the ceremony. Darnell pulled up right on time with his Black Tie motor coach. The photographer, Erin, also came to the house early to take the required pictures of bride donning her dress, bridesmaids smiling as they help, mother and father pacing. I noticed she took pictures of the bridal garter, the bridal bouquet, the bridal veil. I thought that she had forgotten to capture the panties and slips, but I later found I was wrong. Annie wasn't wearing them at the time of the photographs. I think the shoes were chronicled.

Marty was put on flower and transfer duty. He picked up groomsmen at the hotel in Green Valley, took them to Anne's house, then picked up all the flowers, installing them in the church and bringing the bridal flowers to the house, where he dressed, picked up a tuxedoed Josh and Father Waldie to go to the church. He then picked up Erik and the boys and brought them to church. Meanwhile Annie and the girls were primping and posing, finishing precisely at 1:00 p.m., the time designated to get in the bus.

The rehearsal must have worked because we pulled off everything in the real thing to the complete satisfaction of Rosemary, who paced the area like an expectant father. She got us all through a side door into the children's crying area and there we stayed until almost all of the attendees were seated in the church. I have to admit that I sneaked out a time or two but finally was told not to talk so much because people always wanted to socialize. Here we go!

Peter, Paul, and Mary opened the ceremony with "The Wedding Song." My pride and love for Mary grew at the church because I peeked out and could see the astonishment on the faces of everyone there when "her boys," Marty and Josh, escorted her down the aisle. It will remain one of my best memories for the rest of my life. My sister Janet described Mary's entrance to the church beautifully: "I've got to say, my high moment of the year, actually as far back as I can think right now, was seeing our beautiful Mary walk down the aisle at Annie's wedding. Mary was absolutely stunning. She glowed—the picture of beauty, happiness, spirit, and returning health."

Sadly, Erik's mother, Gail, took a fall at the hotel this morning, badly breaking her hip, which landed her in the hospital in Fairfield, so she would miss the wedding. But Aunt Midge stood in for Gail, to be led down the aisle by Clayton, who is the most beautiful little wisp of a boy, a spitting image of Erik. And then Josh was called back into duty to escort Kinsey, the flower girl, and Hunter, the ring bearer, neither of whom would make the walk without him.

To the strains of Stephen Curtis Chapman's "I Will Be Here," the three bridesmaids in their vivid watermelon-colored gowns, entered the church—Annie's high school friend Gwen; her college friend and fellow teacher, Katie; and our Kasey, who looks far more mature than her current 16 years. It is Kasey's first wedding, and she was by far the most nervous person in the wedding party. Lastly came Nancy, who was also stunning as the Maid of Honor. I was already in tears watching all three of my beautiful girls walk down that aisle before I was to escort the fourth.

As Rosemary had commanded we waited in the back, "to increase the expectations," but finally "Bittersweet Symphony" melded into Keith Urban's "Only You Can Love Me This Way," and we began our walk down the aisle. I didn't even have to see Annie's face to know how beautiful she looked on that walk. She has been dreaming of her wedding day since she was a teenager. Today is fulfillment.

We have always been so comfortable together, Annie and I, sharing word games and odd jokes all of her life. We always seem to be on the same wave length and today was no exception. When she was little more than a toddler, she and I agreed on a way we could always say "I love you," no matter where it was and how many people were around. We did that today just before we headed down the aisle, and again before I handed her over to her husband. Neither of us could have said it out loud because both of us would have broken out in tears. I expected I would anyway, later in the ceremony.

Father Paul Waldie said he was merely assisting Erik and Annie to marry themselves. Father Paul is one of our dearest friends. In my mind, he is the essence of what it means to be a priest—thoughtful, caring, and extremely human in his approach. He takes every liturgy he performs with great seriousness, seldom arriving at anything that one would expect, but always focusing on the exact point of importance. I have watched him as a teacher, administrator, parish priest in Los Angeles and Seattle, as well as in the many times he has cared for our family.

He spoke to Annie and Erik as though they were the only ones in the church. Then he turned to the audience, telling everyone that they were there, not to witness a marriage, but to assist Annie and Erik in marrying themselves. He added an addendum—Nobody should be allowed in the reception if they didn't attend the marriage ceremony. "You aren't coming to Anne's and Erik's wedding just to eat some food." Right there he put everyone on notice that this was not a free meal they were having today. I could feel everyone letting out a deep sigh of relief that they hadn't skipped the church service and gone straight to Green Valley Country Club.

Jim Schafer opened the liturgy with the first reading, from John 15:9-12. Nicole Anthony, another of Annie's college friends, did the second reading, a lovely poem about love and marriage. Then came

Paul's homily. Of course it centered on Annie and Erik and what they had to do now that they have committed to each other. But Paul went one or two steps beyond that. His microphone falling off, he stormed over to the pew where the groomsmen were sitting and informed them in no uncertain words what he expected of them in supporting Erik and seeing that he didn't stray from his responsibilities to Annie. He then reversed course and said the same to the bridesmaids. Marriages survive, he said, because everyone who knows the couple helps to get them through the tough times. All of those in the church who have been married a while could only nod in agreement. He let loose one final volley at Erik, which I think startled the groom a bit, but he took Paul's words well, as Erik always does. I really think Paul missed Annie on purpose, but who can give advice to a beautiful woman all dressed in flowing white?

And then Annie and Erik married themselves. They announced their vows without prompting and worked their way through the ring ceremony with a bit of help from Father Paul.

"You two can kiss if you want."

"Are we allowed to do that now?" Annie asked with a grin, a bit uncertain because it hadn't been in Rosemary's rehearsal.

"You can kiss anytime now, Annie."

Brian and Deb then gave the Prayers of the Faithful, and it was my turn. I have always written something for any ceremony in the family. Most of the time it is for funerals, but it was a joy this time to be able to write for a happy event. I wanted to tell the kids a few of the things that Mary and I have done and learned over the past 47 years.

ANNIE & ERIK

"If I only knew then what I know now!"

Erik, Annie, on behalf of Mary and me, and Gail, I'm going to tell you today, on this wonderful day, a few of the things we think we know now. For almost 48 years we have been learning things about ourselves, and we have a couple of suggestions for the two of you.

What does it mean, to love someone else? We think it is actually rather simple—in whatever you do together, think of your partner, not yourself. Annie, when you were a little girl, we always told you to look at whomever you were with and try to discover what they needed, what you could do for them. In doing things for others, you derive happiness for yourself. It's the same thing with marriage. If, in whatever you two choose to do, you will consider each other, you will grow your love. And that love will increase over the years.

Love is not some poet's creation; it's not some lyric in a country song. Love is always considering what your partner needs. Love is forgetting your ego in the cause of bringing joy to your mate. In the course of your life, you are most certainly going to have conflict. I urge both of you—give in, walk away, for the sake of your love. Both of you. If you both walk away from conflict, you'll work your way to solutions. Love isn't always winning, but love is always giving.

Life and love are not going to be what you think today, on your wedding day. Real love is not driven by dreams or testosterone. Real love is facing life problems together with trust in each other, and hard work, and without blame. Real problems are resolved with trust, work, and respect for each other.

But classic love, the Shakespeare sonnet kind, can still live and grow throughout your lives. Always think about your mate. Erik, do you remember I told you that you should always do the unexpected? Don't buy a single rose and expect a heart throb; bring her a green carnation for St. Patty's day or an incredible jack-o-lantern for Halloween. Don't buy Annie a dozen roses; buy three roses, four times. And take my advice, always carry a supply of odd gifts in your trunk just in case you missed something. Annie, learn to fly fish or pitch a tent, and how to tie a Green

Highlander or a Bivisible Badger, and then catch a trout he'll be proud of. Both of you, do things that your mate might not expect, but will brag about, to all of your friends. Always consider each other. Never forget that—it's the first law of marriage.

The second law—I just made these up—is that you are always better together than you are alone. You should each be your life-mate's biggest fan. Annie, your success is Erik's, and Erik, when you do something great, Annie should exult. Your success as a man and wife will be measured by how well each of you turns your ego over to the other, but it also depends on how well you let each other succeed. In your marriage, no one should win; both of you should.

Our third law—as a family, create your own traditions. It doesn't matter what they are, just do your own thing. Wear pink every Monday if you want to; go to a ball game the third full moon of every year; whatever. Just create a life that has a tiny bit that is only you, no one else. Annie, you know that you and I can say "I love you" anywhere, anytime, without a soul knowing it. Do things like that for your own children. Celebrate things. Create our own excitement; you'll find it is infectious. Those traditions will help to bind you ever tighter, will help you smile at times when maybe you're feeling down.

We are a big family, one who works hard, and shares, and cries together, and hugs (all the time, you'll get used to it Erik!), and above all, one who loves. You are part of us now, a new family to add to our spirit, to increase our love. Mary and I can't even begin to tell you how thrilled we are to welcome you, as man and wife, to our family.

At this point we were supposed to watch the lighting of the Unity Candle, but Paul was moving too fast and went right into the Nuptial Blessing and pronounced Annie and Erik to be Man and Wife.

"You can kiss him again, Annie."

And to the tune of Sinatra's "Fly Me To The Moon," they walked out into their new life.

Being one of eleven kids, I have always been comfortable with the natural crowd we create, but others are sometimes surprised by the Dold clan. We are loud, happy, garrulous, smiling. We hug all the time, no matter what the generation. Sadly, only Aunt Cecilia remains of Dad's generation, the last of fifteen siblings born to Anton and Mary Dold. She was able to come to the wedding with Uncle John, but didn't feel up to the reception. Eight of my brothers and sisters and their spouses have come together, only Tim and Caroline missing. And of course we miss brother Tom, who passed away in 2003 and Janet's Dave who died in 2005. A whole bunch of the cousins are here. We are top-heavy in vibrant women and they are a formidable force at any celebration—Lisa, Amy, Sue, Jen, Bobby's Jen, Cyndi, Melissa, Nancy, Annie, Leslie, Julieanna—those ladies can party! I think I better add Kasey and Michelle to that group as well.

The first dance, of course, was for Annie and Erik, who had agreed on Chris Connell's "Finally Forever" for their song. Shortly after I had the wonderful experience of holding my daughter tightly through "Annie's Song," one of my all-time favorites. The DJ, Steve, did a fabulous job all night, keeping the music flowing from the very start, breaking only for the traditional moments of cake-cutting and garter and bouquet tossing. And, of course, the toasts.

Nancy opened the toasts with a remarkable speech. I have always told my girls never to turn down a chance to talk, and it made me burst with pride to watch her give her talk with such confidence and skill. She opened by thanking me for taking care of Mary, but especially thanking Mary for being such an incredible inspiration to our whole family. "She is one tough cookie," she declared, which got a rousing ovation. Nancy spoke from the heart of her unbreakable friendship with her sister, and her respect and growing affection for Erik. She spoke of "friendship on fire," which displays quiet confidence: contentment in the present, hope in the future, and doesn't dwell on the past.

Justin Ellis, the best man, came next. Justin is not accustomed to public speaking and had written out his speech, something I assured him is perfectly acceptable. I had read my speech in church, I told him, but he still found Nancy a difficult act to follow. His sentiments were right from the heart, finishing with a quote, which described his cousin Erik: "Never above you; never below you; always beside you."

From the very first song, the dance floor was packed and it remained so until the very end. Perhaps the greatest surprise was a remarkable demonstration of the Texas Swing by Josh and Kasey. We in California never see that dance at all, but in the country it is almost second nature. I don't think I have ever seen Josh dance before, but Kasey has been working on him, and they astonished the crowd with their moves, some of which should certainly have tied both of them up in double half-hitches. The best part of it was that Josh was so "country cool" about the whole thing. It did my heart good to see a brother and sister in tune enough with themselves to be able to pull off such a complicated dance, for that matter, to pull off any sort of dance.

The other exciting dance moment for me was to watch my fellow teacher, Eva Kastel, thrill the crowd with her yoga version of contemporary dance. Eva is 88 years old, and she floated through a long number literally in the center of the floor, the center of attention. And she wasn't even breathing hard at the end of it. I had worried that she would want to leave early, but she stayed right to the end of everything, another of those inspirations that seemed to fill our day and night.

But the DJ never played "YMCA!" How can you have a wedding without the Village People? I think I saw them outside, dressed and ready to join us. At least Annie could have let them slip in a "Macho Man" or "In the Navy." Come to think of it, I never heard "Shout" or "Louie Louie," "Mony Mony," or even the "Macarena." Somehow we still managed to have a great time.

What a day! All of Annie's hard work and attention to detail paid off, because I can't think of how anything could have come out better. It is a day I will always cherish, because of her and Erik's happiness, because Mary was able to enjoy it to the fullest, and because our family and friends, more than a 150 of us, were able to come together again in a happy event.

Family Picture
(Left to right: Jack, Mary, Annie, Erik,
Clayton, Marty, Nancy, Kasey, Joshua)

Sunday, April 10

Brunch after a wedding has become a sort of tradition in the greater Dold family, a final time when everyone from out of town, which means just about all of us, gets together. As was the case with the rehearsal dinner, the girls, Deb, Marcia, and Donna pretty much took care of everything, ordering Mary into a chair for the duration of the party. Mary showed no signs whatsoever of the strenuous day she had yesterday, is still very much up and alive, thoroughly enjoying everyone's company. I have decided that the thing that is making her so sparkling is that she has discovered an entirely new level of confidence. I am going to have to think about it a bit, but Mary has to have a source for the incredible strength that she is exuding. I think it stems from the fact that perhaps for the first time in her life, her illnesses have made her the absolute center of attention for all of her family and friends. Everyone right now is totally focused on her, and I think that is a powerful source of her strength. And the fact that she has succeeded, not only in dealing with her maladies, but in overcoming them better than anyone could expect, has given her a degree of self-confidence she has never had before. I have watched her closely for almost a year of confinement and I have seen the changes. She has developed a shy little smile that just lights up her face and her sense of humor has expanded considerably. She talks and talks now whenever she gets the chance, in person or on the phone. She is thriving on all of the attention, not in a bad or conceited way, but she is taking the attention and transforming it into energy. If ever someone said that good wishes and prayers are the best medicine, they have only to look at Mary to believe that. I don't think that she will ever again be considered a quiet wallflower, content to sit in the background and watch others perform. When she is finally finished with all of the medicine and chemo and x-rays and scopes and scans, Mary is going to be a dynamo.

After everyone left in the early afternoon, Mary and I went over to North Bay Medical Center to see Erik's mom, Gail. The first thing we noticed was how different the feeling there is from that Mary had experienced at John Muir Hospital. North Bay is a fine hospital, but it is dreary, with small rooms, not nearly as well equipped or furnished as what Mary experienced. We found Gail in good spirits, considering she had broken her hip in three places. We assured her that Erik and Annie had gotten off well and were on their way to Durango. We spent about an hour and had a very good visit. I spoke with the Facilitator or whatever the title is, the nurse who takes care of making the ongoing arrangements for patients. She said that as soon as Gail was ambulatory they would move her to a rehab hospital where the physical therapists would take over. She mentioned three in the neighborhood, one of which we were familiar with. I told Gail I would check with friends to see what their recommendations were.

Thursday, April 14

We are off to Eureka again, this time to help Kasey celebrate the prom, a tradition at Eureka High School that is quite a bit different from other schools, primarily because of the small number of students.

Before we left town, Mary and I paid a visit to Erik's mom, Gail, at the North Bay Medical Center. I have stopped in every day, and she has steadily progressed as her hip gets stronger. Today we found her out of bed and sitting up, a major accomplishment with all of the pins she has is in her hip. She was very upbeat, saying she didn't understand it but she was having a very good time accepting the confines of the hospital. The nurses said that she was being moved this afternoon to the rehab facility just down the street, where they would begin the therapy she needed to become mobile again. We left her in very good spirits.

Friday, April 15

Today we suffered through Josh's two baseball games. This has been a three-sport varsity year for him, something to be proud of since he is just a freshman and hardly the normal jock type. We thrilled during the one football game we saw him in; had a rollercoaster ride with his basketball where he jumped from JV to Varsity every game; and now there is baseball. He didn't want to play, but this is Eureka where there aren't even 100 kids in the whole high school. Josh wasn't going to play, but without him there wouldn't have been enough boys in that tiny school even to field a team. He was approached by the coach first, then by one or another teacher and finally by Mr. Fujii, the principal. What can you do when you are so badly needed?

It has not been easy for anyone, players, coaches or fans. Eureka hasn't fielded a baseball team for at least three years, and it shows in their play. Of all of the sports, baseball is the one that is most based on practice and playing. Players have to respond naturally to every situation, have to know when to run, where to throw the ball. There are a thousand little things that are taught only by experience, which none of the players on Josh's team have had. The first game today was ended by the "Mercy Rule," the other team reaching 20 runs before the 5th inning or something like that. In the second game, Eureka played much better, but still gave up thirteen runs in the first inning. After that they kept it reasonable. I feel so bad for the kids, who want to play but simply have to play more games to become competitive. I give great credit to the coach, Mr. Hicks, who doesn't seem to get down, certainly not on the players and who maintains a smiling, encouraging attitude throughout, no matter what the score, carefully taking each player aside to explain what they just did or didn't do. Only time and practice can help this team, but unfortunately, because of Eureka's remote location, they will only play about ten games in the entire season. Which means competition against only five schools, because they always play two. Ernie Banks would have loved that part of it!

Saturday, April 16

Annie and Erik arrived this morning, driving in from Durango, Colorado, where they spent their honeymoon. Erik originally lived there and they decided to make the honeymoon a nostalgia trip and save a few dollars at the same time. Annie has always done the make-up for Kasey and her friends as they get ready for the prom, so of course they designed their return to go through Eureka.

Prom Day in Eureka involves the entire community in the most refreshing way. The event is held in the old Opera House in town, a nicely restored building dating back to the 19th century. There they have a dinner put on by the junior class, who traditionally spend the year on fund raisers to get the money to pay the bill. The dinner is for the senior class students and their parents, as well as for the junior students. That's all the Opera House can hold.

After dinner, all the friends and family of the kids pack the place for the Grand Entrance. Each student and their date are introduced to the crowd, the girls entering stage left and the boys to the right. They meet in front of the photo backdrop, this year a fountain garden largely created by Josh and Kasey. There they get their pictures taken by the professional photographer and all the parents, sisters, aunts, uncles and grandparents. The procession starts with the seniors and then moves to the other grades, with oohs and aahs, cheers and applause as each enters, at least as each girl enters, because they are much more photogenic than the boys. This year there was a spectacular succession of elaborate ball gowns, most of them quite stunning. Of course we wait for Kasey and her friends, who by our unbiased consideration are the most beautiful of all. The best entrance of the night was achieved by Josh's freshman buddy Andrew, who was invited by one of the senior girls. Taylor, the center on Kasey's basketball team, stands a head taller than Andrew. When they met in the middle of the floor for their picture, Andrew jumped into Taylor's arms with the greatest Cheshire grin ever seen, and fine applause from the balcony.

Pictures snapped, there is the parent-student dance, where the dads and moms are escorted to the floor by their young man or woman for a very beautiful first dance. After that, everyone above eighteen years old is kicked out and the serious dancing begins. Because the school is so small, all high school students can attend the prom. One exception this year was Josh, who really wanted to take Beth, but she is still in the 8th grade. Josh, big sports star, was invited by more than one of the girls, but finally simply announced he wasn't going and that ended the whole thing.

After the dance, the kids go off in various directions, usually for an overnight party. Kasey and her friends organized their own this year at one of the houses, because the general party usually takes place in some remote mountain valley away from the prying eyes of parents and, truth be told, police. We were all thrilled that our kids were more reasonable.

This is a wonderful community tradition, the Eureka prom,

one that all of the kids, their parents and grandparents can enjoy. Everyone in town knows most of the kids, having watched them grow up as toddlers. Even Mary and I know many of them from the games, the school activities, 4th of July, and other events we have attended. Eureka is a throwback to Main Street America, a joy to be part of.

Sunday, April 17

An unspeakable tragedy occurred today. Erik's mom, Gail, whom we just left in the hospital in Fairfield, died this morning in the rehab facility. I received a call from Erik's cousin and knew immediately that something bad had happened. Erik is in a state of shock, not knowing what to do. It is bad enough to lose your parent, but to be informed in this way, just as you are in the high point of your honeymoon, is almost more than a person can bear. We know none of the details, but all of us made quick plans to leave immediately for the Bay Area. I strongly suspect that she was hit by a blood clot, which seems the only explanation for so sudden a death. Last Thursday, we had left Gail in good spirits, ready to begin the rehab of her hip fracture. All we can do is put our arms around Erik and provide as much love and support as he needs.

Monday, April 18

It's back to the medical wars today, as once again we drive into the Cancer Center in Pleasant Hill. It is interesting how the various events of Mary's illnesses have bounced us around from doctor to doctor. This whole thing started with Mary's doctor, Vanita Jain. She transferred us to Shoba Kankopati, who has been the medical focal point in all of the cancer treatments, prescribing the chemo cocktail, ordering scans, blood work, and follow-up. She is also the doctor who recommended us to Rakesh Donthineni. Once the chemo was finished, Shoba turned Mary over to Donthineni for the surgery, and Mary remained his patient until he was satisfied with all of the results and then returned us to Dr. Shoba. We remained in her care until Mary's unfortunate trip to John Muir Emergency Hospital, where Dr. Brian McGuinness took over. Shoba visited Mary several times after her colostomy, but she always deferred to McGuinness if there was anything she wanted to suggest or prescribe. McGuinness had the final say in all things medical until he released Mary back to Dr. Shoba to determine the next stage of the cancer treatment. Dr. Shoba will eventually relinquish authority to Dr. Chao, who will be directing the radiation treatments, thirty-four of them in all that will run into the middle of July.

I must say, it is a very impressive team that has passed Mary around, and kept her heading toward the ultimate goal of renewed good health. We have come so far from the days of Dr. Quinn, Medicine Woman!

Today we officially move from the McGuinness team back to Dr. Shoba Kankopati and the ebullient ladies of the Epic Care Center. Mary is scheduled for blood tests, once again to be sure that her cell counts are in the right place. Her "Homecoming" was quite a scene, where Alice and Lily both rushed to embrace her and welcome the two of us back. The story of Mary's ordeal with the colostomy is common knowledge around here, including the role that was played or not played by Dr. Patel. The staff was not only thrilled to see Mary walk in, but as has been the case with everyone we know, they are astounded by how positively healthy she looks. Mary was wearing that very distinctive smile that transforms her face whenever someone starts praising her appearance. She positively glows in the face of compliments. I think that smile is a combination of shyness and confidence, the confidence that comes from accomplishment. She is wearing it often these days. It is an interesting part of healing. Because Mary has consistently exceeded people's expectations, she has been bombarded day after day with compliments about how great she looks. If you hear anything often enough, you are bound to start believing it, and I believe that has happened to Mary, and it is totally causing her evident confidence. Compliments are powerful medicine and Mary has taken the strongest of doses.

Of course Alice found her cell counts to be fine, so we received one more loving hug from the ladies and moved to Dr. Shoba's office. She was as thrilled to see Mary as the ladies in the infusion center. She has been very much involved in Mary's recovery at John Muir, and welcomed her back almost as a lost daughter, or given her age, as a lost mother. She told us that we would have a couple of weeks off to continue the recovery from the colostomy, that she was putting in the request with Medicare for another PET scan to see what the condition was of the tumors following surgery and the last round of chemo. It has been more than two months since those last chemo sessions. It seems more like a year. For those two months, in the face of the terrible ordeal of the emergency colostomy, we have really put cancer completely out of our minds. We always knew we would have to go back, and today begins that journey again. It will require another change of mental focus, to start thinking about the PET scan and what it will show. Except for the reality of that bag hanging on her side, we are back to the point we left two months ago, having stopped one cycle short of the chemo that Dr. Shoba had envisioned. For now, that last cycle is on the back burner and we are praying for a clear PET scan to keep it there.

Erik is completely devastated by the loss of his mother. There is no way to express our support except to wrap him up in the family and let time work its healing ways. Gail was victim to a blood clot, something that is always feared when an older person breaks a hip. The hospital had moved her to a rehab facility to keep her blood moving through exercise and therapy. What makes it particularly difficult for Erik is that he is just starting a new life and is torn between a hospital investigation and beginning a family life with Annie. He is being hit with advice from all sides. My suggestion to him this morning was to focus on his new wife and begin to live again. I'm sure Gail would want that.

May

Monday, May 2

They do the scans on the first floor of the Cancer Center where Mary gets her chemo treatments. The various offices and functions are joined by computer and therefore able to access information immediately. Not only are they able to access Mary's chemo history here, they also have all Mary's records from her two surgeries at John Muir Hospital and Alta Bates. The actual PET scan takes about an hour and a half, but it will be several days before Shoba can tell us the results. Those are not going to be easy days to endure, because this scan will tell us if all that Mary has gone through with her cancer has been worthwhile. Of course, now that she has thrown a colostomy into the mix, we have no idea what other things might have affected her. I think we'll just focus on that big tumor and put all of the other stuff out of the way.

Tuesday, May 3

I got called for jury duty this morning. That summons from Superior Court that seems to arrive in the mail box every other month, is one of those things that ruins your day, like an envelope from the IRS, or one with a procession of lawyers' names on the return address. When you are working, jury duty is a major pain in the butt and for most thinking Americans a complete waste of time.

Oh, I know, we are told it is one of our sacred duties, one of those things that mark us as a free people. That's probably true, but the fact is most of the decisions that juries make get thrown out five years later, after an endless parade of appeals of one sort or another, or some future judge decides that everything has been done wrong and only he knows how to do it right.

In a dozen opportunities, I have never actually sat on a jury. I used to get thrown out because I had been a dean of boys of a high school, and they want nobody that is an authority figure on their panels. One time I told the judge I thought it was a waste of my time. He told me he could hold me in contempt of court for a statement like that. I told him I *was* in contempt of court and he got so mad he threw me out with a dreadful scolding. I exited past several smiles from other prospective jurors. The last time I was called I was leaving in two days to take a Cal group to Bhutan, an excuse the judge quickly accepted. It was my easiest exit ever.

But times have changed. This time I hope I get on the jury, a hope that comes as a considerable shock, mostly because it is a sure sign I have become a senior citizen. I now have time! I can't think of a single reason why I would not be able to serve. I can't even use Mary's cancer as an excuse because after her PET scan yesterday, she won't need me as chauffeur for at least two weeks. No, this time I am more than willing to find out how the system works.

So about seventy-five of us assembled in the jury room at the Solano County Courthouse in Fairfield and were ushered to the courtroom where twelve of us would be empanelled. The trial was for a convict in the Vacaville Prison who was accused of possession of marijuana. That's ridiculous, I thought. All convicts in our prisons are in possession of marijuana. Where's the crime? I was thinking such a thought when my name was called and I was ushered up to the jury box.

"Is there anyone called so far who thinks this matter is not important?" asked the prosecutor.

I couldn't help myself. "I think it is not only not important. I think it's ridiculous."

"Why do you say that, ….Mr…Dold," she asked looking at the jury roster.

"First of all, I thought marijuana was completely common in all of our prisons. And second, in my mind, this is a prison matter. You have him. Can't you control what gets into his cell? It's the prison's problem, not the court's. I would think the judge here has plenty of other more important crimes to deal with."

I hadn't meant to give a speech, and I still was hoping that I would not be kicked off the jury because I was interested in seeing why this man was brought here in the first place. It was not to be. The prosecutor used me for one of her peremptive discards. Her mistake, I thought, because I was probably the most likely juror in the room to seek a conviction. As I left the courthouse, two other men who had been excused were leaving.

"Hey, man," the younger of the two said, holding out his hand. "I would have backed you in there. This whole thing is stupid." The other man nodded his head in agreement.

I guess I'm never going to learn how a jury works. One of the officers told the woman sitting next to me that she didn't have to serve on jury duty anymore because she was over 70. Who ever knew that?

Friday, May 6

Mary's tumors are gone! Shoba called last night to give us her unofficial reading of the PET scan.

"I know you are probably nervous so I thought I would phone you. Your PET scan came back beautifully. There are no tumors shown anywhere. The large tumor is completely gone and there are no new tumors visible anywhere."

The relief can't be measured. All along there has always been the fear that Mary's sarcoma had grown so fast and spread so quickly that perhaps there would be other tumors surfacing besides those in the lymph nodes and lungs. But Shoba says there is no sign of spreading. Wonderful news! She set an appointment for next Monday when she would go over the scan completely with us.

We immediately took off for Nevada. What better way to celebrate than with the kids? Those seven hours of driving just flew by.

Saturday, May 7

Josh plays his last two baseball games today at Round Mountain. When you attend Eureka High School you have to be ready for long bus rides. There is no school that is closer than about a hundred miles away, with the closest towns being Ely, Austin, and Carlin. They sometimes have a four-hour ride to get to a game, so of course they "play two." We saw Josh's team play a few weeks ago, and I have to be honest, it was awful to watch, but he reported last week that they won both games they played. So today I have high hopes at Round Mountain.

It is difficult to get more remote than Round Mountain, a town lost in Smoky Valley in the shadow of the Toyabee Mountains, on the way to Tonapah from just east of Austin. It is a town that couldn't exist except for a huge hole they have dug in order to extract a couple million ounces of microscopic gold, one of more than twenty such cyanide leaching gold mines in Nevada. I think I drove though Round Mountain once, but can't be sure because it is easy to miss. At this time of year, it does have a wonderfully scenic backdrop of the snow-clad mountains.

I can't believe that this is the same team we watched a while back. Josh's teammates were actually fielding grounders and throwing runners out at first. They caught fly balls! Twice Josh, playing second, raced back to pick off pop-ups. In the last game I gently criticized him for not even running to try and catch such pops. In the month or so since we last saw them play, Coach Hicks has taught them more than the rudiments of the game; he has them playing decent baseball. True, the first game was called when the margin was ten runs after the 5th inning, but the Eureka boys battled well and at least made it a game. They won the second game! It was truly exciting. Round Mountain had the tying run on third with one out in the 7th inning. The last time I saw the kids play, that run would have scored on the next wild pitch. Instead, the batter hit a hard grounder to Josh, playing third this time, and he fired home where Mike Damele applied a difficult tag. Two outs! The next batter bashed the ball that Tanner knocked down on the mound. He scrambled around and barely caught the runner at first. Game over! Those two plays made the season for these kids, and they showed exactly how far they have come in a few games and a couple of months. From being totally clueless at the beginning of the season, the Eureka boys have become a baseball team, not a great one, but one where all of us fans can sit and cheer and be proud. What more can we ask? They finished their season 3-4.

Saturday, May 8

Mother's Day has very special meaning this year. It is nice to be with Nancy, Marty, and the grandkids who showered Mary with attention today. The highlight of the day, however, was a Mother's Day 5k race that Nancy entered in town. The run went from the high school up the hill toward the old gold mine. It would have been fine except it was extremely cold, and raining fairly hard. A few hardy souls showed up anyway, including our daughter who bravely trudged up the mountain and back to the school.

"I came in first in my age group," she announced proudly to anyone who would listen. A true statement, though she neglected to add that she was the only female runner in her age group. It doesn't matter though, because she got out there and did it. Mary and I were there as well, but we never left the shelter of our car.

Monday, May 9

Dr. Shoba confirmed her phone call today—Mary is free of detectable cancer! This medical campaign, which started on October 25 with the first infusion of Gemzar, can now be declared a success, six and a half months of strength, patience, and endurance on Mary's part, interrupted in the middle by two months of colon problems. Dr. Shoba carefully explained the findings of the PET scan, telling us that there were no detectable tumors left, but cautioning Mary that there are undoubtedly still cancer cells at work in her body. All along she has told us that she would recommend radiation after chemo and surgery if both were successful. With that in mind, she sent us to the first floor office of Dr. Kenneth Chao, with whom we met last month. The last lap of Mary's race will be radiation treatment on the tumor exposed by the surgery.

At least for a moment however, I have some good news to convey to all of our friends and family.

Tuesday, May 10

Hi All:

I have very good news about Mary. Last Monday she had a PET scan to find out if there were any more cancer tumors floating around. She was completely clear. So she is finished with chemo. Today we met with the radiation oncologist. Next Monday she will start a radiation schedule which is aimed at reducing the chances that her sarcoma will return. She gets a radiation treatment daily for about six weeks. On the other front, she has adjusted remarkably well to her stoma bag and life is almost back to normal. Of course, she is still very much up from all of the wedding excitement.

Once again, we thank you for all of your love, support and care. We have found that this whole experience has brought everyone in our lives closer together. That is especially gratifying since Mary has made such a remarkable recovery.

With our love,
Jack

I told Mary today that she is going to have to come up with another illness of sorts, something benign but impressive, if she wants the emails and cards to keep coming like this. I think next to the miracle of her recovery, the response of all of her friends and family has been very moving and heartwarming. From that standpoint, there never was anything quite like email. With one message you can get the word out to any number of people, and they are able to respond immediately, something that the good old institution of letter writing never could do. There is an immediacy with the internet that we never had, and while that is sometimes awful if you are a politician in a scandal or someone on trial for some heinous crime, it is great for the type of correspondence we have had.

In the past we have often been a bit reluctant to phone someone who is sick, not wanting to intrude, but with emails there is no such problem. They can be read whenever the recipient feels like it. Mary has had so many good thoughts through emails that I think she has to give some of the credit for her good fortune to the messages that were sent. People bemoan the death of letter writing, but the email is at least a written form telling someone you care about them, and that makes it a wonderful thing in my mind. Even little boys can handle emails! In particular I like the fact that a person can, by using an email, be as enthusiastic or phlegmatic as he/she wants. I just have to look at the ones Mary has received, more than 200 of them to date, and I can read all sorts of personalities into the form and contents. I included a few in this journal, using our niece Susie's as an example of pure unadulterated enthusiasm and love of life, and my sister Janet's as the voice of experience. But I could easily have included all of them because each has a personality that is purely individual. All are expressions of love.

Today we have an appointment with Dr. Chao at the Epic Center. He will outline Mary's radiation program. We laughed when he went through all of the details. Suddenly he got very serious, telling Mary that there was one thing they had to do which would be irreparable. Both of us kind of shuddered, but then he described three or four "tattoos" they were going to have to apply to align the laser for the treatments. Mentally I said, "Great, Mary has always said she wanted to get a tattoo." But then he said that each tattoo was about the size of the head of a pin, and both of us felt let down. I figured that they could maybe do an American flag or a Byers' Choice caroler, but these things are just chicken little dots.

Her program will have thirty-four treatments, starting tomorrow. She will come in five days a week, with the weekends off. We figure the new "Coming Out" date for her will now be July 17, because we will definitely take a few days off for the 4th and then resume afterwards. She won't be starting the radiation for a couple of weeks.

They have to run her through another MRI to get an exact map of the tumor beds they intend to attack. Dr. Chao said there would be no problem radiating the two areas of Mary's surgery, and that he intended also to radiate the skin areas of the incisions, which he said are particularly vulnerable to cancer recurrence. Because the main tumor was in such an inaccessible location, they will have to design a sort of foam chair support which will enable Mary to remain still long enough for the radiation treatments. I looked up the whole process on the internet but this is far too complex for me to figure out.

Wednesday, May 25

Mary began her radiation today, at an ungodly 8:15 a.m. She will generally have it at 9:45 every weekday morning. It takes only a couple of minutes, but we have thirty minutes of driving each way and maybe a few minutes for dressing and undressing. They molded a sort of Styrofoam-cardboard chair for her to use. The site of the tumor on the inner thigh is very difficult to reach with the laser, so she has to assume a difficult pose and hold it for several minutes.

Dr. Chao said she would eventually get fatigued as the radiation builds up in her body, and there is a chance the skin will start to leather a bit. There is also the danger of permanent swelling in her leg, but he said that is somewhat rare. I asked Dr. Chao to get in contact with Dr. McGuinness to determine the areas where he will be working on the reverse of Mary's colostomy. He agreed to do that and adjust his radiation accordingly. Radiation is a sort of preventive medicine for future tumors. Everyone expects the cancer to return at some point, because they almost always do, but the radiation can extend the period of good health above that afforded simply by chemo and surgery. At this point we are going for good health!

Friday, May 27

Tom Meschery and I went to Pacifica to a dinner honoring Bob Hagler and an old basketball friend, Ken Grider, a man who played at Lowell High in SF a couple of years before Tom. Grider was a high school All-American and in the first varsity game that my brother

Bob ever played in high school. Bob Hagler was my algebra teacher in high school back in 1955. He left St. Mary's High that year to become the freshman basketball coach at St. Mary's College. He recruited an incredible freshman team, the centerpiece of which was Tom Meschery, one of the most sought-after high school players in the country. Bob has remained a close friend of both of us all these years. He was a high school principal after he left St. Mary's and then became superintendant of schools of Castro Valley.

Curiously both men are being honored as Men of the Year by the San Francisco Old Timers Baseball Association, odd because both of them are really associated with basketball. But Hagler belongs to just about every organization in Northern California and has worked his whole life for whatever cause gets his attention. In this case, he and Grider began the scholarship program for this group and hence the honor.

For Tom and me it was a fine day of pure "philosophical discussion." Tom and I have been political and sometimes philosophical opponents since college. We were classmates and teammates on St. Mary's best ever freshman team, a team that was undefeated and generally considered the best in the U.S. Tom was the real force on that team. He went on to become an All-American at St. Mary's and was the first round draft pick of the Philadelphia Warriors. Both of us got good grades, something of an oddity among the players. We have resumed that old friendship in the past few years. As it turns out, Tom is a card-carrying liberal and I am a staunch conservative. Politically we agree on nothing, "but we're both romantics," Tom asserts, and the friendship endures. At the moment, both of us are busy writing novels which we will try in our old age to get published. We exchanged rough drafts of our books today, promising to read them and lie to each other about how much we love them.

June

Wednesday, June 8

Mary showed the first signs of fatigue today as a result presumably of the radiation treatments. This was her tenth today. By 9:00 she was in bed reading, pretty much exhausted. Dr. Chao had told us this would be the case, that the radiation would slowly build up in her body and take much of her energy. We are a bit leery that this will build to the point that she will be exhausted all the time, but there is nothing to do but wait and see. With both the chemo and the radiation, Mary's fatigue takes the form of dull ache in her back and shoulders. "It feels like I have a heavy weight on my body," is the way she describes it.

We have started to schedule things separately a day or two a week—lunch with friends, shopping, chores for me around the garden. Most mornings I go down to Lim's coffee shop in Rockville to spend an hour with all the old farmers, "old" meaning my age. I love to hear the stories of life in Suisun Valley half a century ago.

It was late in the day when Mary first started wearing out. I think it is important that she starts to have time for herself, since she has been cooped up with me and other family members for months and months. I find that my inclination is to continue to do just about everything for her, but I am not sure that is in her best interests. Eventually our goal is that Mary returns to her normal life, and that means independence.

Driving is not a problem for her these days, and it is nice to see her starting to schedule meetings and meals with her friends.

Sunday, June 12

Mary got very sick tonight, "up-chucking" to use her word, several times in late afternoon and over night. We discussed what she had eaten that could have caused it, the nausea preceded by sometimes severe stomach cramps. It occurred to me in the morning that we were doing the same thing we had done with the pain that led to the emergency hospital and colon surgery. We are assuming it is food poisoning. Maybe it is something else. I am nervously watching her tonight.

Monday, June 13

We agreed that Mary should ask Dr. Chao today about the vomiting yesterday and last night. He asked whether this happened from cramps or nausea. When Mary described the cramps, he immediately said it was caused by the radiation, and wrote out a prescription for Dicyclomine, a rather strong drug she was to take three times a day. We are getting used to the disclaimers on all of these drugs, but this one seemed extravagant even by modern standards. Mary took one capsule and decided she didn't need any more. The bottle was deposited on the shelf with all of the unused Vicodin they keep throwing at her. The nausea has not returned.

Saturday, June 18

Today is a watershed moment for Mary—she officially went out to a public event with no head covering but her reemerging hair. For some days now she has given up her wigs and hats in favor of what only can be called "a pixie cut." She looks great! I can see the uplifting of her spirits now that she can claim her old hair back again. Before the chemo, people commented on how beautiful was her hair, a silvery gray that women pay big bucks to achieve with their hairdressers. To see her hair growing back so well is wonderful. Now everyone who sees her makes the same comments as before.

The public event this evening is a dinner-fund raiser for the Ritter House in San Rafael, a charity that treats the homeless. Jim and Donna Schafer have been heavily involved with Ritter House for years. Mary, dressed in her bright red shower dress, was striking with her short-cropped white pixie cut. Before we left for dinner she asked Donna if she thought it would be better to wear her wig. Donna gave her an emphatic "NO!" More verbal support!

Sunday, June 19

It's Father's Day, and I got the greatest gift a father can be given. Annie and Erik came by for a barbecue. Annie wasn't in the house two minutes when she gave Mary a box to open. Inside was a lovely little outfit that read, "I love my grandmother."

It takes a minute for something like that to register, but even at our advanced age, we figured it out. Mary let out a squeal that matched her daughter's and rushed over to give her a hug, while I shook Erik's hand and gave him a hug. Does it get any better than that? Now that's some real medicine!

"Not too far along, are we, Annie?" I asked sheepishly.

"No, it's probably too early to announce, but I just couldn't hold it anymore."

In fact, Annie is a bit over a month along by the way I figure it. They were married April 9, two months and ten days ago. It will be a February baby. I did that by using my fingers the way Mary taught me to do it.

This year is getting more and more crazy. We have had all of the trauma swirling around Mary's illnesses and surgeries. Annie and Erik got married and brought Clay into the family, a new grandson for us. Erik lost his mother a week after the wedding. And now we have another grandchild coming to us. Life is a wonderful thing, always with its highs and lows but always with hope and love, sometimes when you least expect it. Annie has dreamed of being a mother since she was a little girl. She more or less warned Erik and all of us that she wasn't going to wait long after the wedding. At the time I crossed my fingers and prayed because young people don't always get what they are expecting along those lines. What do I know?

Annie, who approaches everything she does with planning and research was loaded with answers for any question we had.

"I did three tests, Mom. I'm pregnant!"

"Have you seen a doctor?" I asked

"No, I'll do that in a couple of weeks."

"How did you find this out?"

"I have an email program that tells me what's going on. Right now the baby is only the size of a sesame seed."

Life has gotten way too complicated for me.

Thursday, June 23

The radiation is beginning to burn the skin around Mary's incisions. This was one of the side-effects that Dr. Chao had told Mary to expect, that the skin would get sensitive or even leathery. She has had a variety of samples of ointments to apply to the area, but today she pointed out a couple of spots where the skin was encrusting. She was given a new medication, Biafine ointment, with instructions to "slather" it all over the region. There seems no end to the progression of medicaments we are discovering during this whole experience. Whatever happened to good old aspirin? I looked at her radiation area this morning, and it is positively black, not only on her left leg but on the right one as well. Dr. Chao said that the color was normal, but that he could see the pink areas around the incision which were signs of new skin growth. I can see them too, but it still is unsettling to observe the effects of the radiation.

Sunday, June 26

Things are starting to perk up for the upcoming 4th of July bash at Nancy and Marty's. Our tradition of spending the 4th in Nevada goes back more than twenty years, to when the kids got engaged. Mary and I and Annie joined them there as a way to introduce ourselves to the family and their friends. Nancy was entering a world completely different from ours, one to which we were amazed she was going to try. Love conquers all! I have to admit, the isolation of the place is daunting, just passing through. The idea of living in such a remote area never occurred to me.

But the 4th of July celebration in this small community of farmers, cowboys, and miners is right out of Norman Rockwell's America, a slice of the past that is very much alive, a celebration of living, mostly centered around families, where all generations come together and have fun. Nothing complicated. Just gather up all of the fire engines in the county, have the kids decorate their horses or bikes or ATVs, stick a few folks on a flat bed truck, and call it a parade. Take some fire hose and measure off foot races on Highway 50 starting with the six-year olds and going up to the young adults. Drop a hatful of nickels on the ground for the toddlers to snap up. Pull out some cases of beer quarts for chugging contests for men and women, cokes for the kids. Oh, don't forget the women's nail driving contest. Start the day with hot, hot Bloody Mary's from the Owl Club and finish with cold Coors from the Keyhole. That's the 4th of July in Eureka. Pure fun. We always get a bizarre hat for Jim to wear; the townsfolk are starting to look forward to his annual chapeaux.

Thursday, June 30

The end of June already! Incredible! Life really is like a roll of toilet paper—the closer you get to the end, the faster it goes. It has been just about a year since Mary first realized the symptoms of her cancer, beginning her weight loss, dry mouth and loss of appetite. It doesn't seem that long, so much has happened in between. But here we are, getting close to the end of her treatment. She goes today for her 26th dose of radiation.

She is getting pretty sore and tender around her leg from the daily assaults of the radiation. Jim says he expects her to start glowing in the dark. But the area of the upper thigh/groin is getting extremely sensitive, almost raw. We will have to ask Dr. Chao tomorrow what he can do to help alleviate the discomfort. Otherwise, Mary is feeling fine, not experiencing much of the fatigue she once had and none of the nausea. Eight doses to go!

July

Friday, July 1

It's "Moving Day" in Montreal. Really! July 1 is Canada Day north of the border, when they celebrate Confederation. But in Montreal, it's the day when all rental leases expire and everyone has to move. Because of renter protection laws, anyone whose lease runs more than a year can only be removed from their apartment with dynamite, so no lease runs more than a year unless you want to adopt your tenant. As a result, the whole city becomes one huge traffic jam of moving vans, pickup trucks, trailers, vans, anything that will hold more than a cribbage board. I have no idea why I am including that in this journal except that I saw myself print July 1 and that always triggers this story.

I took Mary into the radiation lab at 8:00. She only as eight more treatments left after today. But her leg is getting pretty sore and raw from the daily bombardment as well as the position of the scar in the upper thigh. Dr. Chao met us after the treatment. He is a very human young man, genuinely interested, not only in Mary's condition but also in her life in general. He was most concerned about the sore on her leg and gave her an ointment to apply very similar to the zinc oxide kids used to put on their noses to block sun burn. Mary has five days off now with the holiday weekend, so it should heal pretty well over that time.

"I really like Dr. Chao," Mary said after we had left him. "He is so humble."

It is a great word to describe him. He is very caring and not at all full of himself, but on the other hand he is extremely confident in his profession. It is a nice combination. A while back he told Mary to drink more green tea because it is very good for your health. Today I presented him with a poem I wrote in China about all the claims they make there of the therapeutic effects of green tea and silk blankets. He got a great laugh out of it and thanked me heartily.

Annie, Erik, and Clayton are with us today on the ride to Eureka, a crowd to be sure, but we made it with no problems, a nine-hour jaunt including a lunch and shopping stop at Cabela's near Reno. Clay is a neat little boy, full of spunk, talk and with an imagination that is remarkable in many ways. The only time he stopped talking was when we put "Finding Nemo" on the VCR in back and he and Annie settled into the story.

Nancy got the same treatment that Mary received on Father's Day—this time a little outfit that said, "I love my aunt." Patrick and Deb had arrived at the same time as we did, and they understood the gift several seconds before the meaning got through to Nancy. True to expectations, she let out a huge squeal and rushed her sister to give her a joyous hug. It was a moving scene. Kasey and Josh were right behind Nancy with the hugs and screams. Well, Josh didn't really scream, but he did come right over with the hug.

Annie gets daily updates from her email program. Today, little Gibson is the "size of a lentil," so he/she is growing at a geometric rate. I hope that doesn't continue for 7.58 more months. Things are so precise these days.

Speaking of growing, Josh has added a couple of inches just since the wedding. It looks like Marty and Nancy are putting him on the rack every night and stretching out his legs. He has passed Deb and Mary and is getting close to Patrick now. He took me out for a tour of his new moto-cross course this evening. It has doubled in size, now almost encroaching on Marty's hay circle. There are huge jumps now, a "table-top," where you can land anywhere in case you're short off the jump, some moguls that Josh calls "oopsies," a bunch of wicked turns and banks. Josh designed the course based on actual professional courses and constructed the whole thing himself, using the loader and backhoe. It is scary looking at it, and he's not even riding it yet. Later on he donned his riding gear and helmet and roared into the course. He does it at full speed. There are at least a dozen jumps, one of which takes him about 10' high and about 30' long, another landing him over the platform because he never comes up short. It is wondrous to watch him fly.

There is also a very large gravel pit on the farm, to which Josh applied his loader. The pit is about 20' deep, and Josh has fashioned jumps all around its perimeter, some of them propelling him 30' or more out to the land above. I think they are going to have to consider finding him some competition because he certainly has the skill. Nancy no longer cares to watch him, but secretly, in spite of her protests, she is as proud of him as a mother can be.

As usual, Patrick and Deb filled their van floor to roof with fireworks for the 4th. This year they flew to Las Vegas instead of Wyoming. Last year they nearly ended up in jail trying to smuggle the explosives across Utah. Patrick was stopped but wouldn't let the patrolman inspect his car. He found that his supplier also had a shop in Las Vegas so that was an easier choice this year.

Jim, Donna, Eric, Sully, Kinsey, and Addison arrive this afternoon, as will Nancy and Brian Bagnato with his friend Conner. That will be our crew this year. We almost always hit twenty these days, as our families are growing.

This is always nervous time for Nancy. I understand her feelings because this is her holiday, just as Mary's is Christmas. We missed our annual Christmas party this year because Mary just didn't have the energy to pull it off, although she really considered braving her way through it. I nixed that. For the women of the family, these annual celebrations are their time to shine. Nancy goes all out, with tons of food and drink. She must have spent hours weeding and planting because the garden is gorgeous. And she has at least ten bedrooms to work on for all of the guests. She put Annie and Erik in the new office, prodding Marty until he had at least installed a toilet and sink.

"I put you there, with Clay in Josh's room, because I thought you might want the privacy, but you have already taken care of that."

She said it so seriously that Anne and Erik were happy that the Empress was already happy and they had nothing more to prove, or produce.

"Why did you put your mother and me where we are, Nan?"

"Don't even go there, Dad!"

Nancy dredged up *The World's Greatest Jokebook* for me and it was waiting in our room. Clay is amazing with the hundreds of jokes he tells, none of which have a punch line or make the least bit of sense, but all of which are imaginative. I want to teach him some actual jokes that are funny, and Nancy's book, which was used by Josh and Kasey way back when, is perfect.

'What do you call a skeleton that won't get out of bed, Clay?"

"Lazy bones."

"What can a school kid give away and still keep for himself?"

"A cold."

Now those are perfect for Clay. I intend to stuff that whole book inside that active little brain.

Saturday, July 2

Everybody has a job today. It's Marty's birthday, #46, but that only means that his do-list is the longest. This is, according to Nancy, the Sixteenth Annual Eureka 4th of July Celebration for what started as the Dold-Plaskett-Schafer families. Over the years we were joined by the Joyces, and now include the Gibsons and the Bagnatos.

What a joy just to sit around and do nothing! Well almost nothing. Nancy fired up her new margarita machine, a swirling dervish of a contraption that conjures up five gallons of concoction in a single mix. We polished off two of those and were still doing fine. Other than that, we just sat around in the deck chairs doing nothing, enjoying the afternoon and evening air, watching the sun set, with the kids playing on the lawn in front of us. It is as good as life can be.

Sunday, July 3

Jim came out of the bathroom this morning, fully dressed, with shaving cream all over the perimeter of his face, splotching down to disappear onto his shoulders under his shirt. Patrick gave him a hand motion that he had something on his face, and he crossed his forearm over the spot, sending the foam to his ear.

"Don't you wash off the shaving cream?" I asked.

"No, I'm taking a shower next."

"But you already have your clothes on, and the shaving cream is getting all over them."

"How else can I walk through here?"

"Why do you shave before you shower? If you shower first, it softens your beard." That was Patrick.

"I do things my own way."

"I shave in the shower," Deb offered, rubbing her chin.

"Me too," Donna backed her up, patting her bum.

I didn't want to agree with them, but I do too. I touched nothing.

A while later, Jim strolled out of the shower, wrapped in a towel, the shaving cream at least gone.

"Why would you dress going into the shower and not coming out?"

"I put my clothes in the sink and they got all wet."

"He's not standard issue," Donna disclaimed over our laughter.

Today is a day for purely slugging around, with nothing to do but relax, take a nap or two, have a beer and talk. All the jobs Nancy assigned yesterday got finished, and now we just wait for the 4th parade. We went down several times to look at the great horned owls that nest in Marty's barn. They are magnificent birds that return annually to have their chicks. They produced two this year and the juveniles are almost as big as their parents now. Further on the bird front, we have noticed a pair of killdeers in the area of the fire pit. They call loudly whenever one of us walks down the path, sometimes even putting on their broken wing display to lure us away from wherever we are. I assumed their nest was somewhere around the tall grass near the office, but Donna discovered three perfectly camouflaged eggs lying right in the walkway on the gravel. Thank

God they laid them near the rocks that line the path or we would have stepped on them. Nature is amazing!

The boys—Josh, Conner, Brian and Erik—all took their shotguns to the gravel pit for a little clay shooting this afternoon. For the rest of us, it is just too hot to go outside. I can't even get up any enthusiasm for rock collecting for my various wall projects.

Our non-efforts are building for a big party tonight. Nancy is throwing a wedding shower for Anne and Erik, inviting all the many friends we have met over the years—thirty of Nancy and Marty's neighbors and their children. More than fifty of us assembled for a true country feast. The highlight was the new wedded couple, Annie in full wedding gown and Erik in his tux shirt and tie (of sorts) with jeans.

Kasey and Josh set up the volleyball net this afternoon, and before long the lawn was full of players, bridging three generations, many of whom are current players on the Eureka girls' team. Fred, Lester, and Moody held up the old folk's end, achieving a smash now and then, finishing in triumph just by being able to stand up. Patrick is the chef tonight, offering up great country tri-tip and chicken. As usual, Nancy has enough food to feed a hundred hungry people, so starvation will not be an issue for the next week or so.

The best thing about the night is the fact that in this country setting there are no generations. The teens talk to the little kids, their parents, and grandparents in complete harmony. It is so unlike city living. Josh ignited a blaze in the fire pit, attracting at first the teenagers, and Clayton, and gradually many of us older folk. Mark Damele and I watched him take a five-gallon can of diesel and pour it onto the already vigorous fire, causing a violent flare-up that illuminated much of the farm.

"Well, none of the girls ran away, so I guess it's not too dangerous out there," Mark observed with a bit of astonishment.

Patrick gave everyone a pre-taste of his 4th fireworks once it got dark, filling the sky with several of his complex rocket displays.

Of course Annie was the focus of the evening, (and Erik by association) but Mary, as has been the case since she has been sick, came in a very close second. All of the women can identify with Mary, with the tremendous challenges she has faced, and they are in total admiration, not only of how she has handled all of that, but in the obvious spirit in which she is waging life these days. Mary draws in the women as kindred spirits, but she also amazes the men because of her obvious strength and toughness. She was sitting at the end of the table with many of our family, and suddenly got up, turned her chair around to a table of the Eureka friends, declaring to the family table, "I can always talk to you guys; I want to say high to our friends in Eureka." It is hard to imagine how she could be any more full of life than she is. I think the pixie cut of her reemerging hair is inspiring her to be more outgoing and daring.

If the party was great fun, and the fire, the fireworks, the food and festivities were memorable, the margarita mixer was the silent star of the program. Folks started out with a tentative sample taste, but then they realized that here was a real-live fountain of great flavor, and Marty was refilling the thing before long. Mark, Lester, and Fred were seriously considering settling in for the night, but the demands of their wives, and the prospect of early morning hay baling finally pried them all away.

Monday, July 4

Happy 4th of July! Nancy handed out our annual T-shirts yesterday, this year's version bright red with exploding rockets on front and back. This, according to the T-shirts, is the Sixteenth Annual Eureka 4th of July get-together for the family. There are lots of traditions involved, the first of which, after the T-shirts, is the annual picture. This year's pose is in the front of the house because the Plasketts completely redesigned that area, installing a beautiful stone entry, with Nancy outdoing herself on the landscaping and porch décor. Patrick has a new camera, but couldn't figure out the time delay key so we have one family picture without Patrick and another without Nancy. But we may decide to reassemble tonight at dinner time.

Marty and Josh arrived back at the house barely in time for the picture. Marty has the field next to the house mowed, and he and Josh were up at 4:30 a.m., raking the circle, combining two windrows into one for easier baling and to help dry the grass. Everyone worries for Marty, that his crop will get rained on, with thunder cells cavorting around all over the sky. Last night there was fairly hard rain on both ends of the valley, but Marty's mowed field was somehow missed, receiving just a few drops. There is a higher percent chance of rain today, so we all have to pray one more day because he wants to bale tomorrow. Rain is the annual conundrum of the hay farmer, fantastic when the crop is in the ground growing; awful once it is lying around helpless waiting to be baled, barned, and sold.

The parade seemed subdued this year. Of course we found our traditional spot on the shady side of Highway 50, near the Mexican restaurant. And of course we made an immediate run to the Owl Club for beer and Bloody Marys. And of course Jim was up front and resplendent in his traditional 4th of July hat, this year's model a fine elephant head with upraised trunk, perfectly in keeping with the 4th theme. Actually he got two hats this year, but opted for the elephant because it allowed him to bellow out challenges to the fire trucks and police chief. And as always, candy is thrown for the little kids from the fire trucks and floats, along with T-shirts, sun glasses, little dolls, and other such throwables. Kasey's FFA team handed out cowbells. Clayton set a record with his haul, easily ten pounds of stuff from blue sun glasses to yellow Frisbees to more Tootsie Rolls than his teeth can ever get stuck in.

Erik was nervous before the parade because he always coaches Clay to get the full value out of whatever activity he is engaged in. I helped this morning as well, running Clay through a series of calisthenics to be sure he was properly stretched and limber. He was a dervish of candy collecting. At one point I watched him snag seven pieces in one hand before depositing them in the sack that Nancy had made for him. Another highlight was when he went after a Fire Department T-shirt that was lying about 15' away. He swept in just as a mother and her two little girls were angling for the Tee, with his right arm he blocked them off as he skidded between them and the prize, plucking the treasure with his left hand as he completed his slide. It will be on ESPN's "Top Ten Plays of the Week" for sure.

All of this is standard fare for our 4th, but something seems more subdued. First, there weren't as many people as in the past. The parade usually attracts lots of folks from other towns, and maybe the gas prices held some back. Then too, we only really have Clay and Kinsey as our young contestants these days. Josh was wiped out from the raking this morning and didn't enter any of the kids' races. Kasey was not feeling well and only managed the three-legged race with her friend Lydia. Kinsey and Clay picked up a lot of loot in the nickel toss for the little tykes, and Conner and Brian entered the beer-drinking contest, but they really only wanted a quart of beer for $3. That contest, by the way, was won by a huge outsider, who downed his quart in an amazing twenty seconds.

It was a sure sign that the family wasn't in proper form when we only made two beer runs to the Keyhole Bar. Normally there would have been half a dozen forays in that direction, with Jim just going in for no other reason than to show the toothless ladies his hat of the year.

In spite of the fact that our liquor consumption was far less and our athletic prowess almost non-existent, we still came home this afternoon and all fell asleep. That is also one of the traditions. In the past, all of us adults used to sack out, leaving Kasey and Josh the only ones awake to answer the phone and tell visitors that none of us could see them at the moment. Essentially we turned the defense of the estate over to the pre-teens. Now they fall asleep too.

Our traditions are not over. Before she passed away, Marty's mom, Tommye, always made brisket on the 4th, smoking it up the day before and bringing it for dinner the next evening. Marty and Nancy bought a small smoker to be able to carry on the tradition, and Nancy has her mother-in-law Tommye's BBQ sauce recipe. This year, Erik and Patrick got the brisket duty, smoking three huge slabs of beef yesterday. Both of them take such a responsibility seriously, and you could see them, heads together, talking quietly about the correct and reverent technique of smoking meats. Erik is a perfect partner for Patrick, because he can actually voice philosophy where brisket and tri-tips are concerned, fashioning a personal relationship with the slabs that almost produces tears when people utter compliments to the chefs.

And lastly there are Patrick's Pyrotechnics, now assuming the form of institution. The weather has been questionable all day, with hot sunshine most of the time, the skies clouding up and threatening rain in the afternoon. The wind was blowing hard by dinner time, and Patrick wasn't at all sure that he could set off his charges with strong gusts blowing directly at the house. Around 9:00 the town's considerable fireworks started in the distance, but our field was quiet. It was killing Patrick, who regards this annual display as one of the highlights of his year, as it is ours. Finally he consented to go and fire a couple of trial rockets, which arched high into the sky, exploded, sending a wave of smoke over the roof of the house. But no embers survived to landfall and it was deemed by Marty to be safe. Patrick then put on a sensational show. Several times there were half a dozen explosions at once, with the sky above us completely filled with colorful blossoms. By now the folks in the valley are used to the Plaskett farm fireworks and several cars were parked on the road near the farm. One flashed its lights in thanks when the show was over.

It was only the next morning, when we were leaving to go home and drove past the "launching pad" for Patrick's show, that we could get an idea of the complexity of his efforts. There in a mowed area of crested wheat are dozens of big square boxes that once contained explosives. All we see during the show are Eric's and Patrick's lights walking around in the darkness, and of course the result, shooting gloriously into the sky.

Tuesday, July 5

The day after the 4th is usually hell on the highway going over Donner Summit, as the Reno and Tahoe revelers try to head home to the Bay Area. We left Eureka before 8:00, hoping to hit the summit around noon, before the rush starts, but today there was no rush. There wasn't a single slowdown until we reached Roseville, almost in Sacramento. We figured that maybe most people had to be back to work today, or possibly the economy and $4 gas gallons deterred some. Whatever the reason, it was a pleasant ride, at least as pleasant as seven hours in a car can be, especially with Mary and her tender rear end and Annie beginning the process of early pregnancy queasiness.

It occurs to me that one of the best things about this weekend was that Mary is almost back to normal. She was by no means the center of attention, except with the folks in Eureka who hadn't seen her in a while, but for the most part, she was her natural, normal self in all of the family proceedings, "puttering" in the kitchen, bent seriously over her traditional jigsaw puzzle, lounging out back with a gin and tonic or margarita, reading one of the dozen books she brought. It is great not to concentrate solely on her health situation, and I think she finds it nice to be back, almost, to normal. I'm not sure if I was expecting to see this again, certainly not as quickly as it has happened, although nine months ago, we set the Eureka 4th of July as Mary's projected "Coming Out Party." I think it will actually be her 70th birthday, August 2, when we can finally say, "Done!" to all of her travails.

Wednesday, July 6

Forty-eight years of marriage! That's incredible. I can't say "Where has the time gone?" because there are so many wonderful things crammed into those forty-eight years, and it does feel like a very full lifetime. We have raised two beautiful daughters, been gifted with two loving and loveable grandchildren, now suddenly grown to three, with yet another on the way. We have had a successful business in American Field Studies and Golden Gate Tours. We have visited probably eighty countries and have hundreds of memorable friends all over the world. Life has been so good for Mary and me, two young kids in Berkeley, who never had much of a vision of where that life would take us. I always used to kid Mary, when we were in some exotic or famous place.

"Mare, in your wildest dreams, did you ever for a minute expect that you would be walking down an Athens street in the shadow of the Parthenon? Or walking on the Great Wall, or watching a blue-footed booby on the nest in Galapagos?"

Always she would roll her eyes and her answer would be the same.

"I never expected anything."

And I guess I didn't either, never expected anything, but always was excited by whatever turned up. And Lord knows, a great deal has turned up in these forty-eight years.

There have been times when I forgot that July 6 sometimes falls over the weekend of the 4th and I have been stuck in Eureka without an anniversary present. I got in the habit of keeping a stock of Mary-presents—Beanie Babies, carolers, nativity sets, red-white-and-blue whatevers—in my trunk just for such occasions. It is advice I freely give to all guys. But this year, I have a whole day to get something, so naturally I headed for David M. Bryant in Walnut Creek which has a fine inventory of useless glass by Waterford, Baccarat, Lalique, and such. They always make hearts and syrupy stuff that are perfect for anniversaries. I am, at heart, a heart person. Just ask Kasey, to whom I give a heart fashioned out of stone or glass nearly every time I see her. And Annie too is a fellow hearter. Flowers always work, too.

I tried to reserve a bunch of wine country restaurants only to find them all booked solid, so I decided on a nostalgia trip—dinner at the Claremont Hotel with a nice view of the Bay. It was perfect. Mary used to live just a couple of blocks away, and the Claremont was an institution for us growing up. As a young boy I used to sneak in there with my friends and spend the day coming down their spiral fire escape slides, until they heard us and poured a bucket of water down to stop us from sliding. The Claremont was also valuable as our source of tennis balls, because their tennis club members consistently hit balls over the fences and we only had to scour the junipers to get a dozen new balls. Over the years, the hotel, which is of the same vintage as the Del Coronado in San Diego, the Mountain View and the Balsams in New Hampshire and others around the East Coast, experienced a roller coaster ride of success, almost decaying into bankruptcy more than once. We found the restaurant to be outstanding, with good service and fine food. It was a very fine evening.

Saturday, July 9

Nancy arrives this evening with the Eureka High basketball team and a few others. The boys are going to a basketball camp in Lincoln on the other side of Sacramento. There will be seven boys in all, five of them bunked in our living room, where blow-up mattresses cover the rugs. The two youngest boys, Gage and Chase, are in the TV room. Cher, mother of Gage and Andrew, is upstairs with Nancy.

They didn't get to our house until almost 8:00, and we had a barbecue waiting for them with Erik in charge. Then, in something that isn't even conceivable in Eureka, we all walked next door to swim in the Adair's backyard pool.

Sunday, July 10

Baseball today! Nancy bought a block of tickets for the Giants-Mets game, a game that begins at 5:05 because it is the national Game of the Week on ESPN. It is no easy thing to get tickets these days, now that the Giants have won the World Series. Every game this year has been sold out and they are reaping the benefits of success. Parking around the park is now $20 - $40. Food prices are through the roof, but it doesn't intimidate the fans who dutifully line up to pay $10 for garlic fries, $9.50 for a small beer, and $165 for a Buster Posey uniform top. $90 secured a ticket in the last section of the second deck behind the foul pole in left field, actually good seats to watch the game, but hardly what anyone could call an intimate look at the nation's pastime. No, today was a good lesson in the rule that in sports success is expensive. And nobody, even in an economy of increasing unemployment, seems to care.

It was fun to watch the Eureka boys enjoy the scene at AT&T Park. For at least one of them, this was the first venture to California, and it must have been a little scary.

Mary made it through the whole game with no problem, dutifully remarking on the batter's count, the pitch speed, and who struck out or walked. The soreness from the radiation seems to be easing a bit and she was able to sit for almost three hours and then walk the four or five blocks back to the car. I think it was a good decision to opt out of Nancy's morning activity. She took the boys to Alcatraz, leaving fairly early this morning. Even the young guys were dead tired by the time we got home. There was little conversation along the bank of sleeping bags in the living room tonight.

Tomorrow morning everyone gets up around 6:00 a.m. to pack and leave for their basketball camp in Rocklin.

Friday, July 15

The last radiation treatment! Thirty-four radiation treatments started seven weeks ago. Except for the inconvenience of having to drive into Pleasant Hill every weekday, the treatments themselves have gone fairly well, with few drastic side effects. Her skin got pretty tough and leathery and black around the incision; she had a few days of fatigue which only occurred in the evenings and one day she was nauseous. Nothing like the chemo. The Epic Care Center is as good a place to be treated as we have ever seen, the same good-natured and happy service in the radiation section as Mary received in the chemo section. The folks there welcome you by name, are always upbeat and very professional. We could not have stumbled on a better place.

More than a year has gone by since she began the examinations that have led her through serious cancer, with a detour for colon problems. It seems like longer in some respects, but at other times it seems like it just started. Of course, I'm not the one who has had to endure the pain, ache, nausea, uncertainty, or despair. It has been a very long grind for Mary, one that has been made considerably easier in many respects by the love and attention given to her by her greater family.

On Monday, we meet with Dr. Shoba to see what comes next, if anything. I consider that to be Mary's "Freedom Day," when she is told that for the present she is cancer free. Of course, then she can start thinking about getting her colostomy reversed.

Today is also special because it is the beginning of the 50th Reunion of my college class. Imagine, fifty years since we got out of St. Mary's College! I can't imagine it. How could the time fly by so fast? Half a century! I think there were only about a hundred or so members of my graduating class. Half of them will be at George's house tonight for a special BBQ. Clyde Figone will bring his smoker to cook the meat, and we will all tell tales that have grown considerably over the years. The fact is however, that in 1957-61, St. Mary's was an all boys school of about 350, plopped out in the country a good fifteen miles from any sort of civilization. We did have some great stories because there was nothing for us to do but sit around and plot some pretty bizarre activities. I think we were the last of the "happy day" classes; college actually became serious sometime after we left. How could we possibly be serious when tuition was only $440 a semester? After us, college started becoming expensive, which is probably why

St. Mary's decided to introduce girls to the student body. Today the women outnumber the men, and the college isn't nearly as interesting as back when we were roaming the Moraga hills.

One of the nice things about our class is that most of us are still married to our original wives, so we will know everyone at a party like tonight. Most of us married high school or college sweethearts and the marriages have held. Of the forty-five guys here tonight, only two have been divorced, a remarkable statistic in today's world. Most of us are nearing 50th anniversaries in the next couple of years. Mary and I, at 48 years, were among the last of our crowd to get married. Tomorrow all of us will gather again at the college for a Mass in the chapel and dinner following. But the real reunion is tonight, because none of us think that the college is the same place today that we knew fifty years ago.

Monday, July 18

Mary gets her blood work done this morning and Lily at Epic Center also flushed out her port, which they have to do about once a month when it is not being used frequently. After that we had a consultation with Dr. Shoba to see what comes next. The last PET scan showed no tumors so, while Shoba didn't say it today, Mary is cancer free. I got the feeling that it was considered bad luck or something to say that before a couple of scans showed no new tumors. But Shoba is thrilled with the way Mary has responded to everything that has been thrown her way. She is more like a friend now than just a doctor.

So here we are—without anything to do until September! It seems like it is almost an anticlimax. Suddenly there are no doctors' appointments, no chemo, no radiation, no blood tests. There is nothing to do but go home and sit around and figure out what to do with ourselves. At least this week, I think Mary has to relax and do nothing. The radiation, which builds in your body, causes quite a bit of fatigue, and I think she has to take it easy and let her body come back to normal.

Friday, July 29

Mary had a follow-up appointment with Dr. Chao today and received a clean bill of health. She is now free from all doctors until early in September so she has a full month to let her body relax and begin to come back to normal. All treatment is now on hold until after the next PET scan in early September. Of course we hope that the scan reveals nothing new and she can settle in on a three-month cycle of cancer-free living. Next week, we will contact Dr. McGuinness to start thinking about reversing her colostomy. I think that once that is removed, she will be able to declare herself free and clear of everything. Her travails have thus far stretched out more than a year. The dry mouth and weight loss actually goes back to April or May of last year, but the genuine concern and testing started after our July 4 time in Eureka with the family.

August

Tuesday, August 2

It is Mary's birthday today! Not just an ordinary birthday, today is #70! That's a major landmark for anyone, and particularly important for her since the past year has been about as traumatic as any in her life. It has been a year of wrenching pain and spirit-lifting joy, a year of fear and hope, of tragedy and triumph, of gain and loss. Through it all, Mary has emerged as an inspiration to everyone she knows, most especially to us in her family. Through it all she has persevered without complaint, her sagging physical strength buoyed by her incredible resolution and acceptance. Her illnesses have brought her family together as a solid unit around her, and her triumph is ours as well. When we first learned that she had cancer, the family's spirits plummeted, but they have been gradually lifted. Our confidence in each other and in the medical profession has become part of our being. At no time during her long ordeal did Mary ever voice the slightest doubt that today would arrive. She accepted her condition without the tiniest hint of a complaint, calmly accepting whatever she was told with a trust that is difficult to believe but uplifting to observe. For her, it is enough that the doctors in whom she placed her trust have done their job with great skill. She has been supported by an incredible network of love and affection, and those who gifted her with their support can also claim their vital role in her cure. Life is not always this distinct, but in Mary's mind, it is clear as a bell. Doctors and medicine worked their magic with Mary, and her family can also claim a major part in the final triumph.

Postscript

February 13, 2012

Emma was born today!

She is a perfect baby. Of course. But no, really, she *is* perfect. She has a perfectly round face, unblemished by the friction and trauma of birth canal passage. She has perfectly long fingers and toes, properly blueish when contrasted with her pink face. She is perfectly verbal, with a fine yell that sounds like music rather than complaint. When she cries, her little face brightens like a rosy sunrise, her thin tongue massages the air outside and her eyes close so that all of her concentration is focused on the sound.

Emma was born this morning at 8:19 at John Muir Hospital in Walnut Creek. Because she refused to unbreech, the doctor performed a C-section, saving Annie the discomfort and pain of natural labor, and allowing all of us to be ready to greet her when she was presented to the outside world. The sound of that presentation alerted us in the family waiting room when Annie pushed the lullaby button as she exited the delivery room, announcing to the hospital that a new soul was entering our world. They paraded down the hall, Annie pushed on her gurney, Erik, a bundle of pride and released emotion, pushing his wondrous daughter in a glass-sided bassinette. Nancy, Mary and I constituted Emma's first appreciative audience. It won't be her last!

What a miracle is tiny Emma, a miracle that occurs every time a child is fashioned from the love of her parents. But Emma may be a greater miracle because she has been so anticipated, so much hoped for. Since she was a pre-teen, Annie wanted to be a mother, so much was she drawn to the little ones around her. As a child, she was always the caretaker of her smaller cousins, and they were always drawn to her. Even as a teenager, she could always be found at family gatherings in the room with the little kids, usually opting for them rather than her peers or the old folks. She became a natural teacher in her first job. And she never lost the vision that some day she would have children of her own.

And now she has Emma!

I have watched Annie since the day she was born, because she herself was a miracle to us, coming nearly ten years after Nancy, and almost as an unexpected gift. But I have watched her especially over the past nine months, an easy thing to do because she lived with the glow of life in her. From the day, on Fathers' Day, that she announced she was pregnant, I never once saw her down in the dumps, or upset in any way. Two nights ago I asked Erik if she was ever cranky, during the long months of preparation and growth. He said she didn't have a glum time since she found out she was pregnant. She has filled her world with joy. I am so proud of her.

She was a marvel to watch as her baby grew, constantly consulting her repertoire of websites to announce the current status of Emma's growth, from a sesame seed to a pumpkin. That little girl traveled the route of seed to grape to plum to banana to winter melon to eggplant to pumpkin. Annie and Erik didn't want to know the sex, so Anne joyously accepted the experiment of every old wife who happened to have a tale or scheme to arrive at the sex of her child. She consulted Chinese proverbs, dangled wedding rings and needles over her stomach. She asked herself dozens of questions: Do I look pregnant from behind? Is my skin smoother? Do I crave sugar or salt? Do I have a high belly bump? Amy Damele, who according to Nancy is always right, gave her the ring test and declared the baby to be a boy. But she issued a disclaimer that perhaps she did the test too early. I gave her my test: It's either going to be a girl or a boy—50% accuracy rate with a standard deviation of 5%.

About the 35th week, Annie's doctor informed her that the baby was in breech position. Of course she went to the Internet, discovering a bewildering array of schemes to make the baby flip. She stuck clothes pins on her little toes. She searched for a moxa stick of incense to use to heat up the acupuncture point on her little toe in a process called moxibustion. She drank orange juice while lying on her side with her knees propped up. She even crawled down the stairs in her house on all fours. Unfortunately, she didn't have a pool where she could stand on her head for a while. And she decided that lying head down on an ironing board that was slanted off the couch to the floor was a physical impossibility.

No, Annie wrang every ounce of maternal joy out of her pregnancy, reveling in her growing girth, thrilled with each new stage of development. Like a boastful prize fighter that thrusts his chest out to the world, Annie thrust her stomach out with pride and told her world that she was ready to become a mother. She could not have been more beautiful.

And Erik did just as well, as far as that is possible for us guys who only offer life but don't carry it. He has been in wonderment since he realized he would be a father again. This morning, clad in translucent hospital white, he lunged into our waiting room gushing tears of joy.

"It is a girl, her name is Emma Jane, she is 8 pounds 6 ounces, 18 inches long. Anne and she are perfect!"

And he is right. Does life ever get any better than it was this morning? Mary would say it couldn't possibly be better.

Mary and Emma

T0895326

THE
DISAPPEARANCE
OF HARRY DAVIS

T.N. DAVEY

iUNIVERSE, INC.
NEW YORK   BLOOMINGTON

The Disappearance of Harry Davis

Copyright © 2009

All rights reserved. No part of this book may be used or reproduced by any means, graphic, electronic, or mechanical, including photocopying, recording, taping or by any information storage retrieval system without the written permission of the publisher except in the case of brief quotations embodied in critical articles and reviews.

This is a work of fiction. All of the characters, names, incidents, organizations, and dialogue in this novel are either the products of the author's imagination or are used fictitiously.

iUniverse books may be ordered through booksellers or by contacting:

iUniverse
1663 Liberty Drive
Bloomington, IN 47403
www.iuniverse.com
1-800-Authors (1-800-288-4677)

Because of the dynamic nature of the Internet, any Web addresses or links contained in this book may have changed since publication and may no longer be valid. The views expressed in this work are solely those of the author and do not necessarily reflect the views of the publisher, and the publisher hereby disclaims any responsibility for them.

ISBN: 978-1-4401-2405-1 (pbk)
ISBN: 978-1-4401-2406-8 (ebk)

Printed in the United States of America

iUniverse rev. date: 3/10/2009

For R.C.

who was an important part of this story

as of all the rest

To see what is in front of one's nose needs a constant struggle.

George Orwell

The annals of the Central Intelligence Agency are filled with folly and misfortune....

Tim Weiner

Legacy of Ashes

PRELUDE

As usual when such matters were to be addressed, the meeting was held in a conference room in the basement of the White House. Ordinarily the group convened at 4 p.m., but that day, owing to the conflicting schedules of the officials involved, it was set for 7. A regulation 30 minutes before that time a uniformed guard, tall, trim and smartly outfitted in starched white shirt with military shoulder straps, coal black tie, charcoal gray woolen trousers and brightly shining black patent leather shoes took up position at the doorway. A .38 caliber pistol was strapped tightly to his right hip. In his left hand he held a clipboard to which was attached a computer printout list of the attendees.

The list was short but long in titles: the Deputy National Security Adviser, the Central Intelligence Agency's Deputy Director for Operations, the Senior Deputy Assistant Secretary of Defense for International Security Affairs (substituting for the Assistant Secretary), the State Department Assistant Secretary for Intelligence, a Deputy Assistant Secretary of State for Africa (substituting for the Assistant Secretary), and the National Security Officer for Africa. Senior level bureaucrats gut nobody with a name widely known to the public. These six were the only participants that evening for a gathering once known as the Forty Committee, now re-christened the National Security Planning Group, names intended to obscure the nature of its business.

First to arrive, at three minutes before the appointed hour, was the Senior Deputy Assistant Secretary of Defense, the participant with the least interest in the matter. A retired three star admiral, upon seeing himself alone in the room, he ostentatiously checked his watch and muttered a complaint about civilian inattention to punctuality. As if to answer, he was joined promptly by the National Security Officer for Africa, an eager young man in his early thirties who had done some small service in helping win Tennessee for the president and was now on a two year leave of absence from his job as assistant professor of political science at the state university. But for his thinning hair he could easily have been mistaken for a college freshman.

Then came the two State Department representatives, both career Foreign Service Officers in their early fifties and both dressed in charcoal gray suits, white shirts and conservative ties. They had ridden over together from State. Having been unable to meet earlier, they had conferred in route about the business to be transacted, full well knowing that discussing a covert operation in the back seat of a car, even an official car and even in whispers, was a violation of security.

At ten minutes after the hour, the Deputy National Security Adviser, a former Marine lieutenant colonel whose ambition to become National Security Advisor was widely broadcast, entered with the flourish he thought befitted his role as host and presiding officer. He proceeded to shake hands all around the table, greeting all by their first names, though in the case of the admiral – to whom in other circumstances he would have owed deference – the familiarity cost him a certain effort. He had been told by his staff assistant that attendance was complete. When he realized that the CIA's representative had not yet arrived he made no effort to hide his annoyance.

"Anyone heard the story about the spook who had himself driven to Dulles and took a plane to Paris when he was scheduled to be at a meeting at the White House? Nobody ever knew whether it was absent mindedness or clever subterfuge."

The sally drew polite chuckles from all but the National Security Officer for Africa, who laughed his appreciation loudly.

"Maybe we'll just have to decide this issue without the Agency. On its merits, shall we say?"

The Deputy Director for Operations arrived well before this threat, which in any event all knew to be empty, could be carried out. The DDO was one of the CIA's "old boys." He came to the Agency in the early days when it recruited almost exclusively from ivy league universities. He disdained he dress code that called for senior bureaucrats to outfit themselves in suits. Double breasted blue blazers, blue and white striped shirts and polka dot ties were his trademark. In his New England high establishment accent he set out the details of the proposed operation, the means to be employed, the dollar cost figure, the duration and the goal to be achieved.

"Let me add," he said gravely in closing his presentation, "that the Director considers this a very important operation. The previous administration was derelict in its duty in failing to use the very effective weapon of covert action against a regime so clearly communist in nature and so closely allied with the Soviet Union. He is sure that no one in a position of responsibility in this administration would wish to see that mistake repeated."

There was a moment of silence as the others digested these ominous words. None of those present needed be told that the Director of Central Intelligence was a powerful figure. He had played a key role in the president's electoral victory, and he was a long time friend and advisor of the president's. He was, moreover, a man used to having his way, ruthless if need be. He had more than enough influence to block any appointment, including that of the next National Security Adviser.

Not in his most rash moment would the Deputy National Security Adviser have thought of putting himself at cross purposes with the Director of Central Intelligence, even had he considered the proposed operation a disaster waiting to happen. In this case, however, he felt no need to. He agreed wholeheartedly with the Director and the Agency and went one further in his view of the previous administration's inaction: it was tantamount to treason. His thoughts on the matter were summed up in the briefing paper his staff had prepared for the meeting. The target regime was "a clear threat to United States national security interests. It rules a country that is strategically located, cutting across possible wartime lines of U.S. military communications. It borders on and threatens to infect with the communist virus three countries governed by friends of the United States."

If pressed, the Deputy National Security Adviser might have acknowledged that the proposed operation hardly seemed to have the potential, which the Agency claimed for it, to bring down the target regime. But that mattered little. What was important was to do something.

The two State Department representatives had long had reservations about the operation. Each in his own capacity had employed the various subterfuges of bureaucracy to delay its being brought up for decision. They viewed it, in State Department speak, as unlikely to achieve any significant purpose and at worst capable of creating a variety of complications – or more plainly, as dumb. They would have liked to kill the operation outright. In theory State could do that, but given the politics of the issue they would need the full backing of the Secretary of State. The Secretary was a reasonable man. He would almost certainly have agreed with their view, if they had had the opportunity to present it to him. They had not, however, had that opportunity, and being realists they knew it to be very unlikely that they could expect it. The Secretary of State had no time for minor matters. He was the administration's chief fire marshal, and as blazes broke out across the globe his attention shifted from one alarm to the next. And even he had to exercise a certain caution in his relations with the powerful Director of Central Intelligence. Unless his representatives were prepared to forecast a major disaster they stood no chance of getting his backing. That they assuredly would not do, for it would seem a rash judgment and tarnish long and carefully cultivated reputations for balance. People who offered rash judgments did not get ahead at State.

But that was not the whole of it. Both men were angling for ambassadorial appointments. The Assistant Secretary for Intelligence was at the top of the list for ambassador to a major NATO ally, a plum that only rarely fell to a career officer. The Deputy Assistant Secretary for Africa had been in Washington for six years, had a son and daughter in college and desperately needed a posting abroad to pay the bills. He was slated for an important African embassy. It would do neither of them any good to incur the displeasure of the Director of Central Intelligence, who in any case would have his way in this particular matter.

For all these reasons – the career ones left unspoken – they had agreed between themselves that they would not oppose the operation in this meeting called for its final approval. Instead they would put questions they hoped would show up its flaws, in the aim of gaining a further delay, or barring that, of winning mitigating concessions.

"You haven't discussed the risks," the Assistant Secretary for Intelligence objected. " How are you going to run this operation in a city that is so heavily policed, with the Soviet and East German services backing up the locals at every turn?"

The DDO was not about to be drawn into offering a serious response to such a puerile question. How the Agency ran its operations was not the business of State or anyone else. He knew the wimps at State were not comfortable with the operation, and he knew they would back off rather than risk crossing the Director. He savored the opportunity to lecture them a bit.

"There are always risks," he said, cracking a sardonic half smile. "If we are going to be deterred by risk, we would never run any operation. Without risk there can be no gain. Our boys are trained to handle risk. In any case, this is a situation that warrants risk. Do you really want to say there is nothing we can do to make it tough on this tin horn commie dictator, that it's too dangerous?"

The National Security Officer for Africa had written his doctoral thesis on Soviet efforts to penetrate third world regimes. That, he considered, gave him more than sufficient standing to intervene in the discussion and, not coincidentally, to score points with his boss and with the Agency.

"If we don't stop this regime now," he interjected breathlessly, "we'll find ourselves confronted with communist subversion all over Africa. Whatever the risks, I regard this operation as essential."

The Defense Department representative had not planned to take sides in this debate, but these remarks struck him as too foolish to let pass unchallenged. Defense had long ago written off this renegade African regime. It mattered not a hoot to those who ruled the Pentagon what shenanigans the CIA wanted to try to oust it. But the admiral had spent most of his career in naval intelligence. He was one of the few people in or out of government who knew the secret history of the Agency's many fiascos. He had come to regard the CIA as amateurish, bungling and not infrequently more dangerous to the national security of the United States than to any foreign government. He himself, alone of those in the room, had no further career aspirations. Three star admiral was quite all he needed in life. They could fire him if they wished. He could make a lot more money on the outside than in government.

"May I suggest," he boomed in a mellifluous southern drawl, "that we not let ourselves be carried way by considerations of ideology. I have heard nothing so far that would persuade me that this operation has the potential to cause any serious damage to the target regime. If successful, at best it might become a minor annoyance. At worst it could become a serious embarrassment to our government."

"Then perhaps, admiral," said the DDO, "I should explain it again, so that you may better understand it. But first, may I ask if you have instructions from the Secretary of Defense to oppose it?"

"Sir, I do not. Defense takes no position in this matter. I assume, however, that does not bar me from expressing a personal opinion."

"You may be assured that your personal views have been noted," the DDO added acidly, "for whatever they are worth."

It cost the Deputy National Security Adviser some effort to disguise the satisfaction he felt in seeing a much too outspoken admiral put so neatly in his place. But it was time to close. There were only a few minutes left for him to change into formal evening dress for the president's dinner for the King of Thailand. Being late for an official function was a sure way of putting oneself in the bad books of the first lady. Under no circumstances did he wish to risk it.

"Let's sum up. I cast my vote with the Agency. Defense takes no position, which I gather means it interposes no objection. Where does State stand?"

The Assistant Secretary of State for Intelligence had built his career on a clever ability to avoid giving direct answers to unwelcome questions. By force of exercise over three decades in the bureaucracy of diplomacy this had become an ingrained habit. A straight yes or no was out of the question.

"We have an important substantive issue we want to raise. We think it very important to be assured that the operation will be confined to the distribution of anti-regime propaganda and the organization of opposition cells, and that no arms of any sort be provided."

The Deputy National Security Adviser turned to the CIA representative. "Farnsworth, what do you say to that?"

"State drives a hard bargain, but the Agency can live with that."

"Then we are agreed. Unless I hear a nay from the State side, the operation is approved. I'll see that a finding is issued."

In the official car that carried them back to their offices, the two State Department officials congratulated themselves on having won an important concession which, they assured one another, amply justified their role in the matter.

The Deputy Director for Operations whistled a tune all the way back to Langley. Not only had he accomplished what the Director had sent him to do but he had given away nothing in the process. The plan that he presented had no provision for the supply of arms. It covered only the initial stage of the operation. The Agency had a draft operational plan for the second stage in which opposition cells, once set up and solidly established, would be supplied the necessary means to pass to armed resistance. But that would be for another meeting. There was no need to talk about it now.

ONE

Even years later, when over and over again he tried to fit the pieces together to make sense of what had happened to him, Harry Davis would recall that early December evening in the African city at seven thousand feet altitude only a few hundred miles shy of the equator. He would recall how in winter the sun plunged beyond the horizon on the hour promptly at 6 p.m. and darkness followed with the speed of a curtain dropping on a stage. And he could still feel the chill of the forty degree cold that as night fell descended upon the city with almost equal suddenness.

On that particular evening, which both was and was not the beginning of his story, Davis left his house at seven for his appointment. By then it was pitch black. There was no moon, and the lights of the night sky – the planets and stars that seen from great altitude blaze like neon – were obscured by a thick smog, the product of the tens of thousands of brushwood and charcoal fires that erupted throughout the city to cook the meager dinners and warm the hovels of the great mass of the poor. The nearly two million who lived in the teeming slums where open sewers ran down the middle of the streets and children with untended sores wandered aimlessly about.

Because Harry Davis thought of himself as short – though at 5 feet 7 inches he could qualify for medium height – he liked to turn up the high collar of the trench coat he customarily wore for such wintertime evening appointments. It made him look taller, he thought, but it also had the virtue of obscuring his face from side view. All that could be seen were a few unruly strands of hair shooting out of the pale top of an otherwise balding head. He preferred this to the alternative, his latex mask. The mask gave him the smooth dark skin and the aquiline features of the people one saw in the offices and on the city streets. It was artfully done. It had been made to measure for Davis, in a laboratory somewhere in Germany by master craftsmen. No expense had been spared in its execution. Davis thought of it as a condom. Sometimes he had to wear it for protection, but he never enjoyed it. It took away all pleasure.

There was a reason for dispensing with the mask that evening. If Davis were going to be driving around the city making dead drops or pick-ups – Hawke, his boss,

considered the city, with its chaotic jumble of infrequently and dimly lit streets, ideal for dead drops – the
mask would have been useful, practically mandatory.
But that was not what Harry Davis set out to do on that
particular evening.

Davis fumbled in the dark to fit the key into the ignition of the 1960s model Volkswagen beetle he drove
on such occasions. By the early 1980s small Japanese
cars were more and more seen around the city. But
the beetle's durability and the scarcity of foreign ex-
change to buy even cheap Japanese imports made it
still the most common vehicle on the road and therefore the least likely to be noticed. That at least was
what the green eyeshade boys back in Langley were
forever telling the station – as though in Langley they
knew exactly what traffic looked like in this city seven
thousand miles distant. The problem with the beetle
was that it was old, very old. Its vital parts, its motor,
transmission and brakes, were in no better shape than
its battered exterior. Barely a month earlier it stalled
on him, luckily just as he was headed into the parking lot at the International Hotel. Langley now had
"under consideration" the Station's urgent request for
an upgrade. In some things the Agency could act with
lightning speed, but in others its bureaucracy was on
a par with that, say, of the Labor Department.

Davis checked his watch as he headed out onto the
airport road, in the direction of the city center. He
was not expected at his appointment for another half

hour, but he would need time to cruise around the city a while, to make sure he wasn't being tailed. Traffic was hardly ever anything but light in this paradise of African socialism. But as he passed the Indian ambassador's residence Davis had to slow for a line of cars, mostly ambassadorial limousines flying their national flags, that edged into the front gate for a reception. Davis spotted Ambassador Herbert Dawson's armored Lincoln Continental inching forward toward the gate. Davis was not much for irony, but he congratulated whoever it was who had the bright idea of sending out to sport the American flag abroad a car that two years earlier had been confiscated from a New Orleans drug lord.

Sticking to the main arteries, Davis turned left onto Roosevelt Avenue, officially renamed Lenin Road a few years back though hardly anyone called it that. As he did, he saw that the headlights of another car followed his turn some distance back. The headlights stayed behind Davis but moved in closer. Now he could see it was a black Mercedes with two figures in the front seat. A knot tightened in Davis's stomach. Never in the months that he had been running the operation had he been so brazenly tailed. There had been times earlier when he suspected he was being followed, but none in which he could be sure he wasn't simply imagining things.

That evening's meeting was important. The last one had to be cancelled when the host's father died and a new meeting place couldn't be quickly found. So Davis hadn't sat down with the group for several weeks and Langley and Hawke were impatient for a first hand progress report. Davis slowed the vehicle to see if the Mercedes would pass, but it stayed some fifteen yards behind, moving now at the exact same pace as the beetle, as though pulled along behind by an invisible tow line.

If that's what the bastards were going to do, Davis thought, he would do them one better. He threw the transmission into second gear and pressed the accelerator to the floorboard. For what seemed a very long moment the engine rattled as though it was about to break apart but nothing happened. Then the beetle shot forward, so suddenly that Davis had trouble controlling it. At that moment a tall figure wrapped in a dirty white blanket emerged from the smog into the full glare of the car's headlights. The man swayed drunkenly, obviously unaware that Davis was bearing down on him. There was no time to brake or even to calculate. Davis jerked the car left into the oncoming traffic lane, only to find himself directly in the path of a very large truck that was moving very fast down upon him.

At that instant, when it seemed that he would die, needlessly, senselessly, stupidly, Harry Davis felt no fear. It was only moments later, after the beetle and the truck had somehow scraped past one another, avoiding by inches a collision Davis knew not how, that he found himself shaking, his body drenched in sweat and his hands gripping the steering wheel so tightly that it took an effort to free one to wipe his face.

The Mercedes was gone now from Davis' rear view mirror but another car had taken its place, a dark Peugeot, in its front seat two men who might have been twins of those in the Mercedes. Obviously there was going to be no way to shake this tail. He would have to abort the mission. Hawke would be furious and Langley probably even more so, but there was nothing to be done about it. As for the people he was to meet with, if he didn't arrive by eight they would know something was amiss and would disperse.

Davis felt the urgent need of a drink. He guided the beetle around to the International Hotel. The Peugeot followed him all the way. As he pulled into the parking lot it circled past and Davis managed a mock friendly smile and a wave to its two unsmiling occupants. He headed for the cocktail lounge, wondering whether they would follow him there and whether he might just offer to buy them a drink. They didn't, and when Davis emerged some two hours later, in a happy glow now but not too drunk to drive (he seldom was), there was no sign of the Peugeot or of the two men, or of anyone watching him.

*   *   *

Black velvet curtains, half an inch thick, were drawn tight across the windows of the office of Randolph

H. Hawke III in the south wing of the chancery. No natural light entered. The room was brightly lit by two overhead racks of florescent tubes. The door to the office was half open. Harry Davis stood there a moment, hesitating before knocking gently, three times, to signal his presence.

Hawke didn't look up. He was seated behind his desk, his head bent over the Monday morning cable traffic which, as usual, was stacked several inches high.

"Got a minute," Davis asked as he took a seat in the left of the three regulation imitation leather government armchairs that faced Hawke's desk.

"Yeah," Hawke answered, still looking under a pink cover sheet stamped SECRET/CODEWORD, "but hold on a second. Maybe you can help me with this. Who or what the fuck is REDHAND?"

"REDHAND is the code name we've given one of the people I was supposed to meet with last night."

"That's what I thought but it doesn't make any sense."

Davis shrugged. Unless Hawke let him see the cable, which Hawke made no move to do, there was nothing more he could offer.

Hawke put the cable aside.

"You were supposed to meet with? You mean he didn't make the meeting?"

"No. I'm the one that didn't make the meeting. I was tailed. I had to break off."

Davis expected an explosion, but Hawke replied quietly, with a question that seemed to reflect only incidental curiosity.

"Did you get a good look at the tail?"

"Yeah, better than I wanted. They came right up close. There were two of them. The first was a Mercedes, the second a Peugeot. Each with two guys in the front seat. Looked like thugs. They stuck to me like glue. The first one tailed me a couple of miles, then the Peugeot came on. I led them around to the International Hotel like I was headed there anyway and I went in for a drink. They were gone when I came out."

Davis didn't mention his attempt to elude the tail and his near accident. Trying to break away from a tail, in the way he did it, invariably ended up in a chase and often in an accident, was generally futile and always gave you away. Unless done to avoid capture it was against regulations.

"Harry, are you sure it was a tail, not some guys out to rob a foreigner?"

"You know this country better than I do, Randy. Crime like everything else is a government monopoly. The private sector criminal has gone the way of the small businessman. The few still around don't drive Mercedes or Peugeots."

"So what's your assessment," Hawke asked.

"Things are getting dicey, Randy. I don't like the looks of it. This was the first time I've been followed, and it was brazen. It was more than a tail. It was a statement, maybe even a warning. They're saying loud and clear that they're on to the operation, they're closing in and they're going to shut us down."

A wonder it hadn't happened earlier, Davis thought. Not that he considered that a few people in the dead of night dropping leaflets or sticking them on walls were a great threat to the regime. Hawke's favorite was the one with the picture of the Great Leader, as he was called, with a snarl on his face, looking like a crazed animal. For sure it was a retouch job done in an Agency lab; the regime would never have allowed such a thing to be published. It had a red circle around it and a thick red line drawn diagonally through the man's face, like a no smoking sign. It was laughable, but dictators didn't like to be laughed at. According to the high level source whose existence and identity were the station's most closely guarded secret – even Davis wasn't supposed to know who it was, though he did – it made the Leader boil. And if something angered the Leader it was a sure bet his security services would attend to it.

"So what do you propose?"

"We need to lie low for a while. Let things cool down. I'll drop a signal to the group to shut down until further notice."

Hawke's features tightened and a hard edge came into his voice.

"Hey, aren't we getting a little ahead of ourselves. Let's not jump to conclusions, just because you think you were tailed this one time. This operation is the most important thing we have going here. I don't need to tell you that, do I Harry? The Director considers it our top priority. Besides, we've got the commie bastard on the run now. This is no time to get cold feet. Just a little more and we'll have him. All we need to do is shake the tree for the fruit to fall right into our laps."

Hawke had been saying that for months now. Davis was tempted to tell him he was deluding himself, but he didn't have the nerve to do it.

Hawke tilted his leather cushioned swivel armchair back and rested his right foot on a drawer opened at the bottom of his desk. He now assumed an earnest, almost pleading tone.

"Harry, maybe you're being too cautious. Think about it. Why not make one more try? If you're tailed again, you can break off. If not, keep your appointment. See what your guys think. We can decide after that."

Harry Davis was thirty-six. He had been with the Agency for eight years and had the better part of his career ahead of him. It was what he wanted to do. The new Director had made it very plain that what he prized above all else in his men was toughness, daring and the readiness to take risks. Getting tagged as cautious was, these days, likely to get you sent back to Langley to some job shuffling papers, if not worse.

"Alright, I'll try it."

No sooner had Davis said it than he regretted it, but there was no taking it back.

"Harry, are you sure you want to keep on this job? I know it's a tough one. Maybe you should try something less demanding for a while. I can get Al to fill in for you while you get some rest. How about it?"

Davis felt betrayed. He had agreed to do what Hawke asked, even though it was against his better judgment. Now Hawke was rubbing his nose in it.

"Look, all I wanted to do was let you know there are some real danger signals out there. I'd be derelict if I didn't, wouldn't I? I know the job's important. Anyway, this isn't a time to change case officers. I've got the group's confidence. I'm close to them and they trust me. So let's leave it at that."

Hawke was pleased. It was just what he wanted to hear. He liked Davis but sometimes wondered if he hadn't made a mistake in assigning him to this particular operation. You had to be tough for it. Hawke wasn't altogether sure Davis was tough enough. But for now he was ready to set aside his doubts.

"Okay," Hawke said. "Good man. Go at it."

        *   *   *

Harry Davis told himself it was the cold that made him shiver as once again he wedged himself into the driver's seat of the beetle. After all, it was now less than a week away from Christmas. Davis checked his watch, turned the key in the ignition and let the motor idle for longer than was needed. Then hesitantly, slowly, he backed the car into the street and headed off into the smog and darkness.

TWO

The spacious, expensively appointed lobby of the downtown Washington, DC hotel that Ambassador Herbert Dawson had checked into late the previous evening was garlanded with yards upon yards of evergreen trimmings tied with thick red nylon ribbons. Pots of blood red poinsettias were crowded onto the floor in no particular order, like an unruly gathering of children. To one side stood a twenty foot high Christmas tree decorated with huge imitation pine cones.

Dawson strode briskly through this garish display of seasonal spirit – too garish for his taste – across the lobby toward the finely polished brass doors leading out onto Connecticut Avenue. As he neared the doors he caught his reflection in one of the glass panels. Good height, pleasing (would he say handsome?) face, no sagging jowls or other sharply recognizable signs of deterioration, still reasonably trim, ageing, if at all, elegantly, comfortably, no matter the thinning hair. A man very much in command of his world, or so it seemed.

It was a flattering snapshot and Dawson took comfort from it, for he was keenly aware that the decade of forty-five to fifty-five was a dangerous one. Up to forty-five, almost everyone he knew (he didn't count the women, he meant the men) had looked better with the years, still young but with a few gray hairs more distinguished. It was after forty-five that the decay set in, not for everybody, but for many. There were classmates of his who had grown fat and bald, whose features had changed so much, had become gross and distorted, that he would hardly have recognized them had he not seen them in intervening years. A few had died. Out of his entering Foreign Service class of twenty-seven, four were gone already. One of a heart attack, another of what was politely called a liver ailment, another dead in a crash on a mountain road in Peru, and one in a suicide.

Dawson had survived to his mid fifties pretty much intact. He congratulated himself again, but uneasily, for he was too much a realist to ignore the fact that the pleasing reflection he had just glimpsed was only partly true. And he knew it meant only that the worst was yet to come.

Stepping into the street, Dawson drew a cashmere scarf, a gift of years earlier from his former and now late wife, closely around his collar and tucked its two ends inside his midnight blue lamb's wool overcoat. A misty gray cold fitting for a late December morning enveloped the capital of The Greatest Nation on Earth. The air, sharp and bracing, lifted his spirits.

Taxi, sir?" a doorman called out solicitously as Dawson crossed onto the sidewalk. The man was short, heavyset and graying. Dawson noted that they seemed about the same age. He wondered what this man had done with his life, or what his life had done with him, to end up like that, fetching taxis at a hotel door.

Dawson waved a no, thanks. He had decided to walk to the State Department, partly because he felt the need for exercise after fifteen hours spent sitting in airplanes the previous day, partly to save the taxi fare (he was, now and then, frugal), and partly to see how the city had changed during his two years abroad. In the past when he had returned from overseas postings he had been struck by the city's dynamism and its growing prosperity. The expensive shops along Connecticut Avenue, the new office buildings going up along K and I streets, the renovations and construction in the George Washington University district. Where once a decrepit old pile had stood there would be a vast hole in the ground. A teeming construction crew, so far down in the hole that from the street they looked like ants, would be busily at work laying the foundations for a gleaming new structure.

Now there were plenty of gleaming new structures. A few actually showed architectural flair. But from first exposure to the capital city's richest thoroughfare it was obvious to Dawson that history had taken an unexpected turn. The third world had infiltrated here into the very heart of the first world and seemed poised to take it over. It was only 9:30 but already street vendors – Africans, Middle Easterners, Asians – were setting up their stalls, laying out cheap costume jewelry, fake name brand watches, imitation leather briefcases and handbags, phony silk ties in cellophane wrappers, scarves, umbrellas that would rip apart at the first hefty gust of wind, sweat shirts, you name it. Street vendors, a little Dakar, in the center of town, just three blocks from the White House.

The thought of it appalled Dawson but did not prevent him from stopping in front of a display of watches. He picked a large gold Rolex from the table.

"How much?" he asked the vendor, a tough looking dark haired man with a thick beard who from his appearance and his dress might have been transported unaltered from a stall in the Kabul souk.

"Thirty-five dool-lars," came the guttural reply.

"Fantastic bargain. Up the block they go for five thousand." Dawson motioned to a jewelry store he had passed on his way out of the hotel.

The man did not appreciate irony. He looked dourly at Dawson. "Here better," he replied.

If I wanted to spend a few minutes haggling, Dawson thought, I could have it for twenty-five. But then what would he do with it. Give it to his son who was in school over at Georgetown University? Better not, he thought. It looked enough like the genuine article to get the boy mugged, even killed.

Dawson headed down the avenue to K street through a crowd of well dressed, prosperous looking citizenry, late arrivals for work or early shoppers. At the entrance to the metro station at Connecticut and K two ragged, miserable looking black men were panhandling people getting on and off the escalators. Off to one side a young woman sat on the sidewalk, a faded torn blanket, draped around her. She leaned against the wall of a high rental office building and cradled a baby on her lap. In front of her lay and open shoe box that showed a scattering of small change. Beside her a large strip of brown cardboard announced, in magic marker, I AM HOMELES PLESE HELP ME.

It would have troubled Dawson, but it would not have surprised or particularly shocked him, had the woman been black. But she was not. She was white, and the baby, whether hers or not, was white. A white woman with a baby, begging at the intersection of two of the richest streets in the country, within view of plush mahogany paneled offices of lawyers who charged $400 and up an hour and lobbyists who could rake in a cool million and complain that it had not been a good year.

That appalled Dawson. It was something he had never before seen and had never expected to see. He dropped a five dollar bill in the shoebox and the woman cried out a blessing on him. Whether he would have been equally generous had the woman been black he did not stop to reflect. He hurried across Connecticut Avenue as the light was changing and made his way west down K street between a row of sidewalk vendors' stands to his left and offices and shops on his right – an airline office that advertised Caribbean vacations, a store that sold expensive men's shoes, and several fancy women's shops. At the corner of 18th and K he dodged a dangerous looking young black panhandler, crossed and walked up 18th toward I street. At the entrance, literally next to the door, of the International Club, where congressmen, ambassadors and the elite of Washington's legal and lobbying professions congregate to consume expensive lunches charged to someone else's tax exempt expense account sat an unshaven young white man. Hunched over inside a dirty, torn army greatcoat, he balanced in front of him a crudely lettered sign announcing "I AM HUNGRY."

Dawson had exhausted his charity. He moved quickly on.

After that the coast cleared. He was able to cover the three blocks to 21st street and then another five down through the George Washington University district to Virginia Avenue, perhaps a whole quarter of a mile, without once being accosted by a panhandler or even spotting a derelict sleeping in an entrance way.

Relief ended at the corner of 21st and Virginia. Dawson had remembered the triangle formed by the intersection of 21st street, Virginia Avenue and E street as a pleasant little park of well kept lawn, shrubs and trees. Now it screamed neglect. Styrofoam cups and plates, broken plastic knives and spoons, empty soda cans, sandwich wrappers, old newspapers, strips of toilet paper and a profusion of refuse so degraded as to be unidentifiable were scattered among weeds and wildly overgrown bushes. Four unshaven men in filthy tattered clothing warmed themselves over a yard wide roaring hot air vent. All this not thirty yards from the nerve center of the Free World, the Department of State. One among them, an elderly white man with craggy features and long dirty white matted hair, was laid out flat across the vent, face up and eyes shut tight. A man amazingly like the figure of Uncle Sam in World War II recruitment posters; he even had a clump of straggly white whiskers descending from his chin. Cleaned up and re-outfitted, he would have made a fine model for the national incarnation. Except that in his present wretched condition he was perhaps an equally apt metaphor for the direction in which the country seemed headed.

To one side stood two rusted supermarket shopping carts filled to overflowing with what might have been debris from a trash heap but more likely were the sum total of someone's worldly possessions.

The sight of these four men made Ambassador Herbert Dawson acutely uncomfortable. Asked why, he would no doubt have said that it was because of the fortune that people in New York were making in mergers and takeovers, and in Washington in lobbying, since the new president took office. Even his own salary had risen by more than forty percent over the past year. Dawson would have accounted for his unease by the simple feeling of shame that so many others were being left behind. He would not have wanted to acknowledge that fear that he too could find himself plunged into such misery, such disgrace, could have anything at all to do with it. The idea itself was preposterous. The idea that The Honorable Herbert Dawson, with the security of his career employment rights, backed up by a comfortable assured pension, by his bank and brokerage accounts, by the house he owned free and clear of mortgage in fashionable Chevy Chase, Maryland, and the other one in Italy's lake district, could ever find himself in genuine want simply defied reason and logic. Yet there it lurked, somewhere in the murky recesses of his subconscious, a primal terror of a reality whose outlines he could only vaguely imagine.

Dawson looked away and hurried past. He decided it would be worth the money to take a taxi back to his hotel at the end of the day.

The building across the street toward which he was now rapidly striding was undistinguished except for its size. Its plain concrete and glass exterior looked like that of any other dour 1960s Washington office complex, but it was larger, much larger, than the ordinary. It squatted eight stories high over two full city blocks. Every weekday morning year round some three thousand earnest beavers, the male majority of them attired in standard coat and tie uniform, streamed through its portals and would make their way to their offices, cells of varying size and distinction that defined with absolute precision the place of the occupant within a rigidly structured hierarchy. So rigidly structured that any variation from the norm immediately drew attention. Dawson recalled the case of two office directors responsible for neighboring groups of countries who fell into a bitter feud over a second armchair that one of them had somehow managed to acquire for his office. The other insisted that he too should rate a second armchair, or failing that, that his colleague should be reduced to one. The movers arrived one afternoon to cart the extra armchair off to a warehouse. The loser felt the loss in his flesh. He never again spoke to the victor, and he celebrated the day his antagonist perished in an airplane crash.

A colleague once called the State Department a fudge factory. He didn't mean candy. It was the other kind of fudge he was talking about. It came in words, many spoken and vanished into air but many more printed and shoveled out in immense quantities of paper. In pyramid like progression, each day millions of minute electronic signals sent from embassies and consulates across the globe were transmitted into millions of words, which became tens of thousands of telegrams, which after digestion by an army of analysts and mid level managers would be reborn as thousands of memoranda. The telegrams and memoranda were distributed to be read, scanned or ignored. A fortunate few were chosen to be tucked away in files; the rest were bundled off to the shredder. Like some hungry animal, the Department of State each day ingested tons of raw paper which it then spewed out into a diarrhea of tiny shredded feces.

Once Dawson had looked upon the building with awe. To be a young man fresh out of middle America and to be a part of this place from which the world was run, where the great decisions that shaped the second half of the twentieth century were made (or so he imagined) had been pure exhilaration. Dawson had thrown himself into his career body and soul, had lived and breathed it, waking and sleeping, twenty four hours a day, for more years than he liked to remember. In that time he had travelled to a great many places, some of them utterly exotic; he would never forget the moment the mists of Darjeeling suddenly opened to reveal before him, as though within reach, the Kanchingjonga, the majestic snow clad mountain of Sikkim. He had been witness to a few of the great scenes of the century's history. He had been in the auditorium of the United Nations General Assembly when Nikita Khruschev, the ruler of the Soviet Union, suddenly took off his shoe and banged in on the desk in front of him in protest. He had been on duty in the State Department's executive secretariat on the night first word came in that the Berlin wall was going up. He had been Lyndon Johnson's interpreter when he visited Lebanon in the summer of 1963, had accompanied Henry Kissinger on his first visit to Syria and had listened, in mild disbelief, as Kissinger pompously declared "It is my destiny that has brought me to this place." He had been at Camp David for the Middle East peace negotiations and at the White House when Jimmy Carter brought Anwar Sadat and Menachem Begin together for their famed handshake. Through it all he had been one of those whom the television cameras caught inadvertently, for a fraction of a second, who appeared in newspaper pictures as the back of a head, half an anonymous face, a possibly identifiable shoulder or arm somewhere in the neighborhood of a secretary of state or a visiting dignitary. And he had gloried in it. In his scrapbook he had invitations to White House receptions and dinners from three presidents.

Ultimately, however, there had come a time of disillusionment, the product of too many compromises and small betrayals of principle accepted in the name of personal advancement, of a feeling that his life had been spent too much in striving to be something and not enough in trying to do something, of having surpassed his superiors and achieved his goals only to see himself in turn surpassed by his own subordinates. But which coincided with a thickening of the waist, the humiliating appearance of a small paunch that would prove resistant even to the wonders of a highly touted and ruinously expensive exercise machine, the alarming retreat of a hairline, the slow but inexorable shrinkage of a physical vigor that once had seemed inexhaustible, all signposts of approaching mortality that could be ignored for only so long.

Dawson had arrived at the Department's diplomatic entrance, its lobby broad as half a football field, with a ceiling three stories high hung with flags of some 150 nations. A mere two decades earlier, it had been possible to move through it unfettered and unchallenged. By the early 1980s that freedom was gone. The lobby's shiny marble floor was cluttered with the paraphernalia of the early Age of Security. Moveable steel frame barriers prettied up with false wood panel fronting, metal detectors that screeched if you tried to carry your house keys through with you, and the obligatory x-ray machine for looking inside your briefcase. And guards, guards everywhere, all very black and very big, decked out in blue police officers uniforms with side arms. Looking both somewhat fierce and very bored.

"Where your chain?"

Dawson had been caught in transgression. He should have been wearing his identification card from a chain around his neck. This was the latest, and the most humiliating, edict of the administrative types who now ruled the Department. It applied to everyone except the secretary of state and the deputy secretary. At their posts ambassadors might be little gods, but in Washington they were mere mortals.

"What do you mean?" Dawson knew exactly what the guard meant.

"You don have no chain?" The guard frowned now, bestirring himself, emerging from his somnolence. "Lemme see your card 'gin. Everybody 'posed to be wearin a chain."

"I've just come from abroad."

The explanation seemed to satisfy the guard. He dug his hand into a box on the desk next to him and pulled out a thin strand of aluminum beads. "Okay, now you got one. Next time you be wearin it."

Dawson took this rebuke and headed off toward the east bank of elevators where, once out of the guard's sight, he deposited the chain in a trash can.

Two of the four elevators were out of working order. The administrative types were very efficient when it came to running people but they couldn't keep the elevators running. While Dawson waited for one to come a small crowd gathered, a cross section of the Department at that time of day: two very plain looking secretaries carrying trays of coffee in large Styrofoam cups alongside heavily sugared soggy donuts; a trim neatly dressed young man, evidently a junior officer, holding a suit and two shirts encased in plastic wrap that he had just retrieved from the dry cleaner in the basement; an electrician in overalls, long hair falling rebelliously down to his shoulders, with an assortment of pliers, cutters and screwdrivers dangling from his belt; a short bald man with a paunch and a soft face whose polyester jacket and badly adjusted knit tie marked him as someone from the research branch; a tall distinguished looking gray haired man who wore a finely tailored double breasted suit and dark tie and who Dawson thought he recognized but was uncertain whether to greet; and two foreign diplomats, Asians of some variety, labeled with visitors tags.

After stops at the third and fourth floors the elevator deposited Dawson at the fifth along with the two Asians. Dawson turned left out of it and proceeded down a corridor painted blue on one side and white on the other. Each corridor announced a different color, a scheme ordained by a secretary of state of an earlier decade who on the only occasion in four years in which he left his office unaccompanied got lost finding his way through the buildings nondescript arteries.

Along the corridor a short dark woman of indistinct age was guiding a buffer back and forth across the hallway's cream colored vinyl floor tiles. It was a common sight. The State Department seemed to have an enormous budget for polishing corridor floor tiles. The woman was bringing them to such a brilliant shine that Dawson could actually see his reflection move down the hall with him.

Dawson pushed through a door marked CONFERENCE ROOM.

The meeting to which he had been summoned from seven thousand miles distant was already in session. Three rectangular tables were set together in the middle of the room. Around them were two rows of chairs, comfortably padded high backed swivel armchairs at tableside for the executive set, and uncomfortable metal folding chairs in back for the flunkies. Dawson recognized most of the occupants of the armchairs, ambassadors to a dozen countries and as many senior Washington officials, from State, Defense, the CIA and the NSC. Only a few of the faces of those in back, desk officers and similar minor officialdom, were familiar.

Dawson made his way down the room and slipped into one of the armchairs. The assistant secretary for Africa, an academic who had come in as a political appointee with the new administration, was speaking in a softly aggressive voice. He held a cigarette in his left hand while discoursing contemptuously about the policies of the previous administration.

"We are not going to make those mistakes," the assistant secretary intoned. "It has to be understood that in this administration issues are going to be viewed not just in a regional framework. Our approach will be global. The big picture is the one that counts, and I don't want any of you to forget it. That's the context in which issues are going to be decided from now on. Another point of our policy that I want to stress is that this administration knows who America's friends are and is going to stand by them. We are going to show the world that there is a lot to be gained by being the friend of the United States and a lot to lose by being our enemy or antagonist. We are not going to make it easy on those who oppose us. I want that to be clear to all of you."

Dawson was well aware that the new administration was infested by people who saw the world in black and white, polarized between friend and foe, devoid of subtle shades. The only wonder of it was that there seemed so many of them. In whose woodwork had they been hiding all these years when America had seemed one of the few sane places on the face of the earth. Obviously his time overseas had made him lose touch with the country.

But it was clear to all, even to the two dowdy looking young female junior officers seated on the folding chairs to the rear, what the assistant secretary meant when he trashed regionalism and hailed globalism. Regionalism was, approximately, the view on which the previous administration had based most of its policy decisions. It stood for judging what one should do by what was happening in the region itself, something that to the uninitiated might seem merely common sense. Globalism was code for the crusade against communism, for the Cold War. The regionalist was a small minded individual too dense to know friend from foe. The globalist grasped the Big Picture.

The assistant secretary's eyes lit up and a look of near ecstasy superimposed itself upon his cold features as he continued. He spoke excitedly.

"It's time we flexed our muscles, and we are going to be in a position to do it. With defense spending at the levels projected in the president's budget requests over the next few years, by the middle of the decade we'll be in a position to fight two and one-half wars simultaneously! The other good news, which all of you already know, is that the chains have been taken off the Agency. It's free now to do the job it was intended to do. It goes without saying that I expect all my ambassadors to give it their full support. Anyone who doesn't isn't doing his job. We're not going to sit back and let the Soviets run roughshod over us any more or the non-aligned beat us over the head, in the

UN or anywhere else. We're going to hit back hard. A government that votes for a resolution that attacks us is going to find out….."

It went on and on in this vein. Just to listen to it tired Dawson. His attention drifted to Sally, to her funeral in Paris two months earlier that he had not attended. Not that he truly blamed her for what she did. He recognized that in his own single minded pursuit of career he had neglected her and the children year after year. It took two decades but finally she left. For six weeks he heard nothing from her, then a letter from Paris advising coldly that she was living with her French boyfriend from her college junior year abroad over twenty years earlier. "The true love of my life," she called her Frenchman. She had wanted to marry him in the 1950s, but in the 1950s sons of the French haute bourgeoisie married for social connections and money. They didn't do rash things like marry more or less indigent Americans. But even in France things changed. Sally finally got him, though for hardly more than a year and not in marriage. She died of a rapidly spreading cancer just as the divorce proceedings drew to a close. Dawson hadn't quite known whether to call himself divorced or a widower.

The assistant secretary had sat down. Benchley Barder III, the ambassador to a neighboring country, was now speaking. Ben Barder was tall and angular, with a big shock of hair – which Dawson noted was now a deep dark brown, after having been turning to gray a few years earlier – brushed up in the pompadour style of the 1950s. His face was skeletal. Imprinted upon it, as though to offset the macabre impression it created, was a perpetual half smirk. He was picking up on the themes the assistant secretary had just enunciated, so crudely that it was almost embarrassing.

"Now in Mosala, that is where we face the test. We have no better friend on the entire African continent than President Aslama. He is with us one hundred percent. But I have to say, with regret, that the question in his mind – and he put it to me very candidly when I met him before returning for this conference – is whether we are with him one hundred percent. He is not asking a lot. A twenty-five million dollar increase in our military assistance program for the current fiscal year would assure his army the weapons he needs to face down the communist threat. It would show him, and it would show the rest of the world, clearly where we stand. It would show that it pays to be our friend, not our enemy."

Dawson had known Barder for at least twenty years. He had known him from the beginning as the ultimate careerist, the black belt of careerists in an organization where careerists abounded. In Barder's life there was virtually no activity that was not meant to advance his career or to assert his will over someone. For in government, where money could be no more than a marginal consideration, what it was ultimately all about was power. Earlier Barder had been known as a writer of flattering notes to superiors and peers he thought could help his advancement. Even Dawson had once upon a time received one of Ben's saccharine missives.

Benchley Barder could spout the official line on any issue you could think of. He was the ardent defender of whatever the administration then in office chose to say or do and an acerbic critic of past administrations. Better than anyone Dawson could think of he knew how to move with the times. In the previous administration he had been an ever so slightly left of center liberal. Now he was a solidly right of center conservative. He had made the transition with such naturalness, like an animal changing color with the season, that it hardly seemed fair to object.

But truth to tell, what Barder had done was unusual only in degree. From the moment it became evident that the former president was not going to be re-elected, a massive shifting of political ground had got underway among the senior officers of the career service - for the juniors it was not so important to be precisely attuned to the new administration. Those who declined to shift, or who wanted to shift but had the ill luck to become too much identified with the previous administration's policies, had either left the service or been sent off to the equivalent of Siberian exile, to jobs well below their rank and ability. Dawson too had shifted, just enough to avoid standing out. But nobody, absolutely nobody, had made the shift more perfectly, with greater aplomb, and with greater disregard for principle, than Benchley Barder.

Barder had finished speaking. The morning session was about to close. The assistant secretary asked if there were questions. A hand went up at the back of the room.

"It's about what Ambassador Barder just said." The speaker was a woman, short, dark haired, perhaps in her late thirties. She wore a fuchsia blouse and a dark blue skirt and was attractive and just a bit sultry behind lightly tinted glasses. Her voice betrayed a shade of nervousness, but she was obviously determined to make her point.

"Now if we increase military assistance to President Aslama by twenty-five million dollars, that will bring the fiscal year total to over one hundred and fifty million. The question is, why is it truly needed? Even the one hundred and twenty-eight million we are giving now isn't being used mainly for defense against the threat of external aggression that he claims to see. It's being used to put down internal dissent."

A dozen heads on the front row turned and focused a collective glare of disapproval on the woman. "Who is that?" someone asked in a whisper.

Whoever she was, she continued, undeterred.

"There have been reports of very large numbers of arrests in Mosala in recent months. I'd like to ask

Ambassador Barder, how many political prisoners are there currently, and what about the stories of torture and killing of political prisoners? Unless I'm mistaken, this is becoming a really serious problem."

Barder had been lounging in his chair, relaxing after his presentation. He pulled himself up, pushed his chin out and cleared his throat.

"Madam, you are indeed mistaken."

A gale of laughter swept the room. The woman turned crimson and sat down, a look of confusion on her face.

Barder grimaced, put on his best tough look and brought a fist down hard on the table. No upstart female from the Bureau of Human Rights, for that was where Barder supposed she must be from, was going to challenge him and get away with it.

"These reports are greatly exaggerated. The president has personally assured me that there are no more than a half dozen political prisoners, er, I mean detainees. They are people who have been caught trying to overthrow the government. Let me ask, are we supposed to tell our friend President Aslama that he cannot defend himself against people who go around trying to overthrow his government? What kind of sense does it make? And all these stories about torture and killing! It's nonsense! We know where they come from, and we know what their purpose is. It's to drive a wedge between us and a government that is our friend, our true and loyal friend, a government that is on our side in the struggle for the preservation of freedom. A government whose friendship we need."

Here it comes, Dawson thought, Barder's ultimate trump card, The Base. A wonder Ben hadn't brought it up earlier.

"I hardly need point out how important the naval and air facilities in Mosala are to our global defense strategy. In making them available to us President Aslama has put himself at considerable risk. He is attacked for it by Moscow and by every communist pinko or crypto communist across the African continent. There is even some criticism at home." Here Barder halted, then resumed anxious to reassure. "But it's not much, its not serious, and it won't be serious as long as people see that their president is getting something from us for his country. That's what it's important to understand."

The mention of the base nearly brought the Defense Department representatives to their feet. There were two of them, an Air Force major general, resplendent in his sky blue medal bedecked uniform, and a strident fresh faced young deputy assistant secretary come to government out of the Heritage Foundation and who, like the NSC officer for Africa, looked barely of age to be served a drink in a bar. The deputy assistant secretary immediately took the floor. He expatiated so passionately and at such length on the vital importance of the bases – "more than vital," he called them – that the group was half an hour late in breaking for lunch.

THREE

As the group rose to go to lunch Dawson approached Barder.

"Congratulations, that was a great performance."

Barder blinked. "You thought so?" Praise from Dawson was to be greeted with suspicion. Barder had a fear of being mocked.

"Masterful. You really put that woman in her place. But you know, I think maybe she does have a point. Maybe we are being just a little simplistic when we...."

Barder could see that it was going to be another of Dawson's snide criticisms of administration policy. He didn't intend to be caught even listening to it.

"Excuse me," he said with deliberate sententiousness, " but I've got to have a word with Dick."

Dick was the assistant secretary. Barder always referred to the top officials of the Department by their first names. The secretary of state was Allen, the deputy secretary Hal, and the undersecretaries were Clayton, George, Mike and Ron. Except of course when Barder was in their presence.

A buffet lunch was served the conferees – those who sat in the front row in the armchairs – in the Department's exclusive eighth floor dining room, which offered distinctly mediocre food but a fine view of the mall, the Lincoln memorial and the Potomac even on this gray overcast day. Nobody talked about issues. Dawson was seated next to another ambassador, a political appointee, a dentist from Indiana in his early forties who was earning his title in one of the countries of Africa that was then suffering a severe drought and famine.

"Ya know, there's nutin t'eat there," the man complained as he cut off a very large piece of baked ham, piled mashed potatoes onto it and shoveled it all into his mouth. "An egg, one tiny little egg, costs a dollar. Can ya believe it! A dollar for an egg practically the size of a pebble! A chicken is twenty dollars, and boy, just try eatin it. Like chewing leather." To emphasize his point he waved his fork in the air, unaware that in doing so he had deposited a blob of gravy onto his tie.

Dawson looked at his politically minted colleague. He was bursting out of his shirt. A fold of fat hung over his collar and a little further down he looked eight months pregnant. He was at least fifty pounds overweight. Obviously food was coming from somewhere.

"So what do you do?"

"Yeah, well, ya know, we bring it in. We gotta great commissary, the best in all Africa, I bet. All the big brand names, just like here in the States. Our Christmas turkeys arrived a month ago. Flew 'em in from Frankfurt in deep freeze. Lemme tell ya bout my admin officer. That guy, he's a miracle worker. He can get anything done. The other day we had this problem with the filtering system in my swimming pool. The pool hadda be drained and there wasn't nuff water in the god damn reservoir to fill it up again. An my wife, she was bout to have a heart attack, cause she had a diplomatic wives luncheon planned the next day at poolside. So what kindda poolside luncheon do ya have round the side of an empty pool? The admin officer, he's a real savy guy, on a Sunday morning he rounds up three tank loads of water and fills the pool right up."

"I thought you had a drought."

"Yeah, well, ya know, for a price ya can always get it somewhere."

The man winked and grinned broadly, displaying a mouthful of the worst teeth Dawson had seen on anybody outside the Third World. Dawson wondered if this political ambassador missed his former profession. Prudently, he decided not to ask.

"Terrific. Sounds like your admin officer should get an award."

"Yeah, ya bet he should. An believe me, he will."

Dawson wondered where in the embassy's budget the administrative officer had hidden the payment for the three tanks of water. They must have cost an arm and a leg on a Sunday morning in a country with a drought. And he wondered what the people of Adeleh thought of this specimen of an American Ambassador Extraordinary and Plenipotentiary. The man was said to have given $50,000 to the president's election campaign. If it was in fact that much he had not got his money's worth with Adeleh, for it decidedly was not a pleasant place. Other administrations had brought in political appointees, but never so many as the current one, and seldom of such abysmal quality.

The meeting resumed at three. Dawson was the last scheduled speaker. He was careful to strike the proper note of belligerence toward Moscow and its principal African surrogate, the government to which he was accredited, which he full well understood to be in high disfavor with the current administration. Having thus covered himself, he felt confident in proceeding to his central point.

"On the matter raised this morning by Ben of increasing our military aid to President Aslama, of course I'm not able myself to offer an opinion on just how serious the human rights objections are." Dawson noted that the woman in the fuchsia blouse, obviously pleased by this none to subtle re-opening of the issue, was smiling warmly at him.

"But there's another problem I can comment on," he continued, "and that is the likelihood of aggression against President Aslama's government. I don't for a moment doubt that the so-called Great Leader would like to get rid of our friend Aslama. But he's fighting a civil war in the north and has too many other problems on his platter. He doesn't have the means to invade anybody and the Soviets are complaining already that he's costing them too much. As things stand, they show no inclination to expand their military aid to him. But if we step up our weapons deliveries to Aslama they may feel obliged to match us and possibly go one further. The result could be another war between the two countries. And if that happens," Dawson turned toward the two Defense Department representatives and spoke directly to them, "our bases could be put in jeopardy. We might have to step in to defend them."

That would cool Defense's ardor, cool it very fast. The last thing the Pentagon wanted, Dawson knew, was to have to put troops on the ground in the middle of a fight between two Third World neighbors. He concluded his remarks with a request for restraint and sat down, reasonably well satisfied that if he had not demolished Ben Barder's arguments he had at least damaged them. He looked at the woman in the fuchsia blouse and saw that she was looking, and again smiling warmly, at him.

Barder's hand was in the air even before Dawson finished. As he began to speak a note made its way down Dawson's side of the table.

"Ambassador Dawson," it read, "please come to the Operations Center. You have an urgent secure phone call from your embassy."

It was 5 pm in Washington, midnight there. What could they possibly be calling about at midnight? Dawson nodded an apology to the assistant secretary and made his way out of the room and down the hall to a door marked "Stairwell." He took the fire stairs two at a time up to the seventh floor, arriving slightly winded. At the entrance to the Operations Center he produced his identification card for the guard on duty in the outer office and signed in. A low clatter of teletype machines, six of them, ejecting long white tongues of paper, greeted him as he entered the spacious high ceilinged room. A large electronic map of the world pulsated on the far wall. Above it were a dozen clocks set to the hour of the major capitals. Dawson's wasn't important enough to be included among them, but he noted that in Moscow it was a few seconds before 1:10 am.

The Operations Center ran a kind of 911 service for the State Department. It was supposed to be the first to receive word of a crisis overseas and to alert those in Washington who should respond to it. It ran twenty-four hours a day but came into its own mainly at night and on weekends. A call from the Op Center with news of a coup, an attack on an American embassy or consulate, or the kidnapping of a US ambassador somewhere in Africa, Asia or Latin America would bring an office director, sometimes even an assistant secretary, barreling in from the Maryland or Virginia suburbs at 2 o'clock on a Sunday morning. At that moment, however, the regular work day hadn't quite finished, so things were quiet. The senior watch officer had his feet propped on his desk and was talking on the telephone in a way that suggested the conversation had nothing of business to it. One of his assistants was reading a newspaper and another was going unhurriedly through a stack of incoming telegrams.

A young black secretary with straight set hair led Dawson to an adjacent cubicle whose only furnishings were a metal frame chair, a narrow Formica desk and a very large and heavy looking green phone. The green phone was the secure line. It scrambled the speakers words before sending them bolting skyward toward a satellite emplaced somewhere over the south Atlantic. Anyone listening in heard only a babble of unintelligible noise. A similar device unscrambled the word when they came down at their destination. Except that the technology was new and did not always work as intended. Sometimes the words came out on the two ends as unintelligible as they had been rendered in the middle, or so faint as to be inaudible.

Dawson picked up the receiver.

"You have a call from your deputy chief of mission, Mr. Kooper," the Washington operator announced. "He is on the line. Go ahead."

The apparatus clicked, gurgled, emitted a series of duck-like squawks and fell silent.

The operator came back on the line. "We're having a little trouble, sir. I hope we can fix it without too much delay. Can you stay with us?"

"I'm here." Dawson imagined technicians laboring away furiously to make the blasted thing work, changing codes and pressing buttons on great banks of blinking electronic gear, somewhere out there in the bowels of a large building in the city's vast suburbs. A quarter of an hour elapsed, then twenty minutes. The machine returned to life.

"Boss, are you there?" It sounded like the voice of Dracula emerging from the tomb, but it had to be Kooper.

"Yes, Bill. Tell me what this is all about."

"I'm sorry to call you out of your meeting. I've got bad news."

Dawson was accustomed to this. Wim Kooper always prefaced his reports with a characterization of their nature – good news, bad news, not so good news, not so bad news.

"Let's have it."

"Harry Davis is missing. He went to meet with his group last night – I guess by now it was the night before last – and didn't come back. Hawke found out that the house was raided. At about noon yesterday Hawke got a telephone message from Davis saying he would make it back on his own later in the day, but so far he hasn't shown up."

"What happened to the others, to the group Davis was meeting with?"

"Hawke thinks they were arrested."

"So what is he going to do?"

"There's nothing he can do right now. He thinks Davis can handle it."

"What does that mean?"

"I'm not sure."

Dawson paused. There went his plans for Christmas dinner at his daughter's apartment in Bethesda, with her husband, and with his son.

"You don't need to come back right away," Kooper said, reading his thoughts. "We can manage for now. I just wanted you to know."

Solicitousness for the comfort of one's ambassador was a quality cultivated by all successful deputy chiefs of mission, but there were times when it was misplaced and this was one of them. With a member of his staff missing, and not just any ordinary one, it would hardly do for Ambassador Herbert Dawson to be sitting in Washington eating turkey and enjoying Christmas cheer. Maybe Davis would come walking in the door tomorrow morning. Maybe, but more likely not. Even if Davis was hiding somewhere, if they were looking for him, Dawson thought, there would be no way he could make it back. The city was simply too heavily policed, and a white foreigner stood out too clearly among the population not to be noticed. And if they had Davis, well, God knew what might happen.

"I'll be on the first flight out of here. I'll cable you my arrival time."

Dawson had a fleeting moment of regret. He realized it was less for the Christmas dinner that he would miss than for the attractive woman in the fuchsia blouse.

FOUR

The first person to suspect that Harry Davis was missing, perhaps surprisingly given the circumstances, was his wife.

Harry and Barbara Davis were a study in contrasts. Harry was relaxed and easy going, and his excess pounds made him look a bit soft. Barbara was perhaps only half an inch taller than her husband but she was wiry and taut, like a steel spring. One imagined her breaking bricks with the butt of her hand. When she and Harry were side by side, which rarely they were these days, she seemed to tower over him.

Harry smoked and drank, sometimes drank more than he knew he should. Barbara was hyperactive, with a cheerfulness that seemed more like a frenzy. She didn't smoke, and she took a drink only when she felt it was absolutely required. Even then she only pretended to drink, a touch of the lips to the glass, a very small sip at long intervals, the glass still nearly full when she left the party. It wasn't the taste of alcohol that put her off. It was simply that she felt it her duty to keep always alert and in condition. Because she had a mission.

These days when Harry didn't come home at night she only wondered if it was because something had happened to him. He spent the night out more and more often lately. He would explain these frequent absences by saying that he had not been able to get away before the government's midnight curfew and had slept over at the house of one of his people. Barbara no longer believed it, but she didn't argue with Harry or accuse him. She was pretty sure she knew were he was when he didn't return after an evening business appointment, but her pride forbade her to call there or even to complain afterwards.

Still, Harry's absence that night, which Barbara discovered only on waking early the next morning because they now kept separate bedrooms, worried her. She knew, as another officer's wife would not have known, just what assignment her husband had that evening. Another officer's wife would have been shut out from her husband's work, or at least should have been. The rule was hard and fast. An officer of the Central Intelligence Agency could not tell his wife about his work. She was allowed to know that he worked for the Agency – there had been a time when wives were not supposed to know even that much, but the prohibition was so ridiculous and so widely ignored that it was eventually rescinded – but that was all she was allowed to know. And even that much she had to keep carefully to herself, from parents, from friends, even from her own children until they reached an age at which they could be deemed mature enough to handle the information. A woman had not only to accommodate herself to his but to accept the fact that, because an officer's job required that he do a great deal of his work at night, her husband was going to be away many evenings. She had to be strong – or weak – enough to live with that and take it as the truth.

But Barbara Davis knew about Harry's assignment that evening. She knew about it for the simple reason that she too worked for the Agency. Harry's cover was his being the embassy's commercial attaché. Barbara's cover was Harry. She was notified to the Leader's government as the dependent wife of Harman Davis. On the diplomatic list issued by the foreign ministry she appeared alongside her husband without even a given name, simply as "Mrs. Davis." On the personnel rolls back home, at Agency headquarters, she was carried under her own name, Godziak, a good Polish name.

That morning after discovering that Harry hadn't come home, Barbara dressed and breakfasted even more hurriedly than usual. She knew, without ever articulating the thought, that only by getting to the embassy could she, just possibly, quell the anxiety that the discovery of Harry's absence caused her. Going to the embassy was a daily habit. Now suddenly it became a pressing necessity.

Barbara guided her Peugeot 404 sedan hurriedly but expertly – she was a better driver than Harry or most other men – through the city's anemic morning traffic, dexterously skirting potholes, passing under rickety wooden arches draped with sagging dirty white banners that commanded "Workers of the World Unite" and proclaimed (ludicrously, she thought, in this country where there was none) that "Heavy Industry is the Motor of Socialism" and "We Build Socialism for the Greater Good of Humanity." At the traffic light stop at Revolution Square she did not bother that morning to look left at the billboard likenesses of Marx, Engels and Lenin that towered above the square. The trinity, people called them, jokingly, father, son and holy ghost. They filled Barbara Davis with loathing when she looked at them.

When the light turned green she pressed the car into third gear to begin the long climb up the mountainside past the thirty food high cast iron statue of Lenin, a gift of the Leader's Soviet friends, past the stereotypically modern International Hotel, past seedy gray government office buildings, past the ornate palaces of the former ruler – a great friend of the West, he, and benevolent – now occupied by the current one, past the tottering abandoned national museum, condemned for some obscure architectural defect, its garden over-grown with weeds. Past the vast new Party congress hall that was being rushed to completion for the tenth anniversary of the revolution, with no expense spared. Past the university campus recently adorned with an imposing black marble bust of Karl Marx and where, in the library, a portrait of V.I. Lenin hung laconically alongside a bust of John Fitzgerald Kennedy.

Beyond the university the mountainside leveled off momentarily and the city began to peter out. To the right there came into view a stone wall, intimidating in its massive height, its evident thickness and its great length. Atop the wall stood, like sentinels with bayo-nets drawn, three double strands of barbed wire, and behind them, in second echelon defense, thick spools of concertina wire whose razor edges gleamed icily in the faint smoke filled morning light.

Barbara turned sharply into the gate that broke the wall approximately at its midpoint. She brought the Peugeot to a halt inches from the thick steel boom, pained a candy cane red and white, that blocked the entrance. A burly very black United States Marine, dressed in combat fatigues pressed to a razor crease, M-16 rifle slung over his shoulder and 45 caliber revolver at his hip, sauntered over to the car to greet her.

"Hi, Mrs. Davis." The Marine bent down and scru-tinized the underside of the vehicle. "You look clean there. Anything inside to declare this morning?"

The Marine guards had instructions to search the interior and the trunk of all vehicles coming into the compound, against the possibility of a bomb, in the case of embassy staff, presumably, one that might have been planted without the driver's knowledge. For Barbara Davis, however, there was no need to go to the trouble. She was that particular kind of person who impressed all as so wholly competent that her word was not to be doubted. And who, though a woman, was tough.

"No, Joe, I've already checked. There's just me, and I'm not very explosive this morning."

The Marine chuckled and gave a signal to two unarmed local guards in slack brown uniforms who stood by the weighted end of the boom looking, compared to the Marine, underfed and ethereal. With a great show of effort the two leaned heavily on it and the boom swung high into the air. The Marine awarded Barbara a glistening white toothed smile and waved her into the American embassy compound.

Outside, on the road she had just left, small wizened women who were perhaps thirty years old but looked every day of sixty plodded single file, zombie like, down the mountain through the gray morning light, each bent low under a pile of neatly packed and tightly bound brushwood half her height. They were headed for the open air market a hill and two miles beyond, to feed the city's insatiable appetite for fuel. Scruffy animals shuffled by, donkeys, mules and cattle, ridden or driven by a scrawny dark humanity wrapped against the morning cold in thick, stained, tattered cotton shrouds. The animals now and then halted to nibble at a bit of brown weed, or raised their tails to leave evidence of their passage in pungent steaming piles. A stream of ancient, lurching smoke belching trucks roared past. Neither humans nor animals paid them heed.

The instant it took Barbara Davis to cross inside the American embassy compound transported her into a world that might have been thousands of miles removed from the street she had just left. For anyone coming from outside, the meticulously groomed twenty acre spread was an hallucination of well kept buildings, of manicured green lawns dotted with profusions of flowers of the tropics and the temperate zone. There were blood red hibiscus, lavender wisteria and purple and orange bougainvillea, lilacs, red, white and yellow roses, pink geraniums, multi colored carnations, chrysanthemums, marguerites, marigolds, zinnias, cornflowers and languid blue irises.

The morning sun was just beginning to add a golden laminate to the compound. Inside this haven of quiet, cleanliness, order and unashamed prosperity, this fortress against the noise, the filth, the disorder, the disgusting odors and the poverty that reigned beyond the wall, everything smelled sweet. The compound's thick high walls seemed even to shut out the acrid morning smoke that lay so heavily over the rest of the city.

Soaring fat trunked eucalyptus trees shaded a circular driveway whose circumference the joggers among the embassy staff measured at a quarter of a mile. At the high end, a football field's remove from the gate but facing down toward it and dominating the whole like a temple dedicated to some god of antiquity stood the ambassador's residence, a majestic white structure whose ample twenty foot ceilinged reception rooms could accommodate several hundred guests. To one side, partly hidden from view by pine trees and flanked by magnificent hydrangeas and beds of yellow cannas, the embassy's two macadamized tennis courts and swimming pool were being swept clean of their nighttime debris by a local work crew. Below the tennis courts and the pool lay the chancery and various administrative buildings, ponderous gray stone structures that looked as though built to withstand heavy weapons assault.

Barbara Davis parked her car in its assigned slot and walked quickly up a neatly pebbled path bordered on each side by delicate pink and yellow daisies, past a gardener who popped up from his task of spading and pruning to give her a comic opera salute, to the chancery. As she came into range of the two video cameras affixed to the building's eaves her image appeared in stark black and white, stunted by the cameras' downward angle, on one of the three television screens in the cockpit, the bulletproof glass cage in the lobby that was manned twenty-four hours a day by one or another member of the embassy's Marine guard unit. The guard on duty that morning, a slender brown skinned young man who wore a corporal's stripes and who looked latino but was in fact American Indian, pressed a button that with a resounding click released the latch on the entry way door. As Barbara stepped inside the lobby, the Marine pressed a second button that set another click echoing through the foyer. With the agility of a ballet dancer, Barbara turned right, seized the handle of the four inch thick bomb and bullet proof steel door, heaved it open and proceeded down a corridor that smelled strongly of a fresh coat of government green paint.

Arriving at a second bomb and bullet proof door, she punched in an entry code at the box to one side, arm wrestled the door open and stepped into Hawke's outer office. There was no one there. Barbara picked up the first telephone that came to hand and dialed Harry's other office, the one in the suites on the opposite side of the Marine guard cockpit.

A secretary answered cheerily: "Mr. Davis is not in yet. May I have him call you?"

For a few minutes Barbara paced nervously. Then she sat down and drummed her fingers loudly against her attaché case. Yes, she thought, she and Harry were breaking up, and that was probably the best for both of them. But tough as she knew herself to be, it wasn't easy. And now that she was frankly worried about

Harry, she was almost ready to forgive him everything and wish they could make up.

Hawke arrived before she could carry the thought further. Hawke had no news of Harry either. So they walked back down the hall together, each thinking about Harry, Barbara anxious, Hawke annoyed, to the Marine guard station. There Hawke drew out the log kept by the guards who stood duty during the night. Together they scanned through the clumsy scrawl of handwritten entries.

Barbara finished first. "There's nothing there," she said bleakly. "He didn't call in."

Sometime between 10 and 11:30 the previous evening Davis should have gone to the International Hotel or one of the other bars frequented by the diplomatic set and called a message to the Marine guard on duty to confirm his safe return from his mission. Since all telephone calls into and out of the embassy were listened to by the Ministry of State Security – this was always assumed, but Hawke was proud to know it for a fact because he had a source in the department that did the monitoring – it was important that Harry's messages should be of a kind that plausibly might come into an American embassy during the night. Harry would alter his voice, a technique taught in the Agency's training program but that he had learned on his own much earlier. It was a thing for which he had a real talent. Sometimes he was a drunk Marine calling to invite his buddy on duty to come have a few drinks with him. Sometimes he was the girlfriend of one of the Marines, cooing suggestively into the ear of the guard who answered. At other times he was a visiting American with a bad case of diarrhea who wanted the embassy to send someone to fix it for him. Harry enjoyed inventing these verbal disguises and the Marines enjoyed them too and joked about them among themselves.

Once this procedure had produced an unintended result. The message devised for an evening some months earlier was to be from a Mr. Brown, a businessman transiting the city who had lost his passport and needed to see a consular officer right away to get a replacement. The Marine guard got the call twice, first from Harry and then a half an hour later from a real Mr. Brown, actually Braun. The guard assured the caller that he already had the message. The caller's voice was quite different, but that was no surprise. Harry always sounded different. The guard thought Harry had had a little too much to drink, which was known to happen, and had forgotten that he had already made his call.

Mr. Harwood Braun, a big beefy man who sported alligator skin cowboy boots under the cuffs of the trousers of his London tailored suits, had done yeoman fundraising service for the Colorado Republican party during the previous presidential election campaign. So he was not greatly puzzled to learn that his message had already been conveyed. No doubt his secretary in Denver, with whom he had spoken a quarter of an hour earlier, had telephoned Washington. The White House, eager to help a party stalwart, would immediately have alerted the US embassy in this faraway African capital.

Impressed by the speed with which the White House had acted, and reinforced in his opinion of his own importance, Woody (to just about everybody) Braun settled, drink in hand, into a comfortable chair in the lobby of the International Hotel to await rescue.

The next morning, after he had missed his flight out, a furious Woody Braun stormed into Ambassador Herbert Dawson's office, indignation radiating from his person as fiercely as gamma rays from an exploded nuclear reactor. It took Dawson and his deputy chief of mission, a tall, gangly man named Kooper, the better part of a day to calm the Denver businessman to the point where he would renounce his threat to write a nasty letter of complaint to the president. After intensive stroking, a tour of the city with Kooper as guide, and an elaborate dinner at the ambassador's residence featuring a hastily acquired Nile perch and two bottles of Moet Chardonnet, topped off by several snifters of Courvoisier, Woody Braun departed the following morning with a new passport in his pocket, a bit hung over but pacified and oozing praise for his new friends, Herb the ambassador, and Bill the counselor.

*   *   *

It took Hawke most of the rest of the morning to establish that the others at the meeting had been arrested but Davis had somehow escaped capture. Hawke was unable to learn how Davis had escaped or where he was but he was sure Davis would make it back safely. For now, however, he had reluctantly to report to Langley that Harry Davis was missing.

FIVE

By the time Dawson's secure telephone conversation with Kooper ended it was almost six o'clock, which in practice meant that it was too late to catch a flight out to Europe that evening. And which was just as well. The long trip back and the day he had just spent in Washington left Dawson with a kind of feverish exhaustion. He had no wish to turn around and fly another twelve or thirteen hours, through seven time zones, hardly more than twenty-four hours after having arrived. A decade earlier he would have done it without a moment's thought. Now it challenged the weight of his fifty some years.

Anyway, the extra day in Washington could be put to good use. Dawson dialed his desk officer, an eager young man in his late twenties, four years into his career.

"Art, I've got to head back early. I'll tell you later why. Book me out tomorrow evening to London and then onward. One more thing. Call the agency and see if you can set me up with Peterson tomorrow, any time that's good for him up to mid afternoon. Yeah, that's it. Keep up the good work. One of these days I'll write you a commendation."

Ambassador Herbert Dawson was not above reminding Arthur Nelson Blakemore of the rather vast difference in their status. But he liked Blakemore. In the way of many older men, he fancied finding a bit of himself in the younger man, for Blakemore was one of the ambitious ones. He had just made the passage from the junior to the mid level, and Dawson was sure he would move up fast in the years ahead.

The personnel system adopted in the late seventies had split the Foreign Service into junior, mid and senior tiers. Unless you were really dumb or had a severe personality disorder – in which case you presumably, though not assuredly, would not have been accepted into the Service in the first place – it was no particular feat to graduate from the junior to the mid level. Once at the mid level, you were guaranteed – short of committing a crime, developing a disabling mental illness or becoming a total goof-off, which did at times happen – another twenty years and a pension after that if you didn't make it into the senior ranks. The leap across the senior threshold was the hard part. Competition for the senior service was fierce, and making it there was tricky too, because you had to pick a date to declare your candidacy, and after that you had four years in which to be promoted. If you weren't promoted in the four year window, you were out.

This Byzantine system was the brainchild of the management experts. They loved complicated schemes. During the decade of the seventies, while others were busy at work on policy, the managers quietly took over the State Department and made its personnel system a labyrinth of new rules and requirements which not coincidentally justified their own existence and made their jobs impregnable. The diplomatic service, once a proud elite, was rapidly becoming just another sclerotic bureaucracy, like the Information Agency or AID, where people spent more time writing reports about what they were doing, or were supposed to be doing, than in actually getting on with the job.

Roughly speaking, the new system spawned two types of young Foreign Service Officers. There were those who figured why break a sweat, I'll take my twenty years and my pension and in the meantime see the world and have fun. The Department and the embassies were full of them now, seat warming clock watchers who looked deeply pained if you asked them to work late or on a weekend, and who could be counted on to file a grievance if you gave them a bad report. Then there were the others, like Blakemore, like Dawson himself when he was a young officer. They were fast and smart and hard working. They stayed after hours and showed up on weekends without ever being asked. When you gave them something to do you could count on its being done ahead of time and right.

But Dawson realized that for all Blakemore's ability and drive it wouldn't be as easy for him to make it to the senior level as it had for himself. The social engineers were moving in on the heels of the administrators and were wreaking their own particular brand of havoc. The Foreign Service was to be made over into "the image of America." Women, Blacks, Hispanics and Asians were already beginning to be singled out for preference. Dawson could see the day coming when quotas would be set up – secretly, no doubt – and ability would become a secondary consideration. Blakemore was white and Anglo-Saxon. It was a serious handicap. He would have to hustle to overcome it.

These thoughts cast a gloom over Ambassador Herbert Dawson. The Foreign Service decidedly was going to hell. Was it time to start thinking about getting out? He dismissed the thought as promptly as it had arisen. Whatever the future might hold, this was now, and for now there was nothing quite so good as being ambassador.

Dawson took the elevator down to the fifth floor, turned left onto the two hundred corridor and passed three short brown women in pale smocks who were gathered around a janitor's trolley speaking softly in

Spanish. He scanned the signs beside the doorways and stopped when he came to the one that announced: Turkish Affairs, Richard B. Purling, Director.

Dawson approached the outer office desk of a middle aged woman whose small gray head popped up alertly the moment he entered.

"Is Mr. Purling free to see a visitor?"

"May I tell him who it is?" Purling's secretary exuded a powerful protective coloration.

"Just say its Ambassador Dawson come to take him out for a drink."

"Is he expecting you?"

The woman was not to be intimidated by titles or swayed by jocularity. This was her turf and she patrolled it with the alert and grim purposefulness of a Rottweiler. She was, Dawson could see, one of that numerous breed, the secretary whose greatest satisfaction in life lay in not letting anyone past without a struggle.

The incipient deadlock was broken by Purling's appearance in the doorway of his office.

"Do I hear Herb Dawson out there? I thought it was tomorrow that we were getting together."

"Hello, Dick, good to see you again." Dawson didn't just say it, he meant it. He genuinely liked Purling.

They had entered the service together more than twenty-five years earlier. Their careers had gone separate paths, but they had stayed in touch at every turn and each thought of the other more as a friend than as a colleague. The fact that they had always worked in different areas made it easier for them to stay friends. If you were smart, you were on cordial terms with all the people in the area in which you worked. You lunched and networked with them, but you never truly opened up to them. There was simply too much competition for good jobs and promotions for that, and too much backstabbing.

"It was tomorrow, but I've got to cancel. Let me take you out for a drink instead and I'll tell you why."

"Give me fifteen minutes and I'll be with you.

Dawson sat in Purling's outer office under the glowering eye of the Rottweiler and skimmed through the day's New York Times. He wondered how long it would be before the Times, and the rest of the American press, would be reporting Davis' disappearance.

When Purling finished they crossed twenty-third street to Columbia Plaza, to a bar and restaurant tucked into one side of the immense complex. The bar was dimly lit and at that hour nearly empty. They slid into a corner booth, well away from the few other customers. To one side, behind a glass case, gold and black damselfish, thin as knife blades, glided nonchalantly in and out of crevices in a submerged rock garden.

Dawson ordered a vodka on the rocks and Purling a beer.

"Dick, can I go on deep background."

"You mean not for attribution?"

"Deeper than that. Not to be repeated anywhere."

Purling held up his right hand in mock seriousness. "I swear." He was a tall, slender man with thick curly blond hair going to gray. He wore steel rimmed glasses, had a deeply lined face and a pleasant and not particularly pronounced southern accent.

"It looks like I've lost a spook. One of the men in the station, name's Davis. His cover is commercial attaché, but he ran the station's only covert operation. He was meeting with the group he's running when they were busted by the security police, night before last. The others were arrested. The station doesn't know what happened to Davis, but I'd be surprised if he weren't picked up too. I'm sorry to break our lunch date, but I've got to keep the day free to go out to the Agency."

"What kind of operation was it?"

"The silliest goddamn thing you ever heard of. The people Davis was running were sneaking around the city in the middle of the night dropping leaflets and putting up a few posters here and there and slapping on bumper stickers. They had a nasty picture of the

Great Leader inside a red circle with a red line drawn through his face. The operation was supposed to spark a popular resistance movement but that was laughable. There was never any chance it could happen. People are too scared, and there are too many police and informers around. You've served in eastern Europe. You know what its like. It's a wonder they got away with it as long as they did."

"So why didn't you stop it? What happened to your ambassadorial veto?"

"Don't be naïve. Do I have to tell you there's a new administration in office, and a new Director at the Agency? Who is very powerful" – Dawson stretched the words out for emphasis – "and who just loves covert action. I did what I could. I warned. I told them the city was too heavily policed, that the operation would end up being busted. I told them the risk was greater than any reward they could realistically anticipate. I know the rule book gives the ambassador a veto over covert operations, but these guys haven't read the rule book and wouldn't give a hoot about it if they had. They have only one thing on the brain, fight communism. Half of them are thugs. If this was Germany in the 1930s, they'd all be big in the Nazi party."

Purling laughed. "Hey," he said, "don't talk like that to anybody around here but me. Others might not understand. You don't think you're exaggerating just a little?"

"Maybe just a little, but not more than that. Anyway, the order that came down from the new Director was that we had to have a covert operation. The Leader and his regime are communist – well, you can quibble about that, but there's no question he's sold to Moscow. Ergo, we had to have a covert operation, and of course the previous administration was derelict in failing to mount one. Even if the only thing it would accomplish is getting a lot of people tortured and killed. The really sad part of it is that the people involved would very likely never have got into this sort of thing if we hadn't organized, directed and supplied them. From what I've been told, they are basically middle class types, professionals, doctors, lawyers, accountants, business people. They didn't do it for money. They did it for a lot of reasons, but mainly, I guess, because they hate what the regime has done to their country."

Dawson paused long enough to follow the movements of a brilliant gold damselfish as it slid behind a piece of imitation coral.

"The worst of it is they probably imagined that because they were working under the Agency's wing they would be protected by our government. By now they must have had quite an awakening. I hate to think what must be happening to them."

"How many are there, or should I say were there?"

"Oh, maybe two dozen at most in the core group. Supposedly there are hundreds more sympathizers affiliated on the fringes, ready to pitch in and help when needed, but that's just what I've been told. The station chief likes to think it's so, but I've seen no evidence for that and I seriously doubt it's true. My guess is that the core group has been rounded up by now. If I know that regime probably a lot of other people have been hauled in too, people who didn't have any connection to the operation. All to be tortured and a lot killed."

Dawson drained the last of the vodka from his glass and ordered another. The metallic taste the grain alcohol left in his mouth was mellowed by the warm glow stoked in his stomach and brain. Ordinarily, Dawson was not much of a drinker. In recent years he had found that alcohol hit him too fast and too hard. Out of necessity he had learned the art of nursing a drink through an hour's stay at a diplomatic reception – the time you had to spend if you wished to avoid offending your host – without ever finishing it. But that evening he relished the vodka's effect.

"Look, I've got to admit something."

Purling smiled. "Go ahead, confess. I once thought about becoming a priest."

"Then take me into your confession box or whatever they call it. Here it is: I tried to stop the operation, but I didn't try hard enough. I sent in my objections, and what I got back was a letter from Foster. You know him, don't you."

"Yeah, he's a certified shit."

Dawson was tempted to agree, but he could not. Foster could indeed at times be thoroughly unpleasant but he was not a careerist or a hypocrite.

"No, I have to defend him. He's a very able bureaucrat. Maybe he just believes more in the orders he's given to carry out than you or I might. Maybe he's just more ruthless that we would be. Anyway the message he sent me – I wish I had the letter here to show you – was that the president had signed off on the operation and therefore it was a done deal and there was no appeal from it. If I didn't like it, maybe it would be time for me to look for another job. Foster didn't quite say it in those words, but that was the import of it. He did assure me that we wouldn't be sending arms to anybody or sponsoring violent actions. That was the bone they threw me. I took it as my excuse to lie down and be quiet, to accept something I knew was wrong, because it was only half as wrong as it might have been. What I have to confess is that the threat in Foster's letter scared me. You don't get your first embassy after twenty some years in the service just to throw it away. And looking for a job on the outside, at my age, I don't have to tell you, that's hardly an attractive proposition."

Dawson's second vodka arrived. He took a hefty swig.

"Go easy there," Purling offered. "I'll have to carry you home."

"And the other part is that I didn't keep close enough control over the operation. I tried. I had session after session with Randy Hawke, the station chief."

"Excuse me," Purling broke in, "but you have a station chief named Hawk?"

"Yes, Hawk, but with an e at the end. Randolph H. Hawke. Handsome guy. Looks like he could have been cast as James Bond."

"Terrific name for a spook, Hawke."

"I guess you could say he lives up to it. Basically what I wanted to do was hammer as much caution into him as possible, but it was a lost cause. He'd hear me out and then he'd say – I heard it so many times I can quote from memory: 'If you have the right training and the methods you can do anything. We have the training and the methods. We won't get caught.' He wasn't just bullshitting. He believed it. You can imagine, I didn't buy it, not right away anyway, it all seemed so unreal. But as time passed and the operation developed and nothing happened, much longer than I ever thought possible, I began to wonder. Maybe Hawke was right and I was wrong. Then I got a real shock, just a week before coming back here. Hawke showed me some of the leaflets that were being sent by the Agency to the station to deliver to the group. They were done on this beautiful paper, and the print job was the very finest. It was absolutely obvious they couldn't have been printed locally. There was no way. Nobody had paper of that quality, and nobody had the machinery to do that kind of print job. It turns out that the Agency was having the things printed in London. They must have chosen the Queen's own stationer to do the work. It was a dead giveaway. It was as if they had sent someone to the State Security Ministry to say that these things were being printed abroad and brought in via diplomatic pouch by a foreign embassy. So whose embassy would they think that might be? I couldn't have believed the Agency would be that dumb. But then why was I so dumb? Why did I wait to be shown what a dumb thing they would do? And another dumb thing they wanted to do. They had a lot of money in the project that they didn't know how to spend, so someone in Langley thought up the bright idea of spending it on a local language translation of Orwell's Animal Farm for the group to distribute here, a country with maybe ten percent adult literacy. Fortunately State nixed that one."

"Herb, cut it out." Purling had his glasses off and was furiously wiping them, a sure sign that he was agitated. "You're on a guilt trip. You're blaming yourself for things that weren't your responsibility. You did everything you should have done, really everything you could have done. You spoke up and made known your objections to the operation. When you were overruled you did your best to make sure it was carried out prudently. You've got nothing to fault yourself for."

The vodka lit a new clarity in Dawson's mind. Suddenly everything came into sharp focus.

"No," he said. "I shouldn't have let myself be intimidated by Foster. I should have taken the case to a higher level."

"That's ridiculous, Herb. There was never any chance you could have reversed a presidential determination on a covert operation. I doubt any ambassador has been able to do that, or has even tried. And you know there is no way you could have hoped to exercise tight control over the running of the operation. No ambassador has that authority. Sources and methods are the exclusive territory of the Agency. They have no obligation to tell you how they are managing an operation. That's their business and you aren't responsible for how they run their business. Anyway it sounds to me like your station chief let you in on more than he was strictly obliged to. If you had pushed harder, Langley would very likely have ordered him to cut you out entirely."

"Probably you're right," Dawson acknowledged, "but then there's one more thing I could have done, that I really should have done."

"What's that?" Purling genuinely had no idea what his friend meant.

"I should have resigned in protest."

Had Dawson at that moment pulled out a pistol and shot himself through the head Purling would not have been more astounded.

"Resign! Herb, nobody does that!" Purling almost dropped his glasses. He fitted them hastily back on. It was time to put a stop to this foolishness. He fixed an intent look on Dawson.

"Look, Herb, we're foreign affairs professionals. The job of the professional is to give his best advice and then implement to the best of his ability whatever the duly elected officials of our government decide. That's the code that we as Foreign Service Officers live by. And that's the way it should be."

Dawson stopped short of blurting out a remark that he realized would offend his friend. He fell silent for a moment, searching for other words.

"That's what's wrong with our service, Dick. Nobody resigns. Nobody takes personal responsibility for anything, and most of the time nobody even gets blamed for abetting stupidity. Everybody hides behind the story that we're just carrying out policy. That's bullshit and you know it. If you're the president's personal representative – that's what the statute says and ambassador is – then you're part of the policy. But look at what happens. You – I don't mean you, just anybody – get named ambassador to country X. You go there and faithfully carry out the policy. It's a stupid policy, and you know it's a stupid policy. And then the government we stupidly back gets overthrown or the country erupts in civil war. A lot of people are killed and everyone else is made miserable. But because you carried out the stupid policy you are absolved. You get promoted and sent on to bigger things. Later you may even get sent back as special envoy to try to put the country back together again, and you gather more laurels for that even if you fail. There are plenty of examples of this sort of thing. You know them as well as I do. Take Harrison, the under secretary for political affairs in the previous administration. Before being chosen for his exalted position in the Department he was ambassador to three countries and in each he managed to get out just before things collapsed. They say we have a Teflon president. Harrison was the Teflon ambassador. He presided over ruin and was rewarded with the top career job in the Department. He was really proud of himself. For two years he strutted around Washington like a peacock, even got himself profiled in the New Yorker."

Purling laughed. "Yeah, and then the new administration threw him out."

"By which," Dawson replied, "I suppose you mean to say there's justice after all, even if it's blind."

The bar had begun to fill up. A couple, a flashy looking young woman and a corpulent ruddy cheeked middle aged man, moved into a nearby booth. They ordered drinks, a fancy mixed drink for the woman, and the man laid a fat hand on her thigh. He whispered something in her ear and she giggled.

Dawson and Purling exchanged glances.

"I guess it's time to go," Dawson said. He put a twenty dollar bill on the table. "Jeanne is going to want to know what you've been up to. Tell her she can call me at the hotel. I'll vouch for you."

They walked out into the December blackness and onto 23rd street, to be greeted by a cold drizzle whose droplets painted golden halos around the sodium street lamps and silvery white ones around the lights of oncoming cars.

Dawson hailed a taxi and held the door open while they shook hands and said goodbye. He had made a fool of himself. The exhaustion of the long trip, the tension of the day, the shock of Davis' disappearance and the arrest of Davis' group, all these things had got to him and he had reacted unprofessionally. Resign from the service? What an idiotic idea. Over a bunch of people who were dumb enough to play the Agency's game? Resign over that! Idiotic even to talk about it. A real bleeding heart you're becoming, Herb Dawson. Purling was right. You did what you could and that was all that reasonably could be asked of you.

A little shamefaced, Dawson said: "Dick, thanks for letting me cry on your shoulder. Just forget all the nonsense I talked in there. I should stay away from vodka."

Purling assured him he understood, that he had always admired his friend's readiness to speak his mind.

"Give my best to Jeanne. You've got a wonderful woman there. I envy you. And good luck for next summer. I look forward to seeing you announced for Turkey.

Purling blushed at the complement. Turkey was an important country and he knew the ambassador's job there wasn't going to go to a mere office director. Uganda or Togo would be more in the ballpark. Still it was a nice thought. Purling was sure Dawson meant it in that spirit.

Back at his hotel, Dawson found a message from Art Blakemore. The meeting at the Agency was set. Petersen, the head of the Africa division, invited him to lunch at Langley.

He fell asleep on the bed still in his shirt and trousers.

SIX

Harry Davis thought he had seen it all in his six years in the Marines. On patrol in Vietnam a land mine had killed the man in front of him instantaneously and blown a foot off the guy by his side, and he himself had been wounded. Visiting Cairo on leave from his Marine guard unit at the American embassy in Khartoum Davis had happened to be in the lobby of the Hilton Hotel when Palestinian gunmen from the Black September faction shot Wasfi Tal dead. He had been less than sixty feet from the Jordanian prime minister, and he had watched in amazement as one of the killers knelt down to lick Tal's blood from the floor. And he was in Khartoum when that same Black September band seized Cleo Noel, the newly arrived American ambassador, and Curt Moore, the departing head of mission, and murdered them. Davis had stood guard outside the Saudi ambassador's residence where Noel, Moore and a Belgian diplomat were being held. He heard the shots that killed them.

Violence seemed to pursue Davis who himself was not a violent man, just someone with a slightly immature adventurous streak. Now it truly frightened him, for now he was no longer a young man in his twenties for whom the violence he had witnessed, even the violence that happened to him in Vietnam, could somehow seem impersonal. Could be shed as a dog sheds water after a dousing, with a good shake and gone.

Davis was already sure that this time he was not going to escape so lightly. He stood behind the false wall blinded by darkness, his heart pounding so loudly that he feared it would give him away, listening to the shouts and cries beyond the partition that hid him, the screams of his people as they were being beaten and dragged away. The three he sat with comfortably and quietly just moments earlier.

Judging by the stomp of boots and the general noise level, Davis calculated that there must be at least a dozen men out there, from the security police and the neighborhood watch committee. He braced himself for the moment they would burst through the doorway and drag him from his hiding place.

It did not come. After a time that seemed an eternity but that the luminous dial of his watch told Davis was only a little over an hour, the tumult subsided. Footsteps faded into the distance.

There had been no warning of trouble that evening when at Hawke's instruction he made his second try. He had not been tailed that evening. He was sure of that. His drive through the city had been uneventful. He had taken the extra precaution of making a swing by the house, a large house in the more affluent part of the city, to check for surveillance before coming around again to park in the driveway. He found his three contacts waiting for him, just as planned. The host, a businessman in his early fifties, tall, with bad teeth and a nervous manner. The nobleman, a government minister under the previous regime, thick set and grizzled, who bore his misfortunes stoically, the murder of his son in the violent early days of the revolution, his own long imprisonment, his wife's death from cancer of which he learned only upon his release a year earlier. And the woman, younger, a gynecologist at the city's one and only hospital, quiet but intelligent and fiercely dedicated. Davis brought a bottle of Johnny Walker Black Label from his briefcase and they had a round of drinks before going to the dinner table a little before eight. The meal, prepared by the businessman's wife, was a pasta dish, a choice Davis would recall later as a kind of omen of things to come.

It might have seemed just an ordinary social get-together, the commercial officer from a foreign embassy spending an evening with a local businessman and friends. Except that as they were about to begin dessert the calm of the evening was shattered by a loud noise from outside the house. The host bolted from his chair to a window and came back with news that guards from the local watch committee were at the front gate. Reflexively, without giving it a moment's thought, Davis went for the hidden closet and the host secured him inside. Later, when he had time to think about it he realized that for him to hide had been a terrible mistake. All the more to hide in the very place where the leaflets and stickers were stored, where there was to be found a pistol and ammunition. Because the very fact of hiding was an avowal, a confession that Davis was not a diplomat but a spy, the first of many confessions he would make.

In his meetings with the members of the group Davis had repeatedly emphasized the importance of security. He had warned that if they were caught they could face torture, jail and even death. He himself, however, would be shielded by his diplomatic immunity, given a mere slap on the wrist, expelled from the country in twenty-four or forty-eight hours. He had been told this, and as he had seen it happen to colleagues caught in east bloc countries in even the most compromising circumstances, he had firmly believed it. Now he was anything but sure of his diplomatic armor.

In his hiding place there was barely enough room to turn around and not enough to lie down. Davis sat on the floor, his legs drawn up against his chest, and silently cursed himself. Cursed himself for his weakness in agreeing to go to the meeting against his better judgment. Cursed the senior officer at headquarters who thought up the operation, had the gall to parade it as a realistic way to get rid of the Leader, and had then gone on to a comfortable retirement. Cursed Hawke for ignoring his warnings and for sending him that evening. Cursed Albright his predecessor who set him up for this fall. Albright, the fucking idiot, who spent his days at the station writing spy novels that nobody would publish, who left drafts of his manuscripts in his desk drawer when he shipped out. And who passed on to Davis a bunch of nut cases. One was a crazy man, another an illiterate who handed in written reports. Then there was the one who failed the station's polygraph. Davis was persuaded that he had been doubled. He wanted to drop him but Hawke insisted he continue to see him. Now Davis was sure that was the guy who gave away the operation. It had to be.

As the evening wore on anger gave way to more immediate physical discomfort. The cold made Davis miserable. He had no blanket and dared not even move his arms and legs about to shake the circulation back into them, for how could he know whether the security police had left someone behind inside the house? If so, smoking could give him away, though he ached for a cigarette. Then with growing urgency came the need to urinate. The hideaway had been created to hide things, not people. It had no toilet. The bonds of convention are not easily broken, even in unconventional situations. Davis could not bring himself to soil his host's property, even though now he knew that his host might soon be a dead man. So with the flame of his cigarette lighter as guide he found a box half filled with the Agency's leaflets, opened it, unzipped his trousers and emptied his bladder onto it. With a certain satisfaction he watched the paper absorb the yellow fluid.

It was then that Davis discovered the pistol. It was a .38 caliber revolver, next to it a box of ammunition. He loaded the pistol and brought a bullet into the chamber. He held the weapon in his hand, felt its familiar weight and the coldness of the metal, and he was tempted. He stood erect, shoved the revolver into his belt and pulled his jacket over it. The embassy was not two miles distant. In a run, he thought, he could make it in less than twenty minutes. Better than that, there was a main avenue just three blocks away, and it was just after eleven, almost an hour left to go before curfew. Once there he could hail a taxi and be at the embassy gate in less than five minutes. If anyone tried to stop him he could shoot his way clear.

Except that he knew that even the neighborhood guards were sometimes armed with AK-47s, and that there had to be guards around, if not inside the house then surely outside. And that even in the dark his white face would give him away. And one more thing Harry Davis knew. He knew that he did not aspire to be a hero. Even less did he want to be memorialized by an anonymous star on the plaque in the lobby at headquarters. He had joined the Agency because he wanted an interesting and exciting life. Now things had gone beyond interesting and beyond exciting to frightening. Now all he wanted was his life. All he wanted was to survive.

Davis took the pistol from his belt, unloaded the bullets and put pistol and ammunition back as he had found them.

At a little after two o'clock Davis heard his VW beetle start up and drive away. Toward morning he dozed off. Then just after daybreak he awoke with a start as the door to his hiding place opened.

It was the businessman's son, a slender doe-eyed boy who the previous evening had brought glasses and ice for the Johnny Walker and had cleared the table after the pasta dish. The boy, Davis thought, would be his salvation. With a scrap of paper torn from one of the leaflets, Davis quickly wrote out a telephone number and a few words and pressed the paper into the boy's hands along with money.

"Don't call from here," he instructed. "Go to a public telephone booth. Dial the number. An American will answer. Speak the words into the receiver in a normal voice. When the person on the other end of the line says thank you, hang up. Can you do that?"

Thinking of his father now, imagining that the words on the paper, words that looked like ordinary conversation, could rescue his father, he said yes he would do it.

Davis made a quick visit to a bathroom and then to the kitchen where he scooped a plate full of cold pasta from the evening before. With it in hand he retreated to his hideout to await rescue by his colleagues at the station.

SEVEN

The first person at the embassy to learn what had happened to Harry Davis was Judith Berhman, who in any rational order of things should have been the last to come into word of a CIA covert operation gone wrong. A petite, attractive dark haired woman in her early forties, she was the embassy's public affairs officer and as such was shut out from knowing about the station's activities.

Many regarded Berhman as the smartest person on the embassy staff. A plain spoken New Yorker, she had a way of cutting through cant and hypocrisy - those overused tools of the diplomatic trade - that could be absolutely terrifying. So it hardly needed saying that Judith Berhman was not a member of the career service. She came to the embassy's public affairs job from journalism, through a chance offer of hire that she accepted both for the challenge of a new line of work and because the move afforded her a convenient way out of a marriage that had turned sour. It did not take long, however, to become clear to Behrman and to others, that she had no patience with the protocols of bureaucracy. Or for the never ending stream of reports that Information Service officers were required to write to justify their programs and their jobs, for all the mutual back scratching, the sugary letters they wrote to tell one another how wonderful they were and what terrific work they were doing. Behrman simply believed in getting on with the job. In the nearly two years that she had been in it she had, to everyone's surprise, succeeded in putting the embassy's public affairs program back in business in this otherwise hostile territory. She had made more contacts and more friends beyond the walls of the compound than all the other members of the embassy staff combined. And because of this, some in the city were persuaded that Judith Behrman must be the Agency's station chief. Told of the suspicion, she was at first horrified, then amused. And also perhaps a bit flattered.

It was because of this suspicion that at the exact moment that Hawke and Barbara Davis were inspecting the Marine Guard log and puzzling over what had happened to Harry, Behrman was well on her way to finding out. Her first telephone call of the morning came from the treasurer of the Crenshaw Foundation, a local charity that provided shelter and rehabilitation for blind children, blindness being a common affliction in this country where nutrition and sanitation were woefully deficient and proper medical care available only to a favored few. Soon after arrival at post Behrman had volunteered to be the embassy's representative on the Foundation's board. Recently she had headed a fund-raising drive, collecting money from the international agencies, the embassies and those few Western firms that had managed to survive and even prosper through the rigors of Marxism-Leninism.

Behrman had in her safe a substantial amount of cash from the fundraising drive ready to be handed over to the treasurer. She assumed that to be the reason for his request to see her that morning. She had met him only once or perhaps twice, and she understood him to be an accountant for a large government operated business. She had never seen him at board meetings held at the American embassy but found nothing unusual in that. The Leader's long suffering subjects rarely felt comfortable visiting the American embassy, even to apply for a visa to visit a relative in the United States. The state security police kept round the clock watch over the embassy's the front gate. From a small building across the street it photographed all those going in and coming out. Frequently it called them in for questioning, which was never pleasant and sometimes far from gentle. Behrman assumed this to be the reason for his evident nervousness when he stepped into her office shortly after ten o'clock.

The treasurer was an extraordinarily tall man, with broad shoulders, a large strong head with dense growths of curly gray hair spouting from each side of his bald pate. He wore thick lens glasses, a mark no doubt of his profession. They made his eyes seem to bulge out of their sockets. Behrman judged him to be a man in his early fifties.

The treasurer pulled his chair up near Behrman's desk. He turned and inspected the room anxiously, as though to satisfy an urgent need to assure himself that the door was shut and no one else present. He spoke without preface in a barely audible voice.

"I have something important to tell you. They have arrested ----." He spoke the names of three persons, two men and a woman, whom Behrman did not recognize. For people to be arrested in the city was commonplace. Behrman did not understand why the treasurer was telling her this as thought it were some great secret that she should know. But she said nothing.

"I think they may also have arrested your man, the American. I need to know what to do."

The mention of an American seized Judith Behrman's attention. "My man? What is it that you're talking about?"

The treasurer repeated what he had said. He seemed sure that Behrman in fact understood perfectly what he was talking about, that she was merely bluffing and that by repeating his words, slowly and deliberately, he could call her bluff.

It did not work.

"You had better tell me what American you mean," she replied.

"What!" The treasurer raised his voice cautiously. "You do not know? You are not one of them, the people in the other part of your embassy?"

Now she understood. She examined the man's anguished features. Small beads of sweat had begun to glisten on his deep brown forehead. The whites of his bulging eyes cut a sharp contrast with his chocolate complexion.

"No," Behrman replied emphatically. "I am not. But I can speak with them. Tell me, please, what has happened."

The treasurer recounted the events of the previous evening, the raid on the house and the arrest of his three colleagues. He wrote their names out on a slip of paper and gave it to Behrman. The American's name was Jack Higgins, but the treasurer was not sure he had been arrested. "Perhaps," he added nervously, "he hid behind the false wall."

"You had better tell me about that too."

He reached into his briefcase and extracted a sheet of stained, cross-lined paper, produced a cheap plastic ballpoint pen from the inside pocket of his jacket and began to draw lines. The sketch of the interior of a house emerged.

"There. There is where he may be, your American." With his pen the treasurer pointed to a walled off closet inside one of the ground floor rooms. He added a rough street map showing the location of the house and handed the paper to Behrman.

"I need to know if I am in danger. If I am to leave the city, please tell me where I should go." He looked at her pleadingly. It seemed a paradox that such a large, seemingly powerful man should be so frightened.

"I do not know," Behrman said, "but I will ask and I will let you know." It was all she could offer. Behrman wondered but did not ask: When they drew you into their net, did they promise you a safe place to hide?

"Don't telephone," he warned.

"I will come to your office," she assured him.

"Not too soon. Not today. Come tomorrow. It will look less suspicious."

As she showed the visitor out of her office, Behrman spoke loudly, perhaps too loudly, so as to assure that her two local secretaries would hear.

"Yes, thank you for reminding me. The fundraising drive is completed. We will have the money ready in a day or so. People have given generously and I know the board will be pleased with the results."

From her office window, Judith Behrman watched the treasurer as he walked down the driveway back toward the gate of the compound, a big man suddenly pathetic and drooping and diminished under the brilliant December sun and the broad turquoise African sky. Behrman turned away from the window to survey for a moment the papers on the desk before her. From the moment she took the public affairs job at the embassy she had done everything she could to lay down a broad moat between her operation and Hawke's. She was determined not to allow her program to be tainted in any way by his. She found the opportunity to make this clear to Hawke one morning not long after her arrival, when he asked her to his office following the ambassador's daily staff meeting.

Hawke as usual came straight to the point. "There's a guy I'd like to meet that you know. The one you went to school with in New York. The senior official in the Ministry of Information."

Twenty years earlier, as a graduate student at Columbia University's school of journalism Behrman had met a short, wiry young African who had come to the school on a scholarship. In those days he was an ardent Marxist-Leninist. Up to that time Behrman had led a sheltered middle class life. Never before having met a revolutionary, she listened in fascination as he declaimed his communist faith eloquently over coffee in the student cafeteria and long walks up Broadway. He went back to Africa and she went on to a career in journalism and had almost forgotten about him when she got the job offer from the Information Service and learned that her posting would be to his country. She asked after him shortly after arriving in the capital and found him now a bitterly disillusioned revolutionary.

"Why do you want to meet him?"

"He might be interested in working with us. Three years ago he made contact with us in Paris. He was there for a meeting at UNESCO. He went to the embassy and spoke with one of our people." Hawke kept to the rule of never saying more than necessary. He stopped, and there was a moment of silence.

"What happened at the embassy in Paris?"

"Nothing much. He wanted asylum in the States in return for what he could tell us about the regime here. He wasn't important enough for that, so we proposed to him to come back here and work for us. He wasn't interested at the time. Maybe now he's changed his mind. I gather he is very disaffected."

The thought of it appalled Behrman. She was being asked to do a repugnant thing, to invite someone she considered a friend into a trap that could cost him his life. She looked at the heavy black velvet curtains drawn tightly across the windows to one side of

Hawke's desk. Only barely did she suppress an urge to rise and throw them open, to let in the bright morning sun.

"Look," Hawke said, feeling expansive and sensing nothing of Behrman's mood, "let's cooperate on this. You hold a party, invite him and anybody else you want, whoever is useful to you, and I'll pay for it."

Judith Behrman suddenly had the sense of looking upon the scene from a great height. "How kind of you," she said in a voice heavy with sarcasm that seemed to her almost to belong to someone else. "But you can save your money. I like to pay for my own parties. And when I hold them you can be sure I won't invite you or any of your people."

She got up to leave, but as she did she hesitated. Even without her assistance, Hawke could still try to recruit her friend. She searched for a word or gesture that would seal the matter beyond appeal. "There is one more thing I want you to understand," Behrman said, her voice infused with emotion. She raised her right arm, held it out straight and pointed her index finger at Hawke's head as though it were a pistol. "If you touch that man, if ever you try to blackmail him, Randy, I will find you and I will do you bodily harm."

They looked at one another in silence, intently, Behrman astonished by her own audacity, Hawke plainly struggling to keep his composure.

On the face of it, the threat Judith Behrman fired off that morning like some kind of thunderbolt was ludicrous. She was a small rather delicate woman with soft unmuscled flesh, in no sense physically strong and in no way inclined to violence. Randolph J. Hawke III was over six feet tall, weighed in at just over 180 trim all muscle pounds, jogged five miles a day and years back had qualified for a black belt in karate. What bodily harm could someone like Behrman do him? Still Hawke was stunned and even a little anxious. He dropped the idea of trying to recruit the senior official of the Ministry of Information.

But it didn't become a case of open warfare. At times after that, when Behrman and Hawke found themselves together at embassy parties, they talked, even joked and flirted a bit. Hawke did, Behrman discovered, have a sense of humor. He would open by proposing that they hold a party. She would shoot back a wry answer. What was on Hawke's mind in these exchanges she did not know. For Behrman, jousting with Hawke broke the otherwise agonizing boredom of these embassy gatherings. She had always imagined diplomats to be sophisticated, elegant people, the kind you saw in those old 1950s David Niven movies, intelligent and witty, or if not that then at least interesting and elegantly dressed. A great disappointment awaited her. With the exception of the ambassador (who had a way of being cordial and distant at one and the same time) and Hawke, the people at the American embassy were a bunch of rubes. The women talked of bake sales and children and complained endlessly about their servants. The men gossiped endlessly about assignments and promotions. And everybody made endless fun of the natives' strange ways and counted the days until they could fly out for leave to Europe, or better yet, to the States.

Why was it, Behrman wondered, that Americans sent overseas to represent their country to other peoples so compulsively mixed among themselves? Why did they insist on bringing with them their own foods, processed and packaged to a uniform blandness, when there was so much new, diverse and interesting to be had locally? Why was it that they celebrated American holidays with such energy and devotion and worked so hard to create a little America in their midst? The answer, Behrman deduced, quite obviously was that they were afraid to leave home and frightened of the people they had been sent to meet.

And why was it that the people at the American embassy were so plain? The women looked as though they bought their clothes at Sears. And the men, well, some wore polyester jackets. Some even wore white socks. Hawke at least was a natty dresser. And Behrman had to admit, reluctantly, a very handsome man. He was almost certainly over forty but could easily pass for thirty-five. Had Hawke been available to screen for the part of James Bond, Behrman thought, Sean Connery might never have had a movie career.

Hawke was drawn to Berhman's company by something in her physical person that he could not readily define, something that spoke to him of luxuriance and sensuality. Still, she frightened him, not because of her ridiculous threat, but because he found her so smart, which was frightening to him in a woman but somehow also attractive. And because they were so plainly on opposite sides of the barricade, which also both frightened and attracted him.

So when Judith Behrman called just before lunch on that late December day, not long before Christmas, and said she was coming to his office – she did not ask if she could come, she announced that she was on her way – Hawke was on his guard.

Behrman fired her question straight away. "Are you missing an American, somebody called Higgins?"

Hawke met the question poker-faced. His eyes betrayed nothing. Behrman saw that they were totally blank, had no light in them whatsoever. They could have been carved from stone.

"Why do you ask?"

"A man came to see me this morning. He said three people had been arrested in a house in town while meeting with one of your people. He thinks your man may have been arrested too."

Hawke stirred uneasily. "Davis is a little late," he said defensively. "That's all. But he's alright, I'm sure of it.

Davis is tough and he knows how to handle himself. In Vietnam even the Vietcong couldn't hold him. Anyway the others would help him."

Behrman found the story about Davis and the Vietcong surprising. She wondered if it could be true. But Hawke offered nothing more on it, or on the others who supposedly would help Davis, and Behrman wasn't going to ask.

"Maybe so," she said, "but I know where he might be." She pulled from her pocket the drawing the Crenshaw Foundation treasurer had given her. In her initial rage she had torn it in two and crumpled it. She spread the two pieces on Hawke's desk. "Here," she said, pointing to the false closet.

Hawke bolted upright in his chair. Carefully, almost lovingly, he smoothed the paper out, fumbled in his desk drawer for a roll of tape and reattached the two parts. Where, he asked, had the drawing come from?

"From the man who came to see me this morning. He needs to know if he is in danger, if he should leave town, and if so where he should go."

Hawke had recovered his poker-faced demeanor. He asked the man's name and received it expressionless. "Yes," he replied after a moment's silence. "He'd better go." But when Behrman asked Hawke had no sanctuary to suggest. The Agency could recruit you, give you assignments and pay you for services, but unless you were someone really big you were strictly a day laborer. The contract didn't include side benefits or a rainy day provision. If you were found out that was your problem, and your tough luck. There was nothing it would do for you.

Behrman started to protest. "Are you telling me that..."

Hawke cut her off. "Look," he said emphatically, "that's just the way the game is played. There's no point in discussing it."

"Would you at least undertake to let the man know that he should get out of town?" she persisted.

"No, I won't."

"Well then I will." She had promised the man an answer, and she was not going to let him down. She would be true to her word, no matter what the risk.

"It won't help," Hawke warned, but he interposed no other objection. If Judy Behrman wanted to so something foolish, that was her problem, not his.

EIGHT

Dawson was picked up at the Department's C Street diplomatic entrance late the next morning by a short, blond, steely-eyed, muscular young man whose handshake was bone-fracturing. The escort, one of Peterson's underlings, drove him to Langley in an ageing cheap model sports car in which both driver and passenger sat half reclining. Dawson made a brief stab at conversation but Peterson's minion may as well have had his jaw wired shut. The twenty minute trip passed in total silence.

The Agency welcomed State Department personnel to its Langley headquarters with approximately the same degree of warmth and openness it might show toward declared representatives of the KGB. Peterson's man deposited Dawson in a small room to one side of the broad, high ceilinged entrance hall. There he was required to fill out a questionnaire and wait twenty minutes before, from some invisible quarter, clearance came to admit him. A clerk pinned to Dawson's jacket a large red badge that warned that he was a visitor, and also, Dawson thought, just possibly that he was the carrier of some dangerous communicable disease.

Dawson had the fault – he understood that for a diplomat it was a dangerous fault – of at times allowing his annoyance to vent in sarcasm.

"Do I go now for fingerprinting and polygraph?" Dawson asked. The short blond young man looked at him hard, ignored the remark and ushered him into the entrance hall to an elevator and up to Peterson's office.

Harvey Peterson, though in his late forties or early fifties, had coal black hair, probably dyed, and a badly pocked face that made him look like a 1930s Chicago gangster straight out of one of those old George Raft movies. Except that Peterson was not a fancy dresser. His polyester/wool jacket, polyester/wool slacks and polyester/cotton button down drip dry shirt and knit tie could only have come from some discount outlet in the northern Virginia suburbs.

The contrast between Peterson and the ivy league type with Peterson could hardly have been more stark. Peterson introduced him as John Duke, "a colleague," but Dawson noticed that the monogrammed initials on the man's shirt didn't match the name. Whoever he was, John Duke combined an almost juvenile face with a full head of gray hair. He was attired in a finely tailored blue wool flannel blazer, a white collar sitting upon a sky blue cotton shirt, gold cuff links, a purple patterned Italian silk tie, creamy gray wool flannel trousers, black cashmere socks and tasseled black loafers. Dawson asked him what he did?

"Oh, I just help out from time to time."

Was Dawson becoming paranoid, or was it simply that Peterson wanted a friendly witness to the meeting so that nobody could later accuse him of having turned the Agency's secrets over to the opposition? And was John Duke, so called, wearing a wire? When Dawson asked to use the men's room before lunch, the short blond escort was called to take him there. Dawson wondered whether the man was going to go inside and watch to make sure he peed into the urinal. But the escort waited outside and led Dawson back, no doubt less out of concern that he might lose his way – Peterson's office was right around the corner – than to make sure Dawson didn't dart into some nearby office to filch the Agency's secret documents.

For lunch Peterson had reserved a table in the Agency's top floor executive dining room. The place was darker even than the bar where Dawson and Purling had drinks the night before. Peterson leading the way, the three of them stumbled among tables until, somehow, they arrived at the one designated for them. Without night vision glasses it would have been impossible to identify anyone more than a table removed. Dawson assumed that was the point.

"Is this the place you guys bring your girl friends?" he asked.

Neither Peterson nor Duke so much as cracked a smile.

As they took their seats Peterson leaned toward Dawson and in a voice barely above a whisper announced: "I've got good news. We think Davis is going to be okay."

"I sure hope so," Dawson replied after a moment's hesitation, "but what do you mean exactly. Have you located him?"

"No, but we're pretty sure he escaped capture, ninety-nine percent, I'd say. And we know how he did it. I can't give you a lot of details – can't reveal sources and methods, you know. But I can tell you one thing. We've been able to find out that the house where Davis was meeting with his group had a room behind a false wall. Davis hid there when the house was raided. We even have a drawing of the place, with the false wall and the hiding place and everything." Peterson smiled in self-congratulation. "Damn good intelligence, eh? Not easy to get in a place like that."

Dawson realized there was no point in asking where this information came from or how reliable it was.

Peterson had already covered himself in the cloak of sources and methods.

As soon as they ordered Peterson launched into a heated defense of Davis' operation. Dawson hadn't criticized it; he had in fact decided before coming that he was not going to criticize it, but apparently Peterson expected he would and meant to stay a step ahead. Peterson cast his defense around the themes of being tough, winning and risk taking. These evidently had been elevated to the status of high philosophy at the Agency. Risk taking, Peterson declared, was part of being tough. And being tough was the true measure of virtue.

"To win you have to take risks. If you don't take risks, you don't win anything. And when you take risks you realize that once in a while you're going to get burned. It's inevitable. It's just part of the game. You have to count your losses together with your wins. The important thing is the bottom line."

A game, Dawson thought, maybe for Peterson and his like, but for those caught in it? But he found it interesting that spooks talked of their profession in that way. He recognized the source of the particular brand of nonsense that fostered the game metaphor. It came from the Agency's new Director, a man who had made millions in the financial markets less by taking legitimate risks that by dealing on the edge of the law, only micro millimeters away from the criminal.

After Peterson had repeated his lines about winning and risk taking three or four times, each slightly rephrased, Dawson became impatient. He did what he had told himself he would not do.

"Look, don't tell me about taking risks. This was a dumb operation. You know it, or you should know it, and I know it. But let me put it your way: the risks surpassed the potential reward by a factor of hundreds, if not more. There was never any chance that operation could be pulled off without being busted. And there was never any serious possibility it could accomplish anything. I mean, accomplish anything beyond getting a lot of people arrested, tortured and killed."

A look of the most profound disdain settled upon Peterson's pock marked face. The so-called John Duke cleared his throat repeatedly, like a horse hawing. They looked at one another and then at Dawson, who was now marked as not being tough, as a bleeding heart, and worse still, as not a team player.

On his way out of the building that afternoon Dawson stopped to inspect the Agency's statue of Nathan Hale. The blackened bronze representation of America's First Spy was tall, trim and handsome. He looked nothing at all like Harry Davis, except, Dawson thought, possibly for one feature. The bronze figure had his hands bound behind his back, and Dawson imagined that Davis might also at that moment be in one of the Leader's jails with his hands tied behind his back. Dawson somehow doubted, however, that Davis would be holding his head high, as Hale was portrayed in the statue.

Hale's famous words were engraved on a plaque on the pedestal: "I regret that I have but one life to give for my country." That at least was what he was supposed to have said; one of Dawson's history professors had insisted that Hale's last words were in fact unprintable and not in the least uplifting. Whether or not this was true, it was said the new Director didn't like the statue of Hale. Not because he found anything wrong with the sculptor's rendition, but simply because Hale had been caught and hanged. Hale had been a failed spy, no matter his alleged noble sentiment. The new Director wanted only successful spies – the kind that would escape capture, as Peterson was so sure Davis had done.

Dawson's nineteen year old son picked him up at the hotel at 5:30, in winter's premature darkness, for the drive to Dulles airport. A freezing drizzle was falling, so light that at first it was hardly noticeable. There was not a lot for them to talk about. Dawson didn't want to burden the boy with the secret of Davis' disappearance. He said he was returning early because of an emergency at the embassy; one of the employees had got himself into trouble. It wouldn't have done either to talk about the boy's mother, her Paris escapade and her sudden unexpected death, so the conversation quickly lagged. Which was just as well, for his son needed to concentrate his full attention on the road. The drizzle was affixing a razor thin film of ice to the highway's surface. Homebound commuters were skidding their cars off into the drainage ditches right and left. Vehicles stood stalled at crazily skewed angles on the shoulders and in the roadway itself. Dawson admired his son's skill in navigating a treacherous path over the ice through out of control traffic. He wondered if he himself could have done so well.

From downtown Washington the drive to Dulles airport normally was a matter of forty-five minutes, give or take a few. That evening it took more than double. Still, Dawson arrived with forty minutes to spare before the 8 p.m. Pan American flight to London, only to learn that the flight had been delayed for an hour. The hour's delay became two, then three. By the time the flight was cancelled for the night, because a work crew couldn't get to the airport to clear the runway ice, taxis were no longer operating out to Washington and the airport hotel was full up. Dawson dozed, unambassadorially, on and off through the small hours after midnight in the passenger lounge, in a chair designed quite deliberately to prevent sleeping. By morning the work crew had made it in and had cleared the runway. A little after 8 a.m. the Boeing 747 lumbered out onto it, revved up and heaved itself skyward. It arrived at Heathrow airport just after 8 p.m. London time. As the plane taxied toward the docking gate Dawson looked out a window and spotted his connecting flight for Africa heading out for takeoff.

He was left with an enforced twenty-four hour layover in London. The British capital was even grayer and more depressing at that time of year than Washington. Dawson was assailed by that particular brand of anxiety, a hollow deeply uneasy feeling, that comes from being in a place one hadn't expected to be and unable to get to the place where one should be. He thought to exorcise it by going to the American embassy, on Grovesnor Square, where he could check the cable traffic coming from his embassy and put through a secure phone call to Kooper.

The British complained that the U.S. embassy, a modern office building with more style than most, clashed with the square's stately architecture, and they ridiculed the large tin eagle that crowned the building. Dawson didn't disagree, but it struck him as odd that the British should mind these American architectural intrusions; they who wherever German bombs had struck in World War II had put up the most unspeakably plain and ugly structures one could imagine. London, Dawson thought, must have been a beautiful city before the war.

Kooper had no news to offer. Davis was still missing. Dawson told himself he shouldn't be too worried. He didn't for a moment share Peterson's certainty that Davis had escaped capture. But even if the Leader's security police did have him, Davis was a duly accredited diplomat. They might rough him up a bit but they would hand him back after a few days at most, no serious damage done. The Leader was ruthless, at times even bloodthirsty, but he craved respectability and legitimacy. It was a common trait for dictators. Once they sat in the seat of power for a while and became accustomed to its honors the thing they wanted most was to be accepted, at home and abroad, as belonging there legitimately, not simply by right of force. For that, they had to obey the rules. And the rules were unambiguously clear. A diplomatic officer could not be arrested or otherwise detained by the government to which he was accredited without the prior agreement of his own government. It didn't matter that Davis had been accredited under false pretenses. All that mattered was that the Foreign Ministry had put him on the diplomatic list and given him a diplomatic identity card.

As his flight winged east and south over France and Italy, then onward across the Mediterranean and above the empty blackness of the Sahara desert, Dawson had ample time to reflect on Davis. Of all the station officers, Davis was the one he found most appealing. He had a humanity and a wholeness about him that the others didn't. Hawke and his other acolytes were strung so tight they often seemed caricatures. Davis wasn't. And Davis was the only one among the station's officers who could be counted on to work conscientiously at his embassy cover job. The others would put in a few hours at most and then slip off to Hawke's office to read the Agency's cable traffic, finish some report or talk shop. It didn't seem to matter to them that by being absent from their desks so often they were blowing their cover. Davis was not only on the job but did it well. A few months earlier he had helped an American company win a contract financed by the World Bank for the building of a road in one of the country's more inaccessible regions. It was a breakthrough of sorts. Dawson was so pleased with Davis' work that he offered him a recommendation if he ever wanted to transfer from the Agency to Commerce or State, and Davis had seemed to be thinking seriously about it.

Dawson wondered, had Davis really managed to take refuge behind the false wall? And even if he had, how would he get out of the house without being discovered? The Leader's security police must know that he was there somewhere. They would take the others, pull out a few fingernails or attach electric wires to penises and ears and switch on the current. In a few hours at most they would know where Davis was and come and drag him from his hiding place. That is if they didn't already have him.

To believe that Davis could escape, you had to believe in miracles. Dawson didn't believe in miracles.

*　　　　　　　*　　　　　　　*

As her driver sped her down into the heart of the city that afternoon, Judith Behrman was too distracted to notice the work crews painting fresh white traffic lines on the main avenues. The Leader's government, it seemed, equated traffic lines with modernity and civic progress, a face it was desperately eager to display to the world. The appearance of work crews painting lines on the streets invariably heralded the imminent arrival of important foreign visitors more unmistakably than swallows the spring. But since the paint was locally produced and of poor quality it faded within weeks even in dry weather, within days under rain. No matter. It would be applied again, along with a coat or two for the storefronts and buildings of the main avenues if the occasion were of particular importance, before the coming of the next batch of foreign dignitaries.

The driver, a short, chubby, ebullient man who considered it a signal honor to ferry Behrman to her appointments here and there in the city, decided that she should know why paint was being streaked down the middle of the road this time.

"It is for tripartite summit, Madam."

What in the world was the tripartite summit? Behrman dismissed the question the moment it was posed.

It was within seconds of 4 p.m. when the driver pulled the black Chevrolet Citation to a halt in the dusty unkept courtyard of the building where the Crenshaw Foundation's treasurer had his office. Thorny dry weeds, rejected even by the neighborhood goats, rose in tangles along the walls while to one side lay a mound of what might have been taken for trash had the concept existed in this country where nothing was too old, dented or rotted to be put to some use. A tough looking muscular man, short and squat, his head shaved, emerged from a white Volkswagen van parked near the mound and approached with a bow-legged gait. Making no effort to hide what he was doing, he drew a pad from his rear pocket, squinted at the diplomatic license plate on Behrman's car and carefully wrote down the numbers.

For the first time Behrman was frightened. From the car window she called out: "What are you doing that for? Do you want me to write down your license number? I am coming for the Crenshaw Foundation."

The man ignored her. When he finished his task he turned and waddled back to his vehicle.

Self-consciously now, Behrman crossed the courtyard to the building and climbed two flights of narrow stairs that smelled heavily of urine. A sickly green paint peeling from the walls showed a base of dingy white underneath.

There were three secretaries at desks in the accountant's outer office. To the first that looked up Behrman announced, too loudly, that she had come for the Crenshaw Foundation, to deliver the money from the fund raising drive. The accountant emerged from his office and just a bit too ostentatiously introduced her to the secretaries.

"This is Mrs. Behrman who has headed the Foundation's fund raising drive."

The introduction produced inscrutable polite smiles from the three secretaries, meek looking young women with smooth glistening brown skin and carefully styled hair. Behrman shook hands with each of them, wondering if they sensed her anxiety. It was impossible to tell. They had on the expressionless mask that came so naturally to the people of the country.

Inside the accountant's office, with the door closed, Behrman drew a thick envelope from her briefcase and extracted several large wads of bills bound with rubber bands. She laid the money on the accountant's desk along with a typed sheet of paper on which were listed the names of the donors and the sums contributed. Behrman and the accountant chatted, awkwardly and too loudly, about the success of the fundraising drive. While they spoke she took a scrap of paper from her briefcase, wrote four words on it and held it up for the man to see.

"Get out of town," it read. Behrman crumpled the paper and put it in her purse. "But be careful," she added in a whisper. "The security people are downstairs."

"Where should I go? Didn't they tell you?"

"No," she said, suddenly feeling terribly ashamed. "I'm sorry," she whispered, "I've done everything I can."

The man's face seemed to collapse. After a moment's silence he whispered: "Then tell them I am lost."

They spoke again loudly of the success of the fundraising drive. The accountant escorted Judith Behrman through his outer office and out the door to the stairwell where they stood together for a moment. "Please call me if you have any questions about the accounts," Behrman said at last.

"Of course," he replied stiffly. "And thank you for all that you have done."

They shook hands and she turned down the stairwell, fighting a nausea that she feared might overcome her if she did not quickly reach her car.

The bald muscular man was lounging by the White Volkswagen van when Judith Behrman emerged into the courtyard. As her car pulled away she saw him enter a notation on a pad which he then returned to its place in his rear trousers pocket.

NINE

"Are you going to kill me now," Davis asked.

He was on his knees leaning precariously against the back seat of a van between two guards armed with AK-47 assault rifles, blindfolded, his hands bound behind his back by electric cord and a thick blanket over his head. His question, though ill advised, no longer seemed unrealistic. The van lurched at high speed along a road that was either unpaved or poorly so. Davis was persuaded that he was being taken to the place outside the city where opponents of the regime had been killed and buried during the bloody early years of the revolution. He had seen it, a broad field crowded with little pockmarked mounds, like the face of a heavily pimpled teenager.

As the fear of dying there consumed him, Davis began to hyperventilate and shake, uncontrollably for a moment until shame overcame fear. Was that what they were going to tell the world about him, in his final moments, that he had gone to his death a coward, trembling and whimpering? No, if he was going to die he would do it the way it should be done. Nothing heroic, for there could be no heroism in being cut down by a shot to the back of the head, as Davis imagined the death that awaited him. But he would not disgrace his country, the Agency or the Marine Corps, above all not himself.

On the morning of his second day in hiding Davis heard a vehicle pass near the house. He was certain he recognized it as the van of one of the station officers. Momentarily his spirits lifted, only to dive once again when nothing followed. By that afternoon he had lost hope of rescue. Several times he picked up the revolver and loaded it, then – after moments of reflection – unloaded the weapon, wiped it clean of his fingerprints and put the ammunition back in its box. Resistance would be futile and very likely fatal. It surprised Davis that his three contacts had not already given away his hiding place but he knew they would not be able to hold out long against torture. He still hoped his diplomatic immunity would shield him from the worst.

When the door of his hideaway finally opened, this time with a crash, Davis stood with his hands raised high in surrender. Facing him were a half dozen security men armed with AK-47s and nine millimeter pistols. One grabbed him and tied his hand behind his back while another slapped him around, ignoring his protest that he was an accredited diplomat. Then they sat him down on a stool and proceeded to play Russian roulette with him, using the .38 caliber pistol they found in the hideaway. His captors roared with laughter when Davis flinched at the pull of the trigger. They continued with the game until finally, not believing they would actually shoot him dead then and there, Davis began to accept it unflinchingly. At about 11 o'clock they left him bound securely on the floor of one of the bedrooms, guarded by a young security man armed with an AK-47, a bayonet affixed to its barrel. During the night, as he squirmed to find a less uncomfortable position, the guard stabbed him in the chest. It was only a superficial wound but it hurt. Even more, it frightened him, for it told him that his life could in fact be in danger.

Still, Davis vowed the he would say nothing beyond giving his name, his diplomatic accreditation and his job as commercial attaché at the American embassy. The vow lasted only briefly. The next morning they brought in his three contacts and seated them around the dining room table facing Davis. The three had blood blisters where once fingernails had been, and they looked wretched from a night of torture and questioning. When Davis refused to talk they took the three to an adjoining room. Their screams under torture quickly brought Harry Davis to make the confession his interrogators sought. He admitted that he was an officer of the Central Intelligence Agency engaged in a covert operation against the Leader's government.

They filmed his confession and put him in the van and drove off with him, but they did not kill Harry Davis. They took him to a house in a town some forty miles outside the capital near a military airbase to which civil aviation flights into and out of the country were being diverted while the city's airport was closed for runway renovations. The next day, his first of what was to be an extended captivity, was Christmas eve. Davis' interrogation that day was punctuated by the roar of large aircraft taking off and landing. Among them that same morning was the plane that brought Ambassador Herbert Dawson back to the country.

TEN

Kooper led the way down the narrow, winding, faintly lit stairwell, his left hand gripping a heavy brass ring from which dangled a dozen keys of uneven length, and his right hand a graphite barreled flashlight. Hawke followed and Dawson brought up the rear. Darkness and a powerful odor of mold and stale air closed around them at the bottom of the steps. Kooper groped along a damp wall until his hand found a light switch. A single bulb, hanging ethereally from a wire running up to the low ceiling blinked on and dimly illuminated a jumble of paraplegic desks and chairs, battle scarred filing cabinets and safes. All had once served proudly. Now they resided in humiliatingly disordered retirement in this dank cellar storage room beneath the chancery.

Each time Dawson visited the place he wondered how in the world these large pieces of office furniture had got there? Was it possible they could have been brought down the narrow stairwell? Surely not. Each time he made a mental note to instruct Nelson, the administrative officer, to sell them off or give them away. Each time he forgot.

The three of them, Dawson thought, might be burglars breaking into someone's basement, or boys exploring a haunted house. His infrequent forays into the chancery's basement did in fact remind Dawson of boyhood adventures exploring the uninhabited wing of his widowed aunt's Cleveland home where one door led to the next in a seemingly endless progression of dark, musty abandoned rooms.

They picked their way across to a steel door at the far end. There they halted while Kooper searched through the key ring, made two tries before opening the first lock but got the second with only one try. The door creaked open heavily to a narrow corridor that once, long ago, had been painted white. Kooper switched on another light and carefully locked the door behind him, a precaution against the wholly unlikely event that someone might try to follow them in. One more door now stood between them and their goal. It had three locks. Kooper got the first one open with one try. The second was vanquished almost as easily, but the third was stubbornly recalcitrant. It ceded finally to Kooper's loud threats of imminent annihilation, and to the fourth key he inserted.

Kooper pushed the door open, switched on a light, and there it stood before them, glistening under a battery of florescent lamps like a giant block of crystal. It was the bubble, so called not for its shape – it was rectangular – but because it was translucent, and it was, when properly secured, a perfectly sealed chamber. The bubble was the one place in the embassy where the ambassador and his senior staff could repair when they had matters of the greatest sensitivity to deal with. It was a room inside a room, a shell of thermoplastic acrylic resin, its walls three inches thick. It was furnished with a long low white formica conference table and fifteen distinctly uncomfortable white plastic chairs.

Kooper threw a switch and a motor sprang to life, emitting a low even hum that would thwart any attempt to pick up whatever resonance of voice might shimmer on the structure's walls. He tried another switch but it gave no response.

"It's going to be bad in there," Kooper warned as he pulled open the door of the bubble.

The air inside smelled a thousand years old.

"Can't Nelson get the ventilator fixed?" Dawson groused. "It's been out for months now. Tell him to get on the ball."

Dawson had come off his overnight return flight just two hours earlier. He had not slept. He knew he could not sleep until this meeting was over, until he had reached a sense of direction and movement toward finding out what had happened to Davis and getting him back. Still, his fatigue felt like it weighed a ton and he carried it resentfully. Now there was this extra discomfort, small it was true, just a little stale air, but why did he have to be subjected to it? What the hell was wrong with Nelson anyway? Couldn't he get anything done?

"Nelson is trying, boss, but you know we can't do it locally. We have to get a technician out of London. One was supposed to come this week but he got shifted to Lagos for an emergency job. We'll keep on it. Kooper knew Dawson knew this already. He knew also that Dawson's irritation would pass as soon as he caught up on his sleep, so he felt free, even a little proud of himself, to stand up for Nelson, a slow, plodding man, even though he too considered Nelson lax and often inept.

Wim Kooper was probably the only deputy chief of mission in the business to address his ambassador as "boss." The standard was "Ambassador" or "Mr. Ambassador." Dawson however considered that kind of formality ridiculous in a small embassy. Right from the beginning he told Kooper to call him by his given name unless the occasion required the use of his title. Kooper couldn't bring himself to do it. His Dutch formality – he was ten when his parents brought him to the States – made him feel just too uncomfortable. So he hit on "boss." Somehow, used by Kooper, "boss" seemed to fit.

The job of deputy chief of mission was highly sought after because it was an important step toward the top of the career ladder. Being DCM could be sublime or awful, and if it wasn't wholly one or the other it was a bit of both. For the staff below you were the bad cop to the ambassador's good cop. It was your job to keep the staff in line, but you also had to keep them happy. Your biggest problem was how to deal with your ambassador. Your career could be made or broken depending on how you succeeded in this, and on the kind of person life's lottery gave you for an ambassador. You lived with the knowledge that you were the one person the ambassador could fire at will, for no better reason than he didn't like your looks when he got up one morning with bloodshot eyes and a hangover after a heavy night out. You knew you had better be there when he got to the office in the morning and when he left in the evening, and in between you took whatever crumbs he swept from his desk. And if the ambassador was a woman, which now and then was beginning to happen, it was harder still. You knew from experience, really from instinct, the techniques of male bonding. You were used to having women work for you, but how did you deal with working for a woman?

It was a sudden death situation, hard on the nerves, a little like playing Russian roulette every day. Wim Kooper's nerves weren't the best. The uncertainty of it weighed heavily upon him, more heavily than on most, among other reasons because Kooper didn't have the college education that practically everyone else of his grade in the diplomatic service had. It wasn't that he didn't have a degree from a prestigious university. He didn't even have a degree from a place that everyone considered a joke, that no one had ever heard of. His parents, poor Dutch immigrants, hadn't had the money to send him to a four year college and he hadn't had the grades to get a scholarship. He spent two years in a community college and joined the Service as a communications file clerk.

But what Wim Kooper lacked in formal education he made up for in drive and ambition, and in street smarts. Kooper's advancement from file clerk to deputy chief of mission was extraordinary. There probably wasn't another example of it, at that time anyway, in all the US diplomatic service. He had achieved it through a combination of hard work, quick wits and a talent for flattery that though blatantly transparent was usually remarkably effective. But even after rising to the height of deputy chief of mission Wim Kooper still felt insecure. He could hardly believe his success and was darkly afraid that it might not last, that at any moment he might make a mistake that would wreck everything he had worked so hard to achieve and plunge him back to his obscure origins. He was at the same time painfully overawed by Dawson who came out of Ivy League colleges with bachelors and master's degrees and was – or had once been - fluent in three foreign languages.

They filed into the bubble. Kooper sealed the door with latches like those in securing the hatch of a ship. The three of them wedged themselves into the plastic chairs.

"Alright," Dawson said, "let's get this over as quickly as possible, before we suffocate. Davis has been missing for four days now. What has happened to him?" He looked at Hawke. "Didn't you tell Bill he sent a message three days back saying he was going to make it back on his own?"

Hawke shifted uneasily in his chair. "We thought so. That's what it looked like at first. Now we're not so sure. Maybe it was an appeal for rescue."

"I don't understand. They're hardly the same thing. How could one become confused with the other?"

"Well, these things are in code and the message we got was a little garbled." Hawke paused for a moment and then resumed, resolutely upbeat. "But my bet is on Davis. He's trained, he's tough and he's smart. In Vietnam he escaped from capture by the Vietcong."

Davis qualified for "smart" but "tough" was not a word that readily came to mind for Dawson when speaking of Davis. And what was this about escaping from the Vietcong? Dawson had not heard of this exploit. He tried to imagine Davis tracking through jungle with the Vietcong in hot pursuit, but he couldn't. It was just too unlike the Harry Davis he knew.

"This is the way I see it," Hawke continued. "That second evening, after the telephone call that came in about noon, whatever it meant, Davis makes it out of the house under cover of darkness and gets to the house of other members of the group, maybe just a few blocks away. He knows it's too dangerous for him to try to get back to the embassy, so they take him from there. Now they're hiding him in the countryside."

The story had so many holes in it that Dawson wasn't sure which one to poke through first.

"Who is 'they'?"

"I mean the group, their network."

"Ah, yes, the network." Dawson made no effort to hide the sarcasm in his voice. Did 'the network' really exist, he wondered, other than in Hawke's imagination?

"But tell me, Randy," Dawson continued, "how does Harry get out of a house that's surrounded by security police? We have to assume, don't we that the Leader's goons didn't just go off to bed and leave the place unguarded? And how can you hide a white man in the countryside, where everybody knows everybody else and a white man would stick out like a sore thumb. Davis would be reported to the authorities immediately."

"They wouldn't keep him in the countryside," Hawke objected, conveniently skipping over the ambassador's question about how Davis could have escaped from the house. "They would take him out of the country, they would get him across the border."

"How would they do that?" Dawson searched Hawke's eyes. They showed not the slightest reflection. They were totally dead. Was having dead eyes a requirement for employment by the Agency, Dawson wondered, or did the Agency deaden them for you after you got in?"

"They have their ways," Hawke replied.

That was it. Hawke was pulling down the curtain, saying don't press me too hard. If you do I can retreat into my citadel of secrecy where not even you, the ambassador, can follow. It was the trump card that the Agency held over State.

Still, Hawke felt he should offer something more.

"If necessary they'll walk him out at night."

Dawson couldn't suppress a laugh. "Randy, you've got to be joking. The nearest border is four or five hundred miles away, over terrain like the grand canyon. The last time I saw Davis he didn't look in shape to hike up the hill from Revolution Square."

"Don't underestimate Davis. He's one tough cookie. I'll bet anything that right now he's on his way out to the border. We won't hear from him until he gets across."

It could hardly be coincidental, Dawson thought, that what Hawke was saying was approximately what Peterson had said. Why was it that the Agency did not want even to entertain the thought that Davis might have been captured? The idea that one of their people could be taken was evidently more than they could handle.

"Maybe," Dawson replied, " but we can't just wait to see if Davis shows up one day. We've got to proceed on the assumption that the security police may have him. Do you have any way of checking that out?"

"Let me work on it. I've shut down almost all of my network, but maybe there's something we can do."

Dawson would have liked to ask for more specifics but he knew it would be pointless to do so. That was Hawke's reserved area. He would clam up.

"In the meantime, Bill," Dawson said, addressing Kooper, "we will have to work on the government. That means the Foreign Ministry. Any suggestions?"

Wim Kooper always had suggestions. He had a plan for every contingency. He launched into the subject enthusiastically, chopping his right hand in the air for emphasis.

"We can't just go and tell them they've got to hand Davis back to us, because we don't know for sure that they have him. So let's try this approach. Why don't I go see the Captain?" The Captain was the official in charge of American affairs at the Foreign Ministry. He was a small, wiry absolutely expressionless man, the most poker faced individual Dawson could recall ever having met. He had been a common soldier in the army of the previous regime. The revolution had catapulted him to the rank of Captain. Then in some unexplained way he had managed to land in the Foreign Ministry.

"I'll tell the Captain that we have this man missing, Davis. I'll say Davis drinks a lot" – Kooper smiled and winked, as though to say we know that part is true – "and he had an argument with his wife the other night" – Kooper winked again – "and left the house without telling her where he was going, and he hasn't been heard of since. I'll say we are worried that he might have got drunk and had an accident. Maybe I should give Davis high blood pressure and an ulcer, whadda you think? That way they'll be gentle with him if they think he's got medical problems. They wouldn't want to have him die on them."

"Bill, you're a genius. You should be writing spy novels."

There was more than a hint of irony in Dawson's voice but Kooper either missed it or decided to ignore it. He beamed. Any complement from the ambassador was like sunshine on a winter day in his native Holland though not quite as rare. He was delighted that his proposal had won approval. Early in his career one of his supervisors had told him that the way to get ahead in the diplomatic service was to make proposals that are accepted. The emphasis was on the word accepted. You made proposals you thought the boss would like. You stayed away from those you thought might not find favor, no matter how reasonable they might otherwise be. It was a nice simple rule. Kooper found it worked wonderfully.

"That way," Kooper explained, "if they haven't got Davis we aren't admitting anything. And if they have him, they'll know we expect them to give him back to us, pronto." He smiled, enormously pleased with himself.

Dawson looked at Hawke. "Any problem with that?"

Whatever nutty thing they wanted to do was fine with Hawke. He nodded his assent.

"Alright then," Dawson said, "try it. But if we're going to pretend that Davis just got lost somewhere, let's play the game as though we meant it. Send Karen to see the chief of police and the people at the airport to ask if they've picked up anything on Davis."

Karen Flood was the consular officer. She was tall, had auburn hair, large round deeply blue green eyes, a fresh pretty face and an absolutely knockout body. If God, nature or her parents' genes had given Karen flood an intelligence to match her looks she would have been a certified genius. As it was she had just enough brainpower to be a competent consular officer. For the eight perpetually horny young men of the embassy's Marine security guard unit Karen Flood was the embassy's sex symbol. All they could do, however, was look and lather, for in her physical person she was as remote as a Maryln Monroe poster. She fended off advances from the Marines (she would never have dreamed of going out with them anyway) and from everyone else by pretending to a romance with a high school sweetheart back home. The truth was a bit different. Whenever she could get away for leave Karen flew off to Athens where she did indeed have a very hot romance going with the head of the embassy's political section there, a woman ten years her senior.

But Karen Flood knew how to put her good looks to professional use with men. Even the most hardened Marxist-Leninist ideologues among government officialdom were always ready to give her an appointment and usually to help her. After all, she not only had looks. She could give, or deny, a visa to a relative or friend who needed to travel to the U.S. Even Marxist-Leninists occasionally found themselves wanting that.

"Right boss," said Kooper, with a customary show of enthusiasm. "I'm on to it."

ELEVEN

Such a damned incestuous thing the diplomatic corps was. Did Dawson really have to go to the German ambassador's farewell dinner for the Argentine ambassador? It was sure to be a monumental bore. His trip to Washington had been the perfect excuse for escaping it. Just for that he had been glad of going. So how had Greta Heldenberg found out that he was back? In three days since his early return, Dawson had left the American embassy compound only once, and then only for a visit to the Foreign Ministry. The German ambassador's wife seemed to run the best intelligence service in town.

But it would be unwise to offend her, and Dawson knew he could not get away with pretending to have another engagement. With no real choice in the matter, he decided to make the best of it.

"Greta, what a pleasure," he crooned into the telephone. "How thoughtful of you to include me at this late date. Are you sure it's not a problem? No? See you on Friday, then."

The former Greta von Gobbens – her husband Heinz Heldenberg was a commoner but she made sure everyone knew that she was a von Gobbens – had once been a beautiful woman. That much was amply conveyed by the very large oil portrait of her, radiant in the freshness of youth, a Germanic looking Grace Kelly, clad in a simple white dress with a single string of pearls around her neck, abundant blond tresses resting on deliciously bare shoulders, that hung in the foyer of the German ambassador's residence in a place where no one could miss it.

The painting was from three decades back. The years since then had not been kind to Greta Heldenberg. Somewhere along the way her face had crinkled, perhaps from too much exposure to the sun of the tropics, where Heinz' mediocre diplomatic career had taken her. Or if not that, from the drink that flowed so abundantly in the Heldenberg household. That part of her anatomy that she turned most publicly to the world now looked like a large ball of wadded paper.

Greta's other misfortune was her husband. Heinz Heldenberg managed the physiologically not inconsiderable feat, for a man in his fifties, of being, at one and the same time, a lush and a philanderer. His current affair was with the wife of a senior United Nations official. Word of it could hardly have escaped Greta's sensitive antennae, but if it affected her at all she was careful not to let it show. In an earlier day, Greta had had not a few affairs of her own. Marital fidelity being, after all, a bourgeois virtue, whereas infidelity was a time honored aristocratic vice.

Now she had found other passions in life. She was a dedicated hostess and a compulsive clothes horse. She entertained extravagantly, far beyond her husband's limited ambassadorial allowance for representation. She gave more dinner and cocktail parties than anyone else on the diplomatic circuit, and they were more lavish. Her new year's eve masked ball was the international set's event of the year, the place where everyone who aspired to be anyone had to be. In this city where gasoline was rationed to ordinary citizens and automobiles were a luxury that only a favored few could afford, it created the year's only traffic jam.

The question was, did Greta Heldenberg entertain for the sake of entertaining, or to show off her latest acquisitions from Paris and Milan? The answer, it seemed safe to say, was both. Whatever strange and crazy outfits the gods of European fashion contrived each spring and fall she bought and wore joyously, gleefully, like a child displaying a prized new toy. Her frequent shopping trips to Europe lasted weeks at a time and afforded Heinz ample opportunity to pursue his dalliances. Her latest acquisition was a thing, all in flaming red silk and satin, with football player padding at the shoulders and a skirt so tight that she had to turn sidewise to walk and so short that when she sat down it slithered half way up her thigh. Decked out in it, Greta Heldenberg looked, with her shiny, now dyed, blond hair, her rutted tanned face, her enormous bouffant shoulders and her spindly worn legs, like a giant winged beetle of some exotic tropical variety preparing for flight.

But Greta Heldenber's overriding passion was gossip. Not the idle kind that feeds on whatever morsels come to hand. Greta's gossip was of the energetically entrepreneurial brand. The woman knew everything, literally everything, that transpired within the diplomatic and international community, and much of what went on in the country as well. It was she who had tipped Dawson off, a few months earlier, to the departure of the Cuban heavy artillery brigade. He was immensely grateful to her for it. It was a big scoop and it won Dawson points back at the State Department, where people congratulated themselves on their good fortune in having an ambassador who had been able, despite the restrictions of a Marxist-Leninist police state, to develop inside sources.

It was amazing, indeed uncanny, how much the woman knew. And that was precisely what worried Dawson. Had Greta Heldenberg somehow got wind of Harry Davis's disappearance? If she had, the story could be all around town within hours. At the moment, however, it seemed to be only Dawson's early return that aroused Greta's curiosity.

"Herr-bert!" She greeted him with a shriek and presented her creased cheeks for the obligatory peck on each side as he arrived for dinner. Greta had that too energetically cheery manner that Germanic women in particular seem to affect.

"Vee are zo happy to have you back with us, dear man. You come early, no? Did you not zay you would not return until January?"

A tall, coal black, strikingly handsome servant, outfitted in an immaculate white uniform emblazoned with gold buttons and red braid, his head wrapped in a flaming red turban, came to take Dawson's coat.

"I couldn't bring myself to miss your party, Greta. Washington is so dull at this time, you know." Dawson knew that wasn't going to satisfy her, but it would have to do for the moment.

"Zuch a charming man! But I am sure there must be more to it than my itty-bitty party." She giggled, child like. Greta Heldenberg would never master the pronunciation of the w and the s in the English language, but she delighted in displaying her knowledge of American slang.

Three musicians, brown faces and hands protruding uncomfortably from white tie and tails, were thumping out a tango in one corner of the room. Dawson eagerly seized the opportunity it offered to change the subject. "Truly we do celebrate Argentina tonight, I see."

"Yes, aftervards vee dance. You vill be my first partner, vill you not?

Dawson hated the tango, and he could imagine Greta, with her tight skirt, falling flat on the floor trying to execute its steps. But all he could do was reply, with foolishly exaggerated chivalry, "An honor and a pleasure, Madam."

The Chinese ambassador and his wife appeared in the doorway just at that moment. Greta broke away to greet them, and Dawson was free. He headed for the far side of the spacious, high ceilinged, softly lit and pushily carpeted reception room, admiring on his way, as he did on each of his visits, the richness of the mahogany trimmings and the antiquity of the paintings that hung on the walls. The paintings were of bucolic eighteenth century Germany, the Good Germany, the one that existed before evil spirits invaded its soul, and of proud bemedaled and bewhiskered German noblemen. The very large one in the center of the room, just above the broad fireplace, that imperious looking gentleman holding the handle of his sword as though about to draw it to slay an impertinent challenger, was Greta's ancestor, the illustrious Prince Siegfried von Gobbens.

The room gave off a soothing golden glow of well being and prosperity. Servants resplendent in their starched white uniforms and gold braid darted back and forth among the sleek, well nourished guests, some offering canapés of smoked salmon, lobster and goose liver pate on broad silver trays, others long stemmed glasses of fine crystal bubbling with champagne. The men were elegantly attired in dark suits, white shirts and conservative ties. The women were bursts of color. They were reds, yellows, greens, blues and mauves. From a distance they looked like exotic flowers in a crowded nursery.

And their jewelry! Diamonds, pearls, rubies and sapphires, enough gems and gold to wipe out the annual trade deficit of this medium sized African nation. The paradox was that here in the Third World, amidst grinding poverty, in a country that espoused the theology of communism, these precious stones and metals – adornments, really, from an earlier age – could be worn safely and proudly, whereas in the great cities of the affluent Western capitalist world their owners would scarcely have dared remove them from their vaults, and then would have shown them only blushingly.

And though this was Africa, Dawson noted that the guests, as usual, were almost all white. He counted exactly three black faces, an ambassador and his wife from a neighboring African country, and a black United Nations official. Other than the servants, there was no one from the country in which they happened to be living. This was not wholly Heinz and Greta

Heldenberg's fault. Rarely were officials of the Leader's government permitted to attend Western diplomatic parties. Private citizens who wished to avoid the unpleasantness of interrogation by the State Security police rarely came either. Those who did show up more or less regularly were generally assumed to be informers.

But this de facto boycott was fine with Greta Heldenberg. She had lived many years among Africans but she was comfortable with them only as servants. She had never been able to look on them as social equals. Asians of course were another matter. They were people of Kultur.

These diplomatic dinners all followed a set pattern. They were announced for 8 p.m. but it was bad form to arrive before 8:15 or much after 8:30. Upon arrival the men and women exchanged greetings and then segregated themselves. The women sat on sofas and the men stood talking in small groups while awaiting the call to table. The code was unwritten and unspoken, but to sit before dinner was unmanly, while to stand was unwomanly. Occasionally a woman violated the rule but rarely did a man dare do so. Dinner would be called at around 9:30 and the guests would rise from the table by 11, stomachs congested by too much rich food eaten too late. Then after dinner the rules changed. The men could seat themselves with the women on the sofas or go off to easy chairs in some corner to light cigars, nurse snifters of brandy and talk business. By 11:30

they would be saying their goodbyes, for the regime's midnight curfew applied to everyone, even to ambassadors, and they were grateful for the excuse it gave them to break away.

Greta Heldenberg's table was, as always, a work of art. It was arranged that evening to seat twenty-four. Upon a finely embroidered white damask linen table cloth were set services of exquisite gold rimmed china and von Gobbens crested silverware in an antique German pattern, knives and forks so authentically and heavily silver that one had to grip them firmly to avoid their slipping from one's grasp. Deep blue linen napkins meticulously fashioned in the form of flowers erupted from the mouths of crystal wine goblets. In the center of the table red, yellow and white roseheads floated in shallow crystalline bowls. Delicate yellow flames from half a dozen finely sculpted silver candelabra softly lit the table and threw the diners' shadows dancing upon the room's frescoed walls.

Seating at the table was, as a matter of course, regulated by diplomatic precedence. All was determined by seniority. The longest serving sat to the right and left of the hostess; their wives to the right and left of the host. The most recently arrived were relegated to the insignificant middle of the table. But given the steady rotation of diplomatic personnel it did not take long to move up. In the two years that he had been there Dawson had gained enough seniority to come only two places removed from Greta Heldenberg's left. In this instance, however, his advance served him poorly. He found himself between the wife of the ambassador of the People's Republic of China, Madam Zhao Chin Pei, and the wife of the ambassador of Belgium, Madam Jean-Pierre Dupoids. It would have been hard to draw a worse hand.

From the moment Dawson saw the place cards he realized that he was in for a deadly hour and one-half. He could anticipate his conversation with Madam Zhao, for it never varied significantly.

"How your wife?" Madam Zhao's large round Asiatic face, shadowed by the moving flicker of candlelight, grinned toothily at Dawson.

Sally's fling in Paris had sent shock waves thought the diplomatic gossip circuit, as had her death there. It was obvious that Madam Zhao was blissfully unaware of the stories that had made the rounds months ago. Dawson decided that it would be just as well to leave matters that way. Setting the record straight would take far too much effort and be much too disconcerting for Madam Zhao.

"Oh, she is doing as well as can be expected, thank you."

"I very sad we not see her for long time." Madam Zhao grinned more broadly still.

"Well, she is very much occupied at present."

"I hope she come soon."

"That could be a bit difficult."

Madam Zhao laughed heartily. Dawson had become accustomed to the grins and the laughter. Asians, he had learned from his infrequent contacts with them, had this idiosyncrasy. When they did not know what to say, or for some other reason were uncomfortable, they grinned and laughed.

Dawson knew exactly what the next question was going to be.

"How many children you have?" Another broad grin.

"Two. A girl and a boy."

"Very nice." Another laugh. "They in America?"

Speaking slowly, so as to be sure that she would understand and perhaps this time remember, Dawson began to tell Madam Zhao, for the fourth or fifth time at least, about his daughter who was a lawyer in Washington DC and his son, who was a student of engineering. Madam Zhao inquired, as she had in each previous instance, whether the daughter was married and, as before, was delighted to learn that she was. As before, she asked if there were grandchildren, lamented the fact that so far there was none but sought to console Dawson by saying she was sure this void would soon be filled. All accompanied by another burst of laughter.

Dawson rerouted the conversation to the already well mined subject of Madam Zhao's children, but that vein too was soon exhausted.

As one could not sit quietly at these dinner but had, obligatorily, to appear deeply engrossed in fascinating conversation with one's neighbors, Dawson reluctantly turned to his right, to Madam Dupoids. Jean-Pierre Dupoids had begun his career as a jailer in the colonial service in the Belgian Congo. When that nation became independent he was offered the option of transferring to the diplomatic service, which he eagerly accepted.

That evening, as most, Annette Dupoids was as heavily made up as a Bois de Boulogne transvestite. Bright orange hair was piled in layers atop her head. Her eyes were circled in thick black rings of mascara and her eyelashes were gooey with it; a small gob was stuck on top of her left lid. Her porcine face was layered smooth with pancake and powdered over to a chalk white. She wore blazing red lipstick. Powerful gusts of a potent perfume wafted from her person, and a plunging neckline, decorated by a gaudy diamond brooch, revealed the vast northern approaches of two very fat and unappetizing breasts.

But if one could ignore all this there was compensation to be had from being seated next to Annette

Dupoids. It could be restful there. One did not have to make conversation or even listen with much care. She could chatter on mindlessly with only an occasional encouraging nod and grunt from her audience. Her subjects were, almost invariably, the house she and her husband owned in the south of France, and food. She was a walking encyclopedia of Riviera real estate values and of cheeses, sauces and veal recipes.

Trapped as he was between the puritanical communist East and the decadent capitalist West, Dawson lamented, as he had a hundred times before, having to attend these diplomatic dinners. They were, ordinarily, a terrific waste of time and they were almost uniformly boring. But they were inescapable, one of the tedious necessities of life, like shaving, brushing one's teeth or clipping one's toenails. The fact was you needed your diplomatic colleagues, especially in a place like this, where the government cut you off from contact with almost everyone else. Here the diplomatic corps became your family. Like any other family it could be tiresome, irritating and embarrassing, but it was also a refuge, a warm place to congregate. It was a place to trade information with your colleagues and keep an eye on what they were up to, which also was part of your job. In time of need your diplomatic colleagues might even rally to your side, though that was something you could not prudently count on. So the dismal round of diplomatic dinners and receptions went on and on, relentlessly, at the rate of three or four a week. Everybody met everybody else and had the same conversations over and over again. As if they had never had them before.

Dawson put himself on automatic pilot while Madam Dupoids prattled on about the cold spell in Europe that had made the pipes freeze and burst in their house in Provence, about how difficult it had been to get the plumbers in and what outrageous prices they had charged.

"Cent mille francs, can you imagine it! For a mere week's work! Scandaleux, n'est-ce-pas? But what can one do?"

Dawson was much relieved when, after dessert had materialized as a magnificent ice cream souffle, a tinkle of silverware on crystal rang out, the buzz of conversation died away and Heinz Heldenberg rose to deliver the evening's toast.

The German ambassador rose unsteadily. He swayed to one side and then the other, righted himself, stepped around his chair and with both hands anchored himself firmly to its high back. The assembled guests followed this maneuver in dead silence, holding their breath, like spectators watching to see if a boat caught in heavy surf would make it to a safe landing. Heldenberg was always the best customer for drinks at anybody's party, his own included. He had never yet been seen to fall but it seemed a good bet that one day he would.

"Excellencies, dear colleagues, ladies and gentlemen," Heldenberg bowed to the right and then to the left. "Welcome to our modest abode. Greta and I are so happy that you chose to honor us with your presence here this evening for this most important event. An occasion which I know is a sad one for all of us. Yes, a most sad occasion." The German ambassador's voice trailed off. He halted, trying to remember what came next. Then his face lit and he resumed confidently.

"A most sad occasion, the departure of our dearest friends and colleagues, His Excellency the Ambassador of Argentina, Senor Alfonso Colombo Zemora and Madam."

Eyes turned to the Argentine, a short, rotund, bespectacled and mostly bald man seated to the right of Greta Heldenberg. He nodded and smiled in grateful acknowledgement.

The German ambassador resumed. "For so many years we have been so honored to share the friendship of this charming man and his dear lovely wife, Concepcion, these dear friends, that when the moment of parting comes, it is, how to say it, it makes" – Heldenberg struggled, searching for the right words and not quite finding them – "it makes a sadness for us all. Your Excellency, Alfonso, as your many friends know you, if you will permit the familiarity, we all owe you so many thanks for the wonderful comradeship that you have given us these five years that we have spent together. You have been a true and loyal member of our diplomatic corps. We have enjoyed so many delightful evenings at your beautiful residence."

Heinz Heldenberg looked down at the short, rotund, rosy faced, dark haired woman sitting at his right. "Concepcion, we all know you as a marvelous hostess, as a woman of grace and charm, as a mother of three beautiful daughters, and as a true and most valuable helpmate of your husband through the trials of life and career. Behind every great man, a philosopher once said, is found a strong and loving woman. And that woman is our dearest Concepcion."

Heldenberg paused, took a deep breath, girded for the homestretch and was off again. "And our dear Alfonso is indeed a great and most talented man. Your Excellencies all know the wonderful work that His Excellency Ambassador Colombo has done in building ties between his great nation, that nation of brave men and women who have made Argentina a leader, indeed a beacon, in our world civilization, those brave men who ride the pampas, and the government to which we all have the honor and good fortune to be accredited. And not only between his government and the government of this great African nation, but between himself and all of us who, as I have said, have been favored with his friendship and have had the opportunity of appreciating his many talents."

The crescendo was approaching. The German ambassador's voice rose. "Their departure will leave an empty place in our hearts, but they will not be forgotten. They will be remembered and honored by all their friends and colleagues."

This fatuous nonsense was received by all in the most respectful silence. Overtly at least none among the diplomatically titled guests so much as cracked a faint smile. All knew that Alfonso Colombo Zemora had spent a wholly unremarkable five years in the capital, his time there distinguished by no apparent achievement of any sort. He was a sweet little man. He came to all the diplomatic functions, smiled a great deal and said little. He seemed able to talk volubly on one subject only, gardening, which was his passion and, it appeared, his major occupation. Newly arrived ambassadors who came to pay the ritual courtesy call on the ambassador of Argentina could count on being conducted on the most painstaking tour of his garden. They would be allowed to leave only after having heard the life history and genealogy of each plant. Some found this annoying, others amusing. They would say to recently arrived colleagues: "Have you called on the Argentine yet? No? Oh, you will learn all about his garden."

People wondered why Argentina kept an ambassador in this distant African nation. There was no apparent reason. Speculation that Alfonso Colombo was an out of favor general sent to political exile was belied in the first instance by his improbable physique. The most likely explanation for his presence was also the most prosaic. Many years earlier and for some long forgotten reason the government of Argentina had established an embassy in this African capital. Once established, the embassy had achieved a byzantine permanence. Occasionally someone thought of closing it down, but the bureaucratic obstacles to doing so thwarted whatever faint efforts were made.

But when it came to saying goodbyes none of this mattered. These diplomatic farewell odes were like graveside eulogies. No one expected to hear the truth spoken.

While Heinz Heldenberg discoursed, servants quietly filled champagne glasses around the table. As he reached his peroration, the head servant presented him one that, on Greta's order, was just short of empty. He lifted the glass high before him and called out:

"Excellencies, ladies and gentlemen, I ask you to join me in a toast to his Excellency the Ambassador of Argentina and Madam, for health, happiness, prosperity and great future success. We hope our paths will cross with theirs many times in the years ahead. And so, let us say to our good friend Alfredo" – "Alfonso," Greta barked from the other end of the table – "yes Alfonso, and dear Concepcion, let us make this not adieu but au revoir."

Heinz Heldenberg swallowed the meager contents of his glass and gingerly maneuvered himself back into his chair. A round of polite applause echoed through the spacious dining room.

All eyes now turned to the ambassador of Argentina. He struggled out of his seat and stood, not much more that five feet tall, barely topping the back of his chair. Unlike his host, he appeared to be wholly sober. With a business-like precision of movement he extracted as sheet of paper from the inside pocket of his suit jacket, adjusted his glasses and cleared his throat. Just as it seemed he was about to read he paused reflectively, muttered something to himself, folded the paper and held it in his left hand as he addressed the audience.

"Excellencies, ladies and gentlemen. I want to thank our distinguished host and hostess, the Ambassador of the Federal Republic of Germany and Madam, for this kind and gracious evening. I want to thank our friend Heinz for his generous remarks. I am not so eloquent as he, so I wrote out what I thought I should say on this occasion. But now I think that it is better that I set aside convention and speak from the heart the words that the heart wishes to say. Heinz, you spoke of my achievements during my five years here. It was kind of you to do so, but let us be honest with one another, if only for once in all that time. You know, and I know, and I am sure our other friends here know, that I have achieved nothing of value during these five years."

A burst of nervous laughter interrupted the Argentine ambassador. This was more than self-deprecation. Obviously the man was joking. Or was he? They were uncertain, so like Asians they laughed.

"Yes," he resumed. "You are right to laugh my friends and dear colleagues. It is indeed comic that my government should maintain an embassy in a place where it had absolutely no interests, where it has no conceivable business to transact. But that all too often is the way things are in my country. They are comic, when they are not tragic. At this moment they are tragic, so very tragic, for in my country today people are being tortured and murdered. They are being tortured and murdered by their government. Men and women, even children, are being tortured and murdered, and their bodies are not even being returned to their families. They are simply disappearing."

A grim silence descended over the gathering. The man was speaking in earnest! He was attacking his own government! It was quite unheard of. An outrageous breach of protocol.

"Torture and murder. Yes, they are something that happens in many places. They happen right here, in the country in which we are living, as all of us know. I would like all of you, my friends, to know that I am leaving my post not because the time has come for my transfer – in Buenos Aires they had quite forgotten about me and if they remembered they would have been happy, I am sure, to leave me here. I am leaving because I feel in my heart that I cannot continue to represent a government that tortures and murders. And that I cannot represent it even in a place where that government has no interests and no business to represent. I thank our host for his good wishes that our paths should again cross one day. I too would wish so, dear colleagues, but if it happens it will not be in diplomatic life." The Argentine ambassador paused, then added, barely audibly, "It may not even be in this life." He bowed toward the hostess and then toward the host and resumed his seat.

The assembled excellencies and their wives were stunned. Never had any among them witnessed such a gross violation of the diplomatic code. If one had the misfortune to disagree with one's government one did so quietly. One did not get up and announce it for all the world to hear. Never! One did not embarrass one's colleagues by making them a party to one's grievances.

Still they faced a quandary. Convention required that they should applaud at this time. But should they? On the one hand, the Argentine had spoken sincerely, from the depth of his being, perhaps reflecting some terrible personal tragedy, the loss of a close relative or dear friend. It was a courageous act. If they failed to applaud it would be a discourtesy to the man and a refusal to recognize his courage and offer sympathy for his pain. On the other hand – there was, in diplomacy, always the other hand – to applaud could risk giving serious offense to the government of Argentina! They had to think of their government's relations with the government of Argentina, and also, potentially, of their own, for one never knew what one's next posting might be. Even more urgently they had to consider their relations with the government to which they were currently accredited, which would surely take offense at the Argentine's remarks.

Conscience pulled in one direction, caution in the opposite. Seeking some sign, they looked at one another and at their host and hostess. Greta Heldenberg's face was a mask. Heinz was swigging down a refill of champagne that he had ordered a servant to fetch for him.

Then the American ambassador began to clap his hands loudly. For an instant, an instant that seemed an eternity, he clapped alone, until Greta Heldenberg joined in. The others hesitantly followed. The applause broke the tension and restored the assembled excellencies and their spouses to their customary state of self-satisfied complacency. Greta rose from her chair and invited everyone to move to the drawing room for coffee. A buzz of conversation arose immediately, as though nothing in the least extraordinary had occurred. Madame Dupoids went off in search of Madame de la Rochefort, the wife of the French ambassador, to ask advice on the hiring of a new cook. Others huddled for similarly weighty deliberations. After all, they were diplomats. Nothing could for long disturb their composure. They were adaptable. They knew how to bend with the times and the circumstances. It was the first law of their profession. If the event that had just transpired – later it would become famously known as 'the Argentine ambassador's outburst' – proved that they had not yet seen everything, it also proved that they were capable of seeing everything without allowing themselves to be affected by anything.

Physically they were vulnerable to the terrorist's bullet or bomb, to the ravages of disease, time and misfortune. But emotionally they moved among the ruins unscathed. They were transients, an exalted race of gypsies, spending no more than a few years in any one place, constantly on the move. They could go from posting to posting, from one country to the next, through an entire adult life, accumulating bric-a-brac, rugs, furniture, art, without ever once feeling deeply about the places or the people they had touched in their passage.

Greta Heldenberg quietly dismissed the musicians. Plainly, it was not going to be an evening for dancing.

Dawson had just lit a cigar and was beginning a conversation with the Italian ambassador when she approached. "Gentlemen," Greta said with mock officiousness, "I interrupt a most important discussion, I am sure. But my dear Guiseppi," she addressed the

Italian while slipping a bony hand under Dawson's arm, "please forgive me. Do let me borrow him from you for a moment."

They moved off to one side. Dawson was apprehensive. Now she was going to grill him about his early return, maybe even about Davis. What new story could he give?

"Ach, Herbert, you ver marvelous." Greta Heldenberg would never have admitted it, but she was outraged over what had happened. Why had that miserable little man from the underside of the world had to choose HER party to make his awful confession?

"You saved the evening. If you had not applauded all those idiots vud have just sat there, they vud not have known vat in the vorld to do. You are zuch a smart man." Dawson was susceptible to flattery, especially by women, and he knew it. He tried to smile wryly but in truth he was pleased.

"I would never have thought that our friend from Argentina had it in him to do what he did this evening. He doesn't seem the type. I know it was embarrassing, but I respect him for it."

Greta Heldenberg smiled. Men! They were all alike. Slaves to their preconceptions and to their fine principles. Women, fortunately were more practical.

"I imagine, Herbert," she smiled coyly, "that you are vaiting for me to apologize for putting you in that dreadful company. You looked absolutely bored to tears, about to die. But vat could I do? It vas protocol. The protocol left me no choice. Vee are its slave, are vee not? One day I shall hold a party vith no protocol. Vat a pleasure it vill be!"

"But," Greta continued, a wicked smile crossing her face, "perhaps you vud have been happier if I had put you next to an attractive voman. Vat a fool, that vife of yours, that Sally! Now that she is gone, all the vemen vill be running after you. I know it! But be careful. It can give trouble. Have you heard about the Turkish ambassador and the vife of the minister of justice?"

Dawson had not. Greta plunged gleefully into her story. The Turk, a handsome, virile looking man in his late forties with a thick black mustache, was the diplomatic corps's most eligible bachelor. He was famous also as a palm reader. At diplomatic dinner parties the women lined up for readings which, not coincidentally, involved having their hand held by this most attractive man. Recently the minister of justice had made an unusual appearance at a dinner at which the Turk was present. The minister's wife, a Polish woman he met and married during his student days in Warsaw, was with her husband, and she came to the Turk to have her hand read.

"A few days later," Greta's voice throbbed with excitement as she spun out the tale, "the Turkish ambassador is called by the minister's vife. She vants to come to his residence for another reading. Of course, he cannot refuse, but he thinks she will come with a relative or companion. Imagine his surprise! The voman comes by herself, alone! So vat can he do? He looks into her hand. He zees much sadness in it but before he can think vat to zay she bursts into tears and throws her arms around him. She tells him she loves him. She zays her husband sleeps vith the children's nurse! She vants to leave her husband and go with the Turk to Europe, you know he is being posted to Paris in March. Poor man, he is frightened to death. The minister of justice is a very powerful figure, one of the top people in the government. If the minister finds out about his vife's visit he might think, vell, you understand vat he might think, that the Turkish ambassador has an affair with his vife. Zo the Turk tells her that her hand says that she must be patient, that she vill find great happiness vith her husband and must under no circumstances leave him. She protests. She zays she loves the Turk and cries more. Finally he gets her to her car, but she continues to telephone him, every day, and to send him presents. The poor man is terrified that the minister vill have him declared persona non grata. He has asked his government for permission to leave early."

At that moment the Chinese ambassador and his wife approached to say goodbye. Greta put on her best hostess manner and broke away.

Poor man, indeed, Dawson thought. He pitied the Turk less for the unwanted attentions showered on him by the wife of the minister of justice – she was at least a very good looking woman – than for the fact that Greta had the story. Well, he could be grateful that she had a juicy tale to keep her busy. Busy enough, with luck, to prevent her from picking up the scent on Davis.

Dawson looked around for the Italian ambassador, spotted him and headed off toward him fast.

TWELVE

Her name was Joy but the students in her eleventh grade English class at the International School called her California. Because California was where she came from, but mainly, they said, because she seemed so California. She had frizzled blond hair that surrounded her head like a halo, a small snub nose and a cherubic face. She stood about five feet four and had a nice figure, a full figure, just a little on the lean side of Reubenesque. It was possible to imagine that in twenty years she might lose it, but for now her physical presence suggested only voluptuous delights. The teen aged boys in her classes had wet dreams about her.

Joy Chamberlain had arrived in this African capital a little over six months earlier, while bumming her way around the world. California, she was persuaded, had everything anyone could want in life, except that she needed to see a bit of the rest of the world before settling down there. This particular stop was to have been just like any other on her global itinerary. Very likely she would have scrubbed it had she realized that the country had gone over to the Soviet side, an event that had happened some six years earlier but that somehow had escaped her notice.

Not that communists particularly frightened Joy Chamberlain. Anarchists – she had known a few at UCLA – were far more scary. But she was for live and let live. All this cold war crap was not for her. It was just that she was low on cash and needed to work a while to replenish her treasury before moving on again, and she wouldn't have thought a communist country the ideal place to find a job. When she saw the large hammer and sickle hanging over the arrival hall at the airport, and the red flags with hammer and sickle, and then the banners with "workers of the world, unite!" and those other odd slogans, her heart sank.

But there she was. She couldn't leave for at least another two days so she went through customs and immigration control and out the other side to look for a ride into town. She didn't know where to go, but instinct told her to head for the best hotel in town, even though she knew she wouldn't have the money to stay there.

A taxi, a rattling old Mercedes, driven wildly by a young man who wanted to fix a date with her "just to have coffee" took her to the International Hotel. She knew precisely what to do there. She sat in the bar, a dark place with leather cushioned armchairs that looked like the bars of hotels a cut above the seedy category the world around, ordered a sandwich and nursed a drink for two hours until, at about 7 p.m., a very large American waddled in and immediately spotted her. The American bought her a second drink and paid for her first and her sandwich. He turned out to be the principal of the International School, which in fact was the American School, camouflaged under the name international for purposes of survival in the rather less than friendly environment of a people's democracy.

As it happened the principal had just lost his high school English teacher and was looking for a replacement. Joy Chamberlain had degrees in English literature and education and had taught for two years at a high school in Los Angeles before embarking on her round the world trek. Out of her backpack she produced her diplomas and letters of recommendation, and she was hired the next day. Soon she found herself liking the city. Communism, she discovered, wasn't so uniformly drab as people in the West might imagine. Like everything else, it had its loopholes. If you were a foreigner, a good looking single white female foreigner, there were plenty of places to have fun. All you had to do was get in with the international set. For Joy Chamberlain that was no problem at all.

School too was a snap. That first semester she was supposed to be teaching English and American writers of the nineteenth century but she slipped in John Updike and Philip Roth and had the class reading passages from Portnoy's Complaint. To fill out classroom time she sometimes regaled them with stories about her former boyfriends.

The boyfriend Joy Chamberlain didn't talk about was the one she met there, a couple of months after arriving, Harry Davis. Joy and Harry found one another at a Marine House party, found one another right away, knew from the very beginning that they were matched. They talked all that evening until they realized, with mild embarrassment, that they had spent so long together that others were beginning to comment on it and they broke off.

Until that time Joy hadn't met any man who truly appealed to her. The principal of the International School had made a more than obvious pitch, but he was too disgustingly fat, and besides, Joy soon learned, he kept a local woman. Neither did she intend to hook up with any of the Marines at the American embassy. She was twenty-nine and except for the gunnery sergeant who was older and married, the Marines were just boys, in their early twenties or even younger. All they were out for was a good lay. Joy wanted more.

Beyond the principal and the Marines, however, the market thinned considerably. To be sure, being a young, good looking white female in an African capital gave her a preferred status. And the competition was definitely light. Plain Jane American and British relief workers who smelled the virtuous smell of the countryside, were total strangers to the cosmetics industry and had never known the inside of a stylish piece of clothing; a fading American woman in her early forties who taught English at the local university, had sharp little teeth, was a compulsive bridge player and was looking desperately for a husband; and a few stray European women who worked for international organizations or taught at foreign schools.

But the pickings weren't that great either. The male relief workers were no more with it than their female counterparts. They were tacky and smelled of hay and manure. The missionaries were of course out of the question, they were so fresh and good, looking always as though about to burst into hosannas of praise for the Lord. The diplomats were mostly staid and creepy, and married, or closet gays. The few Western businessmen were middle aged, unattractive and on the make. None was Joy's type. Harry Davis appealed to her because he was older, but not too old, and he held a responsible job, a job that had status and allure, which she liked also. She didn't mind at all that Harry was married. She looked upon Harry's marital status much as she did his encroaching baldness. Both were minor defects, wholly unimportant. Besides, Harry's story about his unhappy marriage seemed sincere and plausible enough to be genuine. Joy had heard enough of these tales to know.

But the thing that attracted Joy Chamberlain to Harry Davis most of all was something she couldn't articulate and perhaps wasn't even aware of on a conscious level. It was that underneath the tough guy image that Harry sometimes tried to project he was vulnerable. He was someone she could nurse. And nursing, though perhaps she didn't realize it, was Joy Chamberlain's true vocation.

For Harry, Joy was everything that Barbara wasn't, and that he wished she were, beginning with the flesh, which was important to Harry. Barbara was tough and wiry; Joy was soft and inviting. Barbara was tense and keyed up; Joy was relaxed and – most of the time – happy. And unlike Barbara, Joy was wholly unconventional, which appealed to a certain side of Harry Davis. She couldn't care less what people thought about her. And political systems and global power struggles held no place whatsoever in her cosmology. The Cold War was just not something she worried about; not once in a year did she give it a thought. What a relief that was for Harry, who for eight years had lived with a dedicated freedom fighting anti-communist, a woman who went to bed at night and got up in the morning battling the Reds, who would talk shop even when making love.

Harry was afraid it would bother Joy to know that he was CIA, but once the relationship turned serious, which very quickly it did, he felt he should tell her even though he knew it was forbidden for him to do so. Much to his relief, she didn't mind at all. For Joy it simply added mystery and excitement. Perhaps Harry also realized that they were, each in his and her own way, outsiders. Perhaps he sensed too that Joy was the nursing type, and that one day he would need her for that as well.

After their first meeting at the Marine House and another at the airport club bar they conducted their affair like a covert operation, with mail drops, coded telephone messages and after dark rendezvous, sometimes in her apartment, sometimes at his place when Barbara was away on temporary duty in a neighboring country, which happened several times that year. One time Harry showed up at Joy's apartment with his mask on. She opened her door to his coded knock and shrieked with fright. When she recovered she thought the mask hilarious. She put it on and paraded around the apartment with it, giggling like a teenager. Didn't Harry's blue eyes give him away, she asked? No, he replied, the Agency had a solution for that too, but Harry didn't say what it was. Could Harry get a mask made for her? Then they could go out together in disguise, or maybe hold a masked ball. They laughed, fell exuberantly on the couch and buried themselves deliciously in one another's bodies.

Their affair had been going on for three months when Harry failed to show up for dinner at Joy's apartment that evening in December, four days before Christmas. She cried, but her tears were for the cold filet mignon and the deflated soufflé on which she had lavished a whole afternoon and now had to throw out. And for the evening spent alone, waiting for Harry. Because never for a moment did she think he had deliberately stood her up. Nothing at all bad had happened between them, never since the moment they met. There had been no disagreements, no fights, none of the tell-tale signs – Joy knew them well – of an affair winding down. If anything, it was the contrary. They were moving closer together. They were beginning to talk about getting married. And it was Harry, not Joy, who first raised the subject.

So Joy was sure Harry's failure to appear for dinner that evening was not voluntary. She was worried, because by then she knew that Harry was involved in dangerous work even if she didn't know exactly what it was. The next morning she telephoned his office and left the message he had instructed her to leave when she wanted to talk with him. No answer came. She called again and was told that he was out. She called his home that evening but hung up when a woman answered. Finally, two days after Christmas, Joy Chamberlain screwed up her courage. She looked at the telephone for a long time, then picked it up, dialed the embassy's number and asked for the ambassador's office. The sugary, too cultivated voice of a middle aged woman came on the line.

"How may I help you?"

"My name is Joy Chamberlain. I teach at the International School. I would like an appointment to see the ambassador."

"Might I tell the ambassador what the subject is?"

Joy hesitated. "Tell him it's a personal matter."

That afternoon the sugary voice called back. Mr. Kooper would be happy to see her, the next morning at ten.

THIRTEEN

The sign on the door of suite 401 of the modern high rise office building in Nairobi announced an occupant of less than eye catching interest: The Agricultural Machinery Marketing Company, Ltd. The company was incorporated in Amsterdam but all it owned there was a post office box. Its branch offices were located exclusively in those few African countries that overtly maintained commercial ties with Israel after African governments broke off diplomatic relations with the Jewish state in 1974.

The Agricultural Machinery Marketing Company did not just sell agricultural machinery. It sold anything and everything that was grown, produced or manufactured in Israel, everything from eggs to toilet bowls to fire extinguishers to military communications handsets, and much more. The company did a brisk business, all the more so as it operated not only in the countries where its offices were located but also in neighboring ones. The main problem it encountered was that governments were slow to pay. This in particular was the case of a nearby Marxist-Leninist government.

The branch manager was a short, heavyset man nearing fifty with thick, curly closely cropped hair who was known locally by the name Albert Klein. The morning of the day before the end of the year Klein got a call from the commercial attaché of the embassy of the nearby Marxist-Leninist government. Klein buzzed his secretary.

"Rachel, our friend the commercial attaché – the one I just spoke with – is coming in today at noon. Notify security to let him pass and get me the billing file on the fifty thousand pairs of military boots we sold them two years ago. Yes, that's right, the delinquent one. The very delinquent one."

Not a cent had been paid on this account since the original ten percent down payment made upon signature of the contract. The uncollected balance amounted to over a million dollars.

"The bastards are marching around in our boots, which by now probably are not worth more than ten cents on the dollar," Klein muttered as he looked over the file. The account had caused Klein considerable heartburn. The manufacturer, Kibbutz Har-Zahav in the Galilee, had filed suit against the government of Israel for payment of the outstanding balance. A court had awarded it compensation but the ministry of finance and the ministry of commerce and industry had immediately fallen to quarreling over which should pay. The two ministries were headed by politicians who, though they belonged to the same coalition government, hailed from rival parties and were sworn personal and political enemies. Each wanted the money to come from the other's budget, and each was far more interested in making the other pay than in compensating the manufacturer. Meanwhile, Kibbutz Har-Zahav was threatening a second lawsuit. And through all of this a good deal of heat had been directed at Klein.

So Albert Klein relished the opportunity to get tough with his delinquent client. Whatever the purpose of the commercial attaché's visit, Klein was going to use it to insist on the long overdue payment. He had a trump card ready to play, the order the commercial attaché had placed some months earlier for a very large quantity of fifty caliber machine gun ammunition. Klein knew the attaché's government needed the ammunition badly. He was going to insist that not one frigging bullet would be forthcoming until the bill for the boots was paid in full.

Klein was about to launch into this subject when his visitor, a tall, slender dark skinned man with finely chiseled features, announced quietly:

"I have come on an urgent matter of a special nature." The man spoke in a pleasantly accented English barely above a whisper. "You have perhaps heard that an official of the American embassy in my country has been missing now for some days."

Klein said nothing. His face revealed neither knowledge nor ignorance of the matter. In fact, however, he could have told his visitor the American's name and the exact number of days he had been missing.

"This person is an agent of the American CIA. He says his name is Harman Davis, but it appears that he also goes by the name Jack Higgins. He had been apprehended in the act of fomenting disturbances against my government."

"Why do you tell me this?" Klein asked. "What does it have to do with me?"

The commercial attaché smiled a thin smile. "If you are not interested, of course there is no need to discuss it."

Klein was very interested. "Go on. I am listening."

The commercial attaché shed his cool, quiet demeanor. Now he spoke heatedly. "My government wishes only to achieve the welfare of the people, to cure the diseases that ravage them and to raise them from the poverty and ignorance imposed upon them by the imperialist tool regime that our revolution overturned. The fact that my government has chosen the path of socialism does not mean that it considers itself the enemy of any other government. It wishes to be the friend of all. It has nothing against America. It seeks good relations with America and with all other countries. Despite this the American imperialists continue to attack us. Why do they want to keep us in subjection? Is it because they fear the success of our example?"

Klein recognized this for what it was, the obligatory preface to settling down to business. Other third worlders required you to take coffee or tea with them and make small talk about family and the weather. These people made you sit through a lecture about ideology. He shifted impatiently in his chair.

"I am still listening."

"I see you wish me to come to the point. Fine. It is this. My government is deeply aggrieved by the actions of the American CIA. This man Davis is guilty of criminal acts. He should be tried and shot. My head of state, however, is prepared to be magnanimous. He is prepared to release Mr. Davis."

Klein, normally a circumspect man, could barely contain his excitement. What a coup for Israel! The CIA loses one of its men and we find him and get him back for them. Once again, little Israel pulls big America's chestnuts from the fire. Klein wanted to shout hurrah. But what a bunch of dolts they were, anyway, these Americans. To lose an officer under diplomatic cover! How clumsy can you be? This time they will owe us a big one, Klein reflected gleefully. Already he was thinking of the cable he would send back to Mossad headquarters. And of the promotion and transfer this coup could win him. For what Klein, whose true name was Shimshoni, Avinoam Shimshoni, really wanted most was to get out of Africa to one of the postings in Europe. He had had ten years of hot, sweaty places, of malaria pills that left a bitter taste in the mouth and made the stomach feel like one had swallowed a pound of lead, of flies, mosquitoes and dirt, of diarrhea and of underdevelopment in all its surreal forms. He yearned for Civilization and Culture, for someplace where you could go to the opera, see the latest movies and eat salad without wondering whether it was going to make you deathly ill. He dreamed of a posting in London or Paris, though Vienna or Rome would do almost equally well.

"There are of course a few conditions."

"Tell me more." Despite himself, an anxious note crept into Klein's voice.

"My government is prepared to release Mr. Davis on condition that the American government repay to us the fifteen million dollars the revolutionary government paid for military equipment that the United States refused to deliver to us after the Russians began providing us arms. That is one condition. The other is that it provide my government a formal letter of apology for the actions undertaken by Mr. Davis, together with the written assurance that it will in future cease all such subversive activities against it. If these conditions are fulfilled we will release Davis unharmed. If not, revolutionary justice will have to take its course."

Klein returned to earth with a thud, his fantasies shattered. The Americans might be incompetent spies but they were not fools. They would not agree to conditions, least of all to conditions like these.

"Your government is not being realistic. This man Davis is an accredited diplomat. You can't hold him or shoot him. Nobody does that to diplomats, not even your Russian friends. You are obliged by international law to let him go, to expel him at worst. Doesn't your government know that?" Klein realized he was practically shouting.

"Mr. Shimshoni," the visitor replied coldly, "those are my government's terms. I was sent here to state them, not to negotiate about them."

Klein hesitated a moment, then smiled. And they say we are a stiff necked people, he thought. Still, there was no reason to despair. There surely had to be a role for a mediator in this affair.

"In consideration of the good relations between your government and mine, I'll do my best to help," he said. "I should be able to get back to you in a day or two."

The moment the visitor was out the door Klein picked up the telephone and dialed a direct line into one of the offices of the American embassy.

"Terry Reams? Al Klein here. A client of mine has just made an offer that I think you'll be interested in learning about. Yes, it's the matter we discussed three days ago. You want to meet now? This minute? That's too soon. I have a luncheon engagement coming up in ten minutes. How about at three? Okay? You'll come here? See you at three then."

Only after he had hung up did Klein notice the file on the long overdue payment of the military boot sale, sitting accusingly on top of his desk. He had totally forgotten to raise it. He swore and pounded his desk so loudly that Rachel called out to inquire if he was alright.

FOURTEEN

For the minister of foreign affairs, a handsome man, broad shouldered and of medium height, only just forty but possessed already of a quiet dignity, it had been a time of deep frustration. That morning, as every morning for the past three days, the American ambassador had telephoned his office and asked for an appointment. And that day, as each day before, the minister had been obliged to instruct his secretary to refer the ambassador to his deputy minister.

At noon the foreign minister summoned the deputy minister. He remained seated at his desk, reading, as the deputy minister entered. With ostentatious deliberateness he allowed a full minute to pass before looking up.

Having to consult his deputy always put the minister in a foul mood, the more so that day as the man, a tall, gaunt, saturnine individual, appeared before him dressed in the party uniform. It was a kind of Mao suit, a high collared jacket and trousers made of rough cotton and dyed to a medium gray. The minister found it absurd; he could not bring himself to appear in it under any circumstance. He exempted himself from wearing it to the office on grounds that it was not suitable for receiving foreign dignitaries. On other occasions he would don the country's traditional flowing white robe. This enraged the party's ideologues, but as the regime pretended to strong nationalist roots no one dared take him to task for it openly.

The deputy minister could have worn a business suit too that day. Instead he chose to flaunt his dedication to the regime.

"What did Ambassador Dawson have to say today?"

As the minister had not invited him to sit down the deputy minister remained standing, a scowl etched onto his face.

"He made an outrageous allegation."

"Please be specific." It annoyed the foreign minister that he literally had to pry information out of his senior subordinate.

"He said the Americans have learned that their man Davis has been arrested and is being held by us. He demanded – those were his outrageous words, he said 'I demand' – that we release Davis immediately. He gave me this diplomatic note that quotes the provisions of the Vienna Convention." The deputy minister waved two long sheets of white paper in the air. "He said that if our government did not like Davis or did not approve of his conduct it was free to expel him but it did not have the right to detain him."

"Do you know of any such thing? Are we in fact holding an American diplomat?"

"I have no information."

The foreign minister examined his deputy's features but they revealed nothing beyond the man's customary ill humor. The deputy minister could have been lying or telling the truth but the minister was ready to believe that he was lying. His resentment redoubled. The deputy minister had been appointed, he knew, to be his ideological watchdog. He had better connections in the party and in the regime that the minister himself. If he wished he could almost certainly find out – if he did not already know – whether an American was being held. But he did not volunteer to do so, and the minister was not going to humiliate himself by asking it of him.

"How then did you answer the American Ambassador?"

"I demanded to know on what basis he made this outrageous allegation. I asked who had told him that we are holding this Mr. Davis? He answered me arrogantly. He said: 'Your own government can answer that question.' I told him that his story has no truth to it. It is an imperialist plot to smear the good name of our government. The American accused us of making Davis a hostage. He raised his voice. He pounded his fist on the coffee table, so hard that the ashtray jumped in the air." The deputy minister screwed his features into a look of the most profound indignation. "It was unacceptable, absolutely unacceptable."

The ashtray jumped in the air? The foreign minister had to suppress a chuckle. He tried to imagine the American ambassador, a reserved, by the book diplomat, pounding his fist on the deputy minister's coffee table so hard that an ashtray jumped in the air. And the deputy minister's astonishment. Few things could give the minister more satisfaction than the thought of his deputy's discomfort.

The deputy minister continued. "This American imperialist has become altogether too arrogant. We must expel him. He is no friend of our government."

Who, the foreign minister mused, could possibly be more arrogant than my deputy minister? One day, perhaps, he would have the opportunity to apologize to the American ambassador for having inflicted the deputy minister on him in such circumstances.

"That is a matter we shall consider later. Please give me the note." The foreign minister quickly scanned the document. He skipped over the obligatory empty courtesies of the opening paragraph – "The Embassy of the United States of America presents its complements to the Ministry of Foreign Affairs of the Socialist People's Republic of.."- and went straight to the paragraph on the immunity of diplomatic personnel.

"Have we in fact given diplomatic accreditation to a Mr. Harman Davis?"

"His name appears on our diplomatic list."

"Then he is an accredited diplomat, entitled to immunity from arrest and detention?"

The deputy minister grunted a reluctant acknowledgement.

"And the quotation in the American ambassador's note, from the Vienna Convention, is it correct?"

"I will check with our legal advisor."

"Please do, and have him report to me. That will be all, thank you." The foreign minister spoke crisply. He handed the note back to his deputy who, still standing, turned and left the room as gloomily as he had come.

The foreign minister swiveled his chair around so that he faced a broad plate glass window that gave out onto the tree lined avenue running in front of the building.

Beyond the avenue, soaring above the trees, stood the naked gray concrete flank of the International Hotel. At that time of day his office window, shaded by the branch of a nearby tree, offered a reflection of his image. The glass, imported from some east bloc country, was heavily tainted by imperfections. The image it projected back was wildly distorted. The minister's eyes looked back at him slant, his fine Semitic nose was mashed flat and his chin had disappeared in a face stretched out like rubber.

The face the foreign minister presented to the world was a far more pleasing one. In a government resolutely aligned with the East, it smiled enticingly Westward. He was the token moderate in a crowd of hotheaded leftists, the man who, it was intended, should give the regime a gloss of legitimate non-alignment so as to keep aid money flowing from the kind hearted Europeans. He was no fool. He well understood that the Leader was using him. But for some rather long time he clung to the illusion that he could use the Leader; that as foreign minister he could keep a lifeline open to the West where he had received his education and where his sympathies lay. Only gradually did he come to the realization that instead he had become the Leader's apologist to the West, stretching and bending the truth, lying even, to defend the regime.

And now with the case of this American Davis, the worst was in prospect, a total break with the United States that could entrain a break with the Europeans.

For the minister of foreign affairs did not for one moment believe that the American ambassador would make accusations, raise his voice and pound the table for no other reason than to create an incident between the two countries. There had to be valid grounds for his conduct.

From the moment the Americans had reported Davis missing the foreign minister had tried to find out what had happened to him. He had called the minister of state security twice. Both times the regime's policeman had given him the same answer.

"I do not know anything about it."

It was an answer that, however unsatisfactory, the foreign minister, had no grounds to dispute. He was not a member of the politburo but a mere technician, kept around only because of his usefulness in dealing with the West and allowed to know only what the higher powers deemed it useful for him to know. But now that it was clear that Davis was indeed an accredited diplomat, the matter came more clearly within his purview. The foreign ministry was charged with the accreditation and protection of foreign diplomats. He had both the right and the duty to know if his government was holding a foreign diplomat. But the thought of calling the minister of state security again, for a third time, tied a knot in the pit of his stomach. The minister of state security was a fearsome individual. The man had a face that could make children burst into tears and a record that could make a strong man cringe. Still, there was no other way.

The minister of foreign affairs lifted one of the several telephones on his desk off its cradle, pressed the intercom buzzer and instructed his secretary to put through a call for him to the minister of state security. He was vastly relieved when, after a few minutes delay, she replied that the minister of state security was not in his office. Still, he knew it was only a brief reprieve. The unresolved tension left him nervous and fidgety through the rest of the day. He barely touched his lunch and sat distractedly through a series of afternoon meetings and appointments. A smoky darkness was falling when his secretary rang to say that the minister of state security would be coming on the line. Ordinarily he would have spoken cautiously but now he could no longer contain himself.

"The American ambassador came in once again today about this man Davis. Now he is saying that we have arrested him and are holding him hostage. The matter is becoming quite serious. I must know. Are we holding the American or not?"

A long silence ensued. Finally the voice came through at the other end of the line barely above a whisper.

"This is not your business. Keep out of it."

The foreign minister was about to protest when he heard a click on the line and then the drone of a dial tone.

*   *   *

Coming to the American embassy made Joy Chamberlain uncomfortable less because of the business she had to do there than for the fact that, from the outside at least, the place looked such a grim fortress. The concertina wire atop the high wall that sealed off the compound from the street made her flesh crawl. The heavy iron gate, kept shut except in the early morning hours when the staff were coming in to work and the late afternoon when they left, struck her as ominous. The Marine guard on duty that morning was so heavily armed that he looked ready to go straight into combat, an assault rifle slung over his shoulder, a very large pistol in a holster flat against his right hip and a nightstick dangling from his left hip.

Joy arrived in a taxi and stood waiting at the gate while the Marine – a new Marine, one she hadn't met before – looked her greedily up and down and then turned to a leisurely study of her passport, examining the many stamps that had been put in it.

"You've been to a lotta places," he remarked finally.

Joy could see that if she let him the clown would keep her there all day and end up asking her for a date. So she said, in the manner that she could summon when the circumstances required:

"Never mind that Jack, you're not the passport officer. Just call Mr. Kooper's office and clear me though.

At the chancery the too polite secretary whose sugary voice Joy recognized from their telephone conversations, a very prim middle aged lady with dyed blonde hair tied in back in a bun, showed Joy to a small waiting room off the executive offices. There she sat, uncomfortably, on a lacquered wooden chair and looked up at the color portrait that looked down upon her from high on the wall. The President of the United States was smiling at her, but it seemed more a grin, a mean grin even, than a smile. Or perhaps he was just squinting because he wasn't so young any more and was having trouble looking into the camera because of the bright lights. In any case it was an odd picture and it didn't make Joy feel at ease.

The announcement came in the same sugary voice: "Mr. Kooper will see you now."

Wim Kooper's desk, like his hair, was a mess. Papers were scattered everywhere about it. The bright early January light filtered in thinly through windows that obviously had not been washed from the outside for a very long time, for the altogether plausible reason that they were covered by heavy steel wire mesh screen on top of which were fastened steel bars. Kooper was slouched in a government issue brown imitation leather armchair that had been made by convicts in a Florida prison. Without bothering to rise he motioned Joy to a seat on the government issue brown imitation leather couch – made in the same facility – facing him. She perched herself nervously on the edge of the couch, her knees almost touching the plain brown wooden coffee table that separated them.

The name Joy Chamberlain had meant nothing to Kooper. He had not known what to expect. This was decidedly a pleasant surprise. Kooper fixed hungry eyes on his visitor. Her fine legs, beneath a skirt that, when she sat, inched up to show the beginnings of perfectly sculpted thighs, the magnetic plump protrusions beneath her turquoise angora sweater, the warm radiations of a soft, wonderfully feminine flesh, left him in a state of incipient arousal. Kooper and his wife had had a child a little over a year earlier. Since then only in rare instances had Wim been able to persuade her to receive him into the sanctuary of her body. He had no idea what might be the personal matter that brought Joy Chamberlain to his office that morning but now he was eager to assist. He was about to open with small talk, a question about the school and how she liked living in Africa, when she broke in.

"I have come," Joy said in as flat and unemotional tone as she could muster, "to ask about Harry Davis."

The words chased away the thoughts that had been running through Kooper's mind. He sat upright in his chair. An inquiry about Davis was serious business.

"I haven't heard from him in almost ten days," she continued. I'm concerned that something may have happened to him. I'd like to know if you can tell me how I can get in touch with him?"

"Harry's away for a while," Kooper answered after a moment's hesitation, as nonchalantly as he could.

"When will he be back?"

"In a few weeks, maybe. Why do you want to know."

It was time, Joy decided, to cut the pretenses. This tall drooling Dutchman with the funny face was stalling and would keep on stalling.

"Look," she said, her voice suddenly stiffening, "I'm asking you to be candid with me. Harry and I have a relationship. He wouldn't leave without telling me. Not if he had any choice. I want to know what happened to him."

So this was Harry Davis' girl friend. Not bad, Kooper thought, not bad at all. Kooper hadn't thought of Davis as a particularly remarkable guy. Now his opinion of Davis soared. He must have something to get a woman like that. Those looks! That body! What a fine time Harry must have had in bed with that! But Kooper, wondered, what exactly was he going to tell her? His fertile imagination quickly supplied the answer. He lowered his voice, as though to impart an important secret.

"Alright, I wouldn't just let anybody in on this, but I guess you ought to know. Please keep it confidential. Harry's gone back to the States to dry out."

"What do you mean, dry out?"

"You say you know Harry? You don't know about his drinking problem?" The State Department has sent him to a program for alcoholics, to dry out."

"I want to speak with him. What's his telephone number there? What's his address?" Joy fired the questions at Kooper almost in panic.

"I'm sorry, lady, I can't give that information out to anybody. He's not supposed to be in touch with anybody while he's in the program." Kooper smiled coyly. "You'll just have to wait until he gets back."

It was all too ridiculously implausible. "Harry drinks," she said, "but he isn't an alcoholic. He didn't tell me anything about an alcoholism program, and by the way I know very well that he doesn't work for the State Department. What is this, anyway? I don't believe you. You're feeding me a bunch of crap."

The sudden stridency took Kooper by surprise. Joy Chamberlain looked so angelic. Kooper equated femininity with softness and malleability, though he found neither of these qualities in particular abundance in his wife. Clearly the woman sitting across from him was not what he had thought. Kooper decided it was time to put an end to the interview.

"Look, lady, I'm not in the lonely hearts business. I've told you all I can tell you. If you're not satisfied, why don't you go see Harry's wife. He has one, or didn't you know? She's right here in town. I can give you her telephone number."

Joy had been on the point of breaking into tears. Kooper's words sobered her. She stood up, stepped around the coffee table and shot a steely glare at Kooper. She struggled to find words for her anger.

"Thank you for your suggestion, Mr. Kooper. I will do just that. And you won't have to give me her telephone number. I already have it."

She swept out of the room and past the prim, middle aged secretary without a word, furious at Wim Kooper but even more furious at herself for not having found a truly devastating remark on which to make her exit.

FIFTEEN

"The Israelis will be coming in on Monday."

Hawke spoke quietly, standing squarely in front of Dawson's desk at the far end of the ambassador's dark wood paneled office. Ever since word had come that Davis had not escaped, as Hawke had so confidently predicted and had so ardently wished to believe, he had been uncharacteristically subdued.

"Maybe now we'll get this thing settled," he added nervously.

Dawson tilted back in his swivel armchair and looked Hawke up and down, as though seeing him for the first time.

"Don't bet on it," Dawson said. "Don't even bet they'll actually get here, but if they do don't expect they'll

be able to get Davis out for us. It's all make believe."
Dawson was twisting the thin unfurled wire of a pa-
perclip. It broke as he finished his sentence.

"Why do you say that?" Hawke asked the question not
in challenge but in genuine puzzlement.

"Because there's nothing in it for the Leader in giving
the Israelis that kind of prize. He needed them only for
one thing: to tell us he had Davis and to pass on his ridiculous demands. That was all. Even for that little he
turned to them because there wasn't anyone else. He
could not have asked one of the Europeans to do that
piece of dirty work for him. Given the way they work
now, all the others would have known instantly and
would have been horrified to learn that he was holding an accredited diplomat, and even more horrified
to know that he was demanding ransom. He couldn't
have asked any of his African brothers to do the job
for him either; they're too untrustworthy and too talk-
ative, and even they would have been shocked. Even
his Soviet masters would probably have objected. And
given the miserable state of relations between us and
them they would hardly have been a useful emissary.
So who could he count on to be discreet, reliable and
not shocked by anything? The Israelis, of course."

"The cable I have," Hawke said, "gives four names."

"Know any of them?"

"One, the Israeli station chief in Nairobi, a guy named Shimshoni, goes by the name Klein there. He's an ex-paratrooper. He loves opera and has a German girlfriend, along with a wife in Israel. They call it German reparations."

It wasn't often that Hawke attempted humor. Dawson considered it a trend worth encouraging. He chuckled appreciatively.

"How about the others?"

"I don't know any of them, and headquarters hasn't sent me anything except their names. I'm instructed to ask the embassy to arrange transportation and lodging for them. They'll come here after they get in, for a briefing. Then they'll meet with the Leader's people, maybe even with him. That's the plan, anyway. For the moment, they're still waiting for their visas."

"I can see them now," Dawson said, "rubbing their hands over the prospect of rescuing the Americans, their bumbling big friends. But it's not going to happen. They won't even get as far as the airport."

Dawson was wrong. They did get to the airport, but nobody from the government would see them and they left after spending four days cooped up in their hotel rooms. Dawson was relieved. Maybe now Washington would stop daydreaming and start looking realistically at ways to make the Leader recognize his error and hand Davis back. Now, before more time passed.

Because the longer Davis was held the greater the likelihood he would be made to talk and that he would give away names and get more people killed. So getting Davis back without further delay was urgent. Did Washington not understand that?

But days passed without any sign that either the Department or the Agency was in any hurry to retrieve Davis from the Leader's clutches. Kooper and Dawson put together a cable setting out all the things that could be done to hurt the Leader's government, from cutting off its coffee exports to the Unite States to blocking loans by international development organizations, to holding up delivery of the two new Boeing aircraft the country's airline had ordered and paid $20 million down on, even to helping the insurgencies, though Dawson considered that option a very last resort. Washington showed no interest in any of these measures. It continued to send Dawson instructions to do things that, to no avail, he had already done; make another demarche to the foreign ministry, ask again to see the foreign minister, request an appointment with the Leader, ask to see the minister of state security.

Dawson had more stormy sessions with the deputy minister of foreign affairs, but the deputy minister didn't budge. He launched into tirades of indignation, refusing even to acknowledge that his government knew where Davis was. Kooper went repeatedly to see the Captain. To back up his cock and bull story about Davis's high blood pressure – if he didn't have it before, Kooper repeated lightheartedly, he surely has it now – and stomach ulcer, Kooper got the embassy's medical unit to put together a large bag of medications. He took it to the Captain's office. The wiry little man looked at it with a horror that a king cobra or a satchel of unshielded plutonium might inspire, but he allowed Kooper to leave it on a table in a far corner of his office. The next day he telephoned Kooper and pleaded with him to come and take it back. On Dawson's instruction, Kooper ignored the request.

None of this, however, brought them any closer to getting Davis back. Dawson hardly knew whether he was more frustrated with the Leader and his regime or with the people back in Washington. At the end of the third week following Davis' disappearance he decided that something had to be done to shake Washington out of its complacency. He sat down at his typewriter, a 1950s manual Remington he had acquired upon entering the Service and had lovingly carried with him from post to post ever since.

Gloria, the middle aged lady with the sugary voice who sat in the outer office, listened anxiously as Dawson labored away at the machine. For the younger staff, even for Gloria, the Remington was an object of undisguised mirth, a fossil from the Pleistocene age of office equipment, the equivalent of hand set type. Dawson endured the jibes stoically. He loved the Remington. He was determined never to give it up. He looked upon it as possessed of a talismanic quality; without it, he was persuaded, composition that involved any complexity of thought would become impossible for him. Because it was such a sturdy hunk of metal he could pound away at its keys without inflicting the slightest damage; and pounding helped him work off the emotions churned up inside him by the words he produced. When he got going on it at high speed the Remington gave off a stupendous clatter.

By the time the clatter stopped and Dawson emerged from his office it was past five o'clock. Gloria took the five yellow legal pad sheets that Dawson handed her and began the task of deciphering the hand written edits he had added to his typed text and transposing it all onto the glossy white telegram forms that were standard for posts that had "on line" communications. An hour later she returned with the finished product. Ordinarily Gloria deposited the cables she typed for Dawson in his in box and left quietly. This time she stood there, obviously waiting to say something.

"Mr. Ambassador," she volunteered after a long hesitation, "that is a fine cable."

Gloria had worked for Dawson for two years. He had never before known her to comment on one of his cables.

"You like it?"

"Oh, yes, I like it very much."

"They may not like it back in Washington. They could decide to get themselves a new ambassador."

"If they do that," Gloria announced defiantly, "then they can just get themselves a new secretary too."

*   *   *

"Tom, you're coming through garbled." Dawson stood in the embassy's communications vault, with the green enameled receiver pressed hard to his ear, trying to shut out the buzz of the two tall banks of blinking communications gear that surrounded him. It was one twenty in the morning, which meant six twenty in the evening Washington time. And it was characteristic of Foster, Dawson mused, to wait until the end of the Washington work day, which Foster well knew to be the middle of the night Dawson's time, to call him on the secure phone. Dawson had been roused out of bed by the communications officer, who in turn had been roused out of bed by someone in Washington, to come to the chancery to take Foster's call. He had hastily thrown on trousers and a sweater and had walked the fifty yards from the residence to the chancery in his night slippers.

"Can you hear me now okay, Herb?" Suddenly Foster's voice came through loud and clear. Dawson was surprised. It even sounded like Foster. He recognized Foster's dour tone.

"Yes, that's fine. Like you're right here in the room. Did someone flip the right switch, or is it technology on the march?"

Foster was not one for small talk. He ignored the question.

"I'm calling about your latest cable, Herb. I have to tell you that some parts of it were not well received here."

With Foster at least you knew where you stood, which was rare in the diplomatic service. Others would hem and haw endlessly rather than say something disagreeable. Foster let you have it right between the eyes. Dawson could picture Foster hunched over his desk in the Department, short cropped curly brown-gray hair, a big square head and a scowl permanently affixed to a permanently red face.

"Tell me what failed to find favor, Tom."

"Several things, Herb. First of all, the bit about America looking like a paper tiger there. I would have thought you knew this administration well enough to understand that a remark like that wouldn't be appreciated."

Now it was Dawson's turn to be direct. "I'm glad to hear it hit home. Don't you think it was time to set off a few alarm bells? Doesn't anyone back there recall that it's been more than three weeks now since we lost Davis, two since we learned what happened to him.

All you've done is send us instructions to do things you know perfectly well won't work, Kooper or I go to the foreign ministry every day. The minister won't see me on this issue, neither will the minister of state security, and getting to see the Leader is out of the question. We've sent notes. We've pounded the table. The deputy minister just tells me we must be deluded, his government knows nothing of Davis' whereabouts. They're thumbing their noses at us, Tom. Meanwhile they've got Davis and they've got to be grilling the hell out of him. I can't understand Washington's complacency. Do people back there think Davis is going to be able to hold out forever?"

Dawson was tempted to go further and remind Foster of a few basic facts: of his warning a year earlier that sooner or later the operation would be discovered and busted; of Foster's heavy handed putdown; and of the uselessness of it all, ending inevitably in getting a lot of people tortured and killed, not even to good purpose. But he held off. It wouldn't help to rub it in. Recriminations could wait until later.

"We had hoped the Israelis would get him out for us." For the first time that Dawson could recall, Foster sounded ever so slightly apologetic.

"We told you they couldn't."

"Okay, so it didn't work. But the way you propose isn't any good either."

"Tell me what's wrong with it?"

"It's bad politics."

"Since when do politics have anything to do with getting back a missing spook?"

"Herb, you disappoint me a times. What's going to happen this year?"

Dawson was in no mood for games. He was ready now to agree wholeheartedly with his friend Purling. Foster was indeed a shit, an unmitigated shit.

"You tell me."

"I'm talking about elections. Eee-lections. The White House is worried that having an American official held hostage abroad will hurt it in this fall's elections. They remember what happened to the previous administration."

If Dawson had not heard it straight from Foster's mouth he wouldn't have believed the cynicism of it. Could it really be that Davis was being sacrificed on the electoral altar?

"They haven't got much choice in the matter, Tom. Davis is being held hostage. We need to get him out. After that the politicos can worry about their elections."

"Okay. We want to get him out, but we want to do it without publicity. What you're proposing would oblige us to go public with the case."

"We've tried reasoning with them. It doesn't work. If you have a better idea I'm ready to listen."

Foster cleared his throat loudly. "Eventually we're ready to go your route, if nothing else works, but before we get there, there's one other thing we could try. The reason I'm calling is to see what you think of it."

"Go ahead. I'm ready to listen."

Foster spun out the proposal.

"Tell me, Tom," Dawson asked, "is this your idea?"

"Mine and some others. Why do you ask?" Foster didn't appreciate the question. There was a mean edge of defensiveness in his voice.

Dawson savored a moment of silence before replying.

"Because it's a stroke of genius. I could kick myself for not having thought of it first. Let's do it."

"So you like it." Foster sounded relieved. "I thought for a moment you were going to take me apart. But let me caution. It won't work unless we can keep Davis' arrest absolutely secret. There can't be leaks anywhere. Can you keep the lid on?"

"We'll do our best but I can't guarantee anything. The rumor is already getting around town that an American embassy staff member has been arrested. It's beginning to be picked up by the diplomatic corps. And Davis' girl friend is hot on the trail."

"I thought he had a wife."

"He does. He has a girl friend too. And she's wild to know what's become of him."

"Well, do something to calm her. And plug the others too if you can.

'We'll try, but you'd better move fast on your end."

"I promise you a cable inside three days."

SIXTEEN

The cable that Foster promised didn't arrive until the fourth day. Gloria typed the message it conveyed on diplomatic note stationery and Dawson carried it to the foreign ministry. The deputy minister read it through and said gravely "I shall pass this to our Great Leader." Dawson noted that this time the deputy minister proffered no denial that his government was holding Davis. His manner in fact was almost civil.

That was the easy part. The hard part was what to do about Joy Chamberlain, about the British embassy commercial attaché who was a genuine commercial attaché and who had picked up the story about Davis and was dropping heavy hints, and about a couple of others in the diplomatic corps who showed signs of being onto the story. How was he going to be able to plug all these little holes in the dyke before the great raging sea of rumor came pouring through and wiped out prospects for the success of the initiative that Washington was proposing?

The key to it, he was sure, was Greta Heldenberg. If she wanted to, she could blow the story all over town and out into the headlines of the world press. If she didn't, she had the social clout to stop it dead, at least inside the diplomatic corps. But could Dawson trust her? He decided he would have to gamble on it.

It would be easy to catch Greta on the diplomatic merry go round but there was too much risk of being overheard at a reception or dinner at someone's embassy. The only way would be to go see her. That entailed complications. Fortunately, Heinz was away in Germany burying a relative. For an ambassador to call on the wife of one of his colleagues while the colleague was in town would be well nigh inexplicable; for him to do so while the colleague was away would cause tongues to wag, but so be it. Ambassadors enjoyed privacy only in the confines of their own bedrooms, if there. Otherwise they lived a fish bowl existence.

Over the telephone Dawson tried to make his visit to Greta Heldenberg sound as innocent as possible. Would she have a moment to speak with him about a ball for the benefit of the local charitable societies? Well of course!

She received him in a small, cozily furnished room, something between a study and a boudoir, off the main salon of the German embassy residence.

"Dear man," she said after the customary enthusiastic greeting and peck on each cheek, "now you organize a charity ball? Is this not new, a bit, dare I zay, unlike you?"

Dawson laughed. "Greta, you know me too well. That was just for the people who listen to our telephone conversations. I've come on a matter that is more urgent."

She paused and smiled coyly. "Is the name of this matter, by any chance, your man Harman Davis?"

"So you know."

"I have known zince the day you returned from the United States. I have been disappointed that you have not spoken to me about it earlier."

"But you've said nothing, to anyone?"

"Nothing to anyone. Heinz even does not know."

"I won't ask how you learned, but I want to tell you something now and ask for your help. We have a plan to get Davis back but it can succeed only if his arrest is kept secret until he is out, and if nothing becomes known of our effort. I need to keep word from getting around the diplomatic corps and from there to the press. Will you help me?"

Greta reached across and took Dawson's hand in hers. "Dear man, I vill of course. I vill do anything you ask of me."

'Anything' was more than Dawson intended. But he felt the warmth of her hand, and he could see now for perhaps the first time that the beauty that had once been hers had not altogether fled her. She wore a light cotton paisley dress with a billowing skirt that was unfashionably but flatteringly long, simple jewelry – a necklace of a single strand of pearls, small pearl earrings and a single silver bracelet – and just a hint of an unobtrusive perfume. Her blond hair fell in tresses onto her shoulders. She was a different person from the Greta Heldenberg of the diplomatic corps parties. Dawson experienced the eerie impression of having seen her years earlier when she was still a radiant young woman. Then he understood. This was the Greta Heldenberg of the portrait in the foyer, the hairstyle, the dress, the simple jewelry, even the manner. It had never occurred to Dawson to guess at her age. Now he supposed she must be his own in years, give or take a few.

"There may be a visit soon by a high American official," he said.

"It vill not be known from me."

Dawson pressed her hand gently and rose. "Greta you are a friend. A true and dear friend."

As he stood to say goodbye she drew close to him, so close that he could feel the contour of her body pressing toward his.

*   *   *

Barbara Davis dismissed her cook and houseboy after lunch that Saturday. They would have half the day off and Sunday too. They left delighted, all smiles and thanks, and headed straight for the state security office to make their reports early so that they could have the rest of the weekend free.

At three o'clock she rummaged through the storage closet, found the album, wiped the dust off its cover and leafed thought its brittle pages. From them she chose three pictures. She had not seen these pictures for a long time. She did not dwell on them, either the three she chose or the others. She was determined not to let herself be affected by them. She needed them for a very specific purpose. That was all.

Barbara continued rummaging through the closet and came across the three frames. One in silver, one in pewter and one in plain dark wood. The silver frame would be for the picture of Harry and her holding hands at their wedding, she in laced billowing white dress, bridal veil thrown back over her hair, Harry in tuxedo, and with such a nice head of hair then, she had almost forgotten. The two of them smiling, blissfully, radiantly. The pewter frame would go for the second, a snapshot of Harry and her with her mother and father in the Chicago suburbs, at a back yard cookout, Harry standing close with his arm around her shoulder.

The third showed Harry and Barbara, arms twined tightly around one another's waists, Harry in swim trunks, the two of them tanned, relaxed and happy on the balcony of their hotel in Positano, against the background of a placid aqua blue September Mediterranean, white sails and the lovely old Italian town climbing out of the sea straight up the mountainside, a jumble of gold domes, red roofs and beige and white walled houses stacked precariously atop one another. It wasn't taken on their honeymoon. In fact it came from only a little over three years earlier and it was even then a bit of a fraud for they were already moving apart. But that didn't show in the photograph, and it was the kind of storybook picture that looked like it might be from a honeymoon. It would be for the plain wooden frame.

She applied polish to the silver frame, wiped it to a shine and then worked on the glass of all three. She spent another half an hour after that deciding where to place the three, going back and forth, changing, looking about, figuring angles. What would be most effective? The wedding picture on the side stand in the foyer, the first thing the visitor would see? It was indeed eye catching there but perhaps too contrived. Should it go then on the lamp table in the living room? Yes, adjusted so that it would be in straight line of view across the sofa where the visitor would sit. Then where to put the two others? After several alternative viewings Barbara finally settled the family picture in the foyer and the Positano picture on the bar, where it couldn't be missed when the visitor's eyes followed her as she went for drinks or tea.

Barbara worried a bit with her hair and her makeup, debated whether to change dresses but decided that what she had on was right. When all was done it was nearly four-thirty. She sat and waited for a knock at the door. It came promptly.

Barbara had seen the woman who stood in the doorway before, months ago at one of the Marine House parties, but they had not met. She looked at her now and thought, yes, Harry must like that.

"I'm Joy Chamberlain, I'm sure you know."

"Yes."

"I won't keep you long."

"That's alright. I have plenty of time."

There was an awkward silence. Barbara motioned to the side table in the foyer on which stood the family picture. "You may leave your purse here," she said.

"Thank you, I'll keep it with me."

"Please come in, then." Barbara led the way into the living room and motioned Joy to the sofa.

"Please sit down. May I offer you something?"

"No thanks."

"Are you sure? I have vodka, scotch, gin, cognac, whatever you like." She pointed emphatically toward the bar. "Or perhaps tea."

"Thank you. This isn't a social call. I've come to see you because at the embassy they won't tell me the truth about where Harry is or what happened to him. That jackass Kooper just lies to me. I've heard rumors, so I guess I really know what happened. But what I want to know now is, is Harry alright, is he going to be released?

"I don't know."

"What do you know?"

"Not a lot that I can tell you. I know Harry's alive. I don't know if he is alright. I can tell you one thing for sure. If you want to see him again the best thing you can do is stop asking about him and not say anything to anyone about him being gone. That's the only way you can help him now. Do you understand that?"

Joy ignored the question. "Is he going to be released?"

"We hope so."

"Soon?"

"I don't know."

"How will I know when he is released?"

"You'll know."

"Will someone tell me that he's been released?"

Barbara smiled wryly, mildly annoyed by the woman's persistence. "I won't. Maybe Harry will."

"That's all you have to say to me?"

"Yes, unless you have other questions."

"No, I'll go now." Joy rose to leave. "I see you have lots of pictures," she said.

"Yes." This was the moment to rub it in. "Do you like them?"

Joy had her answer ready. "They weren't here the times I came before."

"That doesn't surprise me," Barbara replied, struggling to stay cool but manifestly not succeeding. "Harry wouldn't have left them out for you to see."

They were at the door. Joy paused and looked straight into her adversary's eyes. She did not offer her hand in goodbye.

"I don't have any pictures," she said, "but someday I will have pictures."

The remark infuriated Barbara so that it left her speechless. A reply didn't come to her until after Joy was out the walkway and into the street. She wanted to rush out after Joy Chamberlain and shout: Be care-

ful that what happened to my pictures doesn't happen
to yours.

*   *   *

"Boss, I've got news."

Kooper stood a few feet from Dawson's desk, nervously fidgeting with his hands. Dawson wondered if
he should get his deputy chief of mission a string of
worry beads.

"Good news or bad?"

"Good news, boss, good this time. You remember the
New York Times reporter who showed up here at the
beginning of the week, who came snooping around to
Judy Behrman's office and wanted to know what's going on, and we were afraid he'd gotten wind of Davis'
disappearance?"

"Indeed I do."

"Well I just saw him at the International Hotel. He
doesn't know one fucking thing. Says he's found it
boring here. Spent practically the whole time at the
hotel swimming pool. He's leaving for South Africa
this afternoon. Says that's where the action is these
days."

"That is good news," Dawson said. "Now I've got
good news for you. Look at this." He handed Kooper
a sheet of yellow legal pad paper on which he had just

written out the text of a cable to Washington. Kooper scanned the message quickly.

"They've agreed to our proposal. Congratulations, boss."

Dawson was tempted to say don't congratulate me, I didn't do it. But he let the remark pass.

"I've already called in word to Foster. He says the General will be here at the beginning of next week."

*   *   *

Randolph J. Hawke was deeply perplexed. He swore softly at the dirty creased paper spread out on his desk. It had to be a goddamn provocation…but what if it weren't? What if five hundred people were about to get blown up?

"Al, tell me again what that guy said to you."

Alterman Paul was Hawke's deputy. He was one of those people whose names you think you must have got backwards, but that wasn't the only odd thing about him. Even Hawke at times thought him a bit strange. He spoke in a voice so soft and so low that he would have been incomprehensible were it not that he pronounced each word with total precision. When he spoke what came out sounded as though issued from a machine. He was tensely expressionless. His eyes had a faraway look in them. He stood five feet eight and could have weighed no more than 150 pounds but he was fiercely fit. He did fifty chin ups a day, and it was said that he could bench press 250 pounds. Dawson considered him detached from reality and possibly dangerous.

In his metronomic voice, Alterman Paul repeated his story. The man, a slender young man in his mid or late twenties, had walked up to the embassy gate that afternoon just after lunch and told the Marine guard that he had to speak urgently to a political officer. He told Paul that he was from a neighboring country. He had been recruited by the Libyans and brought here to train with a team assigned to blow up the American embassy in Cairo. They were due to depart for Cairo any day now; he did not know exactly when but was sure it would be soon. He was scared and wanted to defect. He would tell everything if the Americans would give him money and help him get away. To prove his story he handed over an architectural drawing purporting to be of the Cairo embassy. He said the team had been given copies of it to study.

"What do you think, Al," Hawke asked.

"Don't know," Paul replied in his barely audible voice. "Maybe it's a provocation. Maybe it's for real."

The man had said it would be too dangerous to come back to the embassy a second time. He had given a telephone number where he could be reached if the Americans were ready to help him. He would meet them anywhere they wanted outside the embassy.

Hawke had spent two years at the Cairo embassy. The drawings looked real to him. But it didn't make any sense that a terrorist in training to blow up an American installation would be allowed to wander into the nearest US embassy to tell all about it. Or that said terrorist would offer to arrange a meeting by telephone, with all lines tapped. And the proposal to meet outside the embassy could easily be a trap. It immediately aroused Hawke's suspicion.

Still, a lot of things in Hawke's profession didn't make sense. He was deeply perplexed. He went off to see Dawson. Maybe the two of them could figure out what to do.

SEVENTEEN

Dawson sent off his cable telling Washington that its proposal to send a high level emissary to meet with the Leader had been accepted. After that he spent the rest of the day drafting another to the emissary himself, a man of many titles but known to most by his former military rank, simply as the General. The clatter from Dawson's Remington rose to a crescendo that did not subside. Gloria listened ever more anxiously as the hours passed. At 5:45 she called to cancel her bridge evening.

Even Dawson conceded that at eleven single spaced pages the cable was long. But the General was an avid reader and Dawson wanted to tell him everything he might need to know, from the brand of cigarettes the Leader smoked to how to handle the various subjects that might come up in the meeting, from the trivial to the absolutely essential. Summed up, however, Dawson's advice was simple and straightforward: be firm but civil and matter of fact, avoid tough talk or threats. The Leader was cruel, ruthless and no friend of the United States. But unless provoked he was sufficiently rational and prudent to recognize that bringing a high level representative of the president of the United States halfway around the world only to spit in his eye would be a dangerous business. If the General played his cards right, there was every reason to believe he could expect to take Davis out with him when he left.

In Washington, however, prudence and rationality were obviously qualities in short supply. Two days after he sent off his cable Dawson received a cable conveying the talking points the Department had drafted for the General. The language was harsh, grating and belligerent. It was the absolute opposite of Dawson's advice. He considered it a sure bet that if the General followed the Department's guidelines he would be thrown out of the meeting with the Leader before five minutes passed. And if that happened, Davis would languish in the Leader's dungeon for a long time to come.

Clearly the Department's cable was Foster's work. The language and the turn of phrase were characteristic of Foster. Dawson couldn't figure Foster out. He had come up with a brilliant idea and now he seemed determined to wreck it. What kind of tactic was that?

It was the General who explained it. They stood together on the tarmac at the airport, under a wing of the General's Learjet, their backs turned to the arrival lounge and the roar of the Learjet's idling engines blanketing their voices. There could be no safer place to talk.

"Your cable was excellent," the General said. "Pay no attention to the Department's. It's all politics, to make a record to keep the White House hardliners happy. It wasn't meant to be taken seriously. We'll follow your scenario."

The General was a great hulk of a man, at least six feet three and as broad as a tank. He spoke a dozen languages and had served almost as many American administrations. He had lived a rich life that anyone might envy. From it he had amassed a bottomless repertoire of stories. As he spun them out Dawson learned that one of his specialties, not known to the public, was getting errant spooks out of jail.

"President Eisenhower sent me to Paraguay where one of our men had got himself into trouble, to see Stroessner. That was back in 1957, and I said to Stroessner, 'General, we'd like to get our man back.' Stroessner said to me 'why do you want the miserable son of a bitch? He's not worth the shirt on his back.' I said 'General, you're absolutely right, but he's our son of a bitch and we think we ought to have him back anyway.' So Stroessner handed him back."

The General's great frame shook with laughter as he recounted the story. It was, Dawson thought, like watching a seismic tremor.

Another more recent mission of like nature had led the General to a meeting with the president of an African country who threatened to put the offending spook in front of a firing squad. "I told him that of course there was nothing we could do if that is what he decided but that it wouldn't be good for his country's image."

The Leader initially had offered to receive the General at his office in the capital. But at the last minute the Leader moved the meeting to the main city of the northern region, presumably for its greater privacy, away from the snooping eyes and ears of the diplomatic corps. By Learjet the northern region city was only an hour's flight distant.

The General explained that he had come as far as Rome by commercial aircraft and had picked up the Learjet there by private hire. Dawson noted that the crew, the pilot, the copilot and the communications officer, who doubled as steward, were all Americans and that the General had no hesitation about discussing classified matters in their presence. He noted too that the plane was loaded with sophisticated communications gear. It had a secure phone that enabled the General to speak directly with the president or the secretary of state. Dawson didn't ask where one rented that kind of executive jet. He could imagine only one address.

In the few days since he had been given the assignment the General had read through the entire bibliography of histories of the country, some of which Dawson only vaguely recalled hearing of. As they flew north over a barren mountainous moonscape he spoke of the country's nineteenth century rulers and wars, recalling dates and events with the clarity and precision of one discussing items from yesterday's newspapers. Dawson listened apprehensively lest the General ask him to contribute a fact or two to the discussion. But the General talked on happily, wholly content with his monologue.

When he finished with history the General turned to rehearsing tactics for his meeting with the Leader and began quizzing Dawson. Who was likely to be at the meeting beside the Leader? The foreign minister, the minister of state security and maybe another senior person from the leadership, Dawson replied. But not one of them would say a word. The Leader would do all the talking.

"No interpreter?"

Oh, yes, Dawson had forgotten. The Leader's interpreter would of course be there.

What kind of person was the interpreter, the General asked? Interpreters, he observed, can make or break a meeting. It's important to get them on your side. Dawson explained that the Leader's interpreter was a small nervous man with a crippled right hand who suffered cruelly under the Leader's frequent verbal abuse. The Leader conducted his audiences only in the national language, in the manner of the former ruler, but he wanted it known that he had a fluent command of English. When the interpreter didn't get his meaning just as he thought it should be he would interrupt, correct and reprimand him unmercifully.

"So the man can use bucking up. What languages does he speak beside English?"

"French, Spanish, Portuguese and Czech," Dawson answered, "and maybe a few more."

The General knew them all. "I will speak Czech with the man. It is not an easy language, you know," the General remarked with unabashed vanity. "I'll congratulate him on his fluency. And the Leader. What great world figure would you compare him to?"

The question aroused Dawson's sense of irony. "Maybe Ghengis Khan," he answered, "or Stalin or Hitler if you want a more contemporary figure. They're the only fitting ones I can think of."

"No, no, seriously. I mean somebody....somebody he would understand that I'm making him a compliment."

"They say he admires Churchill. I can't imagine why. There's nothing in common between them."

"Churchill!" the General exclaimed gleefully. "That's it. You say the Leader smokes?"

Dawson nodded.

"Is it safe to assume that when he lights up he may offer me a cigarette?"

"He did with me the few times I met with him."

"Then here is what I shall do. I do not smoke, so I will thank him and excuse myself. But then I will hesitate for a moment and say, 'Sir, on second thought, may I take one of your cigarettes as a souvenir of our meeting. Winston Churchill once offered me a cigar and I refused it. I have regretted that ever since.' Which by the way is true. He will like that, won't he?"

"He will love it."

"And these stickers you mentioned, about the Boeing 767s coming?"

"Yes, it's a big thing for them. They're very proud of their national airline. They want to have the latest and best planes."

"They've paid twenty million down, you say?"

"I've recommended impounding the money and withholding the planes if they don't release Davis."

"Well, I'll see if I can work in something about that. Not with the Leader, but maybe there'll be an opportunity elsewhere."

The foreign minister and the interpreter met them at the airport. The minister announced that he was inviting them to lunch before the meeting with the Leader. They loaded into black Mercedes sedans and were driven into the city at breakneck speed. There was, however, very little reason to worry about crashing into another vehicle. It was noontime on a weekday but the streets were all but empty and so were the sidewalks. It was easy to guess which were the government buildings; they had to be the ones fronted by sandbagged machine gun emplacements. Obviously the civil war was not going well for the regime. The northern capital was a lovely old colonial city. From the air it had looked well preserved. Up close, Dawson could see that it was crumbling badly. It was a city built for half a million people but there didn't seem to be anybody in it. And plainly no money was being spent on its upkeep.

They pulled up at the city's best hotel, owned before the revolution by a European group and taken over and run since then as a state enterprise. Its lobby was not too badly gone to seed, but like the town itself it was eerily empty.

The foreign minister and the interpreter excused themselves. They would be back in half an hour to join the

General and Dawson for lunch. In the meantime the manager would show them to a room where they could rest and freshen up. Dawson was about to object that the courtesy was superfluous, they could just as comfortably sit in the lobby, when the General accepted. In the room Dawson tried the wash basin faucets. A thin stream of cold water issued from the warm tap. The cold tap gave only a gurgle. They sat in lumpy armchairs that were frayed at the seams.

"You know," the General remarked turning to Dawson and speaking in a volume of voice just short of shouting, "I have great respect for this country. They are a fine people and I don't see any reason we shouldn't be able to get along with their government. But we have to settle this issue first, just this one issue. If we can't, then those 767s – you saw the stickers, didn't you, the ones that say '767s are coming' – well, the 767s will not be coming."

The General winked at Dawson, and Dawson wondered if the monitors at the other end of the microphones would be able to get the General's message to the Leader before the meeting that afternoon.

Lunch was served in a private dining room. Dawson was pleasantly surprised to discover that the hotel's coerced transition from capitalism to socialism had at least done no damage to its cuisine. The dishes were both European and local, and they were superb. And the General was superb. He told jokes and everyone laughed. He stroked the foreign minister and the interpreter until they fairly purred. The foreign minister glowed to learn that his earlier accomplishments as education minister had earned him fame as far away as the United States (where they were in fact quite unknown). The General spoke Czech with the interpreter for thirty seconds and complemented him lavishly on his mastery of that difficult language. After that the little man would gladly have eaten out of the General's hand.

As coffee was being served the foreign minister was called from the room. A moment later he returned to announce, in the reverential tone of a mandarin announcing an audience with the emperor of China, that they had received "the summons." Hastily they abandoned the dining room, made their way to the waiting cars and again careened through the streets of the empty city, the drivers slowing only as they approached the palace gates.

The palace was a large and very ornate structure surrounded by a broad expanse of meticulously kept and exceptionally beautiful gardens that at that very moment were being assiduously attended to by a platoon of gardeners. It dated from colonial times. It had been the residence of the colonial governor general, then of the former ruler, and now of the Leader. It served each master as readily as the next and would serve still others later. It found its services recompensed, for while the rest of the city sagged miserably for lack of maintenance it was kept as though new. Not a fleck of paint or plaster was missing anywhere.

After a brief wait, the General and Dawson were introduced into a room the size of a Versailles palace. Delicately hued frescoes of winged cherubs in amorous pursuit of one another through powder puff clouds adorned the walls and thirty foot high ceiling. On the Italian marble floor lay a rich oriental carpet, by far the largest Dawson could recall ever having seen. Across the room, at the far end, stood the Leader, flanked by his number two, a total nonentity, by the minister of state security and by the foreign minister. The deputy leader looked utterly blank; the minister of state security utterly sinister. The foreign minister had been serene and confident at lunch. Now he looked quite meek.

The incongruity of the scene made Dawson want to laugh. The feared Leader, a man with the blood of thousands on his hands, standing beneath the gaze of innocent cherubs! To say nothing of the minister of state security! And then there was the awkwardness of it. The Leader and his acolytes stood as though at attention, in utter silence, some fifty yards distant. A ribbon of plain red carpet, broad enough for one person only, cut across the room toward them like an arrow. As it was apparent that this was the path by which the visitors were expected to approach the Leader, the General strode ponderously down it, his heavy frame shaking with each step, followed by Dawson straining to slow his pace so as not to overtake the General. The trek to the other end seemed to last an eternity and while it was in progress the only sound heard was the stomp of the General's footfall.

But they did arrive, and after hands had been shook all around, very stiffly and perfunctorily, the Leader motioned the General and Dawson to shiny newly refurbished Louis XV chairs to his right. The deputy leader and the two ministers – the state security minister and after him the foreign minister – seated themselves to the Leader's left, across from the visitors. The Leader's chair, cushioned in an imperial purple velvet, its arms and legs lacquered in gold, was raised above the others in the manner of a throne. As he was a man of only medium stature his feet barely touched the floor, but the chair's height required others to look up when addressing him. Which evidently was the purpose of it.

The Leader invited the General to speak first, and there began an intricate ritual dance of words that each man knew were not to be taken seriously but were required for the occasion. The peace pipe had to be smoked, and the General started off by drawing a hefty puff. He assured the Leader that the United States had no hostility toward his government. Washington desired nothing but good relations. Both countries, the General piously declared, aspired to peace and stability. "I am confident,' he announced, "that this shared aspiration will make for a most fruitful partnership between us. There is only one obstacle. Once it is removed, but it must be removed quickly," the General emphasized quietly, "everything will be open."

The General would have been hard put to elaborate on what he meant by that phrase. The Leader spared him the embarrassment of asking. Both men recognized that it meant absolutely nothing.

The Leader's task was more complex and thus less easily achieved. He had to extricate himself without loss of face from the untenable position into which he had blundered by arresting and holding for ransom an accredited diplomat. He was not the government of Iran with a fanatically loyal populace and vast oil wealth at his beck and call. His government was fighting a civil war. It was wholly dependent on Soviet military assistance and in desperate need of western European economic handouts. Intransigence was a luxury he couldn't afford. Dawson mused that by now the foreign minister must have got across that keeping Davis in jail or otherwise punishing him could cause the government to lose the Europeans' easy millions. The Soviets themselves might already have told him they couldn't back him in his violation of the principles of diplomatic immunity that they themselves honored.

But when it came to gilding the lily the Leader was every bit a match for the General. He bemoaned America's inexplicable hostility toward his government, whose sole and exclusive aim after all was to lift the people from poverty and rid them of ignorance and disease. He regretted the cold war and the great squandering of resources that it entailed when there was so much need for money to feed the hungry and cure the ill. He regretted it all the more as he and his government were strictly neutral in the unfortunate contest between the power hungry West and the socialist East. His country wished nothing more than to be left alone to educate its children, heal its sick, develop its resources and lift its people out of the poverty and ignorance into which the previous regime had plunged them. Its most ardent desire was to have peaceful relations with both contenders in the global conflict.

"But now there is this thing. This monstrous thing, this breach of law and comity that the Americans have per-petrated against my government! How am I to explain it to myself, to my government, to my people, in the light of our genuine desire for peace and good rela-tions with all?" A look of the most profound perplexity spread across the Leader's dark face.

It was now the General's turn. Assuming a manner of the most complete sincerity he assured the Leader that there could be no greater mistake than to think of America as unfriendly to his government. To the con-trary, the United States harbored nothing but the most sincere good intentions toward it! The little thing that Davis had become involved in was truly insignificant! It was a kind of congenital failing that diplomats some-times suffered from! They strayed! It happened all the time, in Washington and in Moscow, that diplomats were discovered to be straying! But neither the U.S. nor the Soviets ever did more than ask the offending individual to leave.

Just as Dawson was beginning to wonder how far this comedy could go before one of the two would blush or laugh he saw the Leader reach into his coat pocket and extract a pack of cigarettes.

"May I offer you a cigarette?" asked the Leader.

"Thank you," the General began his reply, "I don't smoke....but.." the General hesitated an instant, "might I take one anyway, as a souvenir of our meeting. Sir Winston Churchill once offered me a cigar and I turned him down. I have regretted that ever since."

The Leader beamed. He extended the pack of cigarettes to the General and to Dawson and both plucked a single one from it. With a care one accords to a thing of immense value, the General tucked the cigarette into his breast pocket. Dawson followed suit.

The General told funny stories from his vast repertoire. The Leader laughed heartily, and the others too, all but the minister of state security. The General said he would like to take Davis out with him on his plane back to the United States that evening.

"You may have him," the Leader replied, "but his wife will have to leave also. We have discovered that she too was engaged in subversive activities."

"Yes, it does seem to run in the family," the General retorted.

The quip, wholly unrehearsed so far as Dawson knew, made the Leader, a man dreaded by millions, double over with laughter like a child.

The two sides said their goodbyes enveloped in a halo of good fellowship, but as he and the General left the room Dawson saw the minister of state security approach the Leader and whisper something in his ear. The General and Dawson were in one of the Mercedes waiting to leave for the airport when the foreign minister caught up with them.

"Unfortunately," the foreign minister announced, "it is not practical to release Mr. Davis this afternoon, but you may take him away tomorrow morning."

The General had counted on being off that day. This was an unexpected inconvenience, but he didn't protest. He smiled knowingly at Dawson and both understood. They needed a little time to clean Davis up.

On the way to the airport to see the visitors off, the foreign minister waxed enthusiastic about the coming era of harmony in relations between his country and the United States. Dawson could see that at least he truly seemed to mean it.

On the flight back the General crowned his large head with a baseball cap that the steward had given him on the way up and let out a whoop. He had succeeded!

Now he wanted to communicate his success to the president and the secretary of state. The steward bent over the apparatus that housed the secure phone and worked it furiously. Lights blinked and eventually an operator answered on the other end, but neither the president nor the secretary of state was available to take the call. The General decided that transmission of the good news could await the filing of a telegram.

*   *   *

At ten o'clock the next morning Dawson was summoned to the foreign ministry. The Captain met him at the door, inscrutable as always, and escorted him to the office of the deputy minister, who was no more dour than usual. The deputy minister handed Dawson a diplomatic note. It declared Davis, Davis' wife, Hawke, Paul and the other station officers persona non grata. It gave them forty-eight hours to pack and leave.

The Captain then led Dawson back to his car in the ministry's courtyard. After instructing Dawson's driver to follow him, the Captain boarded a Volkswagen beetle – Dawson wondered if it might be the same car Davis had driven to his appointments – and putted out into the street and around the corner to a building hidden behind a profusion of tall trees and shrubs. Dawson had driven by the spot a hundred times, often wondering what lay there. Now, pulling into the driveway, he saw a building that looked like a small apartment house or office complex. The Captain led Dawson inside to an ample and, unlike the common run of government establishments, luxuriously furnished lobby. They sat there, on opposite sides of the room, and waited silently.

After a quarter of an hour Harry Davis emerged at the head of the lobby accompanied by a well dressed sleek dark skinned man of medium height. For six weeks Dawson had strained every thought and nerve toward this moment. He jumped from his chair, rushed to Davis' side and then, unthinking, turned to shake, in thanks, the hand of the man who accompanied him. A small sardonic smile crossed the man's face and his hand was cold and limp. Up close Dawson could see that his skin was extraordinarily smooth and unnaturally shiny, as though oiled with some fine lotion. His person exuded a scent of corruption. Dawson realized, too late, that he was very likely one of Davis' jailers, or if not that someone intimately associated with the apparatus that jailed, tortured and killed people in that country. Dawson recoiled in disgust and embarrassment.

Davis' hair, what was left of it, had been mostly dark the last time Dawson saw him. Now it was almost entirely white, and his skin was of a pallor to match. He walked unsteadily. As they moved out the door and across the courtyard to the car, Dawson took Davis tightly under one arm to support him. Only when they were inside the vehicle, with the doors closed, did the stench hit.

"I'm sorry," Davis whispered, "I know I stink. They didn't let me take a bath until yesterday."

"That's okay, Harry, it'll wash off," Dawson assured.

"They fed me pasta the whole time, nothing but pasta, and they kept the lights on all the time," Davis continued. "I think there's something broken in my head."

"Don't worry, that'll get fixed too. But are you alright except for that?"

"Yes, I think so."

Dawson had to restrain himself from asking more. What exactly had happened? Had Davis eluded his captors for a time, hiding behind the false wall? Or had he been taken along with the others? Where had he been kept, how had he been treated and what had he revealed? But this was not the moment, for it was plain to see that even as it was Harry Davis was struggling to maintain his composure. And the details of his arrest and imprisonment were not something to be discussed in the presence of Dawson's driver. So they rode in silence up the hillside, the American flag snapping energetically from its stanchion on the car's right forward fender, to the embassy compound, through the front gate that was flung open wide as the vehicle approached, past the Marine guard frozen in salute, to the chancery.

The General was sitting together with Kooper and Hawke in Dawson's office as he brought Harry Davis in. It was an awkward moment. The General greeted Davis coldly. For him, Harry Davis was just another job and another success, another notch on a pistol handle already carved full of notches, another good story to tell at the next way station. The only emotion aroused in him by the person associated with that job was contempt. For Harry Davis was a spy who had been caught, a spy who had failed. No matter whose fault that was.

Harry stood for a moment, confusion and embarrassment written across his face. Then Barbara appeared in the doorway. She called out his name and he hers and as they reached toward one another Harry's legs buckled under him and he collapsed onto the floor, like a puppet whose string had abruptly been cut. He sat there looking up pitiable, as though about to burst into tears.

It is a fearsome thing to see another human being fall with no warning, not stumble and fall but plummet to the ground. It violates one's sense of the good and proper order of the universe. Together, spontaneously, Dawson, Kooper, Hawke and Barbara rushed to pull Harry Davis erect. Barbara and Harry embraced tearfully, and the General, Dawson, Kooper and Hawke retreated quietly to the outer office.

As soon as the State Department doctor had examined Davis and found him fit to travel they piled into cars and headed for the airport where the General's plane waited at the ready on the tarmac. Dawson breathed a huge sigh of relief. At last it was over. Or so he thought.

The General was eager to be off, but a stone faced official ostensibly from the airport authority informed Kooper curtly that his aircraft did not have clearance for departure.

"The General has come at your Leader's invitation," Dawson explained with as much patience as he could muster. "Your Leader will be deeply aggrieved to learn that the General and his party are being prevented from departing." Dawson repeated this refrain to two other officials who showed up but it was hard to tell if either of them was even listening. There was, he soon learned, a second problem. State Security had put Davis' name on the list of persons not to be allowed to leave the country. In vain Dawson displayed the foreign ministry's note expelling Davis. The contradiction between the terms of the note and their orders interested the officials not at all. They definitely did not consider it their job to resolve it.

As Dawson's level of frustration rose, he came across the foreign minister in the airport hall. It was sheer luck. The minister had just come from seeing off a visiting foreign dignitary and was on his way back to the office. Dawson explained the problem. The minister promised to set things straight. It was not to be so readily done. Dawson watched apprehensively as the foreign minister argued furiously with the airport authorities. They would not budge. Their orders came from the powerful and feared minister of state security. They were not about to take directions from, or even the word of, the minister of foreign affairs. They valued their freedom and their lives.

After a considerable delay the foreign minister got through to the Leader's office and the necessary instructions were issued. But it was mid-afternoon before the general – who by that time was fuming – was allowed to board his aircraft. Davis couldn't make it across the tarmac on his own. Dawson and Kooper each took him under an arm and half carried and half dragged him to the plane.

EIGHTEEN

The knock was unexpected and therefore startling to Hawke. He looked apprehensively at his watch. It was almost 11 p.m. and he had at least another two hours of packing ahead of him. Cautiously he approached the door and put his eye to the peep hole. It took him an instant to recognize the tall sandy haired figure who stood beneath the yellow porch light. When he did he flung the door open eagerly.

"Yuri, what a surprise! To what do I owe the pleasure?"

"Good evening, my friend. I bring greetings from all your friends in Moscow."

Hawke remembered that the Russian's American English was virtually flawless. Only a somewhat too formal manner and a slight mechanical clipping of his words gave him away as a foreigner, but as one whose national origin was impossible to guess.

"Good of you to drop in on me," Hawke observed. "I suppose you just happened to be in the neighborhood."

"No, my friend, not at all. I arrived only today, from Moscow."

"Then let me take your coat. You can put your attaché case there." Hawke motioned toward a stand in the entry way. He whistled lowly as he looked more closely at the case. "Louis Vuitton. As always nothing but the best for you guys. Pardon the condition of my house. I'm getting ready to move out. You may have heard."

"Somewhat ahead of schedule."

"Yes, somewhat ahead of schedule. That's not a bad way to put it." Hawke paused and looked his visitor up and down. "So how's the boy? I haven't seen you since Lagos. That was five years ago, wasn't it? No, six. A long time in any case, but you don't look a day older. Very fit, as always."

"And you too, my friend. Handsome and trim as ever. There is a lady in Moscow who sends you her most special regards."

"Nice of her. Return the favor for me, will you? But come and sit down. What can I get you to drink? I'm afraid my vodka's warm. It's been sitting in the packing box all evening. But I can get some ice for it."

"Never!" The Russian screwed up his face in mock horror. "Are we savages? No! We shall drink like civilized men. I have brought all we need." He popped open the clasps of this attaché case and extracted an object wrapped in a white towel, stripped off the towel and held a milky white bottle triumphantly in the air.

"Stolichnaya, freshly iced," he exclaimed proudly.

"Just as I said, Yuri. Nothing but the best for you guys."

"True," the Russian replied, digging deeper into the attaché case. "We must drink it now, before it warms. And here I have caviar and brown bread."

Hawke went off to the kitchen and emerged a few moments later with shot glasses, plates, spoons, knives and a stick of butter. The Russian dished caviar onto a plate and poured out two shots of vodka.

"Let us drink," he said, "to your health, Randolph, and to your future." They raised their glasses. "If you make the right move now," the Russian added, "I foresee a great future for you." He swallowed the contents of his shot glass in a single swig. Hawke took a sip of his.

"Just what are you advising me to do?"

"Let us look at your objective situation." The Russian smiled. "That is the scientific Marxist way, is it not? Your objective situation at this moment is not, may I venture to say, such a good one. No, it is very unpromising. Your operation has been busted, all of your assets have been arrested and you yourself and your colleagues are about to be expelled. It is a very big failure, and it is not the first failure. Remember what happened in Lagos."

"How could I forget?"

"By the way, I want to assure you, once again, that I was not responsible for what happened to you in La-gos."

"I never said you were."

"But you suspected it."

"Yes, I suspected it at the time. But I accept your word."

"Good, then we are on a basis of confidence, which is very important." The Russian filled his shot glass a second time and topped off Hawke's. "With two fail-ures on your record you must know that your career with your government is over, it is finished, kaput. There is nothing left for you but to join the swell-ing ranks of the outcasts of capitalism. What a pity it would be to see you with a cup in your hand at the entry to a metro station in Washington."

"Hawke laughed. "I doubt it will come to that."

"Perhaps not. I exaggerate. But it is no exaggeration that your career as station chief is over. Maybe if they are generous they will put you in a little room in Langley with a big pile of papers to read and analyze every day for the next ten years, until they turn you out to pasture with a miserly pension. I come to offer you an alternative. An important position with my ministry, a fine apartment in Moscow, full access to the party stores, a dacha in the countryside, and of course an automobile."

Nothing but the best, eh Yuri."

"You are right, Randolph. Nothing but the best for you."

"You know, Yuri, this is just like the good old days in Lagos, when we used to sit around and try to recruit each other. We had a really fine time then, didn't we? But tell me, why would your ministry want a two time loser like me? I would be a jinx on your operations."

"No, not at all. You will be quite valuable to us. We know that you are a very capable man. The two failures are not your fault. You were the victim of a stupid and incompetent leadership. In Moscow you will be working with true professionals. And I almost forgot, the lady is also there, waiting for you."

"Say, that's very generous of you guys, Yuri. Tell them I appreciate it. I do. I'm flattered. But I just can't accept. I just don't think I'd fit in. Anyway, I don't see a future in it."

"No future? Why not, with all we are offering you?"

"That's right, no future and you know it as well as I do. Your system is corrupt. Your leaders are old and sick, and your society is sick. Your economy is dead in the water. If I'm going to panhandle in front of a subway station I'll take Washington any day over Moscow. Now let me make you and offer. I'm leaving for the States tomorrow night. Come along with me. You're highly respected there. The Agency will be delighted to have you. We'll fix you up very nicely."

The Russian grimaced. "Will I get a dacha and a car?"

"How about an apartment at Rehoboth beach?"

"Not good enough, Randolph. Anyway, I don't think I would fit in in Washington. I suppose we are, as you say in America, back to square one." The Russian downed his second shot of vodka and looked around the room. "I see you have much work. I will leave you to complete it." He rose. "My offer still stands. Think it over. There is still time. You are flying out to Frankfurt tomorrow night and will spend the next day there. I can have someone call you in Frankfurt and tickets for your travel to Moscow can easily be arranged there. It is a good offer."

"Thanks anyway."

"You will regret it if you pass it up."

"I doubt it."

"Well, in any event," the Russian said, extending his hand, "good luck. And no hard feelings, eh?"

"Right, Yuri. No hard feelings. It's all just part of the game."

"Yes, to show that I mean it, I will give you a tip. Tell your lady friend at the Swedish mission, Carla is her name, isn't it, to get out of sight. It might even be a good idea for you to take her out with you when you leave tomorrow night. She is an attractive lady. I know you would hate to see her having problems because of you."

"Thanks, Yuri. That sounds like good advice."

"My pleasure."

They moved together toward the door. Hawke held the Russian's trench coat for him. Then he remembered.

"Hey, what about the vodka. You forgot to take it."

"No, keep it as a souvenir of our friendship. Ciao."

"Das vidanya."

There were times when being on opposite sides of the barricade was less important than sharing a profession. From his doorway Hawke watched almost affectionately as the Russian passed into the street and headed toward a black limousine parked halfway down the faintly lit street.

When the next morning Hawke told Dawson of his meeting with the Russian the Ambassador at first refused to believe him. It sounded too much like an episode from a bad spy novel. Dawson wondered whether the pressure of recent weeks had unhinged the station chief.

NINETEEN

The Revolution Daily News was one of those mind numbing journals common to one man or one party regimes whose sole purpose is the glorification of the leader, the party or the ideology. It was read, if at all, not in the expectation of finding news but for the modest insights its pages might afford into the mood and the inner workings of the regime. Occasionally, however, it did reward its readers with a surprise.

The morning after the General's Learjet knifed upward into the blue early February African sky carrying him off to another top secret mission and Harry Davis to another life, the paper announced in two inch flaming headlines:

COUNTER REVOLUTIONARY ELEMENTS CAUGHT REDHANDED

Beneath the headline, in words of scalding indignation, the Revolution Daily News informed its readers that four leaders and fourteen members of a "gang of feudal remnants" had been "caught redhanded distributing anti-revolutionary pamphlets in connivance with imperialist designs to stifle the Revolution." The ringleaders, it said, were "former landowners, bloodsuckers of the people who had deluded themselves with the chimeric hope that they could thwart the will of the people." They were involved in "rumor-mongering, collecting secrets and passing them over to imperialist agents and distributing anti-people pamphlets." Their cases were "under investigation."

The regime's mouthpiece revealed nothing of the rest of the story. It did not identify the imperialist power behind the plot. It did not reveal that the previous day five officers of the American embassy had been ordered expelled. Nor that the arrest of the eighteen had taken place more than a month earlier. Nor that a great many more than eighteen had been arrested. But it did not matter. All these things were already known to a great many in the city.

A full inside page was given over to photographs of the culprits and the impressive evidence of their guilt: three pistols, a single box of ammunition, two pairs of binoculars, several dozen cassette tapes and two tables stacked high with "anti-revolutionary pamphlets." Behind the incriminating evidence stood the culprits themselves, grim faced, eighteen of them in a lineup so long that the Revolution Daily News had to join two pictures into a composite in order to get them all in. One woman and seventeen men, middle aged looking men, most of them still wearing jackets but, in a country where despite a Marxist-Leninist revolution – and the party uniform – the necktie remained the symbol of respectability, without ties.

Ambassador Herbert Dawson studied the faces for a long time. He studied the features of the grimly defiant woman until he could have drawn them from memory. She seemed to be challenging her jailers to do their worst to her, and when Dawson reflected on it he imagined they most likely already had. He examined the stoic face of the elderly man whose look seemed to say you cannot conquer me because you can hurt me only in my flesh. And the pathetically frightened face of the man next to him, the cowed look of most of the others.

Then there was this big fellow slightly at the left of center, towering over the others, with broad shoulders and large tufts of white hair sprouting like wings from either side of a bald pate, who had hold of his trousers at the waist, evidently to keep them from falling down, caught in a ridiculous pose that for an instant must have erased his consciousness of his far more serious predicament. Dawson had the feeling that something was missing from the man other than his belt or suspenders. He had seen the man somewhere before, of that he was sure. It was, it had to be, the accountant, the treasurer of the Crenshaw Foundation. The missing item, Dawson realized, were the thick lensed glasses that made the man's eyes seem to bulge out of their sockets. Dawson had met the man soon after his arrival in the capital and had put his name on the embassy's reception lists. He had come once or twice but then had stopped coming. Now Dawson understood why.

Dawson wondered whether the treasurer was still alive. He wondered whether any of the eighteen was still alive.

Outside a hard, dry wind blew noisily through the trees. The treetops bent and swayed with the gusts, and as they swayed the afternoon sun pierced the gloom below and played intricate patterns on the ground strewn with pine needles. From somewhere heavy golden rays flickered onto the top of Dawson's desk. As the sunlight reflected itself unevenly off the desk's chipped enamel it caught Dawson's gaze and held it transfixed.

*   *   *

Randolph H. Hawke III read carefully through the story. The headline, or rather the word "redhanded" in it, left him mildly troubled. Redhand was the code name Davis had given the group's leader, but it was also part of another more sensitive code name. In their brief meeting before his departure the previous day Davis had admitted to Hawke that he had talked, that he had given away the identities of the members of the group and of the station's officers. But there hadn't been time to learn everything Davis had revealed. If he had given away only the group leader's code name no particular harm was done. But if he had talked about the other thing, well, that could be serious. Hawke dashed off a quick cable to Langley to ask that Davis be questioned about that in his debriefing.

Hawke was able to identify all but four of the eighteen in the picture. He clipped the story and the pictures and put them in the last pouch that his staff was preparing before all departed that evening. After that he turned to drafting a report on the interesting visit he had received the previous evening, and another tying together all the events of the previous forty-eight hours. The supposed defector who had so much occupied the station's last two weeks had disappeared from view and Embassy Cairo, put on alert, had detected no evidence of a bombing plot. Hawke closed the file on the case with the judgment that it was, almost certainly, a provocation and that he had been wise not to respond to it.

Having accomplished these tasks, Hawke turned to shredding his remaining files and checking his desk to make sure that everything was out of it. After that all that was left for him to do was say goodbye to Dawson and Kooper, pick up Carla from the Swedish mission and take her to get her tickets from the airline office, then spend a relaxed afternoon with her at her apartment before the flight that evening.

It was all routine, the only difference being, as Yuri had put it, that he was leaving a little ahead of schedule. Hawke thought again of Yuri and was grateful for his tip about Carla. It was too bad Yuri had turned down his offer to come along to Washington, but then Hawke had never really expected that he would.

And it was of course too bad about Davis. Basically Hawke had liked Davis, though he had always suspected that Davis was a little soft. It was to be regretted, in particular, that Davis had talked but at least he had been candid about it. As for all the others, those eighteen in the picture and the many others who had also been arrested, well, that too was to be regretted. Judith Behrman had come storming into Hawke's office earlier that morning and had made a scene. She had shouted at him and called him a murderer. What the Judith Behrmans of this world didn't understand was that sometimes these things just happened. They were unavoidable, simply part of the game. You couldn't let them get to you.

Yuri couldn't have been more wrong about Hawke's future with the Agency. Hawke knew now that he had nothing to worry about. In his cable traffic that morning he had found a message from the Director congratulating him on the outstanding work he had done as station chief and the contribution he had made, at enormous personal sacrifice, to the struggle for freedom around the world. The Director had assured Hawke that an interesting job awaited him at Langley and that in another couple of years he could expect another foreign assignment. In the meantime, he and Carla would be married as soon as clearance came through from the Agency. So it was with a rather light heart that he would be leaving. Hawke in fact found himself looking forward to this next step in his career.

The music playing in Carla's apartment may have blocked out for Hawke the sound of the rifle fire that startled many residents of the city that afternoon. It came in three long volleys, spaced almost a minute apart, echoing up the mountainside. It was not uncommon for shots to be heard at night, a nervous watchman letting fly at the shadow, real or imagined, of a curfew breaker, or at a pack of hyenas prowling in too close to the city's periphery. But those were random firings that tore through the night's silence without announcing anything at all ominous. These conveyed a different message. They were meticulously ordered. They came, moreover, in broad daylight. It had been years since anyone in the city had heard rifle fire of that kind in daylight. In the quiet of their separate offices, both Dawson and Judith Behrman heard the volleys distinctly. To both it seemed that the shots had come from half a mile or so down the hill and off just a bit to the northeast. Which both realized was precisely the location of the security police central prison.

That evening a lively party was in progress in the airport lounge as five passengers on the night flight out to Frankfurt gathered, along with well wishers from the American embassy and the international community, to celebrate their departure. Allen, a tall, lanky young man with a casual manner, the youngest member of Hawke's team, happily strummed bluegrass on the guitar that had cost him a cool grand and that he had received through the diplomatic pouch just a few weeks earlier. Peter, whose job it had been to provide support for Harry Davis' operation, paraded about in cowboy boots and a five gallon broad brimmed Texas cowboy hat, occasionally stopping to mimic the fast draw of a wild west gunman. Alterman Paul popped open bottles of champagne, each one with consummate method, and mechanically served the contents around in Dixie cups, measuring out precisely the same portion to each.

Carla, with her thick abundant golden hair, her large very blue eyes and fine lightly tanned skin, was radiant. And Hawke, after the hours that he and Carla had spent together at her apartment that afternoon, looked the happiest man alive. And possibly was.

As the champagne bottles emptied, Allen, by popular demand, forsook his bluegrass to strike up some of the good oldies for everyone to sing. They belted out lustily "I've been working on the railroad." Then came The Battle Hymn of the Republic. Allen had a bit of trouble with that but the chorus carried him along and covered up his mistakes. The Marine gunnery sergeant, there to see the group off, ordered up the Marine Hymn, which was followed by America the Beautiful. "From sea to shining sea" rang out across the lounge, to the amusement of some of those who had also gathered for the flight, and to the annoyance of others.

Just as the flight was announced, Alterman Paul, having proven his own best customer for his champagne offering, burst into a solo rendition of The Star Spangled Banner. The others applauded wildly.

TWENTY

No celebration attended Harry Davis' return. He did not return a hero and not even a free man. He had admitted giving away the secrets, though not precisely how many and which ones. The Agency wanted to know more.

A Learjet dropped Harry off at a military airport outside Washington, DC. From there the Agency took him for medical examination and a long weekend of recuperation. Then it put him back into confinement, in an Agency safehouse in the northern Virginia suburbs where he was grilled for six hours or more a day by two steely faced counterintelligence types. It was called "debriefing," an anodyne name for a distinctly unpleasant process. It was not exactly jail, but it was not freedom, and Davis was kept there longer than the forty-two days of his African imprisonment.

In the Leader's prison Davis had been deprived of sleep for the first eight days. Toward the end of that time he began to hallucinate. Then and later in his captivity he had been beaten with fists (a tooth knocked out), burnt with cigarettes, hit on the back of the head with a rifle butt when he cursed one of his interrogators (a hairline fracture of the skull and a chipped vertebra) threatened with death more times than he could remember, and forced to listen endlessly to the screams of others under torture.

Frequently there was blood on the floor of the room to which Davis was taken for interrogation, but he was spared the more energetic forms of torture practiced by the Leader's security police. His fingernails were not pulled out, he was not cut or hooked up with electric wires to his penis, nipples and earlobes as were those others seized in the roundup of the group he had worked with. But he was made to believe that that too could be his fate. He tried to dole out information slowly, making a show of telling things he knew his captors knew, obfuscating and seeking to mislead, but with little success. He pretended to lose his voice and he went on a hunger strike to protest the torture of his associates. But as the days of his captivity became weeks his will faltered. He wanted to survive, to get out alive, and not as an invalid, but whole.

So Harry Davis talked. He did not give away the man in the Leader's inner circle, the one who was not recruited but who came and volunteered his services and who was the station's only truly authentic source, the man whose code identity included a version of the word "redhand." But he did give away the group he had worked with and what he had done with them. And he gave away officers of the station, not just their identities but their assignments as well. That was more than enough to condemn him in the eyes of his colleagues at headquarters.

Davis' American interrogators did not make him sleep under bright lights, prevent him from washing or feed him nothing but pasta for forty-two days. But they questioned him relentlessly and mostly not in a friendly way, and they hooked him up to the polygraph machine for hours on end. He would later say that he had been "raked over every coal that one could imagine in one's lifetime." For someone already traumatized, as Davis was, it was deeply painful.

More painful still was the ostracism of his colleagues at headquarters. No one would sit with him in the cafeteria or greet him in the hallway. Colleagues he had thought of as friends cut him, would not return his calls. He was called a traitor, obliged to endure the contempt of people who had never experienced anything like what he had been through, who had no idea what he had suffered.

Harry Davis felt that he had served his country faithfully; six years in the Marine Corps and eight in the Agency. He had alerted his superiors to the surveillance and to the impending danger of discovery. When his warnings were disregarded he had been a good soldier and followed orders. What more was wanted of him? That he should sacrifice his life? He would dare anyone to go through what he had experienced and do it better and survive.

He felt betrayed. He was being punished for having survived. Plainly the Agency would have preferred him to come back in a coffin. In which case it would have honored him.

TWENTY-ONE

The rains failed that year. All through February, March and April, when fat gray clouds should have ridden low over the highlands carrying the spring showers, the sky stayed a cruelly unblemished deep blue. In place of the fierce thunderstorms that in earlier years had awakened Dawson in the middle of the night with a start, crashing through the darkness like artillery salvos exchanged between two immense armies, there was only the low whistling of the wind. That year it blew dry and hard from the desert. Easter came and not a drop of moisture had fallen since the previous October.

The sun beat down implacably. The spring crop was wiped out. In many parts of the country the peasants ate their planting seed, and when that gave out they slaughtered their oxen. So that when the summer rains did come, in July, tardy and anemic, many had neither the means to plow or to plant. And the regime, in denial and for long unwilling to admit that under the new socialist order a famine could occur, had nothing to offer.

The Leader's government kept the army fed and the capital adequately provisioned. It wanted neither hungry soldiers nor a rioting urban mob. The rest of the country was left to fend for itself; or rather, was left to the tardy care of Western governments, international agencies and charitable organizations whose conscience forbade them to stand by while people starved. In the south and some parts of the center where the drought was less acute there was only scarcity. In the north, there was catastrophe. At last allowed to travel north, after their repeated earlier requests had been denied, Dawson and Kooper saw that there was hardly anything left there but dust. Even the cactus was wilting.

Entire villages, thousands of them, emptied out. The main towns along the north-south highway drew the rural population like magnets. Some innate understanding told the peasant that there he could find food and water. Hundreds of thousands trekked for days over stony baked brown hills to the feeding centers set up on the outskirts of the highway towns. They arrived emaciated and consumptive, living skeletons, dusty brown skin hanging limply from bones whose contour stood out as though seen on an x-ray screen.

They sheltered themselves from the fierce highland sun and freezing nighttime cold with whatever came to hand, a boulder found here, a piece of cardboard or a few rags there. They stood docilely in line each day, like ghosts, behind a single strand of barbed wire, for a meager handout that for many came too late. Dawson would have thought them ready to storm any barricade. In their passivity he saw the measure of their tragedy. Hundreds died each day.

The famine brought no hardship to the diplomatic corps. In fact the outpouring of international charity that greeted it was in some small ways a boon for the diplomats and others of the international community in the capital. The sister socialist republic of Bulgaria donated two thousand tons of feta cheese – evidently the only item of food Bulgarians enjoyed in surplus – to feed the starving. The government relief agency well understood that there was no way it could get feta cheese to the famine areas unspoiled, and even if there were, the peasantry, unfamiliar with it, would reject it. So it was dumped onto the market. To that time feta cheese had been a rare and expensive commodity in the city. Now, in true capitalist fashion, its price plummeted. Dawson's cook, knowing a bargain when he saw one, immediately stocked a twenty kilo provision. The American ambassador and his guests were served feta cheese until he protested that he would have no more.

A twenty thousand ton shipment of rice purchased for donation by the well meaning burghers of Austria met the same fate after relief officials tried and failed to gain acceptance for it in the feeding centers. The regime found a foreign buyer for most of it but what was left over flooded the city's markets. Suddenly, rice could be had for next to nothing. For months afterwards it appeared in extravagant mounds at diplomatic dinners and receptions.

For the round of diplomatic dinners and receptions continued unabated by the famine. The famine in fact accelerated it. A curious phenomenon was at work. Throughout the ages considered a scourge from which to flee, famine in the era of the jet aircraft and the video camera became the place where everyone who was anyone in the affluent Western world wanted to be, and, more particularly, to be photographed. Famine suddenly was chic. A horde of famous voyeurs descended upon the capital. They demanded of their respective embassies to be housed, fed and feted, and to be promptly transported to the famine camps hundreds of miles distant, there to survey the tragedy and to be photographed doing so. And then to be whisked speedily back to the safety of the capital, to the reassurance of a full meal, a hot bath and a clean bed.

Dawson, who soon found himself managing a food air program that had mushroomed to a quarter of a billion dollars, had also to cope with this flood tide of Very Important Persons. He shouldered the task dutifully but with little enthusiasm. They came in all sizes, shapes and varieties. A famous senator, recently a candidate for his party's nomination for the presidency, flew in by special United States Air Force aircraft. The senator waddled down the arrival ramp like an overweight poodle – Dawson was astonished to see how fat the man had become in recent years – followed by a sub-machine gun toting bodyguard, a retinue of sycophants programmed to laugh at his every quip and a gaggle of television cameramen. The telegram in which the State Department announced his coming advised that he wished no diplomatic functions in his honor but Dawson hastily organized a luncheon for him; and was glad he did, for the senator's vanity would have accepted nothing less. The senator said he wished to spend three days in the field, working in the feeding camps. He curtly countermanded arrangements the embassy had made to put him up at a minimally comfortable government guest house. He wanted a true field experience. He would sleep in the camps themselves, on a cot, on the ground even. Dawson, coping simultaneously with an aircraft hijacking – a plane sitting on the airport runway with several American citizens aboard and a hijacker threatening to blow it up – sent Kooper to accompany the party. Early the morning after their first night out Kooper phoned in with an urgent message. The senator's back was hurting him. The embassy should reinstate the guest house.

The senator was followed by a congressman from the Middle West, a gentle, sincere, well meaning soul whose only request of Dawson was for a hair dryer to fluff his heavily dyed locks following their morning shampooing. Dawson sent a servant with the dryer Sally had left behind.

A delegation of twelve congressmen and women arrived, two of the congressmen battling for leadership of the group and each giving Dawson instructions that contradicted the other. With only one aircraft available, each insisted on flying to a different destination. Dawson tried to negotiate a compromise. One agreed, the other refused and attempted to commandeer a plane that was set to depart with an urgently needed provision of medicine and food for an isolated emergency feeding camp. Dawson was outraged. He put a stop to it immediately and sent the delegation, the two congressmen still squabbling, off to one of the main camps while the second aircraft departed as planned on its mission of mercy.

The frustrated congressman, head of an important committee, complained to the State Department on his return to Washington. Foster called on the open line, where he knew his remarks could be overheard by the regime's monitors, to report the complaint.

"Your stock has fallen here," Foster announced. Dawson imagined he could hear glee in Foster's voice.

Two right wing congressmen from California came. They had no desire to help or even see the starving. They wanted only to be able to say that they had been to the country and to report that communism was the undoubted cause of all its miseries. One, a big man with a red freckled face, a loud voice and a domineering manner, had an even more ambitious agenda.

"You agree," he asked Dawson, "that this discredits the liberal left?"

"No," Dawson replied, "I don't think it's that simple." The congressman turned without a word and walked off in another direction.

A nationally known black evangelist came, with an entourage of followers. They gathered in the broad high ceilinged reception room of Dawson's residence. The evangelist intoned a prayer and Dawson joined hands uneasily with the group as they swayed to and fro and sang We Shall Overcome. Afterwards one of the members of the group approached Dawson to say that, seeing as how this was Africa, maybe it would be more fitting for the United States to be represented by a black ambassador. Dawson thought of asking the man whether he was advocating segregation. Instead he smiled and patted him on the back.

A famous actor came, a man whose ruggedly handsome features were known around the globe and who was a great friend of the president and of that uniquely American phenomenon, the National Rifle Association. The actor carried a fat packet of glamorously posed photographs of himself which he intended to hand out in the famine areas until someone pointed out that starving people wanted food, not Hollywood. He had made his fame in athletic roles, battling gladiators in Roman arenas, rescuing maidens from burning buildings, jumping, diving and lifting great weights. He was now in his sixties and Dawson observed with a certain satisfaction that he had developed a rather noticeable paunch. When he mentioned this to Kooper's wife Katie she vehemently denied it. She had seen no paunch, she assured. Katie was one of the lucky ones who got an autographed photograph. She had managed to keep herself in conversation with the actor for an entire five minutes, though when she approached him at a reception two days later she was chagrined to find that he had no recollection of her.

The actor traveled to the famine camps and returned to the capital. "The trouble with those people," he confided to Dawson, alluding to the starving, "is that they have no get up and go American initiative. They just sit there and wait to be fed. Now if I was in that situation," he said, clearing his throat and standing tall, "I would do something to pull myself up by my bootstraps. For example, you saw all those pigeons that swarm around the bags of donated grain? Well, I would catch the pigeons and sell them."

Dawson nodded gravely. It was, he realized, the job of an ambassador to endure quietly, so long as no other harm was done, whatever nonsense his esteemed guest saw fit to inflict upon him. Later he recounted to himself what he could have said had he chosen to violate that rule: that no one in the famine camps had the money to buy anything; and that for the highland peasant a pigeon was as taboo as a fat pork sausage for an orthodox Jew, he would rather die than eat one.

Many others came. An Italian princess who brought three large suitcases filled with licorice, good for colds and very nourishing, she explained, to distribute to the starving. An Israeli peace activist who had collected ten thousand dollars to contribute to the government's relief commission but spent it on lollypops which he roamed around the famine camps at night passing out to children, narrowly missing getting shot by guards. A Hollywood comic actor who came to announce that vegetarianism was the cure to famine and to all mankind's ills. The black mayor of a major American city reportedly under investigation for drug use and who during his entire stay was glassy eyed and dreamy, though when about to be photographed came to life and screwed up a broad quarter moon smile. Dawson took him on a drive around the capital. As they passed by the monster statue of Lenin the mayor asked "who's that?" and when told mumbled quizzically, "you mean this ain't a friendly country?"

And then there were the two wide eyed Americans from Minnesota who had paid a conman in California a thousand dollars each plus an exorbitant air fare for the privilege of coming to work as volunteers for a famine relief organization that, they discovered upon arrival, did not exist. And many more.

And then, in the spring, just over a year after she had resigned and left quite suddenly following Harry Davis' release, Judith Behrman came. She was, once again, a journalist, and she called from the International Hotel to ask Dawson for a briefing. Dawson was pleased to learn that she was back, if only for a brief visit. Gloria could tell that he was happier that day, after the call from Judith Behrman, than she had seen him in many months.

Dawson invited Behrman to lunch at the residence the next day. When he met her at the top of the steps, under the royal blue canopy that led up from the driveway to the front door of the immaculately white façade of the residence, he was surprised to find that she was prettier even than he had remembered her. Now that she was no longer working for him he felt relaxed in her company and noticed things he did not recall having seen before. He remembered that she was very smart but also a bit of a firebrand. Now he saw that she had nice legs and that behind her lightly blue tinted glasses her dark eyes were warm and inviting and that something about her person that he could not readily define appealed to him in a way that no other woman had for a very long time.

After lunch they sat in a small salon off the large reception room and talked for such a long time, engrossed in a conversation that ranged far beyond the subject she had come to discuss, that Joseph, the head servant, finally peeked in to ask if the staff might be dismissed, for it was after all a Saturday. Dawson gladly assented. It was dark when they finished and Dawson himself drove Judith Behrman back to the hotel rather than get the duty driver from the motor pool to do it. She was scheduled to fly off early the next morning for a look at a famine relief camp. She would be back Tuesday afternoon. Would she, perhaps, he offered hesitantly, searching for any excuse to see her again, like to accompany him to the dinner dance being given by the German ambassador and his wife that evening?

As they pulled into the hotel parking lot Judith Behrman was relieved to see that the place was dimly lit and that at the moment there was no one else around. There was so little time and she had no idea how long it would take to get him there on his own, so she decided to seize the initiative.

"You may kiss me," she said in a voice so soft that Dawson at first doubted that he had heard it correctly. He did not wait to learn whether he had. He put his arm around her and drew her to him, and they stayed there, bodies and lips pressed together in a glow that blotted out everything else.

Dawson was jittery all the next day. A plane belonging to the relief agency with which Behrman was flying had crashed two months earlier and all of its occupants had been killed. Though it was Sunday, finally late that afternoon, painfully embarrassed but unwilling to endure uncertainty any longer, the American ambassador called the agency's local director away from his tennis game to ascertain that the flight had arrived safely at the camp. Still, he was nervous and fretful in the office on Monday and Tuesday. Gloria, who was unused to seeing him other than calm and even tempered, could not imagine the cause. For no apparent reason he had her call Tuesday morning to cancel a luncheon invitation from the Swedish ambassador that he had accepted two weeks earlier to meet the new head of the Swedish foreign ministry's foreign aid department. It embarrassed Gloria to have to offer Helga, the Swedish ambassador's secretary, who was Gloria's bridge partner every Wednesday evening and who sooner or later would surely press her for a better explanation, the feeble and wholly mendacious excuse that "an emergency had arisen."

Dawson slunk guiltily off to the residence, leaving instructions that if any call came for him he could be reached there during lunch hour. When he came back he paced the office for the rest of the afternoon, until just after four-thirty Gloria buzzed on the intercom to announce"

"You have a call from Ms. Behrman from the International Hotel, on extension zero two."

After that, when Dawson dashed from the office, wholly forgetting to put his classified papers away or lock his safe – habits ingrained by a quarter of a century of practice – and muttering that he would not be back for the rest of the day, Gloria understood. Beneath her staid and proper exterior Gloria was a romantic, and she was thrilled.

Dawson found Judith Behrman waiting for him in the hotel lobby and when their eyes met the rest of the room disappeared. "A diplomatic dinner this evening would be just too awful," she said. "Let's go to my room."

They joined hands and walked toward the elevator. From somewhere in the lobby someone called out to Dawson, "Ambassador, hello!" Dawson heard it as a kind of echo, something that came to him from a faraway place. He did not answer or even look around.

TWENTY-TWO

They called one another Mr. Minister and Mr. Ambassador, though they were now neither minister nor ambassador. Their mutual bestowal of past titles stemmed in part from habit and in part from courtesy, but in some measure also from a shared nostalgia for the years, now forever gone and not to return, when they were important men. Men engaged in the secret and weighty business of state. Men whose presence and opinions others eagerly sought.

"When I learned of your decision to defect," Dawson said, "I thought of our meeting that day in the northern capital. It brought back to me the agony of that whole affair. I mean Davis, his detention and release."

The foreign minister smiled faintly. He was surprised how much older Ambassador Herbert Dawson looked, in only four years time since they last met. Heavier, hair thinner, now almost all gray, face lined and skin under the neck beginning to sag. Dawson thought the foreign minister somehow smaller now, his features still handsome but compressed into a look that had anguish etched sharply into it.

A waitress came to clear dishes away, to sweep the crumbs of a late breakfast from the fine white muslin table cloth and offer more coffee. They fell silent in her presence, the foreign minister from the caution ingrained through living many years in a police state, Dawson out of courtesy to him, though he knew the woman would neither be interested in nor understand what they were talking about.

Dawson had learned of the foreign minister's defection over three years earlier, from the deputy assistant secretary who replaced Foster, who by then had gone off to be ambassador to a country that, Dawson did not doubt, would in a few years collapse into chaos as a result of the policies Foster so energetically applied. It was one of those bright, too warm November days when nature seemed turned upside down. Out on the mall in full view from the sixth floor window of what used to be Foster's office, leaves were falling from trees while temperatures soared into the mid eighties. Crawford, the new deputy assistant secretary had just finished telling Dawson, with embarrassed apology, that he would not be getting another ambassadorial posting.

"We think you did a terrific job out there. The problem is the Agency. They say you're not a team player."

This notice came as no surprise to Dawson. He had objected to the Agency's proposal to reopen the station after the expulsion of Hawke and the other Agency personnel but had prevailed for only a few months before a new team was installed in Hawke's offices. The Agency, he knew, would not forgive him that. And he was aware that his efforts to free Davis from the Leader's prison counted for little in Langley, where Davis would have been more welcome returning in a box than alive. Still, he couldn't suppress the urge to ask an unwelcome question.

"Do you mean to say that in this Administration the Agency can blackball ambassadors?"

Foster would have answered Dawson with a blunt "sure." Crawford agreed that it was true – and that it was deplorable. But he was not about to say so. He shrugged and turned to the next item, which he announced as "good news."

"Your friend the foreign minister is on the brink of coming over. But it's really killing him. He was at our mission in New York yesterday afternoon, in tears most of the time."

The waitress finished her task and moved on.

"I was sure you were trying to help us with it, I mean getting Davis released," Dawson said, "even though you sent me off to see the deputy minister every time I asked to see you."

"Yes, well, I suppose you know, or perhaps you don't know, that the whole affair caused me serious problems with the minister of state security and with the Leader. You might say that it was one of my first steps on the road here." The foreign minister lifted his hand in a half wave at the elegant dining room of the Capitol Hilton hotel on Washington's sixteenth and K streets. "Might I ask," the foreign minister continued, "whatever happened to your Mr. Davis?"

Dawson poured milk into his coffee, stirred it until black became a chocolate brown, took a sip and was disappointed to find that it had already turned tepid.

"If you mean where is he now," Dawson replied, "I don't know. I do know that he left the CIA a year or so after the incident. Davis and his wife divorced and he married a woman he met during his time at the embassy."

Dawson in fact knew more. He knew that Davis had come close to having a nervous breakdown in the months following his release, that he had pulled through and put his life back together thanks to the support of his new wife, and that he had left the Agency after being told that his career there was effectively over.

"I never learned exactly what happened to Davis during the time he was held by your government," Dawson said. "I gather he was treated rather badly. He was hit over the head at some point and came away with a skull fracture and some other injuries."

"What Mr. Davis suffered was nothing compared to what was done to the others who were arrested along with him."

"Were they all killed?"

"All but a few. All of those shown in the picture in the party newspaper were tortured, and all but one that I know of were killed or died in prison afterwards. One man you may have known survived, the treasurer of the Crenshaw Foundation. He was released from jail a year ago and died a few months ago. He was a strong man but torture and prison broke his health. But what you may not know," the foreign minister continued, "is that several hundred others were arrested in addition to the eighteen. Those arrests were never reported. Most of them were people who had nothing to do with the group your CIA was sponsoring. Some were killed and some were tortured and later released. I had a friend among them. I do not believe that he was involved in any way but his family was identified with the former regime and therefore he was suspect. We grew up together and went to school together. Later I learned that he had been so badly tortured that he lost his sight in one eye and became paralyzed from the waist down. He was a well known person and healthy when arrested. The security police were afraid of what people might say if they released him in that state. So they hit on a simple solution. They killed him."

The foreign minister paused and averted his eyes from Dawson. "Could you tell me, Mr. Ambassador, what was it that your government got from all this? Who is to answer to all those people, good people, who were tortured and killed? Who is to be called to account for their suffering and their deaths, and for the suffering inflicted on their families?"

Dawson didn't reply. The foreign minister knew full well who was responsible in the government he had so effectively served. On the American side, all Dawson could have said was that nobody was held responsible. From those who made the decision to launch the operation to those who carried it out or were involved in other ways, all but Davis and himself had gone on to greater rewards. A failed operation here or there was just considered a policy mistake. In almost any policy decision too many people were involved for any single person to be held responsible for anything. It was a kind of collective insurance. And there was no mechanism for considering such things as the moral and humanitarian consequences. Once in a while someone was made to pay a price for incompetence or bullheadedness, but it was rare. And when it happened it was usually, as in the case of Davis, the lowest ranking of those involved.

The foreign minister looked at his watch. "It has been good to meet you again, Mr. Ambassador. I hope you will excuse me now. I have an appointment in a few minutes."

Dawson had an announcement before they parted. "I'll be getting married next month. An invitation to the reception will be coming to you. I hope you and your wife will be able to attend."

"Of course, with pleasure. Is the bride by any chance Ms. Behrman?"

Dawson wondered what the regime's spies had reported to the foreign minister about his torrid affair with Judith Behrman, that night at the International hotel, the week they spent together two months later at a secluded hotel on an Indian Ocean beach, then on safari in one of the big east African game parks. He could recall as if it were yesterday the crystal fresh night air of the highland African savannah, the roar of the Lions roaming in the moonlit darkness and their torpor under the midday sun, the purple flowered Jacaranda trees, the elephants that charged their car and stopped just a dozen feet short of it, the herds of black bearded wildebeest running past the low broad branched thorn trees, kicking their heels high into the air like happy children.

Whatever the foreign minister had heard, it would not do for Dawson to try to correct it or finish the story for him now.

Dawson answered as though he had not heard Judith Behrman's name, "It's a woman who used to work at the State Department. We met that December when I was here in Washington, when Harry Davis disappeared." This statement, Dawson realized, was not entirely accurate. They had not actually met on that December day five years earlier, he and the woman in the fuchsia blouse. They had only seen one another, exchanged looks, joined in a common enterprise, he without so much as knowing her name. But that also was something too complicated to explain. So for the purpose of history and tradition the gray December day in Washington and the nondescript conference room in the State Department would become the time and place they first met.

The former foreign minister and the former ambassador took leave of one another in the hotel lobby, with a handshake and a few more polite words. The minister exited quickly. He strode rapidly north up sixteenth street, past the Russian embassy, as though fleeing a ghost of sorts.

Dawson stood in the lobby grappling silently with his own personal ghosts, a rush of incandescent memories crowding his brain. Of the people and of the place. Of the African highland capital, its aroma of coffee and spices, its soaring eucalyptus trees, its smoggy nights, its turquoise midday winter sky, its spring and summer electrical storms booming like none anywhere else. Of Harry Davis, of Hawke, of Kooper, of the

Great Leader and the General, of Judith Behrman and Greta Heldenberg, of the eighteen in the picture in the Revolution Daily News on that second day of a long past February.

As he pushed through one of the heavy brass doors leading out of the hotel he caught a glimpse of his reflected image, one that he no longer wished to examine carefully. He realized that there would be no official car and driver waiting outside to whisk him to an important appointment or back to an office or an official residence or on to an embassy function. The thought filled him with intense happiness. He had played the game long enough, too long really. Now it was over, and even though his nostalgia for the world he had left behind would never entirely fade, he rejoiced in its passing.

For the first time in more than thirty years Herbert Dawson felt himself a free man. He wanted to shout out his freedom as he walked down K street toward the Farragut North metro station, an ordinary citizen, unremarked, looking up at a pale blue April sky that had been freshened by a morning shower, past an airline office that advertized Caribbean vacations, past a homeless wreck of humanity slouched at the corner of a building behind a rusting shopping cart overflowing with worthless belongings, past the expensive shops and the fancy office buildings where lawyers and lobbyists drew five hundred dollar an hour fees, past the stand of a Korean street vendor that displayed costume jewelry, imitation silk ties and scarves, handbags and briefcases, past three black panhandlers camped at the mouth of the metro station, down the escalator, through the ticket gate and onto the platform into the silent crowd of waiting commuters. Absorbing it all, as though he were seeing it now, with bright clarity, magnified in every minute detail, for the very first time.

As he waited for a train to pull in Dawson put out of his mind the lingering image of Judith Behrman. His thoughts turned instead to Greta Heldenberg, and he wondered what had become of her. He could not imagine her tucked away in some dreary German provincial town. Surely, he told himself, she was still out there somewhere, in some embassy large or small, showing off the latest Paris and Milan fashions, hosting elegant diplomatic dinners, knowing all the great and petty secrets of the place. Ready to greet him again with an energetic "Herr-bert!" or a gently stroking "Dear Man."

To have thought otherwise would have shaken his faith in the just and stable order of the universe.

END